MEDIA & CRIME

Key Approaches to Criminology

Series editor: Yvonne Jewkes *University of Leicester*

The SAGE Key Approaches to Criminology series celebrates the removal of traditional barriers between disciplines and, specifically, reflects criminology's interdisciplinary nature and focus. It brings together some of the leading scholars working at the intersections of criminology and related subjects. Each book in the series helps readers to make intellectual connections between criminology and other discourses, and to understand the importance of studying crime and criminal justice within the context of broader debates.

The series is intended to have appeal across the entire range of undergraduate and postgraduate studies and beyond, comprising books which offer introductions to the fields as well as advancing ideas and knowledge in their subject areas.

MEDIA & CRIME

3RD EDITION

YVONNE JEWKES

Los Angeles | London | New Delhi
Singapore | Washington DC

Los Angeles | London | New Delhi
Singapore | Washington DC

SAGE Publications Ltd
1 Oliver's Yard
55 City Road
London EC1Y 1SP

SAGE Publications Inc.
2455 Teller Road
Thousand Oaks, California 91320

SAGE Publications India Pvt Ltd
B 1/I 1 Mohan Cooperative Industrial Area
Mathura Road
New Delhi 110 044

SAGE Publications Asia-Pacific Pte Ltd
3 Church Street
#10-04 Samsung Hub
Singapore 049483

Editor: Natalie Aguilera
Editorial assistant: James Piper
Production editor: Sarah Cooke
Copyeditor: Sharon Cawood
Proofreader: Fabienne Pedroletti-Gray
Indexer: Silvia Benvenuto
Marketing manager: Sally Ransom
Cover design: Wendy Scott
Typeset by: C&M Digitals (P) Ltd, Chennai, India
Printed and bound by CPI Group (UK) Ltd,
Croydon, CR0 4YY

Library of Congress Control Number: 2014945242

British Library Cataloguing in Publication data

A catalogue record for this book is available from the British Library

ISBN 978-1-44627-252-7
ISBN 978-1-44627-253-4 (pbk)

MIX
Paper from responsible sources
FSC
www.fsc.org   FSC® C013604

At SAGE we take sustainability seriously. Most of our products are printed in the UK using FSC papers and boards. When we print overseas we ensure sustainable papers are used as measured by the Egmont grading system. We undertake an annual audit to monitor our sustainability

Contents

Companion Website   ix
Acknowledgements   xi

Introduction   1

1 **Theorizing Media and Crime**   9
   Media 'effects'   12
      Mass society theory   13
      Behaviourism and positivism   14
      The legacy of 'effects' research   17
   Strain theory and anomie   19
   **Marxism, critical criminology and
      the 'dominant ideology' approach**   21
      The legacy of Marxism: critical criminology and   25
         corporate crime
   Pluralism, competition and ideological struggle   27
   Realism and reception analysis   30
   Late-modernity and postmodernism   31
   Cultural criminology   35
   Summary   38
   Study questions   40
   Further reading   40

2 **The Construction of Crime News**   43
   News values for a new millennium   49
      Threshold   49
      Predictability   50
      Simplification   51
      Individualism   53
      Risk   55
      Sex   56
      Celebrity or high-status persons   57
      Proximity   60
      Violence or conflict   63

Visual spectacle and graphic imagery   64
Children   66
Conservative ideology and political diversion   68
The disappearance of Madeleine McCann: a newsworthy
story *par excellence*   70
News production and consumption in a digital global
marketplace: the rise of the citizen journalist   73
News values and crime news production: some
concluding thoughts   76
Summary   78
Study questions   79
Further reading   79

3 **Media and Moral Panics**   81
   The background to the moral panic model   84
      How the mass media turn the ordinary
         into the extraordinary   85
      The role of the authorities in the deviancy
         amplification process   86
      Defining moral boundaries and creating consensus   88
      Rapid social change – risk   90
      Youth   91
   Problems with the moral panic model   93
      A problem with 'deviance'   93
      A problem with 'morality'   95
      Problems with 'youth' and 'style'   96
      A problem with 'risk'   98
      A problem of 'source'   99
      A problem with 'audience'   100
   The longevity and legacy of the moral panic model: some
      concluding thoughts   103
   Summary   105
   Study questions   106
   Further reading   106

4 **Media Constructions of Children: 'Evil Monsters' and**
   'Tragic Victims'   109
   1993 – Children as 'evil monsters'   111
   1996 – Children as 'tragic victims'   116
   Guilt, collusion and voyeurism   120
   Moral panics and the revival of 'community': some
      concluding thoughts   124
   Summary   126
   Study questions   127
   Further reading   128

5 **Media Misogyny: Monstrous Women** **129**
 Psychoanalytic perspectives **131**
 Feminist perspectives **133**
  Sexuality and sexual deviance 135
  Physical attractiveness 140
  Bad wives 141
  Bad mothers 143
  Mythical monsters 146
  Mad cows 148
  Evil manipulators 150
  Non-agents 152
 Honourable fathers vs. monstrous mothers:
  some concluding thoughts **154**
 Summary 159
 Study questions 160
 Further reading 160

6 **Police, Offenders and Victims in the Media** **163**
 The mass media and fear of crime **165**
 The role of the police **170**
 The role of mobile and social media in policing **175**
 Crimewatch UK **179**
  Crimewatching victims 183
  Crimewatching offenders 185
  Crimewatching the police 186
 Crimewatching crime: some
  concluding thoughts **188**
 Summary 189
 Study questions 190
 Further reading 191

7 **Crime Films and Prison Films** **193**
 The appeal of crime films **195**
 The crime film: masculinity, autonomy, the city **197**
 The 'Prison Film' **201**
  The prison film and the power to reform? 203
 The Documentary **205**
  Documentary as Ethnography 206
 The remake **210**
  The Taking of Pelham One Two Three and The Taking
   of Pelham 123 211
 Discussion **214**
 Concluding Thoughts **216**
 Summary 218
 Study questions 218
 Further reading 219

8 Crime and the Surveillance Culture   221
   NSA, GCHQ and the new age of surveillance   222
   Panopticism   224
   The surveillant assemblage   226
      Control of the body   228
      Governance and governmentality   230
      Security and 'cybersurveillance'   232
      Profit   236
      Voyeurism and entertainment   239
   From the panopticon to surveillant assemblage and back again   242
   'Big Brother' or 'Brave New World'?: some concluding thoughts   243
   Summary   248
   Study questions   248
   Further reading   249

9 The role of the Internet in crime and deviance   251
   Redefining deviance and democratization: developing nations
      and the case of China   254
      Cyber-warfare and cyber-terrorism   257
   'Ordinary' cybercrimes   259
      Electronic theft and abuse of intellectual property rights   259
      Hate crime   260
      Invasion of privacy, defamation and identity theft   262
      eBay Fraud   264
      Hacking and loss of sensitive data   265
      Child pornography and online grooming   267
   Childhood, cyberspace and social retreat   268
   Concluding thoughts   271
   Summary   272
   Study questions   273
   Further reading   273

10 (Re)Conceptualizing the Relationship between
       Media and Crime   275
    Doing media-crime research   276
    Stigmatization, sentimentalization and sanctification:
       the 'othering' of victims and offenders   282
    Summary   291
    Study questions   292
    Further reading   292

Glossary   293
References   309
Index   325

Companion Website

This book is supported by a brand new companion website (**https://study. sagepub.com/jewkes3e**). The website offers a wide range of free teaching and learning resources, including:

For Students:

- **Annotated lists of further reading**
- **SAGE Journal Articles:** free access to selected further readings
- **Links to** websites, YouTube videos, blogs and reports

For Instructors:

- **PowerPoint Slides** to accompany each chapter

Acknowledgements

The last twelve months has seen the passing of some of the great names in British media-crime research – Stan Cohen, Stuart Hall, Geoffrey Pearson, Keith Soothill and Jock Young – and this book acknowledges its debt to them all, as well as to Mike Presdee.

I would like to thank Natalie Aguilera and James Piper at Sage Publications for their support and enthusiasm for publishing a third edition of this volume, and to Caroline Porter for her energy and commitment to getting the book – and the whole *Key Approaches* series – off the ground in the first place.

Finally, as always, to David, who isn't much interested in media and crime, and to whom I give thanks for that.

Introduction

I want to start this third edition of *Media & Crime* with the story of an event
that could not have opened the first edition published in 2004. On 15th April
2013, two bombs exploded close to the finishing line of the Boston marathon,
in which some 23,000 runners were competing, with large crowds cheering
them along the 26 mile route. The pressure cooker bombs, loaded with gun-
powder, nails and ball-bearings, and placed in nylon rucksacks, were left on
the street amidst the cheering crowds. They claimed three lives and wounded
up to 200 other people. The following day, and with no claims of responsibility,
FBI investigators announced that they were considering a wide range of suspects. So far, regrettably, so familiar.

But as news emerged of CCTV footage taken from a department store
located near the scene of the second blast, showing a potential suspect carrying and possibly dropping a black rucksack, a swathe of amateur detectives
went into overdrive on the Internet. One group posted a 57-picture album on
website imgur.com featuring people wearing black backpacks, while on social
news site Reddit, more than 100 threads speculated on images captured by
CCTV or on mobile phones, and a dedicated subreddit was set up devoted to
the manhunt called r/findbostonbombers. As a Boston police commissioner
announced that, at the time of the bombings, 'this was probably one of the
most photographed areas in the entire country', the police and hundreds of
Internet vigilantes were simultaneously combing through vast numbers of
photos and video clips of the bomb scene, before and after the explosions.
While the former had the benefits of sophisticated facial recognition technology, the latter were relying largely on guesswork and a misplaced sense of
civic duty.

Three days after the bombings, the FBI held a press conference, showing
photographs and security images of the prime suspects watching the marathon, each wearing a large, dark coloured rucksack. The footage showed
that the suspects acted differently to other bystanders after the blasts,
remaining at the scene to survey the damage before calmly walking away,
rather than fleeing like everyone else. In response to the news conference,
further photographs and movies from mobile phones were provided by the

public, and a wounded victim who lost both of his legs in the bombings, gave a detailed description of one of the bombers to investigators, stating that he saw him place a backpack beside him, approximately two-and-a-half minutes prior to the explosion. The suspects were identified as Chechen-born brothers Dzhokhar Tsarnaev, aged 19, and Tamerlan Tsarnaev, aged 26. Amidst feverish speculation, more details emerged of the events following the explosions. Shortly after the young men walked away from the scene of carnage they created, they killed an MIT police-man, carjacked an SUV and initiated an exchange of gunfire with the police, during which an officer was injured but survived with severe blood loss. Tamerlan was shot several times in the crossfire and his brother sub-sequently ran him over with the stolen SUV as he escaped. He was pronounced dead at the scene. After an extensive manhunt, Dzhokhar was found hiding in a boat in a backyard in nearby Watertown. Despite being wounded and unarmed, the police opened fire on the figure beneath the boat's tarpaulin cover, only ceasing fire when ordered to by a senior officer. By this point, a crowd had gathered and were taking photos and movies at the scene. As Dzhokhar climbed out of the boat and was arrested, a police photographer took several images which he subsequently offered to *Boston* Magazine. His motive was reported to be that he wanted to show the real story of what happened and to counter the 'fluffed and buffed' rock star image used of Dzhokhar on the cover of *Rolling Stone* magazine (www.bos tonmagazine.com/news/blog/2013/07/18/tsarnaev/). Of course, images are endlessly interpretable and many felt that the police officer's photographs showed Dzhokhar in an equally positive light; vulnerable and heroic. The photographer was subsequently suspended from the police and ordered not to talk to the media.

The Boston case raises many points of interest from a criminological and legal perspective, not least the issue of whether the Federal death penalty would be applied (30 charges were brought against him, including using a weapon of mass destruction, more than half of which carry the death pen-alty). The case also raised the question of where execution would be administered, given that the state in which the crime took place, Massachusetts, abolished the death penalty in 1984. But from a media-criminology perspec-tive it is an especially interesting case because of the open access afforded journalists. First there was the excited amateur sleuthing that took place on social networking sites, then faithfully reported in the world's media. This quickly tipped over into more dangerous territory with several 'suspects' being incorrectly identified and libeled online and in the traditional media. One of the early mis-identifications was of a 22-year-old student who had gone missing a month before, having suspending his studies while suffering from severe depression. Users of social media pinpointed this individual as the 'standout suspect', a claim that was proved wrong, but only after the young man's family had endured several distressing days of speculation and accusation. On 23rd April, four days after Dzhokhar's capture, the missing student's body was found in a nearby river and identified through dental records. Although the cause of death wasn't immediately known, foul play was not suspected.

Once the perpetrators had been correctly identified from very clear footage taken by cameras at a store opposite where they were standing and where they left the bombs – itself a stroke of good fortune given that the US has not embraced CCTV to nearly the same extent as the UK – there simply was not enough time for the police to impose reporting restrictions or cordon off sites, and audiences were granted possibly unprecedented access to the events as they unfolded. Social media quickly became inundated with news of developments as they were happening, as the *Chicago Tribune* reported on 19th April 2013:

> It was all happening in a small town near Boston on Friday evening, but social media was the place to be as police in Watertown, Mass., closed in on and then arrested Boston Marathon bombing suspect Dzhokhar Tsarnaev.
>
> @BostonGlobe: Dzhokhar Tsarnaev IN CUSTODY!
>
> @mayortommenino: "We got him"
>
> @SeanKellyTV: Loud applause at end of Franklin Street as SWAT walks out to crowd…
>
> UPDATE: Boston Police are asking social media users not to post information they hear on police frequencies/scanner channels.
>
> (http://articles.chicagotribune.com/2013-04-19/news/chi-boston-marathon-bombing-suspects-social-media-20130419_1_social-media-users-boston-police-boston-marathon)

When the brothers carjacked an SUV in which to escape, the vehicle's owner had left his cellphone inside, enabling the police to track it. Once the police had named the suspects, scrutiny of the brothers' computers, Facebook and vKontakte (a Russian version of Facebook) pages, Twitter accounts and YouTube histories revealed many aspects of their personalities, histories and motivations to commit such a terrible crime. The fact that 19-year-old Dzhokhar seemed a fairly ordinary boy in thrall of his older, radicalized brother did little to dampen the zeal with which the American authorities pursued him. Controversies continued to rage after Dzhokhar was captured, from the FBI's denial of his Miranda Rights (the right to remain silent and have an attorney present) while questioning him in hospital, to debates about whether, despite being an American citizen, he should be tried as an unlawful enemy combatant, preventing him from any legal counsel. In the end, he was granted a defense attorney, but special administrative measures were imposed, leaving him isolated from communication with his family and lawyers, despite no evidence to suggest his credibility as a threat in the future (the measures were lifted in October 2013; they were illegal and could have jeopardized the prosecution).

And so it is that, at the time of writing, the young man who, on 14th April 2013, was a college student, part-time lifeguard and keen skateboarder, and who aspired to becoming a dentist, has been languishing in near isolation at a high security unit awaiting the trial that could culminate in his execution, while his lawyers argue that the statements made while he was hospitalized and in a serious condition as a result of gunshot wounds, should not be admitted because he did not have an attorney present. Meanwhile, inevitably, conspiracy theories abound. Readers' comments on online newspapers, magazines and blogs typically communicate conservative, anti-Islam views in various shades of vitriol, but many sites are devoted to alternative versions of events, including a theory that the US Government staged the whole event. A 'Dzhokhar Tsarnaev is Innocent' Facebook page was set up, and some sceptics expressed incredulity at the events that unfolded in Boston via media blogs:

> When was the last time you saw a whole city on lock down, martial law brought in and rounds fired into a boat at a child who was unarmed?? NONE OF ANY OF WHAT HAPPENED MAKES SENSE TO ME?!! I am afraid of our Government if they can do something like this and no one hold them accountable?? They could do this to me, to you to anyone! There is hardly one shred of evidence linking this kid to what happened!! (www.bostonmagazine.com/news/blog/2013/07/18/tsarnaev/)

The volume

The relationship between crime and mobile/social media is arguably the biggest change that media-criminologists have witnessed in the decade since the first edition of this book was published – and not just in the way that news about crime is reported and circulated, but in the ways in which it is produced and gathered too. Since 2004, we have learned about the lengths to which both journalists and governments will go in order to gain 'secret' information about us (see Chapters 2 and 8 respectively). Social media forums have come and gone (MySpace, bebo), and even the once ubiquitous Facebook and Twitter are in decline and being replaced by more instant, personal, time-limited, image-and-messaging/blogging sites (Instagram, SnapChat, Tumblr, Flickr, WhatsApp, Pinterest and the like). No doubt that by the time this book is published, more newcomers will have come onto the scene. But while means of communication change, the 'message' seems remarkably similar. Everything that appears in the first edition of *Media and Crime* – the theoretical frameworks that help us to understand media influence, the contested terrain of moral panics, the media's bifurcated approach to children as victims and as perpetrators of crime, the frequently misogynist portrayals of women who offend, the preferred meanings with which the police imbue reporting of crime, the insidious surveillance culture within which most of us live, and the news values that determine which events are considered worthy of bringing to our attention – all broadly remain constant. The rise of mobile and social media might mean that everyday crime news is more immediate, more visual and more democratic in terms of its production. It might even be the case that the ante has been upped considerably, in terms of the level of sensationalism required to gain mainstream media attention. Certainly, authorities' ability to starve 'terrorists' of the oxygen of publicity, as Margaret Thatcher once famously put it, has disappeared, at least, prior to arrest and conviction. The camera footage of a ranting Michael Adebolajo, with bloodied hands carrying the large meat cleaver with which he had just brutally murdered British soldier Lee Rigby on a busy street in Woolwich, London in May 2013, is evidence of these tendencies. But, as this tragic story also illustrates, while the vast majority of offenders are viewed as caricatured monsters or pantomime villains, it is still the case that the lives of some victims are regarded as more worthy than others; as a serviceman recently returned from Afghanistan and a keen supporter of the 'Help for Heroes' charity, Fusilier Rigby might be said to be an 'ideal' victim.

Like its predecessors this revised, third edition includes a number of pedagogic features (overviews, key terms which are highlighted at their first appearance in the chapter, summaries, study questions, suggestions for further reading, and a glossary) which, it is hoped, will make it engaging and accessible – as well as being stimulating and intellectually challenging – to students and their tutors. But, like other books in the *Key Approaches to Criminology* series, *Media and Crime* is intended as much more than an overview of the literature or a teaching text. In addition to going over necessary but well-trodden paths, it is hoped that the book will move key debates forward, develop existing knowledge and offer new and innovative ways of thinking about the relationship between media and crime (and, indeed, media studies and criminology). The first two chapters provide the foundation for what follows, and many of the themes and debates introduced here are then picked up and developed in relation to specific subjects and case studies in the remainder of the volume. Chapter 1 brings together theoretical analysis from criminology, sociology, media studies and cultural studies in order to provide a critical understanding of the relationships between these areas of academic study, and to synthesize their contributions to our understanding of the relationship between media and crime. Chapter 2 then discusses the 'manufacture' of crime news, and considers why crime has always been, and remains, so eminently 'newsworthy'. The chapter introduces a set of 'news values' which shape the selection and presentation of stories involving crime, deviance and punishment in contemporary news production. Although the chapter concentrates solely on news, these criteria – which alert us to the subtle biases that inform public perceptions of crime – extend beyond the newsroom, and underpin much of our mediated picture of crime in contemporary Britain.

The next four chapters of the book illustrate the extent to which crime and justice are constructed according to prevailing cultural assumptions and ideologies by examining a number of different issues that have gained significant media attention. Although divergent in terms of subject, the overriding theme of the book is that contemporary media deal only in binary oppositions, polarizing public responses to criminals and victims of crime, perpetuating psychically held notions of 'self' and 'other' and contributing to the formation of identities based on 'insider' and 'outsider' status. The book thus argues that the media, in all its forms, is one of the primary sites of social inclusion and exclusion, a theme that is explored in Chapter 3 in relation to 'moral panics'. So influential has Stanley Cohen's *Folk Devils and Moral Panics* been that a book about media and crime could not have omitted the concept he made famous. The moral panic thesis is therefore discussed, but in such a way as to move beyond the faithful re-writing of Cohen's famous study of Mods and Rockers that is favoured by many commentators, and problematize moral panics as they have traditionally been conceived.

Chapter 4 develops the previous chapter's examination of moral panics over youth, by considering the degree to which, in today's media landscape, children and young people are viewed both as folk devils, and as the victims of folk devils – notably paedophiles. The chapter discusses the extent to which mediated constructions of children in the 21st century are still seen through the lens of 19th century idealized images of childhood as a time of innocence – a (mis)representation that only serves to fuel public hysteria when children commit very serious offences or are themselves the victims of such crimes.

Chapter 5 is also concerned with constructions of offenders (and, peripherally, victims) which remain curiously embedded in the Victorian age, only here the focus is on deviant women, especially those who murder and commit serious sexual crimes. Using psychoanalytical and feminist theories, this chapter introduces a psychosocial perspective to argue that the media reinforce misogynist images of females who fail to conform to deeply-held cultural beliefs about 'ideal' womanhood. For such women their construction as 'others' renders them subject to hostile censure and their crimes can come to occupy a peculiarly symbolic place in the collective psyche.

Our gendered analysis continues in Chapter 6, which considers the ways in which victims, offenders and the police are constructed on British television. The chapter concludes that, in the main, crime narratives are constructed around female victims (usually either very young or elderly), male offenders (often black, usually strangers), either in the victim's home (increasing the impression of personal violation and female vulnerability) or in public places ('the streets', where we are all at risk), and are investigated and brought to a successful and 'just' conclusion by a caring and efficient police force that can trace its lineage back to everyone's favourite policeman, PC George Dixon, who first appeared in the 1950 film *The Blue Lamp*. One of the reasons why Dixon of Dock Green is still regularly evoked is because he seems to hark back to a golden era of policing. Chapter 6 discusses some of the incidents that have recently damaged public confidence in the police and looks at their attempts to manage their reputation via social media networks, including Facebook and Twitter. For the police, new media platforms are a double-edged sword: on the one hand they permit officers to engage in 'open' dialogue with the public; on the other, they can be used to create and circulate ordinary citizens' footage of police misconduct.

Chapter 7 takes up the theme of what representations in films have to tell about the social and political contexts of real policing and changing social attitudes to crime. Given the many thousands of films that could possibly have been discussed in this chapter, it is of necessity highly selective and rather personal in its scope and content. However, the analysis of the appeal of movies about crime and prisons, the focus on ideal masculine types in these films, the reflections on the potential power of documentaries to influence public opinion about offenders, and the discussion of what cinematic 'remakes' have to tell us about changing cultural fears and anxieties, are all intended to chime with themes raised elsewhere in this volume.

Chapter 8 returns to the theme of demonized 'others' in its examination of the extent to which surveillance technologies are employed as repressive forms of regulation and social control. The chapter suggests that, despite recent accusations that we are all under constant surveillance in all aspects of our lives, the surveillant gaze falls disproportionately on some sections of society. The representation of surveillance as panoptic is ultimately challenged because, not only does surveillance raise important questions about social exclusion and 'otherness' (which are especially meaningful given the preponderance of surveillance images on television and in popular culture) but it also may be regarded as something that is desirable and fun. The numerous references to Facebook and other social media that appear in this volume testify to the fact that we have become a society which likes to be watched.

Much of Chapter 8 inevitably discusses the kinds of surveillance facilitated by the Internet and social media and Chapter 9 develops this theme with a chapter on 'cybercrime'. The subject of mixed and contested opinion about its importance and profile in the broader picture of offending behaviour, cybercrime sometimes seems at best intangible to many people. Optimists see computer-mediated technologies as a potential source of democratization and this chapter discusses examples of the 'people power' that has come with mass ownership of computers. However, not only is access to the Internet unevenly distributed across the globe, but it has also become something of an ideological battleground between states and citizens, as the case study of China discussed here illustrates. Furthermore, when we recall some of the arguments made in Chapter 8 and consider the surveillant opportunities that cyberspace brings, we may have mixed feelings about our growing dependence on the World Wide Web.

Chapter 10 attempts to round things off by offering some thoughts and words of caution about conducting research in the field of media-criminology and also by reviewing and reflecting on the key themes and issues that have emerged from the previous chapters. It contends that the media's stigmatization – not only of offenders, but also of those who simply look 'different' – is a necessary counterpoint to their sentimentalization and even sanctification of certain victims of the most serious crimes, and their families. Without 'others', 'outsiders', 'strangers' and 'enemies within', the media would not succeed in constructing the moral consensus required to sell newspapers, gain audiences and, most importantly, maintain a world at one with itself.

1

Theorizing Media and Crime

CHAPTER CONTENTS	

Media 'effects'   12

Mass society theory   13

Behaviourism and positivism   14

The legacy of 'effects' research   17

Strain theory and anomie   19

Marxism, critical criminology and the 'dominant
ideology' approach   21

The legacy of Marxism: critical criminology and corporate crime   25

Pluralism, competition and ideological struggle   27

Realism and reception analysis   30

Late-modernity and postmodernism   31

Cultural criminology   35

Summary   38

Study questions   40

Further reading   40

OVERVIEW

Chapter 1 provides:

- An overview of the theoretical contours that have shaped the academic fields of criminology and media studies during the modern period.
- A discussion of the 'media effects' debate; its origins, its epistemological value and its influence on contemporary debates about media, crime and violence.
- An analysis of the theories – both individual (behaviourism, positivism) and social (anomie, dominant ideology) – which have dominated debates about the relationship between media and crime within the academy.
- An analysis of the theories (pluralism, left realism) which have emerged from within the academy but which have explicitly addressed the implications of theory for practitioners and policymakers.
- An exploration of new, emerging theories which can broadly be called 'post-modern', including cultural criminology.

KEY TERMS

- anomie
- behaviourism
- crime
- criminalization
- critical criminology
- cultural criminology
- 'effects' research
- folk devils
- hegemony
- hypodermic syringe model
- ideology
- late modernity
- left realism

- Marxism
- mass media
- mass society
- mediated
- paradigm
- pluralism
- political economy
- positivism
- postmodernism
- psychoanalysis
- reception analysis
- stereotyping
- youth

Why are we so fascinated by *crime* and deviance? If the media can so success-fully engage the public's fascination, can they equally tap into – and increase – people's fears about crime? Is the media's interest in – some would say, obses-sion with – crime *harmful*? What exactly *is* the relationship between the *mass media* and crime? Students and researchers of both criminology and media studies have sought to understand the connections between media and crime for well over a century. It's interesting to note that, although rarely working together, striking parallels can be found between the efforts of criminologists and media theorists to understand and 'unpack' the relationships between crime, deviance and criminal justice on the one hand, and media and popular culture on the other. Indeed, it is not just at the interface between crime and media that we find similarities between the two disciplines. Parallels between criminology and media studies are evident even when we consider some of the most fundamental questions that have concerned academics in each field, such as 'what *makes* a criminal?' and 'why do the mass media *matter*?' The reason for this is that as criminology and media studies have developed as areas of interest, they have been shaped by a number of different theoretical and empirical perspectives which have, in turn, been heavily influenced by developments in related fields, notably sociology and psychology, but also other disciplines across the arts, sciences and social sciences. Equally, academic research is almost always shaped by external forces and events from the social, political, economic and cultural worlds. Consequently we can look back through history and note how major episodes and developments – for example, Freud's 'discovery' of the unconscious, or the exile of Jewish intellectuals to America at the time of Nazi ascendancy in Germany – have influenced the intellectual contours of both criminology and media studies in ways that, at times, have synthesized the concerns of each. In addition, the interdisciplinary nature of both subject areas and their shared origins in the social sciences, has meant that, since the 1960s when they were introduced as degree studies at universities, a number of key figures working at the nexus between criminology and media/cultural studies have succeeded in bringing their work to readerships in both subject areas – Steve Chibnall, Stanley Cohen, Richard Ericson, Stuart Hall and Jock Young to name just a few.

The purpose of this first chapter is to introduce some of this cross-disciplinary scholarship and to develop a theoretical context for what follows in the remainder of the book. The chapter is not intended to provide a comprehensive overview of all the theoretical perspectives that have shaped media research and criminology in the modern era – an endeavour that could fill at least an entire book on its own. Instead, it will draw from each tradition a few of the major theoretical 'pegs' upon which we can hang our consideration of the relationship between media and crime. These approaches are presented in an analogous fashion with an emphasis on the points of similarity and convergence between the two fields of study (but remember that, in the main, scholars in media studies have worked entirely independently of those in criminology, and vice versa). In addition, the theoretical perspectives discussed in this chapter are presented in the broadly chronological order in which they were developed, although it is important to stress that theories do not simply appear and then, at some later date, disappear, to be replaced by something altogether more sophisticated and enlightening. While we can take an overview of the development of an academic discipline and detect some degree of linearity in so far as we can see fundamental shifts in critical thinking, this linearity does not mean that there were always decisive breaks in opinion as each theoretical phase came and went. In fact, there is a great deal of overlap in the approaches that follow, with many points of correspondence as well as conflict. Nor does it necessarily indicate a coherence of opinion within each theoretical position or, even any real sense of progress in our understanding and knowledge of certain issues. As Tierney puts it:

> There is always a danger of oversimplification when trying to paint in some historical background, of ending up with such broad brushstrokes that the past becomes a caricature of itself, smoothed out and shed of all those irksome details that confound an apparent coherence and elegant simplicity. (1996: 49)

Notwithstanding that what follows is of necessity selective, condensed and painted with a very broad brush, this chapter seeks to locate the last 50 years of university-taught media studies and criminology within over 100 years of intellectual discourse about the theoretical and empirical connections between media and crime. We will start with one of the most enduring areas of research that our discussion of theory begins: that of media 'effects'.

Media 'effects'

One of the most persistent debates in academic and lay circles concerning the mass media is the extent to which media can be said to cause anti-social, deviant or criminal behaviour: in other words, to what degree do media images bring about *negative* effects in their viewers? The academic study of this phenomenon – *'effects research'* as it has come to be known – developed from two main sources: **mass society** theory and **behaviourism**. Although deriving from different disciplines – sociology and psychology respectively – these two approaches find compatibility in their essentially pessimistic view of society and their belief that human nature is unstable and susceptible to external influences. This section explores how mass society theory and psychological behaviourism gave rise to the notion that media images are responsible for eroding moral standards, subverting consensual codes of behaviour and corrupting young minds.

It is often taken as an unassailable fact that society has become more violent since the advent of the modern media industry. The arrival and growth of film, television, computer technologies and social media, have served to intensify public anxieties but there are few crime waves which are genuinely new phenomena, despite the media's efforts to present them as such. For many observers, it is a matter of 'common sense' that society has become increasingly characterized by crime – especially violent crime – since the advent of the mass media, even though crime surveys show declining rates of offending in many jurisdictions. For example, the Crime Survey for England & Wales, published in April 2014 by the Office for National Statistics showed that overall crime rates fell by 15 per cent in 2013, and violent crime has dropped by 22 per cent.

Nonetheless there is a persistent mythology that crime rates continuously climb and that this sorry state of affairs is inextricably linked to an insufficiently regulated media. Yet as Pearson (1983) illustrates, the history of respectable fears goes back several hundred years, and public outrage at perceived crime waves has become more intensely focused with the introduction of each new media innovation. From theatrical productions in the 18th century, the birth of commercial cinema and the emergence of cheap, sensationalistic publications known as 'Penny Dreadfuls' at the end of the 19th century, to jazz and 'pulp fiction' in the early 20th century, popular fears about the influence of visual images on vulnerable minds have been well rehearsed in this country and elsewhere. As significant advancements were made through the course of the 20th century in photography, cinema, the popular press, television and, latterly, mobile communication technologies and the Internet, it became common for writers and thinkers to mourn the passing of a literate culture, which was believed to require a degree of critical thinking, and bemoan its replacement, a visual popular culture which was believed to plug directly into the mind of the masses without need for rational thought or interpretation.

Mass society theory

Emerging in the latter years of the 19th century and early 20th century, 'mass society' became firmly established as a sociological theory after the Second World War. The term usually carries negative connotations, referring to the masses or the 'common people' who are characterized by their lack of individuality, their alienation from the moral and ethical values to be gained from work and religion, their political apathy, and their taste for 'low' culture. In most versions of the theory, individuals are seen as uneducated, ignorant, potentially unruly and prone to violence. The late 19th and early 20th centuries marked a period of tremendous turbulence and uncertainty, and mass society theorists held that social upheavals associated with industrialization, urbanization and the Great War had made people feel increasingly vulnerable. Within this atomized society, two important strands of thought can be detected. First, it was believed that as communities fragmented and traditional social ties were dismantled, society became a mass of isolated individuals cut adrift from kinship and organic ties and lacking moral cohesion. An increase in crime and anti-social behaviour seemed inevitable, and as mass society took hold – in all its complex, over-bureaucratized incomprehensibility – citizens turned away from the authorities who were seen as remote, indifferent and incompetent. Instead they sought solutions to crime at a personal, community-orientated, 'micro' level, which included vigilantism, personal security devices and, in some countries, guns. The second significant development that emerged from conceptualizations of mass society was that the media were seen as both an aid to people's well-being under difficult circumstances and as a powerful force for controlling people's thoughts and diverting them from political action.

Behaviourism and positivism

In addition to mass society theory, models of media effects have been strongly influenced by behaviourism; an empiricist approach to psychology pioneered by J.B. Watson in the first decade of the 20th century. Deriving from a philosophy known as *positivism*, which emerged from the natural sciences and regards the world as fixed and quantifiable, behaviourism represented a major challenge to the more dominant perspective of *psychoanalysis*. Shifting the research focus away from the realm of the mind with its emphasis on introspection and individual interpretation, behavioural psychologists argued that an individual's identity was shaped by their responses to the external environment which formed stable and recognizable patterns of behaviour that could be publicly observed. In addition to emulating the scientific examination of relations between organisms in the natural world, Watson was inspired by Ivan Pavlov, who was famously conducting experiments with dogs, producing 'conditioned responses' (salivating) to external stimuli (a bell ringing). The impact of these developments led to a belief that the complex structures and systems that make up human behaviour could be observed and measured and predictions of future behaviour made. In addition to stimulus-response experiments in psychology and the natural sciences, developments were occurring elsewhere which took a similar view of human behaviour; for example, the modern education system was being established with learning being seen as something to be tested and examined.

Meanwhile, in criminology, the search for objective knowledge through the positive application of science was also having a significant impact. The endeavour to observe and measure the relationship between 'cause and effect' led to a belief that criminality is not a matter of free will, but is caused by a biological, psychological or social disposition over which the offender has little or no control. Through gaining knowledge about how behaviour is determined by such conditions – be they genetic deficiencies or disadvantages associated with their social environments – it was believed that problems such as crime and deviance could be examined and treated. The most famous name in positivist criminology is Cesare Lombroso, an Italian physician who studied the bodies of executed criminals and concluded that law-breakers were physically different to non-offenders. He claimed that criminals were atavistic throwbacks to an earlier stage of biological development and could be identified by physical abnormalities such as prominent jaws, strong canine teeth, sloping foreheads, unusual ear size and so on. Although in more recent years positivist forms of criminology have become theoretically more sophisticated, Lombroso's rather crude approach to biological criminology is still evident today, particularly in popular media discourses about women and children who commit serious and violent crime (see Chapters 4 and 5).

While criminologists in the early decades of the 20th century were concerning themselves with isolating the variables most likely to be found in criminals as distinct from non-criminals, media researchers were also developing new theories based on positivist assumptions and behaviourist methods. The notion that all human action is modelled on the condition reflex, so that one's action is precipitated by responses to stimuli in one's environment rather than being a matter of individual agency, made the new media of mass communication an obvious candidate for concern. Amid rising levels of affluence, advertisers were to become regarded as 'hidden persuaders' who could influence people to purchase consumer goods almost against their better judgement. Additionally, experiments were conducted under laboratory conditions to try to establish a direct causal link between media images and resultant changes in behaviour, notably an inclination among research participants to demonstrate markedly agitated or aggressive tendencies.

One of the most famous series of experiments was that conducted by Albert Bandura and colleagues at Stanford University, California in the 1950s and 1960s, in which children were shown a film or cartoon depicting some kind of violent act and were then given 'Bobo' dolls to play with (these were large inflatable dolls with weighted bases to ensure that they wobble but do not stay down when struck). Their behaviour towards the dolls was used as a measure of the programme's effect, and when the children were observed behaving aggressively (compared to a control group who did not watch the violent content) it was taken as evidence that a direct relationship existed between 'screen violence' and juvenile aggression. Although these studies were undoubtedly influential and, indeed, have attained a certain notoriety, they are hugely problematic and have been rejected by most contemporary media scholars on the grounds of their many flaws and inconsistencies. Bandura and his colleagues have been widely discredited for, among other things: failing to replicate a 'real life' media environment; reducing complex patterns of human behaviour to a single factor among a wide network of mediating influences and therefore treating children as unsophisticated 'lab rats'; being able to measure only immediate responses to media content and having nothing to say about the long-term, cumulative effects of exposure to violent material; using dolls that were designed to frustrate; praising or rewarding children when they behaved as 'expected'; and overlooking the fact that children who had not been shown any film stimulus were nevertheless found to behave aggressively towards the Bobo doll if left with it – and especially if they felt it was expected of them by the experimenter.

Effects research is sometimes termed the **hypodermic syringe model** because the relationship between media and audiences is conceived as a mechanistic and unsophisticated process, by which the media 'inject' values, ideas and information directly into the passive receiver, producing direct and unmediated 'effects' which, in turn, have a negative influence on thoughts and actions. Anxieties about media effects have traditionally taken one of three forms. The first is a moral or religious anxiety that exposure to the popular media encourages lewd behaviour and corrupts established norms of decency and moral certitude. A second anxiety, from the intellectual right, is that the mass media undermine the civilizing influence of high culture (great literature, art and so on) and debase tastes. A third concern, which has traditionally been associated with the intellectual left, is that the mass media represent the ruling élite, and manipulate mass consciousness in their interests. This view was given a particular impetus by the emergence of fascist and totalitarian governments across Europe in the 1920s and 1930s, which used propaganda to great effect in winning the hearts and minds of the people. The belief that the new media of mass communications were among the most powerful weapons of these political regimes was given academic attention by members of the Frankfurt School – a group of predominantly Jewish scholars who themselves fled Hitler's Germany for America.

A famous example from America that appears to support mass society theory's belief in an omnipresent and potentially harmful media and behaviourism's assumptions about the observable reactions of a susceptible audience, concerns the radio transmission of H.G. Wells' *War of the Worlds* on Halloween Night in October 1938. The broadcast was a fictitious drama concerning the invasion of aliens from Mars, but many believed they were listening to a *real* report of a Martian attack. While the broadcast was on air, panic broke out. People all over the US prayed, cried, fled their homes and telephoned loved ones to say emotional farewells (Cantril, 1940, in O'Sullivan and Jewkes, 1997). One in six listeners were said to have been very frightened by the broadcast, a fear that was exacerbated by the gravitas of the narrator, Orson Welles, and by the cast of 'experts' giving orders for evacuation and attack. As one listener said: 'I believed the broadcast as soon as I heard the professor from Princeton and the officials in Washington' (1997: 9). This case provides a powerfully resonant metaphor for the belief that the modern media are capable of exerting harmful influences, of triggering mass outbreaks of negative social consequence and of causing damaging psychological effects. However, to characterize the episode as 'proof' of the hypodermic syringe effect of the media would be very misleading. The relationship between stimulus and response was not simple or direct because the panic experienced by some listeners was not without context. It was the time of the Depression, and American citizens were experiencing a prolonged period of economic unrest and widespread unemployment and were looking to their leaders for reassurance and direction. War was breaking out in Europe and many believed that an attack by a foreign power was imminent. It is of little surprise, then, that the realistic quality of the broadcast – played out as an extended news report in which the radio announcer appeared to be actually witnessing terrible events unfolding before him – powerfully tapped into the feelings of insecurity, change and loss being experienced by many American people, to produce panic.

The legacy of 'effects' research

Scholars in the UK have strongly resisted attempts to assert a direct, causal link between media images and deviant behaviour. The idea of isolating television, film or any other medium as a variable and ignoring all the other factors that might influence a person's behaviour, is considered too crude and reductive an idea to be of any epistemological value. Much effects research that cannot adequately address the subtleties of media meanings, the polysemy of media texts (that is, they are open to multiple interpretations), the unique characteristics and identity of the audience member, or the social and cultural context within which the encounter between media text and audience member occurs. It mistakenly assumes that we all have the same ideas about what constitutes 'aggression', 'violence' and 'deviance', and that those who are susceptible to harmful portrayals can be affected by a 'one-off' media incident, regardless of the wider context of a lifetime of meaning-making. It also ignores the possibility that influence travels the opposite way; that is, that the characteristics, interests and concerns of the audience may determine what media producers produce.

But despite obvious flaws, behaviourist assumptions about the power of the media to influence criminal and anti-social behaviour persist, especially – and somewhat ironically – in discussions within the popular media, which are frequently intended to bring pressure on governments and other authorities to tighten up controls on other elements of the media. Of particular salience in the public imagination is the notion that media content may lead to copycat acts of violence. This view is prominently aired when spree killings occur, especially those on school and college campuses perpetrated by disaffected students, and when new films and computer games are released that are clearly aimed at consumers younger than the official age classification awarded them. Assumptions about harmful media effects draw on Lombrosian ideas about the kinds of individuals most likely to be affected. In addition, they dovetail neatly with mass society theorists' fears that institutions such as the family and religion are losing their power to shape young minds, and that socialization happens instead via external forces, notably the media. Whether assessing the effects of advertising, measuring the usefulness of political campaigns in predicting voting behaviour, deciding film and video classifications or introducing software to aid parents in controlling their children's exposure to certain forms of Internet content, much policy in these areas is underpinned by mediacentric, message-specific, micro-orientated, positivist, authoritarian, short-term assumptions of human behaviour.

The ongoing political debate about censorship and control of the media tends to periodically reach an apotheosis when serious, high-profile crimes occur, especially those perpetrated by children or young people. For example, following the tragic death of two-year-old James Bulger at the hands of two older boys in February 1993, there was a great deal of speculation in the popular press that the murderers had watched and imitated *Child's Play 3*, a mildly violent 'video nasty' about a psychopathic doll. Despite there being no evidence that the boys ever saw the film, and consistent denials from the police that there was a connection, the insidious features of *Child's Play 3* were soon ingrained in the public consciousness:

> Our gut tells us they must have seen the evil doll Chucky. They must have loved the film. And they must have seen it over and over again, because some of the things they did are almost exact copies of the screenplay ... We all know that violence begets violence. (Anne Diamond, *Daily Mirror*, 1 December 1993, quoted in Petley, 1997: 188)

This appeal to common sense ('we all know ...') is a perennial feature of what has come to be known as the 'copycat' theory of crime and is seen by its adherents as natural and unassailable. However, it is instructive here to remember Gramsci's definition of the term 'common sense': 'a reservoir of historically discontinuous and disjointed ideas that functions as the philosophy of non-philosophers', a folklore whose fundamental distinction is its 'fragmentary, incoherent and inconsequential character' (Gramsci, 1971: 419). Others, meanwhile, have demonstrated how the unquestioned truths which we accept as common sense are, in fact, culturally derived mythologies specific not only to individual cultures but also to particular points in time (Barthes, 1973; Foucault, 1977; Geertz, 1983).

The link between screen violence and real-life violence was given a gloss of academic respectability when, following the Bulger case, Professor Elizabeth Newson, head of the Child Development Unit at Nottingham University, produced a report that was endorsed by 25 psychologists, paediatricians and other academics. Despite extensive and sustained publicity in the media, it turned out that Newson's report was just nine pages long, contained no original research, and concluded – as these things inevitably do – that more research was needed. But despite the highly-questionable evidence for the potentially harmful effects of media content, the proposition that media portrayals of crime and violence desensitize the viewer to 'real' pain and suffering, and may excite or arouse some people to commit similar acts, persists in the popular imagination where it is rarely applied universally, but tends to be tinged with a distinct class-edged bias. Echoes of both mass society theory and criminological positivism can be detected in the lingering notion of a threatening 'underclass' who pose the greatest threat to society. This view, appealing to common-sense notions of 'intelligent people' versus the dark shapeless mass that forms the residue of society, also has a gendered bias. The contemporary culture of blame is frequently directed at the 'monstrous offspring' of 'bad mothers', a construction that combines two contemporary *folk devils* and taps into cultural fears of the 'other', which will be explored further in Chapters 4 and 5. Consequently, when particularly horrific crimes come to light, the knee-jerk reaction of a society unwilling to concede that depravity and cruelty reside within its midst, is frequently to turn to the familiar scapegoat of the mass media to attribute blame.

Another version of this approach, which also has its roots in mass society theory, concerns a broader preoccupation with the globalization of cultural forms and products and, in particular, the American origin of much popular global culture. Television, cinema, video and latterly the Internet, have come in for particular criticism by those who view anything American in origin as intrinsically cheap, trashy and alien to British culture and identity. Fears dating back more than a century have become crystallized in the view that the popular media are slowly corrupting the 'British' way of life by importing values that are altogether more vulgar and trashy from the other side of the Atlantic. The concerns of the Frankfurt School theorists Adorno and Horkheimer about the debasement of 'high' culture by 'low' popular cultural forms found synthesis in the UK with élitist expressions of concern about an American-inspired *youth* culture in post-War Britain. Since that time, a variety of moral panics have reached these shores only months after their appearance in America, and a wide range of phenomena – rock and roll music, mugging, dangerous dogs, car-jacking, satanic child abuse, gun crime, gang warfare and crystal meth addiction – have been characterized by our media as essentially 'un-British'; an unwelcome and alien crime-wave from the US (see Chapter 3).

Strain theory and anomie

By the 1960s academic scholars were turning their backs on positivist, behaviourist research, believing that it attributed too much power to the media and underestimated the importance of the social contexts of media consumption, the social structures which mediate the relationship between the state and the individual, and the sophistication and diversity of the audience. Similarly, positivist approaches to explaining crime in terms of its individual, biological roots were giving way to more sociologically informed approaches which originated in the work of the Chicago School in the 1920s and 1930s. The overriding concern of Chicago School sociology was to understand the role of social environment and social interaction on deviant and criminal behaviour. In other words, it was recognized that where people grow up and who they associate with is closely linked to their likelihood of involvement in crime and anti-social behaviour.

Limitations of space preclude a full discussion of sociological approaches to crime here, but one important early theory that has a bearing on the present discussion of the relationship between media and crime is Robert Merton's (1938) strain theory, or 'anomie'. Like mass society theory, strain theory takes as its starting point a decline of community and social order and its replacement by alienation and disorder. Whole sections of society are cut adrift, unable to conform to the norms that traditionally bind communities together. Yet, within this state of normlessness, society as a whole remains more or less intact. Social cohesion may be partly accounted for by the pursuit of common objectives, and anomie draws attention to the goals that people are encouraged to aspire to, such as a comfortable level of wealth or status, and their means of attaining those goals; for example, hard work. Through socialization, most come to accept both the goals *and* the legitimate means of achieving them; a process summed up in the notion of the 'American Dream'. But anomie describes a situation where a society places strong emphasis on a particular goal, but far less emphasis on the appropriate means of achieving it. It is this imbalance that can lead some individuals, who Merton terms 'innovators', to pursue nonconformist or illegal paths to achieve the culturally-sanctioned goals of success and wealth and one of the key factors involved in the internalization of cultural goals is the media which, it might be argued, instil in people needs and desires that may not be gratifiable by means other than criminal. The anomic drive might thus be less concerned with feelings of desperation and more to do with conspicuous consumption and the desire for peer approval. Coleman and Norris (2000) even suggest that strain theory may help to explain serial killing, arguing that the growth of the American economy since the 1960s has resulted in a commensurate rise in the numbers of serial killings. Inevitably, some sections of the population will be excluded from the general rise in living standards which, in a culture that glorifies violence, may lead some disaffected individuals to a (usually misdirected) desire for revenge.

Anomie has fallen in and out of favour with remarkable fluidity over the years, but from its nadir in the 1970s when Rock and McIntosh referred to the 'exhaustion of the anomie tradition' (in Downes and Rock, 1988: 110) it has recently enjoyed something of a revival thanks to two diverse phenomena. The first is the emergence of interest within cultural criminology in transgressive forms of excitement, ranging from extreme sports to violent crime, as a means of combating the routinized alienation that besets contemporary life. The second is the growth of the Internet and social media, which seem to offer a solution to the problems of dislocation by fostering a sense of community across time and space. In the world of virtual reality, anomie is both 'a condition and a pleasure' (Osborne, 2002: 29).

Marxism, critical criminology and the 'dominant ideology' approach

It is clear from the discussion so far that the mid-20th century saw a change in focus from the individual to society. This *paradigm* shift led to the predominance of Marxist-inspired models of media power and, in particular, to the writings of Karl Marx (1818–83) and Antonio Gramsci (1891–1937). Their theories of social structure led to the development of an approach known as the 'dominant ideology' model, which was taken up enthusiastically by both criminologists and media researchers in the 1960s and dominated academic discussions of media power for over 20 years.

Marxism proposes that the media – like all other capitalist institutions – are owned by the ruling bourgeois élite and operate in the interests of that class, denying access to oppositional or alternative views. Although the media were far from being the mass phenomena in Marx's lifetime that they are today, their position as a key capitalist industry, and their power to widely disseminate messages which affirm the validity and legitimacy of a stratified society, made his theories seem very relevant at a later time when the mass media was going through a combined process of expansion, deregulation and concentration of ownership and control. Gramsci developed Marx's theories to incorporate the concept of *hegemony*, which has played a central role in theorizing about the media's portrayal of crime, deviance, and law and order. In brief, hegemony refers to the process by which the ruling classes win approval for their actions by consent rather than by coercion. This is largely achieved through social and cultural institutions such as the law, the family, the education system and the media. All such institutions reproduce everyday representations and meanings in such a way as to render the class interests of those in power apparently natural and inevitable. The media thus play a crucial role in the winning of consent for a social system, its values and its dominant interests, or in the rejection of them. This is an important refinement of Marx's original formulation, for Gramsci dispensed with the idea that people passively take on the ideas *in toto* of the ruling élite (a position usually termed 'false consciousness'), and instead established a model of power in which different cultural elements are subtly articulated together to appeal to the widest possible spectrum of opinion.

The writings of Marx and Gramsci inform the theoretical organization of much of the most important and influential work which emerged within the social sciences in the 1970s and 1980s. For example, although Marx himself had little to say about crime, the rediscovery of his theories of social structure gave impetus to a new 'radical' criminology that sought to expose the significance of structural inequalities upon crime and, crucially, upon *criminalization*. Also drawing heavily on labelling theory, which posits that crime and deviance are not the product of either a 'sick individual' or a 'sick society' but that 'deviant behaviour is behaviour that people so label' (Becker, 1963: 8), a new generation of radical criminologists such as Taylor et al. (who, in 1973, published the hugely influential *The New Criminology*) took this proposition and gave it a Marxist edge, arguing that the power to label people as deviants or criminals and prosecute and punish them accordingly was a function of the state. In other words, acts are defined as criminal because it is in the interests of the ruling class to define them as such, and while the powerful will violate laws with impunity, working-class crimes will be punished.

Inspired by the 'new criminology', a number of further 'radical' studies emerged which drew attention to the criminogenic function of the state and the role of the media in orchestrating public panics about crime and deflecting concerns away from the social problems that emanate from capitalism. This work became known as *critical criminology* and of particular importance is Stuart Hall et al.'s *Policing the Crisis: Mugging, the State and Law and Order* (1978/2013), which remains one of the most important texts on the *ideological* role of the media in defining and reporting crime and deviance. In media research, the work of the Glasgow University Media Group (GUMG) is also of note. The GUMG produced a series of '*Bad News*' studies based on empirical and semiotic analysis looking at bias in television news coverage of industrial conflicts, political disputes and acts of war. The central finding in these studies is that television news represses the diversity of opinions in any given situation, reproduces a dominant ideology (based on, for example, middle-class, anti-dissent and pro-family views) and silences contradictory voices. Another important perspective that influenced studies of media power throughout the 1980s and beyond was the *political economy* approach, which claims that the undisputed fact of increasing concentration of media ownership in recent years makes Marx's analysis all the more relevant to contemporary debates about the power of the media. Political economy focuses on relations between media and other economic and political institutions and argues that, since the mass media are largely privately owned, the drive for profit will shape their output and political position. Concentration of ownership, it is suggested, leads to a decline in the material available (albeit that there are more channels in which to communicate), a preoccupation with ratings at the expense of quality and choice, and a preference for previously successful formulae over innovation and risk-taking. The net result of these processes is that the material offered is reduced to the commercially viable, popular, easily understood and largely unchallenging (Golding and Murdock, 2000).

Some writers go as far as to suggest that the 'dumbing down' of culture is part of a wider manipulative strategy on the part of the military-industrial complex to prevent people from engaging in serious political thought or activity. For example, Noam Chomsky's 'propaganda-model' demonstrates how certain stories are underrepresented in the media because of powerful military-industrial interests. In a content analysis of the *New York Times* he shows how atrocities committed by Indonesia in East Timor received a fraction of the coverage devoted to the Khmer Rouge killings in Cambodia. Chomsky claims that the reason for this imbalanced coverage is that the weaponry used to slaughter the people of East Timor was supplied by America, Britain and Holland (Herman and Chomsky, 1992).

There are countless other examples that could be drawn on to make the point that, when it comes to global power structures, the media are highly selective in what they report. On the other hand, it is sometimes the case that journalists go where politicians fear to tread. The diplomatic protocols surrounding East–West relations, and the shifts in global power that have taken place over the last two decades, have resulted in a situation where leaders in the West have become cautious about criticizing other nations' human rights records. The news that US President, Barack Obama, cancelled a visit by the Dalai Llama to 'keep China happy' (*Daily Telegraph*, 5 October 2009) was treated with scorn by many news outlets, who recalled that 18 months earlier, Obama had lobbied his predecessor, George W. Bush, to boycott the Beijing Olympics opening ceremony in protest at the bloody repression of a popular uprising in Tibet.

Although not without their critics, the Marxist-inspired works discussed in this section were among the first to systematically and rigorously interrogate the role of the media in shaping our understanding, not only of crime and deviance, but also of the processes of criminalization. The common theme in all these studies is that information flows from the top down, with the media representing the views of political leaders, military leaders, police chiefs, judges, prominent intellectuals, advertisers and big business, newspaper owners and vocal opinion leaders. At the same time, they reduce the viewer, reader or listener to the role of passive receiver, overshadowing his or her opinions, concerns and beliefs. Thus, a hierarchy of credibility is established in which the opinions and definitions of powerful members of society are privileged, while the 'ordinary' viewer or reader is prevented by lack of comparative material from engaging in critical or comparative thinking (Ericson et al., 1987).

This structured relationship between the media and its 'powerful' sources has important consequences for the representation of crime, criminals and criminal justice, particularly with respect to those whose lifestyle or behaviour deviates from the norms established by a white, male, heterosexual, educationally privileged élite. For example, in *Policing the Crisis* (1978/2013), Hall and his colleagues demonstrate how the press significantly over-reacted to the perceived threat of violent crime in the early 1970s and created a moral panic about 'mugging', but only *after* there had been an intensification of police mobilization against black offenders. The net result of these forces – public fear and hostility fuelled by sensationalized media reporting and heavy-handed treatment of black people by the police – combined to produce a situation where more black people were arrested and put before the courts, which in turn set the spiral for continuing media attention. But as Hall et al. explain, this episode can be set against a backdrop of economic and structural crisis in 1970s' Britain, whereby the disintegration of traditional, regulated forms of life led to a displaced reaction onto black and Asian immigrants and their descendants. The central thesis of the book is that by the 1970s, the consent that might previously have been won by the ruling classes was being severely undermined, and the state was struggling to retain power. The birth of the 'law and order' society, evidenced in the development of a pre-emptive escalation of social control directed at a minority population, served to divert public attention from the looming economic and structural crisis, crystallize public fears in the figure of the black mugger, create a coherent popular discourse that sanctioned tougher penal measures, and ultimately justify the drift towards ideological repression. All these developments were disclosed, supported and made acceptable by a media that had become one of the most important instruments in maintaining hegemonic power.

Critics of the hegemonic approach suggest that it overstates the *intent* of powerful institutions to deceive the public. They argue that it is not the case that media industries maintain a policy of deliberately ignoring or marginalizing significant portions of their audience. The tendency of professional communicators to perpetuate the taken-for-granted assumptions of consensus politics is not something that is necessarily overt, deliberate or even conscious, and certainly can rarely be described with any certainty as conspiracy. Rather, it may be attributed to an underlying frame of mind that characterizes news organizations (Halloran, 1970). In other words, journalists are like those who work within any organization or institution in that they are gradually socialized into the ways and ethos of that environment and come to recognize the appropriate ways of responding to the subtle pressures which are always there but rarely become overtly apparent. In a news room these 'ways of responding' range from the individual reporter's intuitive 'hunch' through perceptions about what constitutes a 'good story' and 'giving the public what it wants' to more structured ideological biases, which predispose the media to focus on certain events and turn them into 'news'. But hegemonists maintain that alternative definitions of any given situation may not get aired simply because there is no longer the spread of sources that there once was. The ownership and control of the mass media is concentrated in the hands of fewer and fewer individuals, and there is a reliance among editors on a relatively limited pool of expert and readily available sources. These official sources and accredited 'experts', together with the journalists themselves, thus become the 'primary definers' of much news and information; a kind of deviance-defining élite (Ericson et al., 1987). Consequently, according to proponents of the 'dominant ideology' approach, there is an increasing risk that culturally dominant groups impose patterns of belief and behaviour which conflict with those of ethnic, cultural and religious minorities. Feminists have argued that gender inequalities in society are also reproduced ideologically by a patriarchal media industry; an issue that will be examined further in Chapter 5.

The legacy of Marxism: critical criminology and corporate crime

As we have seen, the dominant ideology approach has successfully highlighted the extent to which those in power manipulate the media agenda to harness support for policies that criminalize those with least power in society. But Marxist-inspired criminologies have also been useful in raising awareness of the crimes of the powerful themselves; in other words, the offences committed by corporations, business people, politicians, governments and states. Critical criminologists whose intellectual roots lie in Marxism have noted that the media rarely covers 'white collar' or 'corporate' crime unless it has a 'big bang' element and contains several features considered conventionally newsworthy (see Chapter 2). Their reluctance to portray corporate wrongs contrasts with the manufacturing of 'street' crime waves and reflects a pervasive bias in the labelling of criminals. Although this inclination extends beyond the media and arguably constitutes a collective ignorance towards corporate crime on the part of all social institutions, there is little doubt that the media are among the most guilty in perpetuating very narrow definitions of crime. In fact, the media might be said to be doubly culpable: first for portraying affluence as the ultimate anomic goal and glamorizing images of offending and, second, for pandering to public tastes for drama and immediacy over complexity. As Steven Box says, 'the public understands more easily what it means for an old lady to have £5 snatched from her purse than to grasp the financial significance of corporate crime' (1983: 31).

In recent years criminologists have sought to redress this imbalance and to expose the crimes of governments and corporations. For example, Tombs and Whyte (2007) have estimated that two million people are killed at work each year. With the exception of high-profile cases such as the gas leak at Bhopal,

India, in 1984, or the collapse of the eight-storey Rana Plaza clothing factory building near Dhaka, Bangladesh in 2013, both of which killed thousands of people, crimes that have occurred as a result of corporate negligence or error fail to attract a great deal of interest. Even the reported deaths of more than 1,000 migrant workers on Qatar building sites as the Gulf state prepares to host the FIFA World Cup in 2022, has received a fraction of the media coverage devoted to other issues, including the heat in which the qualifying football teams will be expected to play in. Like allegations of corruption and bribery (now so commonly associated with FIFA that they barely raise a quizzical eyebrow), the migrant slave-labour used to build the infrastructure for the World Cup may only become prominent in the news if the decision to hold the event in Qatar is reversed.

But as Chapter 2 will demonstrate, crime is by-and-large portrayed by the media as a matter of individual pathology which mitigates against the investigation and reporting of wrongdoings in a large organization. On the whole, corporate crimes are not the stuff of catchy headlines and tend to be reported, if at all, in such a way as to reinforce impressions of their exceptional nature and distinction from 'ordinary' crime. The underdeveloped vocabulary of corporate crime compounds the difficulty of regarding it as an offence. Words such as 'accident' and 'disaster' appear in contexts where 'crime' and 'negligence' might be more accurate. Where they succeed in making the news agenda, corporate crimes are frequently treated not as offences, but as 'scandals' or 'abuses of power', terminology which implies 'sexy upper-world intrigue' (Punch, 1996). Alternatively, they may be presented as 'acts of God', thus reinforcing the notion that modern life is beset by risks and that actions that result in casualties and/or fatalities are random or preordained, depending on your religious convictions. The choice of this kind of language not only serves the purposes of a commercial media steeped in circulation and ratings wars, but it also suits corporations themselves who are able to secure powerful political allies and carefully control and manage information about damning incidents (Herman and Chomsky, 1992). So, while a few journalists uphold the investigative tradition and are prepared to act as whistleblowers when they uncover corporate offences, the vast majority of media institutions – according to radical crime and media theorists – either ignore the crimes of the powerful or misrepresent them. As a consequence, news reporting remains coupled to state definitions of crime and criminal law.

A related area that does not attract much media attention, although it is a burgeoning field of critical criminology is 'green' crime. A new generation of scholars are examining notions of environmental harm and justice, following the publication of a special issue of *Theoretical Criminology* on 'green criminology' in 1998 (edited by Piers Bierne and Nigel South). Since then, debates about the meaning of 'green' to criminology have resulted in a wealth of scholarship that has taken the discipline into new and imaginative areas of concern, including climate change, air and water pollution, genetically modified food and animal abuse (Walters, 2010; South and Brisman, 2013; White, 2013). Some green criminologists have made dramatic, even apocalyptic, claims about the impacts of environmental harm; for example predicting that climate change will become one of the major forces driving *all* crime over the course of this century (Agnew, 2012: 21). However, like corporate crime more generally, ecological and environmental offences can be difficult to communicate succinctly, attempts to attribute blame can appear tenuous, and audiences may simply fail to connect with stories about issues that do not necessarily seem to affect them obviously, directly and immediately.

Pluralism, competition and ideological struggle

The theoretical models outlined so far share a belief in the omnipresence of the media and hold assumptions about a passive and stratified audience, with those at the bottom of the socio-economic strata being the most vulnerable to media influences, whether they be 'effects' caused by media content or discrimination at the hands of a powerful élite that uses the mass media as its mouthpiece. By contrast, the 'competitive' or 'pluralist' paradigm that emerged during the 1980s and 1990s tends to be a more positive reading of the mass media as an embodiment of intellectual freedom and diversity offered to a knowledgeable and skeptical audience. Given this favourable characterization of the media industry, it is unsurprising that, while the 'dominant ideology' perspective has been influential within the academy, *pluralism* has been championed by practitioners and policy-makers.

Pluralists argue that the processes of deregulation, privatization and technological advancement which have gone on over the last two decades have succeeded in removing the media from state regulation and censorship, encouraged open competition between media institutions and given media users more individual power. Advocates of these processes have heralded a new age of freedom in which the greatly increased number of television and radio channels, magazine titles and, particularly, Internet-based networking services have offered a previously unimaginable extension of public choice in a media market of plurality and openness. The result has been that, in addition to the primary definers already mentioned – politicians, police chiefs and so on – there also exist 'counter definers'; people with views and ideas which conflict with those of official commentators, and which are given voice through various media channels. Consequently it is suggested, while we can still identify a dominant economic class in an abstract, materialistic sense, it rarely acts as a coherent political force and is consistently challenged by individuals and organizations campaigning for policy changes in areas such as criminal justice. Furthermore, traditional ideological inequalities formed along lines of class, gender and race no longer inhabit the static positions suggested by those who favour the dominant ideology approach outlined previously. Thanks to higher education, social mobility, the Internet and the rise of the 'celebrity culture', the contemporary 'ruling class' is more culturally diverse than at any time previously, and the modern media has been at the forefront of the erosion of traditional élitist values (McNair, 1998).

The expansion and proliferation of media channels and the Internet have certainly made more accessible the views and ideas of a greater diversity of people. In the past, the pluralist perspective might have been said to be limited by its sheer idealism because it does not take account of the many vested interests in media ownership and control, or of the fact that, for all the proliferation of new channels, media industries are still predominantly owned and controlled by a small handful of white, wealthy, middle-class men (or corporations started by such men). However, even though the media still may be regarded as a potential site of ideological struggle, proponents of the competitive, pluralist paradigm believe that *all* minority interests can be served by the plurality of channels of communication available. In particular social media is said to have democratized contemporary cultural life, with Twitter and blogs providing powerful channels of influence and offering a form of public participation to those who traditionally may not have had access to it.

However, social media have also joined competition and deregulation in being said to pose a serious threat to informed media commentary and analysis. Following accusations that in a commercial marketplace, competition for audience share leads to 'soundbite' journalism, in which there is little room for background, explanation or context, those who have not embraced social media despair at the idea of communicating anything meaningfully in 140 characters! Further, it is argued, while there may be greater public engagement with shocking or visually dramatic events, there is little evidence of extensive public participation in the issues of policy, politics and reform that underlie such stories, or of a media willing to communicate such a context to the public (Barak, 1994; Manning, 2001). Public participation in *mediated* discourse may *appear* to be more inclusive: after all, more people can air their views on the serious issues of the day – not just on Twitter but also via talk radio, television audience shows, newspapers' reader comments and other online forums. In fact texting and social media have broadened traditional channels of communication to the extent where television news broadcasts now encourage viewers to send in their thoughts and opinions to be transmitted almost instantaneously on air. But the 20- or 30-second viewer contribution has arguably been introduced at the expense of complex analysis or detailed critique, and *media* pluralism – that is, many channels – does not necessarily result in *message* pluralism – diversity of content (Barak, 1994).

Critics argue that the mainstream media continue to provide homogenized versions of reality that avoid controversy and preserve the status quo. Consequently, ignorance among audiences is perpetuated, and the labelling, *stereotyping* and criminalization of certain groups (often along lines of class, race and gender) persists. We might view the success of the *Daily Mail* as evidence of homogenized and stereotyping news output. A British newspaper described by *New Statesman* and *Huffington Post* columnist Mehdi Hasan as 'immigrant-bashing, woman-hating, Muslim-smearing, NHS-undermining [and] gay-baiting', the *Mail* has gone from strength to strength in recent years, under the Editorship of Paul Dacre, the 'man who hates liberal Britain' (www.newstatesman.com/media/2013/12/man-who-hates-liberal-britain). Not only does the paper sell an average of 1.5 million copies on weekdays (2.4 million on Saturdays) but its 4.3 million daily readers include more from the top three social classes (A, B and C1) than the *Times*, *Guardian*, *Independent* and *Financial Times* combined (ibid). Furthermore the *Mail*'s online version has overtaken the *New York Times* to become the world's most visited newspaper website, with 45.3 million visitors a month. Political economists would argue that the increasingly commercialized character of media institutions like the *Daily Mail* results in tried and tested formulae – a focus on entertainment, gossip and celebrity (much of it misogynistically directed at women's bodies), with a good measure of terrifying stories, frequently involving violent and atypical crimes, thrown in.

The tendency to play it safe by offering the shocking, the sensational and the 'real' is also evident in TV schedules where mainstream programming is dominated by seemingly endless and increasingly stale imitations of once innovative ideas. Even 24-hour rolling news services are restricted by the news values to which they have to conform (see Chapter 2) and by the pressures of having to succeed in a commercial environment. As Blumler (1991: 207) observes of American broadcast news media, while they may have a tradition of professional political journalism, it can nonetheless be the case that 'heightened competition tempts national network news ... to avoid complexity and hit only those highlights that will gain and keep viewers' attention'. These 'highlights' will rarely involve in-depth political commentary or sustained analysis. Instead, viewers are fed a diet of 'infotainment' which may have a strong 'human interest' angle, a particularly dramatic or violent element, or a visually arresting component. This trend – often described by its critics as the 'dumbing down' of news and current affairs media – privileges audience ratings over analysis and debate and results in 'a flawed process of public accountability, with few forums in which issues can be regularly explored from multiple perspectives' (1991: 207). Crime is a subject that is especially limited and constrained by a media agenda on an endless quest for populist, profitable programming. One of the few strands of 'documentary' film making that has survived the wave of deregulation celebrated by pluralists is the 'true crime' genre where a serious criminal case is re-examined via a predictable formula, starting with a dramatized reconstruction of the crime itself and then a smug-with-hindsight examination of the sometimes bungled, frequently tortuous police investigation, before the dramatic denouement when the culprit is captured and convicted. Such programmes – which are commonly concerned with highly unusual yet prominent cases involving rapists and serial killers – pander to the thrill-seeking, voyeuristic element of the audience, while at the same time quenching their thirst for retribution.

While pluralism has traditionally been viewed as an expression of how things *could* be, rather than how things *are*, there is no disputing that Internet-based forums are democratizing communication and allowing more freedom of expression. However, sceptics would argue that the apparent openness that social media afford to their users must be squared with a recognition that dominant groups still enjoy structural advantages and that there are ongoing conflictual processes both inside social institutions and within the media themselves.

Realism and reception analysis

Throughout the 1980s established theories were being challenged by new approaches which turned on their heads some previously held assumptions and altered the focus of scholars in both criminology and media studies. In criminology a new perspective called **left realism** emerged as both a product of, and reaction to, what it saw as the idealistic stance of the left represented in works such as *Policing the Crisis* (Hall et al., 1978/2013). Accusing writers on the left of adopting reductionist arguments about crime, and romanticizing working-class offenders, left realists claimed that the political arena had been left open to conservative campaigns on law and order which chose to overlook the fact that most crime is not inter-class (that is, perpetrated by working-class people on middle-class victims), but is *intra*-class (perpetrated on members of one's own class and community). Writers such as Lea and Young (1984) urged criminologists to 'get real' about crime, to focus on the seriousness of its effects – especially for women and ethnic minorities – and to elevate the experiences of victims of crime in their analyses. After all, if there was no rational core to the proposition that crime is a serious problem, the media would have no power of leverage to the public consciousness, and the numerous attempts to theorize the relationship between media and crime discussed in this chapter would simply never have materialized.

Meanwhile, in media and cultural studies a form of audience research called *'reception analysis'*, pioneered by David Morley, dominated the agenda throughout the 1980s and 1990s. Researchers reconceptualized media influence, seeing it no longer as a force beyond an individual's control, but as a resource that is consciously *used* by people. In the modern communications environment where there is a proliferation of media, and the omniscience of any single medium or channel has diminished, most audience members will select images and meanings that relate to their sense of self-identity or to their wider experiences of work, family and social relationships. Furthermore, in an age of democratic, interactive, technology-driven communications, it is argued that media and popular culture are made from 'within' and 'below', not imposed from without and above as has been traditionally conceptualized (Fiske, 1989). By the mid-1990s, researchers had dismissed concerns about what the media *do* to people, and turned the question around, asking instead, 'what do people do *with* the media?'

An example of criminological research using this approach is *Captive Audience* (Jewkes, 2002). Here my aim was to examine the media's role in the exercise of power relations and the construction of masculine identities in prisons. At the time, most prisoners in England had access to television, although for some it was in communal TV areas and for others it was within their own rooms ('in-cell TV' was just being rolled out across the prison estate). The study found that communal TV viewing in prison replicates many of Morley's findings concerning TV within the family: 'We discuss what we want to watch and the biggest wins. That's me. I'm the biggest', is a typical comment from a male respondent in Morley's 1986 study that had resonance in the prison context. In my study, solitary viewing (and reading and listening) revealed a range of motivations and identity constructions, some of which were familiar to all media consumers (passing time, becoming informed, chilling out) and some of which had a particular salience (enhancing one's credentials as a violent man, 'tuning out' of the aggressive prison culture) or poignancy (escapism, evoking memories of loved ones) in the context of the prison.

Late-modernity and postmodernism

There is a clear trajectory that links the theories discussed so far, even if development has come from antagonism as well as agreement between different schools of thought. **Postmodernism** is a paradigm shift that impacted on all the social sciences, becoming a ubiquitous and unavoidable term throughout the 1990s. Postmodernism is frequently presented as an emphatic and decisive break with all that went before, with large-scale theories like Marxism being rejected for their all-embracing claims to knowledge and 'truth'. Most commentators now prefer to describe the current epoch in terms of *late modernity*, to indicate that, while there have been radical changes in patterns of global cultural, political and economic life, they have not entirely *replaced* the structural characteristics associated with 'modern' society; class structure, capitalism, industrialism, militarism, the nation state and so on.

However, traces of earlier theories can be found in postmodern accounts. Like reception analysts, postmodernist writers view audiences as active and creative meaning-makers. In common with realists, they share a concern with fear of crime and victimization, and make problematic concepts such as 'crime' and 'deviance' just as labelling theorists did in an earlier period. Furthermore, like advocates of the pluralist approach, postmodernists suggest that the media market has been deregulated, leading to an explosion of pro-grammes, titles and formats to choose from. All tastes and interests are now catered for, and it is the consumer who ultimately has the power to choose what he or she watches, listens to, reads and engages with, but equally what he or she ignores, rejects or subverts. In this glossy, interactive media market place, anything goes – so long as it doesn't strain an attention span of three minutes, and is packaged as 'entertainment'. Postmodernism, then, is con-cerned with the excesses of information and entertainment now available, and it emphasizes the style and packaging of media output in addition to the actual substance of its content. This is the 'society of the spectacle' (Debord, 1967) a 'hyperreality' in which media domination suffuses to such an extent that the distinction between image and reality no longer exists (Baudrillard, 1981, 1983). Mass media and the collapse of meaning have produced a culture cen-tred on immediate consumption and sensationalized impact but with little depth of analysis or contextualization (Osborne, 2002). It is the fragmentary, ephemeral and ambiguous that are observed, and pleasure, spectacle, pastiche, parody and irony are the staples of postmodern media output. The media's responsibility is to entertain, and audience gratification is the only impact worth striving for.

This abandonment of a distinction between information and entertainment raises two problems, however. The first is the threat to meaningful debate that postmodernism seems to imply. A media marketplace based on a pluralist model of ideological struggle may suffice as a forum for debate, but it relies on the public's ability to discriminate between what is true and what is not; between fact and interpretation. In an early critique of postmodernism, Dick Hebdige warns that:

> The idea of a verifiable information order, however precarious and shifting, however subject to negotiation and contestation by competing ideologies, does not survive the transition to this version of new times ... today aliens from Mars kidnap joggers, yesterday Auschwitz didn't happen, tomorrow who cares what happens? Here the so-called 'depthlessness' of the postmodern era

> extends beyond ... the tendency of the media to feed more and more greedily
> off each other, to affect the function and status of information itself. (1989: 51)

The second difficulty with postmodernism lies in how we define 'entertainment'. As Hall et al. (1978/2013) suggest, violence – including violent crime – is often regarded as intrinsically entertaining to an audience who, it is argued, have become more emotionally detached and desensitized to the vast array of visual images bombarding them from every corner of the world. Many see this as an escalating problem and highlight that it has become necessary to accelerate the drama of each successive action in order to maintain the same level of coverage (Mander, 1980).

It is usually organizations that fall outside mainstream consensus politics which best understand this theory of acceleration. Groups with a radical political agenda are well practised in the art of manipulating the media and will frequently 'create' a story through the use of controversial, but stage-managed, techniques, knowing that it will make 'good copy'. Greenpeace, the Animal Liberation Front, pro- and anti-foxhunting groups, 'Fathers 4 Justice' and antiglobalization, anti-capitalism movements are examples of pressure groups which have been extremely successful in garnering media attention and ensuring attention-grabbing headlines. Even the police have adopted the techniques of heightened drama and suspense to produce spectacular, even voyeuristic television, with stage-managed press conferences involving 'victims' of serious crimes whom they suspect of foul play, and dramatic raids on the homes of suspected burglars and drug dealers in which police officers are accompanied by television cameras.

But it is arguably terrorists who have taken the lesson of sensationalized impact to heart to the greatest and most devastating effect:

> The spectacularly violent acts of terrorists can be viewed as performances for
> the benefit of a journalistic culture addicted to high drama ... the terrorist act is
> the ultimate 'pseudo-event' – a politically and militarily meaningless act unless
> it receives recognition and coverage in the news media. (McNair, 1998: 142)

However, the desire to 'play up to the cameras' may be no less true of state aggressors as it is terrorists and dissidents. For example, military campaigns may also be planned as media episodes, as was witnessed in the 2003 Allied War on Iraq when journalists were 'embedded' with military personnel and were allowed unprecedented access to troops and operations. Similarly:

> When President Reagan bombed Libya [in 1986], he didn't do it at the most effec-
> tive time of day, from a military point of view. The timing of the raid was principally
> determined by the timing of the American television news; it was planned in such
> a way as to maximize its television impact. It was timed to enable Reagan to
> announce on the main evening news that it had 'just happened' – it was planned
> as a television event. (Morley, 1992: 63–4)

But the most compelling example to date of a postmodern media 'performance' occurred on 11 September 2001. The terrorist attacks on the World Trade Center took place when millions of Americans would be tuned into the breakfast news programmes on television. The timing of the actions ensured that viewers across the world who missed the terrifying aftermath of the first attack on the north tower would tune in to see 'live' pictures of the second hijacked aircraft being flown into the south tower 16 minutes later. The television pictures from that day – transmitted immediately around the globe – have arguably become the most visually arresting and memorable news images ever seen, evoking countless cinematic representations from *The Towering Inferno* to *Independence Day*. The 'event that shook the world' had such an overwhelming impact because of the immediacy and dramatic potency of its image on screen; it was truly a postmodern spectacle.

Terrorist attacks on 'innocent' civilians chime with the postmodern idea that we are all potential victims. Postmodern analyses reject traditional criminological concerns with the causes and consequences of crime, pointing instead to the fragmentation of societies, the fear that paralyses many communities, the random violence that seems to erupt at all levels of society, and the apparent inability of governments to do anything about these problems. This concern with a lurking, unpredictable danger is fortified by an omnipresent media. Postmodernist critic Richard Osborne suggests that the ubiquity of mediated crime reinforces our sense of being victims: 'media discourses about crime now constitute all viewers as equally subject to the fragmented and random danger of criminality, and in so doing provide the preconditions for endless narratives of criminality that rehearse this ever-present danger' (Osborne, 1995: 27). Perversely, then, the media's inclination to make all audience members equal in their potential 'victimness' lies at the core of the postmodern fascination with crime. For Osborne, there is 'something obsessive in the media's, and the viewer's, love of such narratives, an hysterical replaying of the possibility of being a victim and staving it off' (1995: 29).

Another aspect of the hysteria that surrounds criminal cases, fusing the fear of becoming a victim with the postmodern imperative for entertaining the audience, is the media's inability, or unwillingness, to separate the ordinary from the extraordinary. The audience is bombarded in both factual media and in fictional representations, by crimes that are very rare, such as serial killings and abductions of children by strangers. The presentation of the atypical as typical serves to exacerbate public anxiety and deflect attention from much more commonplace offences such as street crime, corporate crime and abuse of children within the family. Reporting of the 'ever-present danger' of the predatory paedophile or young thug who is prepared to kill with little provocation are the stock-in-trade of a media industry which understands that shock, outrage and fear sell newspapers. In recent years, interest has turned to the collective outpouring of grief that has been witnessed in relation to certain violent and/or criminal acts, which has resulted in them occupying a particular symbolic place in the popular imagination. It has been suggested that the 'coming together' of individuals to express collective anguish and to gaze upon the scene of crimes in a gesture of empathy and solidarity with those who have been victimized, is a sign of the desire for community; a hearkening back to pre-mass society collectivity or an assertion of 'people power' (Blackman and Walkerdine, 2001: 2). But equally it might be regarded as a voyeuristic desire to be part of the hyperreal, to take part in a globally mediated event and say 'I was there'.

Cultural criminology

The populist, entertainment imperative of the postmodernist approach is central to the developing perspective known as *cultural criminology* most commonly associated with the work of its American originator, Jeff Ferrell, and with the criminology department at the University of Kent in the UK (for example, Ferrell et al., 2008; Hayward and Presdee, 2010). This approach seeks to understand both the public's mediated fascination with violence and crime, and also the enactment of violence and crime *as* pleasure or spectacle. Its debt to earlier work by Stuart Hall, Stanley Cohen, Phil Cohen, and Jock Young (who was himself part of the cultural criminology vanguard) is evident in its proposition that all crime is grounded in culture and that cultural practices are embedded in dominant processes of power. It therefore supports the early Marxist-influenced, critical criminological view that criminal acts are acts of resistance to authority. But unlike earlier accounts that conceptualized resistance as something that was internalized and expressed through personal and subcultural style, cultural criminologists emphasize the externalization of excitement and ecstasy involved in resistance and here their debt is to the work of Jack Katz who argues in *Seductions of Crime* (1990) that crime is not about acquisition, materialism or economic need, but about presence, status and 'sneaky thrills'. Many criminal activities involve risk-taking and danger, but may in fact represent an attempt to break free of one's demeaning and restraining circumstances, to exercise control and take responsibility for one's own destiny. In a world in which individuals find themselves over-controlled and yet without control, crime offers the possibility of excitement *and* control. The rising number of gun crimes and gangland style killings in the UK might be conceived in these terms; as an act of self-expression which, somewhat ironically, makes the individuals involved feel alive.

   In cultural criminology, crime becomes a participatory performance, a 'carnival', and the streets become theatre. Some commentators have found this a refreshing antidote to Marxist-inspired studies such as *Policing the Crisis*, in so far as cultural criminology avoids the condescension of criminal-as-victim (of disadvantageous circumstances) (Jefferson, 2002). Mike Presdee provided some of the most compelling examples from Britain of the carnival of crime. Describing the large-scale ritualized joyriding that occurred on the Blackbird Leys estate in Oxford in the early 1990s, Presdee comments:

> [T]heir joyriding became a celebration of a particular form of car culture that was carnivalesque in nature, performance centred and criminal. The sport of joyriding went something like this: a team of local youths would spot a hot hatch (the car of choice) and steal it (or arrange with others to have it stolen). It would be delivered to another team who would do it up, delivering it finally to the drivers. In the evenings, the cars were raced round the estate, not aimlessly but in a way designed to show off skill. Furthermore, two competing groups (teams) attempted to outdo the other. These displays were watched by certain residents of the estate who, the story goes, were charged a pound for the pleasure, sitting in picnic chairs at the sides of the road. Often after these races the cars were burned on deserted land. (2000: 49)

Similarly, in an exploration of the ways in which fire has become both an important part of the culture of everyday life and an act of rebelliousness, resistance, defiance and destruction, Presdee explains the primeval attraction of arson, via stories from the US and UK:

> On Monday 6 December 2004 in Indian Head, Washington, USA, unknown arsonists put a complete new up-market housing development to the 'torch', burning 26 houses in one spectacular conflagration! It was a five million pound bonfire that was deliberate, and organized, changing both the landscape and society in one swift and totally destructive act...

[Meanwhile in a field in Gloucester on Bonfire night]:

> they got wooden boards and placed those over the fire and as the flames rekindled the fire dance began again. They faced each other bouncing on the bridges of burning boards, jousting with each other with burning sticks as the howling wind made the flames more dangerous. Like mediaeval knights they fought in the fire and the watching crowd feasted on this spectacle of fire. (http://www.culturalcriminology.org/papers/presdee-fire.pdf)

Riots, protests and other outbreaks of disorder can also be viewed in this way. It is not the case that all carnivalesque performances involve crime, but it can be said with some certainty that participation in them can lead to criminalization. It is therefore not just the cultural significance of crime, but the criminalization of certain cultural practices that cultural criminologists are interested in.

While cultural criminology is not without its critics (Mason, 2006, archly refers to it as 'ghettoized '70s retro chic'), it is undeniable that it has had a significant impact on the ways in which connections between crime, media and culture are made. Cultural criminology celebrates postmodern notions of difference, discontinuity and diversity, and breaks down restrictive and negative stereotypes. What were formerly regarded as unconventional interest groups or simply public nuisances have been embraced amidst a renewed verve for ethnographic enquiry and a fascination for the power of the image. For example, in *Crimes of Style* (1996) Ferrell explores the meaning and practice of graffiti: the building up of 'tagging' experience; the mastery of the art; the aesthetic attention to detail; the thrill of getting away with it (or getting caught); and the network of friendships built up with fellow artists, all of which take shape and meaning within the immediate contingencies of boredom, disaffection and alienation. The comment of a graffiti artist in the celebrated documentary *Style Wars* (1983) sums up the feeling of transcendence experienced: 'I think it's something you can never recapture again once you experience it ... even the smell you get, like when you first smell trains, it's a good smell too, like, a dedicated graffiti writer ... you're there in the midst of all the metal and, like, you're here to produce something'. Once viewed exclusively in terms of teenage delinquency and mindless vandalism, graffiti is one of the many 'underground' subcultural practices that has been appropriated by corporations and repackaged for mass consumption. It has even featured on the US version of *The Apprentice* (NBC) in an episode that required the two competing teams to create a graffiti advertisement on a 20-foot wall in Harlem, New York, for the Sony PlayStation game, *Gran Turismo 4*. The show's star, Donald Trump, announced, without a trace of irony, that there is a 'new form of urban advertising – it's called graffiti', before going on to exclaim, 'I'm not thrilled with graffiti. I don't like graffiti, but some of it is truly amazing'. The sums of money demanded for works by British street artist Banksy (some of which have been illegally removed from the buildings on which they were painted) provide further evidence of the transition of graffiti from underground to the mainstream.

The emergence of cultural criminology can be characterized as a challenge to 'crime science' and to the lingering influence of positivism which, it is suggested, has led to a vacuum in so-called 'expert' knowledge surrounding the pursuit of pleasure. The overriding concern with reason and scientific rationality means that traditional criminology has been unable to account for 'feelings' such as excitement, pleasure and desire. The activities described by Ferrell, Presdee, Hayward and others certainly convey the sense of excitement and desire that are at the heart of many criminalized behaviours, but they also hint at the possibility that such pleasures can be transmuted into something darker and more distorted. They recognize that postmodern media – *Big Brother, X Factor* and *American Idol* being prime(time) examples – merge 'fun' and 'hate', 'cruelty' and 'playfulness', 'celebrity' and 'nobody', 'inclusive' and 'exploitative', 'accessible' and 'extremist'. In this respect they share many qualities with the Internet, which celebrates a world of entertainment, spectacle, performance and fetish. When it comes to privatized pleasure and public displays of narcissism, cyberspace is arguably the cardinal site of the carnival of crime (see Chapter 9).

Summary

While of necessity a distillation of the historical development of two fields of enquiry (in addition to noting the importance of the broader terrain of sociology), this chapter has traced the origins and development of the major theories that have shaped the contours of both criminology and media studies, and attempted to provide a broad overview of points of convergence and conflict between the two. In so doing, it has established that there is no body of relatively consistent, agreed upon and formalized assertions that can readily be termed 'media theory' or 'criminological theory'. Although such phrases are widely used, neither field has been unified by the development of a standard set of concepts, an interrelated body of hypotheses or an overall explanatory framework. However, it has proposed that a sense of progressive development is nevertheless evident in ideas concerning media and crime. Despite their obvious aetiological and methodological differences, the theoretical approaches discussed in this chapter have clear points of convergence which have enabled us to locate them in the wider context of social, cultural, political and economic developments that were concomitantly taking place. In summary, the theoretical 'pegs' upon which our analysis has been hung are as follows:

- Media effects: Early theories connecting media and crime were characterized by an overwhelmingly negative view of both the role of the media and the susceptibility of the audience. Like Martians with their ray guns, the new media of mass communications were perceived through early 20th century eyes as alien invaders injecting their messages directly into the minds of a captive audience. Although academic researchers in the UK have strongly resisted attempts to assert the existence of a causal link between media and crime, rendering the debate all but redundant in media scholarship, notions of a potentially harmful media capable of eliciting negative or anti-social consequences remain at the heart of popular or mainstream discourses, including those that have been incorporated into policy.
- Strain theory and anomie: Merton's development of anomie helps us to understand the strain caused by a disjuncture between the cultural goals of wealth and status, and legitimate means of achieving those goals. For those with few means of attaining success through normal, legal channels, the media might be said to place incalculable pressure, creating a huge ungratified well of desire with little opportunity of

fulfilment. It is in such circumstances that some individuals pursue the culturally desirable objectives of success and material wealth via illegitimate paths. Recent commentators on anomie have suggested that disaffected individuals overcome feelings of isolation and normlessness by forming communities based on shared tastes and opinions, and that the Internet has, for some, countered the sense of dislocation that gaps in wealth and status inevitably produce.

- Dominant ideology: With the rediscovery of Marx's writings on social structure, scholars in the 1960s and 1970s focused their attentions on the extent to which consent is 'manufactured' by the powerful along ideological lines. According to the dominant ideology approach, the power to criminalize and decriminalize certain groups and behaviours lies with the ruling élite who – in a process known as 'hegemony' – win popular approval for their actions via social institutions, including the media. In short, powerful groups achieve public consensus on definitions of crime and deviance, and gain mass support for increasingly draconian measures of control and containment, not by force or coercion, but by using the media to subtly construct a web of meaning from a number of ideological threads which are then articulated into a coherent popular discourse.

- Pluralism: This perspective emerged as a challenge to hegemonic models of media power. Pluralism emphasizes the diversity and plurality of media channels available, thus countering the notion that any ideology can be dominant for any length of time if it does not reflect what people experience to be true. Although there is undoubtedly a firm alliance between most politicians and sections of the journalistic media, pluralists argue that the media's tendency to ignore, ridicule or demonize those whose politics and lifestyle lie beyond the consensual norm is changing, precisely because public sentiments have changed. There is growing antipathy to the apparatus of political communication and people's responses to crime will always be much more complex and diverse than any headline or soundbite might suggest. In addition, it might be argued that the quantity and rapidity of contemporary news-making undermines the notion of élite power and ensures that governments are accountable and responsive to their electorate.

- Postmodernism: As far as we can state that there are 'defining characteristics' of postmodernism, they include: the end of any belief in an overarching scientific rationality; the abandonment of empiricist theories of truth; and an emphasis on the fragmentation of experience and the diversification of viewpoints. The postmodernist rejection of claims to truth proposed by the 'grand theories' of the past, challenges us to accept that we live in a world of contradictions and inconsistencies which are not amenable to objective modes of thought. Within criminology, postmodernism implies an abandonment of the concept of crime and the construction of a new language and mode of thought to define processes of criminalization and censure. It is often suggested that, for postmodernists, there are no valid questions worth asking, and Henry and Milovanovic (1996) insist that crime will only stop being a problem once the justice system, media and criminologists stop focusing attention on it.

- Cultural criminology: Media and culture are central to this form of criminological analysis; style is substance and meaning resides in representation. Consequently, crime and crime control can only be understood as an ongoing spiral of inter-textual, image-driven, media loops (Ferrell, 2001). Cultural criminology embraces postmodern ideas and underpins them with some more 'radical' yet established concerns, borrowing especially from the work of British scholars in the 1970s on subcultures and mediated forms of social control. And, in a decisive break with traditional, 'positivist' criminologies which have been unconcerned with 'feeling' and 'pleasure', cultural criminology also draws attention to the fact that crime can have a carnivalesque quality; it is exhilarating, performative and dangerous.

STUDY QUESTIONS

1. Choose one of the theories discussed in this chapter and discuss the contribution it has made to our understanding of the relationship between media and crime.

2. As the *War of the Worlds* radio broadcast demonstrates, concerns about media effects frequently reflect or crystallize deeper anxieties in periods of social upheaval. What examples of contemporary concerns about the effects of the media can you think of, and in what ways might they be attributed to wider anxieties about social change?

3. Conduct an analysis of a week's news. What evidence can you find for the proposition that news is ideology and that the mass media are effectively assimilated into the goals of government policy on crime, law and order?

4. In a challenge to Marxist-inspired critiques, some cultural theorists (for example, Fiske, 1989) argue that all popular culture is the 'people's culture' and emerges from 'below' rather than being imposed from 'above'. It is thus seen to be independent of, and resistant to, the dominant hegemonic norms. What implications does this have for those who hold deviant or oppositional viewpoints? Can 'popular' culture really be described as non-hierarchical when it celebrates power and violence for men, and sexual availability and victimization among women and children?

5. At the heart of postmodern analyses lies the thorny question of why crime is threatening and frightening, yet at the same time popular and 'entertaining'. How would you attempt to answer this question?

FURTHER READING

A good place to start is the collection of readings with annotations brought together by Chris Greer: C. Greer (2009) *Crime and Media: A Reader* (Routledge). Your university library may hold Y. Jewkes (2009) *Crime and Media: Three Volume Set* which is part of the Sage Library of Criminology and is also a collection of readings with original commentaries. In addition, there are now numerous good introductions to criminological theory. The best of them, especially from a media/crime perspective is E. Carrabine, et al. (2014) *Criminology: A Sociological Introduction 3rd edition* (Routledge), which covers all the theories discussed here and also devotes a specific chapter to the relationship between crime and media. The most comprehensive introduction to media theory probably remains D. McQuail (2010) *Mass Communication Theory* (Sage), now in its 6th edition. Covering many of the theories discussed in this chapter and anticipating the discussion of news in Chapter 2, J. Curran and J. Seaton (2010) *Power Without Responsibility Press, Broadcasting and the Internet in Britain* (Routledge) is another classic, now in its 7th edition. For a fun take on media-criminology, which manages to combine theoretical sophistication with its application to cinema, N. Rafter and M. Brown (2011) *Criminology Goes to the Movies: Crime Theory and Popular Culture* (New York University Press) is highly recommended. Finally, *Crime, Media, Culture: An International Journal* is devoted to cross-disciplinary work that promotes understanding of the relationship between crime, criminal justice, media and culture: http://cmc.sagepub.com.

2

The Construction of Crime News

CHAPTER CONTENTS	

News values for a new millennium | **49**
Threshold | 49
Predictability | 50
Simplification | 51
Individualism | 53
Risk | 55
Sex | 56
Celebrity or high-status persons | 57
Proximity | 60
Violence or conflict | 63
Visual spectacle and graphic imagery | 64
Children | 66
Conservative ideology and political diversion | 68
Two examples of newsworthy stories *par excellence* | **70**
1. The disappearance of Madeleine McCann | 70
2. Anders Behring Breivik and the spree killing of 77 people in Norway | 71
News production and consumption in a digital global marketplace: the rise of the citizen journalist | **73**
News values and crime news production: some concluding thoughts | **76**
Summary | **78**
Study questions | **79**
Further reading | **79**

OVERVIEW

Chapter 2 provides:

- An analysis of how crime news is 'manufactured' along ideological lines.
- An understanding of the ways in which the demands and constraints of news production intertwine with the perceived interests of the target audience to produce a set of organizational 'news values'.
- An overview of 12 key news values that are prominent in the construction of crime news at the beginning of the 21st century.
- Discussion of the ways in which the construction of news sets the agenda for public and political debate.
- Two case studies of archetypal newsworthy stories.
- An examination of how new technologies are changing the ways in which news is produced and consumed.

KEY TERMS

- agenda-setting
- audience
- binary oppositions
- celebrity
- citizen journalist
- crime
- crime news
- ethnocentrism
- folk devils
- framing

- ideology
- moral majority
- newsworthiness
- news values
- populism/populist/punitiveness
- public appeal
- public interest
- social constructionism
- user-generated content

The diversity of theoretical approaches discussed in the previous chapter will have alerted you to the fact that the influence of the media can be conceptualized both negatively and positively, depending on the perspective adopted. Those who have attempted to demonstrate a link between media content and crime or deviance have employed numerous theoretical models in order to establish alternative, and frequently oppositional, views, ranging from the idea that the media industry is responsible for much of the crime that blights our society, to the idea that media perform a public service in educating us about *crime* and thus aid crime prevention. Some have even argued that media are redefining and making obsolete traditional notions of crime and deviance altogether. It is clear from these divergent viewpoints that the media's role in representing reality is highly contested and subject to interpretation. Although accounts of criminal activities in film, television drama, music lyrics, computer games and websites are arguably of greatest salience in discussions of media influence, the reporting of *crime news* is also of importance and is no less shaped by the mission to entertain. Indeed, while it might be expected that the news simply reports the 'facts' of an event and is an accurate representation of the overall picture of crime, this is not the case. Even the most cursory investigation of crime reporting demonstrates that crime news follows markedly different patterns to both the 'reality' of crime and its representation in official statistics. Thus, despite often being described as a 'window on the world' or a mirror reflecting 'real life', the media might be more accurately thought of as a prism, subtly bending and distorting the view of the world it projects.

Whether we adhere to the 'effects' theory of media influence, the hegemonic understanding of media power as an expression of élite interests, the pluralist idea of an open media marketplace, or notions of a postmodernist mediascape, we have to conclude that media images are *not* reality; they are a *version* of reality that is culturally determined and dependent on two related factors. First, the mediated picture of 'reality' is shaped by the production processes of news organizations and the structural determinants of news-making, any or all of which may influence the image of crime, criminals and the criminal justice system in the minds of the public. These factors include the over-reporting of crimes that have been 'solved' and resulted in a conviction; the deployment of reporters at institutional settings, such as courts, where they are likely to come across interesting stories; the need to produce stories which fit the time schedules of news production; the concentration on specific crimes at the expense of causal explanations, the consideration of personal safety, which results in camera operators covering incidents of public disorder from behind police lines; and an overreliance on 'official', accredited sources for information. The second factor that shapes news production concerns the assumptions media professionals make about their *audience*. They sift and select news items and – in a process known as *agenda-setting* – will prioritize some stories over others. Then they edit words, adopt a particular tone (some stories will be treated seriously, others might get a humorous or ironic treatment) and decide on the visual images that will accompany the story; all of which constitutes the *framing* of a story. It is in these ways that those who work in the media select a handful of events from the unfathomable number of possibilities that occur around the world every day, and turn them into stories that convey meanings, offer solutions, associate certain groups of people with particular kinds of behaviour, and provide 'pictures of the world' which help to structure our frames of reference.

Far from being a random or personal process, editors and journalists select, produce and present news according to a range of professional criteria that are used as benchmarks to determine a story's *newsworthiness*. This is not to say that alternative definitions do not exist or that other non-mediated influences are at least as important. But if a story does not contain at least some of the characteristics deemed newsworthy, it will not appear on the news agenda. *News values*, then, are the value judgments that journalists and editors make about the **public appeal** of a story and also whether it is in the **public interest**. The former can be measured quantitatively: put simply, lack of public appeal will be reflected in poor sales figures or ratings and is frequently used to justify the growing dependence on stories with a dramatic, sensationalist or *celebrity* component. The issue of public interest is rather more complicated and may involve external interference, such as corporate or, more commonly, political pressures. Although the press are hampered by very few limitations regarding what they may print, the main television channels in the UK, and particularly the public service BBC, are subject to a range of restrictions which are framed by notions of 'impartiality'. Intervention may be coercive, ranging from the control of information to an outright ban on publication or broadcast of material on the grounds that it is not in the public interest – often a euphemism for disclosure of information that is not in the government's interest.

Alternatively, pressure might be so abstrusely exerted as to appear as self-censorship on the part of editors and producers. But as Fowler (1991) notes, the news values that set the media agenda rarely amount to a journalistic conspiracy – they are much more subtle than that. Nowhere in a newsroom will you find a list pinned to the wall reminding reporters and editors what their 'angle' on a story should be. Rather, the commercial, legislative and technical pressures that characterize journalism, together with a range of occupational conventions – which are often expressed in terms of 'having a good nose for a story', but which are actually more to do with journalists sharing the same *ideological* values as the majority of their audience – results in a normalization of particular interests and values (Wykes, 2001). This shared ethos enables those who work in news organizations to systematically sort, grade and select potential news stories, and discard those which are of no perceived interest or relevance to the audience.

While agenda-setting is usually guided by pragmatic concerns, framing is an ideological process. As one US journalist (Scott London) has described, the informational content of a news report is less important than the interpretive commentary that attends it:

> This is especially evident in television news which is replete with metaphors, catchphrases, and other symbolic devices that provide a shorthand way of suggesting the underlying storyline. These devices provide the rhetorical bridge by which discrete bits of information are given a context and relationship to one another... The frames for a given story are seldom conscientiously chosen but represent instead the effort of the journalist or sponsor to convey a story in a direct and meaningful way. As such, news frames are frequently drawn from, and reflective of, shared cultural narratives and myths and resonate with the larger social themes to which journalists tend to be acutely sensitive. (www. scottlondon.com/reports/frames.html)

Arguably even more important than metaphor, catchphrases and other linguistic forms of framing are the visual images that accompany news reports (in the press as well as on television), which will be discussed below.

The first people to attempt to systematically identify and categorize the news values that commonly determine and structure reported events were Galtung and Ruge (1965/1973). Their concern was with news reporting generally, rather than crime news *per se*, and they studied only a limited range of publications (broadcast news was still in its infancy) from the perspective of Norwegian academics writing for the *Journal of International Peace Studies.* Nevertheless, their findings that incidents and events were more likely to be reported if they were, for example, unexpected, close to home, of a significant threshold in terms of dramatic impact, and negative in essence, clearly made them relevant to crime reporting and their research continues to be a touchstone for students of crime news today. Following their classic analysis, another important study was published in 1977 by Steve Chibnall. Despite it being more than 30 years old, and being concerned with journalistic priorities in the post-war period from 1945 to 1975, *Law and Order News* remains an influential study of news values relating to crime reporting and has led to numerous applications of the concept of news values in a myriad of different contexts.

However, Britain is a very different place now than it was half a century ago. The prison population has more than doubled since the 1970s and contemporary news reports contain references to crimes – road rage, air rage, identity theft, online grooming, trolling, revenge porn – not even heard of 25 years ago. Conversely, non-violent crimes such as house burglaries which, in the post-war period constituted nearly a quarter of stories in *The Times* (Reiner, 2001; Reiner et al., 2001) became so commonplace in the 1980s and 1990s that they were rarely considered worth mentioning in the national media; and then, conversely, as the cost of electronic goods plummeted because of cheap imports from China, became so rare in the 'noughties' that they did not warrant much attention in that decade either. The media landscape has itself changed almost beyond recognition. In 1977 there were just three television channels, a fraction of the newspaper and magazine titles, email was used only by a handful of academics sitting in computer labs, and media outlets were far less market-driven or dictated by constant, pressing deadlines. British politics is not as polarized as it was in the 1970s and contemporary audiences are arguably more knowledgeable, more sophisticated and more sceptical than at any time previously. What is more, some critics argue that the pressure on media professionals to produce the ordinary as extraordinary shades into the postmodern, and that what was historically described as news-gathering has, in the new millennium, begun to take on the same '"constructed-for-television" quality that postmodernists refer to as "simulation"' (Osborne, 2002: 131). The time seems right, then, for a reassessment of the criteria that structure the news that we read, hear, watch and browse online at the beginning of the 21st century. So what constitutes 'newsworthiness' in 2015?

Of course, some of the criteria identified by Galtung and Ruge in 1973 and Chibnall in 1977 still broadly hold true and will be drawn on in the analysis that follows. It is also important to remember that different values may determine the selection and presentation of events by different news media (and, for that matter, by different or competing organizations), and that the broadcast media tend to follow the news agenda of the press in deciding which stories are newsworthy. Not surprisingly, the news values of the *Sun* are likely to be somewhat different from those of *The Independent* and different again from those of the BBC – not to mention the *New York Times, Canberra Times* or *Ming Pao*. Even among news organizations which appear to be very similar, such as the British tabloid press, there may be differences in news reporting which are largely accounted for by the house-style of the title in question. For example, some stress the 'human interest' angle of a crime story (with first-hand accounts from victims and witnesses, an emphasis on tragedy, sentimentality and so on) and may be primarily designed to appeal to a female readership, while others sensationalize crime news, emphasizing sex and sleaze, but simultaneously adopting a scandalized and prurient tone.

News values are also subject to subtle changes over time, and a story does not have to conform to all the criteria in order to make the news – although events that score highly on the newsworthiness scale (that is, conform to several of the news values) are more likely to be reported. Newsworthiness criteria vary across different countries and cultures, and it should be noted that the list that follows has been devised primarily with the UK media in mind. Readers in, or with knowledge of, other countries might like to consider how notions of newsworthiness differ across geographical boundaries and perhaps construct their own list of news values pertinent to the area they are most familiar with. The list that follows is, then, by no means exhaustive, but it considers a total of 12 features that are evident in the output of most contemporary media institutions, and are of particular significance when examining the reporting of crime.

One other point that should be borne in mind is that while 'crime' could in itself be classified as a news value, it goes without saying that in a study of crime news, all the news values outlined in this chapter pertain explicitly to *crime*. It is also taken for granted that the vast majority of crime stories are *negative* in essence, and that news must contain an element of 'newness' or *novelty*; the news has to tell us things we did not already know (McNair, 1998). Crime, negativity and novelty do not therefore appear in the list below as discrete news values, but are themes that underpin all the criteria discussed. It is understood that *any* crime has the potential to be a news story, that it will contain negative features (even if the outcome is positive and it is presented as an essentially 'good news' story), and that it will contain new or novel elements (even if it has been composed with other, similar stories to reinforce a particular agenda or to create the impression of a 'crime wave'). This list of news values is concerned, therefore, with how previously unreported, negative stories about crime – already potentially of interest – are determined even more newsworthy by their interplay with other features of news reporting.

News values for a new millennium

The 12 news structures and news values that shape crime news listed below are discussed in the rest of this chapter:

- Threshold
- Predictability
- Simplification
- Individualism
- Risk
- Sex
- Celebrity or high-status persons
- Proximity
- Violence or conflict
- Visual spectacle or graphic imagery
- Children
- Conservative ideology and political diversion

Threshold

Events have to meet a certain level of perceived importance or drama in order to be considered newsworthy. The threshold of a potential story varies according to whether the news reporters and editors in question work within a local, national or global medium. In other words, petty crimes such as vandalism and street robberies are likely to feature in the local press (and will probably be front page news in rural or low-crime areas) but it takes offences of a greater magnitude to meet the threshold of national or international media. In addition, once a story has reached the required threshold to make the news, it may then have to meet further criteria in order to stay on the news agenda, and the media frequently keep a crime wave or particular crime story alive by creating new thresholds. For example, a perennial staple of crime news reporting is attacks on the elderly in their homes but, although serious such assaults might in themselves initially be deemed newsworthy, journalists will soon look for a new angle to keep the story 'fresh' and give it a novelty factor. This might simply involve an escalation of the level of drama attached to the story, or it might require the implementation of other news structures and news values in order to sustain the life of the story. In 2002 the British news media introduced several supplementary thresholds to the story by adding thresholds of *escalating drama* and *risk* ('Attacker of elderly "could kill" next time', *BBC News Online*, 1 August 2002); *celebrity* ('Robbers raid [Bruce] Forsyth's home', *Observer*, 21 July 2002); a *sexual* component ('A 93-year-old woman has spoken of her bewilderment after a man conned his way into her home and raped her elderly daughter', *BBC News Online*, 9 May 2002); the *macabre* ('A teenager obsessed with vampires stabbed to death an elderly neighbour before cutting out her heart and drinking her blood', *Guardian*, 3 August 2002); an *ironic* angle ('Pensioners fight off bogus callers with poker and walking stick', *BBC News Online*, 9 November 2002); and the *counter-story* ('Man, 76, stabs 21-year-old neighbour to death for singing too loudly', *BBC News Online*, 12 November 2002). These additional thresholds may, then, take many forms (we might add to the above list any number of other factors including the 'whimsical', the 'humorous', the 'bizarre', the 'grotesque', the 'nostalgic', the 'sentimental' and so on; see Roshier, 1973; Hall et al., 1978/2013). After several months of press hysteria over the entry into the UK of political refugees and illegal immigrants, the *Daily Star* (21 August 2003) filled their front page on a quiet news day in midsummer with the headline 'Asylum seekers eat our donkeys'. This illustrates the point well: the addition of new thresholds introduce a novel element to a familiar theme and may revive a flagging news story.

Predictability

As the introduction to this chapter suggested, it goes without saying that an event that is rare, extraordinary or unexpected will be considered newsworthy. Like the thresholds outlined above, unpredictability gives a story novelty value. In particular the media's 'discovery' of a 'new' crime is often sufficient to give it prominence. But equally, a story that is *predictable* may be deemed newsworthy because news organizations can plan their coverage in advance and deploy their resources (e.g. reporters and photographers) accordingly. Crime itself is frequently spontaneous and sporadic, but news media will know in advance if a government minister is to announce a new initiative to combat crime or the Home Office is due to release its annual crime statistics and will plan their coverage before the event has actually occurred. This is also true of criminal trials, which can contain an element of predictability. Media organizations can estimate the time that a criminal case will remain in court and, having deployed personnel and equipment, they are likely to retain them there until the end of the trial. Hence a degree of continuity of coverage is also assured.

Another aspect of predictability is that, for the most part, the media agenda is structured in an ordered and predictable fashion. Having set the moral framework of a debate, those who work in the media will rarely do a U-turn and refashion it according to a different set of principles. Put simply, if the media expect something to happen it will happen, and journalists will usually have decided on the angle they are going to report a story from before they even arrive at the scene. One of the first examples of this tendency was the media coverage of anti-Vietnam demonstrations in London in 1968 (Halloran et al., 1970). The media anticipated violence and were going to report the event as a violent occasion, whatever the reality on the day. Consequently, one isolated incident of anti-police violence dominated coverage of the demonstration and deflected attention from its general peacefulness and, indeed, its anti-war message. Another regular event that illustrates this tendency is the Notting Hill Carnival held in London every August Bank Holiday which attracts in excess of 1.5 million people. Crime rates at the carnival remain relatively low compared with those at other musical events attended by far fewer people, but since riots marred the event in 1976 and occurred less seriously in 1977, the media has consistently reported the event within a framework which emphasizes racism, crime and violence, often overshadowing the many positive and joyous aspects of the parade. For example, in 1991, following an isolated stabbing, *Daily Mail* columnist Lynda Lee-Potter described the carnival as 'a sordid, sleazy nightmare that has become synonymous with death' (quoted in Younge, 2002). The broadsheets are as culpable as the tabloids: under the headline 'Police cameras ring Notting Hill' the *Guardian* reports that 'more than 70 closed circuit television cameras were deployed by police at Notting Hill carnival yesterday to help cut crime' but somewhat contradictorily goes on to say that 'the first day of Europe's biggest street party saw just six arrests for minor offences' (*Guardian*, 30 August 1999). In recent years, anti-capitalism and anti-globalization demonstrations around the world (most notably at the annual summit meetings of government leaders) have received similar treatment, leading many to conclude that the media tend to report events in the ways they have previously reported them.

Simplification

Events do not have to be simple in order to make the news (although it helps), but they must be reducible to a minimum number of parts or themes. This process of simplification has several aspects. First, news reporting is marked by brevity in order that it should not strain the attention span of the audience. Second, the range of possible meanings inherent in the story must be restricted. Unlike other textual discourses – novels, poems, films and so on – where the capacity of a story to generate multiple and diverse meanings is celebrated, news discourse is generally not open to interpretation and audiences are invited to come to consensual conclusions about a story (Galtung and Ruge, 1965/1973). Immediate or sudden events, such as the discovery of a body or an armed robbery, are likely to be reported because their 'meaning' can be arrived at very quickly, but crime trends, which are more complex and may take a long time to unfold, are difficult to report unless they can be marked by means of devices such as the release of a report or official statistics. In other words, a 'hook' is required on which to hang such stories in order that they fit with the daily or hourly time-span of most media.

Not only does news reporting privilege brevity, clarity and unambiguity in its presentation, but also it encourages the reader, viewer and listener to suspend their skills of critical interpretation and respond in unanimous accord. As far as crime news is concerned, this usually amounts to moral indignation and censure directed at anyone who transgresses the legal or moral codes of society. In the aftermath of high-profile criminal and terrorism cases, notions of potential 'dangerousness' have come to be applied indiscriminately to whole sections of society. In popular journalism's oversimplified worldview, sufferers of mental illness can be portrayed as potential murderers; asylum seekers as potential terrorists; gun club members become potential spree killers and, most insidiously, children and young people come to be seen as 'evil monsters' with no hope of rehabilitation. Such reproach is particularly evident in the tabloid press, who have arguably taken to heart the words of former Prime Minister John Major, said in the context of the Bulger case, that we should seek to 'condemn a little more and understand a little less'.

Simplification of news can boil down to partiality; an accusation sometimes levelled at broadcasters in the UK and USA said to be pro-Israeli in their coverage of the conflict in the Gaza strip. At other times, simplification takes the form of an unquestioning patriotism; particularly in relation to acts of terrorism. American journalist-turned-media critic Danny Schechter (2003) has observed a sudden early change of focus in news reporting in the aftermath of 9/11. He describes what he sees as a manipulation by the US Government (perpetuated faithfully by the mainstream media) to turn around the initial introspective and disbelieving tone of coverage to an emphatically robust style of nationalism. This easily transmutes into a situation where anyone who opposes the 'War on Terror' is regarded as 'unpatriotic' or treacherously 'anti-American'. At the same time, those who perpetrate acts of terror on the USA and her allies become constructed as cartoon baddies or evil automatons, with little or no discussion of their histories and motivations. Mythen and Walklate (2006) similarly argue that, following terrorist attacks in New York, Washington, Madrid and London by groups claiming allegiance to al Qaeda, the creation of common enemies in these countries and their allies has resulted in a simplification of complex issues and personalities, and a separation of cause and effect, both of which add to the public's perceptions of the terrorist as an irrational 'other' whose motivations are greedy or fanatical rather than socio-economic or geo-political. The experiences of marginalization that such individuals commonly experience are underplayed by politicians and the media who continue to discuss individual moral responsibility as if it exists in a vacuum, somehow detached from the circumstances in which people find themselves. As Mythen and Walklate observe, this leaves little room for rational attempts to understand the values, objectives and grievances of these individuals and instead reduces them to simplified inhuman objects of hate.

The discussion about simplification of news alerts us to the fact the mass media are inclined to deal in **binary oppositions**. Thus, stories involving crime and criminals, including terrorists, are frequently presented within a context that emphasizes good versus evil, folk heroes and folk devils, black against white, guilty or innocent, 'normal' as opposed to 'sick', 'deviant' or 'dangerous' and so on. Such polarized frameworks of understanding result in the construction of mutually exclusive categories; for example, parents cannot also be paedophiles; individuals driven to carry out suicide bombings and other terrorist acts are entirely evil and have no 'good' qualities to redeem them. All these processes of simplification add up to a mediated vision of crime in which shades of grey are absent and a complex reality is substituted for a simple, incontestable and preferably bite-sized message.

Individualism

The news value *individualism* connects *simplification* and *risk* (see below). Individual definitions of crime, and rationalizations which highlight individual responses to crime, are preferred to more complex cultural and political explanations. The media engage in a process of personalization in order to simplify stories and give them a 'human interest' appeal, which results in events being viewed as the actions and reactions of people. Consequently, social, political and economic issues tend only to be reported as the conflict of interests between individuals (the Prime Minister and the Leader of the Opposition, for example), while the complex interrelationship between political ideology and policy may be embodied in a single figure, such as the 'Drug Tsar'. The effect of this is that 'the social origins of events are lost, and individual motivation is assumed to be the origin of all action' (Fiske, 1987: 294).

Both offenders and those who are *potentially offended against* are constructed within an individualist framework. Put simply, the criminal is usually described as being 'impulsive, a loner, maladjusted, irrational, animal-like, aggressive and violent' (Blackman and Walkerdine, 2001: 6) – all qualities which allude to the offender's autonomous status and lack of normative social ties (see Chapter 6). The media coverage of 'lone wolf' Anders Breivik, discussed below, was framed in this way, despite his terrorist attacks clearly being inspired by well-known and long-standing political rhetoric (Berntzen and Sandberg, 2014) and by other mass shootings (Sandberg et al., 2014). Furthermore, news reporting frequently encourages the public to see themselves as vigilantes and positions those who are offended against (or who fear being the victims of crime) as vulnerable and isolated, let down by an ineffective social system and at risk from dangerous predators. Those who try and protect themselves from victimization are frequently portrayed as 'have-a-go-heroes' and, when killed in the commission of an offence, are constructed as 'tragic innocents' (see Chapter 6).

Meanwhile, as discussed in the previous chapter, institutions, corporations and governments may be literally getting away with murder. Even when an offence that occurs within a large organization actually makes the news, it may once again be explained by recourse to individual pathology. The collapse of the British merchant bank Barings in 1995 and a similar case in 2008 involving French bank Société Générale were two such complicated, technical cases which might have seemed somewhat abstract to the general public. To avoid complex explanations, and despite the fact that Parisian trader Jerome Kerviel defrauded the French bank to the tune of 4.9 billion euros (that is, £3.7bn or $7.1bn) the British media constructed *both* stories around the figure of Barings employee, Nick Leeson, the 'rogue trader' who was single-handedly held responsible for the loss of £869 million in the 1995 case, and who became sufficiently famous to have a movie made about him (*Rogue Trader*, 1999). Similarly, a case that gripped the United States in 2009 was a fraudulent investment scheme that paid investors from money contributed by other investors rather than from real profits to the tune of $65 billion (£40bn). Media coverage of this crime focused on the charismatic figure at the centre of the fraud, Bernard Madoff who – unusually for a white-collar criminal – was described by his trial judge as 'extraordinarily evil' (http://news.bbc.co.uk/1/hi/8124838.stm).

For Reiner et al. (2001) individualism is a consequence of the increasing tendency to view society as being obsessed with 'risk' and all its attendant notions, including risk assessment, risk management and risk avoidance (see 'Risk' below). The new vocabulary surrounding this 'foxy but evocative term' (Leacock and Sparks, 2002: 199) highlights a shift in perceptions of how risk should best be dealt with. As social problems have come to be seen as the product of chance or of individual action, and solutions are sought at the level of individual self-help strategies – such as insurance or personal protection – a 'winner–loser' casino culture is created (Reiner et al., 2001: 177). Individuals are held responsible for their fates and the media devalue any styles of life other than spectacular consumerism (Reiner et al., 2001: 178). The outcome of individualism in criminal justice is that deviants are defined in terms of their 'difference' and isolated via policies of containment, incapacitation and surveillance. Popularly conceived as a 'breed apart', many offenders are judged within a moral framework which constructs them as morally deficient malcontents who must be dealt with punitively and taught the lesson of individual responsibility (Surette, 1994).

Risk

Given that the notion of modern life being characterized by *risk* has become such a widespread and taken-for-granted assumption, it is surprising to find that the media devote little attention to crime avoidance, crime prevention or personal safety. The exception to this is if a message about prevention can be incorporated into an ongoing narrative about a serious offender 'at large', in which case the story will be imbued with a sense of urgency and drama (Greer, 2003). The vast majority of serious offences, including murder, rape and sexual assault, are committed by people known to the victim. There are also clearly discernible patterns of victimization in certain socio-economic groups and geographical locations. Yet the media persist in presenting a picture of serious crime as random, meaningless, unpredictable and ready to strike anyone at any time (Chermak, 1994: 125). Such discourse as exists in the media regarding prevention and personal safety invariably relates to offences committed by strangers, thus implicitly promoting stereotypes of dangerous criminals prepared to strike indiscriminately (Soothill and Walby, 1991; Greer, 2003; see also Chapter 6).

The idea that we are all potential victims is a relatively new phenomenon. After the Second World War, news stories encouraged compassion for offenders by providing details designed to elicit sympathy for their circumstances, thus endorsing the rehabilitative ideal that dominated penal policy at that time (Reiner, 2001). In today's more risk-obsessed and retributive times, crime stories have become increasingly victim-centred. Perceived vulnerability is emphasized over actual victimization so that fear of crime might be more accurately conceived as a fear for personal safety. Sometimes, the media exploit public concerns by exaggerating potential risks in order to play into people's wider fears and anxieties. Following the September 11th terrorist attacks in America, the British media fuelled a vision of apocalyptic meltdown with a series of stories ranging from terrorist plots to target the UK, to warnings about falling meteorites heading for earth. Yet it must be remembered that audiences are not passive or undiscriminating. Many crime scares and moral panics simply never get off the ground (Jenkins, 2008), and while it might be argued that the media fail to provide the public with the resources to independently construct alternative definitions and frameworks, people's sense of personal risk will usually correspond to their past personal experiences and a realistic assessment of the likelihood of future victimization above and beyond anything they see or hear in the media.

Sex

One of the most salient news values – especially in the tabloid press, but also to a significant degree in the broadsheets and other media – is that of sex. Studies of the press by Ditton and Duffy (1983) in Strathclyde, by Smith (1984) in Birmingham, and by Greer (2003) in Northern Ireland, reveal that newspapers over-report crimes of a sexual nature, thus distorting the overall picture of crime that the public receives, and instilling exaggerated fears among women regarding their likelihood of being victims of such crimes. Ditton and Duffy (1983) found that when reporting assaults against women, the press frequently relate sex and violence, so that the two become virtually indistinguishable. Furthermore, the over-reporting of such crimes was so significant that in Strathclyde in March 1981, crimes involving sex and violence accounted for only 2.4 per cent of recorded incidents, yet occupied 45.8 per cent of newspaper coverage. So interlinked are the themes of sex and violence, and so powerfully do they combine to illustrate the value of 'risk', that the prime example of newsworthiness is arguably the figure of the compulsive male lone hunter, driven by a sexual desire which finds its outlet in the murder of 'innocent' victims (Cameron and Frazer, 1987). As such, sexually motivated murders by someone unknown to the victim invariably receive substantial, often sensational, attention. On the other hand, sexual crimes against women where violence is not an overriding component of the story (bluntly, sex crimes that are non-fatal) and sexual assaults by someone known or related to the victim are generally regarded as routine and 'pedestrian' and may contain only limited analysis (Carter, 1998; Naylor, 2001). Moreover, the sexually motivated murder of prostitutes – who do not conform to media constructions of 'innocent' victims – also invariably receive considerably less coverage than those of other women.

Bronwyn Naylor (2001) argues that the frequency with which articles appear about apparently random stranger violence against 'ordinary' women and girls not only indicates that such stories fulfil key news values, but also that they permit highly sexualized, even pornographic representations of women. At the same time, these narratives tend to be highly individualized so that offences involving females – whether as victims or perpetrators – are rarely reported by the popular media without reference, often sustained and explicit, to their sexualities and sexual histories. Victims are frequently eroticized: for example, the conviction of Stuart Campbell in December 2002 for the sexually-motivated murder of his 15-year-old niece, Danielle Jones, was accompanied by media reports of their 'inappropriate', that is, abusive, sexual relationship, and photographs of a pair of blood-stained, white lace-topped stockings belonging to the girl found at Campbell's home. Meanwhile, female offenders are often portrayed as sexual predators – even if their crimes have no sexual element (see Chapter 5). This narrative is so widely used that it leads

Naylor to question the purpose of such stories and how readers consume them:

> These stories draw on narratives about particular kinds of masculinity and about violent pornography, reiterating a discourse about masculine violence as a 'natural force', both random and inevitable. They normalize this violence, drawing on and repeating the narrative that all men are potentially violent and that all women are potentially and 'naturally' victims of male violence (Naylor, 2001: 186).

She goes on to suggest that not only does the media's obsession with 'stranger-danger' give a (statistically false) impression that the public sphere is unsafe and the private sphere is safe, but also that it influences government decisions about the prioritization of resources, resulting in the allocation of funding towards very visible preventative measures (such as street lighting and CCTV cameras) and away from refuges, 'or indeed from any broader structural analysis of violence' (Naylor, 2001: 186).

Celebrity or high-status persons

The obsession with *celebrity* is evident everywhere in the media and a story is always more likely to make the news if it has a well-known name attached to it. Put simply, the level of deviance required to attract media attention is significantly lower than for offences committed by 'ordinary' citizens because a certain threshold of meaningfulness has already been achieved. As such, a 'personality' will frequently be the recipient of media attention even if involved in a fairly mundane or routine crime that would not be deemed newsworthy if it concerned an 'ordinary' member of the public. Whether they are victims or perpetrators of crime, celebrities, their lives, and their experiences are deemed intrinsically interesting to the audience. Even otherwise under-represented categories of crime such as libel, perjury and embezzlement are guaranteed widespread media attention if they have a 'name' associated with them. However, it is sexual deviance that dominates the news agenda of the tabloids, and a celebrity or high-status person who unexpectedly takes personal and professional risks by engaging in a sexually deviant act is an enduring feature of news in the postmodern mediascape, providing a titillating juxtaposition of high life and low life for an audience who, it is assumed, lead conventional and law-abiding 'mid lives' (Barak, 1994b).

So elevated has celebrity status become that it even blinds the populace to crimes that may have been taking place quite publicly over several decades and/or been covered up by numerous individuals and institutions who could have intervened. For example, two highly newsworthy cases that came to light in 2012 which, in hindsight, were seemingly obvious to many observers, are the doping scandal perpetrated by American cyclist and seven-time winner of the Tour de France, Lance Armstrong (who subsequently was stripped of his titles), and the Jimmy Savile case, involving an unprecedented number of victims of sexual assault by the former BBC TV and radio presenter. The latter case is one of the most shocking in living memory. Leading to a major criminal inquiry involving 28 police forces, three internal BBC inquiries and the resignation of a BBC Director General, the Savile case has been described by the Metropolitan Police as a watershed moment in child abuse investigations. While the media have, for several years, reported other prolific sexual predators and alleged high-level cover-ups by institutions including schools, care homes and the Catholic church, it seems that it was Savile's celebrity status that allowed him to abuse on a massive scale – police estimate that he may actually have abused well over one thousand victims, most of whom were children and young people.

The star's fall from grace was all the more dramatic for the fact that it was a very long drop from the elevated position he had occupied for five decades. Jimmy Savile wasn't any ordinary celebrity. He was a cultural icon from the earliest days of popular radio and television; part of the cultural fabric of British life. The BBC show *Top of the Pops*, which he presented from the very first edition in 1964 was, in its heyday, watched by 15 million viewers and his other main vehicle, the BBC TV show *Jim'll Fix It*, broadcast between 1975 and 1994, was watched by up to 20 million people. He rose to fame at a time when there were only three (and latterly four) TV channels and his programmes were points of commonality and connection among people of a certain generation (or generations because they ran for so long). On top of this he had a high-profile career as a charity fund-raiser; it is estimated that he raised over £40 million for good causes. He was awarded a knighthood, a papal knighthood, and counted members of the royal family among his friends. He even reportedly acted as some kind of broker in Prince Charles and Princess Diana's failing marriage. Many of Savile's crimes were carried out in places he had privileged physical access to (it has been reported that staff, including senior managers, at Broadmoor Hospital called him 'Doctor' and afforded him free access to the entire site). Meanwhile, Britain's tabloids and TV executives promoted him as a 'secular saint' (Cross, 2013; Furedi, 2013). When rumours of his offences first started to circulate, it was hard to imagine just how far the star would descend. Two years into the police investigation Operation Yewtree, over 500 victims had come forward and, every time we, the audience, thought that the story had reached new depths, it just got worse, with reports that Savile abused paralysed children in spine injury wards, children who were wheelchair bound and had no speech, and even reports that he was a necrophiliac who enjoyed access to hospital mortuaries. Underlining the widespread belief that Savile's celebrity status made him 'untouchable', fellow BBC presenter Jeremy Paxman (whose programme, *Newsnight*, dropped a documentary investigating allegations about Savile's behaviour, much to Paxman's chagrin) asked, 'What was the BBC doing promoting... this absurd and malign figure? They have never felt comfortable with popular culture and they have therefore given those who claim to perpetrate it too much licence' (www.theguardian.com/media/2013/feb/22/jeremy-paxman-on-jimmy-savile).

Further underlining the fact that celebrity status is so powerful that it can give individually powerful men (and it is nearly always men) a sense of invincibility while acting immorally and illegally towards relatively powerless and/or vulnerable victims, in May 2014, publicity agent Max Clifford was sentenced to eight years custody for sexual offences against young women and girls. Summing up at the end of the trial, the presiding judge commented that Clifford's dominant character and position in the world of entertainment meant that his victims believed he was untouchable, as did he. The case followed several other unsuccessful prosecution attempts as part of Operation Yewtree, in which well-known celebrities in the UK were tried in court for historic sexual offences. The securing of a conviction in the case of Max Clifford came as a huge relief to the Crown Prosecution Service who had been facing allegations of leading a celebrity witch hunt in the aftermath of the revelations about Jimmy Savile.

Convicted criminals can also become media 'celebrities' by virtue of the notoriety of their crimes. Sometimes criminals are cast as *folk devils* by the media, and they are deemed newsworthy long after their convictions because the mass media take a moral stance on public distaste and revulsion towards their crimes. One such example is Peter Sutcliffe, known as the Yorkshire Ripper who, in 1981, was convicted of the murders of 13 women in the north of England. After two decades of confinement in a high-security hospital, he remains something of a media celebrity, with endless newspaper column inches and frequent television documentaries devoted to his crimes and his life since arrest. He has even been revealed to have been a friend of Jimmy Savile's who, reportedly, was questioned as a possible suspect in connection with the police investigation into the murders. However, the fact that Sutcliffe is unlikely ever to be released means that the media are able to treat Sutcliffe as a side-show, an entertaining if somewhat macabre diversion to fill media space when there is little else of importance to report. There are a handful of other criminals who occupy a particular symbolic space in the collective conscience of the British public (the Kray twins, the Great Train Robbers, Denis Nielsen, Fred and Rosemary West, Jon Venables and Robert Thompson, Ian Hunter and Maxine Carr, Amanda Knox), but arguably the most notorious figure in the history of the British criminal justice system is Myra Hindley (the 'Moors murderess') who, with her partner, Ian Brady, was convicted in 1966 of her part in the abduction, torture and murders of two children. Until her reported death in November 2002, Hindley was Britain's longest-serving prisoner and was a regular figure in the pages of the popular press, who waged a systematic and profoundly retributive campaign that culminated with front page copy on the day after her death announcing that the 'devil' had gone to hell 'where she belonged' (see Chapter 5). So successful was the campaign to keep her in prison that it became all but impossible for any Home Secretary – relying on public mandate as they do – to authorize the release of Hindley.

It is not just those who represent showbusiness and notorious crime who are elevated to visibility in the news. High-status individuals in 'ordinary' life (businesspeople, politicians, professionals, the clergy and so on) are also deemed newsworthy and are frequently used to give a 'personal' angle to stories that otherwise might not make the news. This is especially germane when such individuals are defined as deviants: the more clearly and unambiguously the deviant personality can be defined (thus reducing uncertainty and reflecting the underlying news judgement of 'simplification'), the more intrinsically newsworthy the story is assumed to be, especially if it intersects with other news values. This is equally true of local media who report the deviant activities of people from the community they serve. Here, the value of 'proximity' comes into play (see below), but the recipient of news attention will normally be of high-status within the community; for example, a teacher, priest or doctor. Paradoxically, then, despite the media's general tendency to portray crime as a menace wrought by a disaffected underclass on ordinary, respectable folk, it is the middle-class, high-status or celebrity offender who is deemed most newsworthy and will have the greatest number of column inches or hours of airtime devoted to their deviant activities.

Proximity

Proximity has both spatial and cultural dynamics. Spatial proximity refers to the geographical 'nearness' of an event, while cultural proximity refers to the 'relevance' of an event to an audience. These factors often intertwine so that it is those news stories which are perceived to reflect the recipient's existing framework of values, beliefs and interests and occur within geographical proximity to them that are most likely to be reported. Proximity obviously varies between local and national news. For example, a relatively 'ordinary' crime like mugging or arson may be reported in local media but might not make the national news agenda unless it conforms to other news values, for example, it was especially violent or involved a celebrity. The converse of this trend is that events that occur in regions which are remote from the centralized bases of news organization or in countries that are not explicitly linked (in alliance or in opposition) to the UK or US rarely make national news. Indeed, there are some areas of the world which are unlikely to be prominent on the news agendas of the UK, US and other industrialized nations, however high a threshold is reached by potential news stories. By way of example, in 2009 the charity Oxfam launched a campaign to 'save' world news. Reporting that 'British television is sleepwalking towards a global switch-off', Oxfam is critical of the two main broadcasters:

Only three out of 52 African countries are currently represented in factual TV programming, and even this focuses on wildlife. Latin America and non-Anglophile countries are currently not covered by British public service broadcasters in factual programming. On ITV, meanwhile, just five hours of programming from the developing world were broadcast throughout the whole of 2007. (www. oxfam.org.uk/get_involved/campaign/actions/help_save_the_news.html)

However, it is the United States that is most frequently accused of **ethnocentrism** for its tendency to look inwards for its news coverage. However, while the American news media (and, for that matter, the American public) come in for criticism for their perceived lack of interest in world affairs, it is with some justification that they focus on events that occur within their own boundaries. For example, the extended global coverage of two hijacked passenger jets ploughing into the twin towers of the New York World Trade Center on September 11 2001, like earlier footage taken in Dallas in November 1963 of the assassination of President John F. Kennedy, illustrates the degree to which America is regarded a world superpower. Their news is our news in a truly global sense, and both of these crimes cast a long shadow in the collective memory of people with no connection, however tenuous, with the events of those days. But as others have pointed out, for those not of the 'First World', there have been other 'September 11ths' which have received little, if any, media coverage in the West (Carrington and Hogg, 2002).

Cultural proximity also changes according to the political climate and cultural mood of the times. There was little media coverage of the Iran–Iraq war in the 1980s, but more recently Iraq has rarely been out of the news. In short, there may be a domestication of foreign news whereby events in other areas of the world will receive media attention if they are perceived to impinge on the home culture of the reporter and his or her audience. If there is no discernible relevance to the target audience, a story has to be commensurately bigger and more dramatic in order to be regarded as newsworthy. Novelist Michael Frayn comments facetiously:

The crash survey showed that people were not interested in reading about road crashes unless there were at least 10 dead. A road crash with 10 dead, the majority felt, was slightly less interesting than a rail crash with one dead ... Even a rail crash on the Continent made the grade provided there were at least 5 dead. If it was in the United States the minimum number of dead rose to 20; in South America 100; in Africa 200; in China 500. But people really preferred an air crash ... backed up with a story about a middle-aged housewife who had been booked to fly aboard the plane but who had changed her mind at the last moment. (Frayn, 1965: 60)

Cultural proximity also pertains to the individual actors in any crime story that receives global coverage. When individuals from different nations are involved, any country's media can appear to 'take sides' to a degree that might, at best, be classified as patriotism and, at worst, xenophobia. In the case of American student Amanda Knox, convicted of the murder of her British housemate, Meredith Kercher, in Perugia in November 2007, it is interesting to observe the different tones adopted by the US and UK media in their reporting of Knox throughout her long court trial. While American media (relying to a large degree on her affluent, middle-class, 'respectable' parents as sources) portrayed her as a wholesome, all-American, girl-next-door, the British press and many Internet sites have persistently concentrated on the sexual proclivities of 'Foxy Knoxy' and portrayed her in an altogether more sinister light. They also made much of pictures she had posted on social networking sites of her posing with a machine gun, and fantasy stories she had composed involving drugs and rape. But Knox's fellow students at the University of Washington argue that there appears to be a thinly-disguised vendetta against Knox in some of the international media simply because she is American; or rather, she is, 'a pot-smoking, unstable, sex-crazed American' (www.com.washington.edu/commIR/vol2/editionOne).

Similar contradictions and biases can be detected in relation to offenders and victims within the UK. When an individual goes missing (whether or not foul play is immediately suspected) the likelihood of the national media lending their weight behind a campaign to find the missing person depends on several interrelated factors. If the individual in question is young, female, white, middle class and conventionally attractive, the media are more likely to cover the case than if the missing person is, say, a working-class boy or an older woman. Even in cases where abduction and/or murder is immediately suspected, the likelihood of media interest will vary in accordance with the background of the victim. If the victim is male, working class, of African Caribbean or Asian descent, a persistent runaway, has been in care, has drug problems, or is a prostitute (or any combination of these factors), reporters perceive that their audience is less likely to relate to, or empathize with, the victim, and the case gets commensurately lower publicity. The compliance of the victim's family in giving repeated press conferences and making themselves a central part of the story is also a crucial factor in determining its newsworthiness, as is their willingness to part with photographs and home video footage of their missing child. Hence, the disappearances of Madeleine McCann, Sarah Payne, Milly Dowler and the 'Soham girls', Holly Wells and Jessica Chapman, were all eminently newsworthy stories: attractive, photogenic girls from 'respectable', middle-class homes with parents who quickly became media-savvy and were prepared to make repeated pleas for help on behalf of the police (and in the case of the McCanns and Sarah's mother, Sara Payne, continued to court the media and political establishment, even after the story would normally be 'closed').

Even the relatively high-profile case of the murder of 10-year-old Damilola Taylor in Peckham, South London was, initially at least, constructed very differently to the murders of the girls mentioned above. For over a week the victim remained virtually invisible as media reports concentrated almost exclusively on issues of community policing and the levels of violent crime on the streets. It was not until Damilola's father flew into the UK from Nigeria (and made press statements and television appearances) and CCTV footage was released to the media that this little boy became a person in his own right – a person worthy of media attention and public mourning and remembrance. Nevertheless, the public grieving for Damilola failed to reach the near hysterical outpourings of anger and sadness that accompanied the deaths of Sarah, Milly, Holly and Jessica.

To further illustrate this hierarchy of media interest in such cases, it is instructive to analyse similar stories from the same time period and compare the level and tone of coverage accorded to them. For example, a short time after the disappearance of 14-year-old Milly Dowler from Surrey in March 2002, the body of a teenage girl was recovered from a disused quarry near Tilbury Docks. Before the body had even been identified, sections of the tabloid press were carrying headlines announcing that Milly had been found. But it turned out to be the corpse of another 14-year-old girl, Hannah Williams, who had disappeared a year earlier. Yet it was the hunt for Milly that continued to dominate the news for the weeks and months to follow. Almost as soon as she was found, Hannah was forgotten. Quite simply, unlike Milly who was portrayed as the 'ideal' middle-class teenager, Hannah's background made it difficult to build a campaign around her. She was working class and had run away before. Furthermore, her mother – a single parent on a low income – 'wasn't really press-conference material' according to a police spokeswoman (Bright, 2002: 23).

Violence or conflict

The news value which is arguably most common to all media is that of 'violence' because it fulfils the media's desire to present dramatic events in the most graphic possible fashion. Even the most regulated media institutions are constantly pushing back the boundaries of acceptable reportage when it comes to depicting acts of violence because it represents a basic violation of the person and marks the distinction between those who are of society and those who are outside it. Only the State has the monopoly of legitimate violence, and this 'violence' is used to safeguard society against 'illegitimate' uses (Hall et al., 1978/2013). However, violence has become so ubiquitous that – although still considered newsworthy – it is frequently reported in a routine, mundane manner with little follow-up or analysis. Unless a story involving violence conforms to several other news values or provides a suitable threshold to keep alive an existing set of stories, even the most serious acts of violence may be used as 'fillers' and consigned to the inside pages of a newspaper. Yet whether treated sensationally or unsensationally, violence – including violent death – remains a staple of media reporting. According to research conducted in the early 1990s, the British press devoted an average of 65 per cent of their crime reporting to stories involving interpersonal violence, although police statistics indicate that only around 6 per cent of recorded crime involved interpersonal violence (Williams and Dickinson, 1993). Since that time, according to the Government's Office for National Statistics, violent incidents have halved and the number of homicides in 2011/2012 was the lowest since 1989 (www.ons. gov.uk/ons/dcp171778_298904.pdf). Yet media depictions of violence suggest precisely the opposite.

Cultural criminologists argue that crime, violence, humiliation and cruelty are objectified, commodified and desired to the extent where they are widely distributed through all forms of media to be pleasurably consumed. Mike Presdee offers numerous examples which, he claims, are evidence of the consumer's need for privately enjoyed, carnivalesque transgression. From 'sports' that, having all but disappeared, are now enjoying a dramatic upturn in popularity (albeit underground), such as bareknuckle fighting, badger-baiting and dog-fighting, to 'Reality TV' and gangsta rap, the evidence of our lust for pain and humiliation is all around us:

> The mass of society bare their souls to the media who, in turn, transform them into the commodity of entertainment. Confidentialities are turned against the subject, transforming them into the object of hurt and humiliation as their social being is commodified ready for consumption. (Presdee, 2000: 75)

Little wonder then, that news has followed a similarly dramatic and vicarious path. With an increasing imperative to bring drama and immediacy to news production, the caveat 'You may find some of the pictures that follow distressing' seems to preface an increasing number of television news reports. This leads us to consider the spectacle of violence as portrayed through graphic imagery.

Visual spectacle and graphic imagery

Television news is generally given greater credence by the public than newspapers, partly because it is perceived to be less partisan than the press, but also because it offers higher quality (moving) images which are frequently held to demonstrate the 'truth' of a story or to verify the particular angle from which the news team has chosen to cover it. Chris Greer has suggested that of all the changes in journalistic perceptions of news value over the last half-century, it is the visual that most emphatically marks the difference between the criteria described by Galtung and Ruge in the 1960s and the ones described here. For Greer (2009) the primacy of the visual has been hastened by technological developments (the exponential growth of mobile digital technologies, the Internet, etc.) and consolidated by the shift to a more explicitly visual culture; we all simply take it for granted that any news story will be accompanied by images, and, increasingly, thanks to mobile phone/cameras, Facebook, etc. images that have not been approved for publication by the subject, as the earlier discussion of Amanda Knox highlighted (see also discussion below about 'citizen journalism'). Quite simply, in the second decade of the 21st century, potential news stories are only likely to make the news if they can be portrayed in images as well as words, and the 'availability of the right image can help elevate a crime victim or offender to iconic status' (Greer, 2009: 227; cf. Hayward and Presdee, 2010). Linnemann (2013) comments that visual representation of the traumatic and grotesque is designed to tap into the same human tendency that compels people to gawp when passing the scene of an accident (see Chapter 10 of this volume). The shocking is a defining feature of spectatorship (see also Brown, 2009).

As described above, violence is a primary component of news selection. But there are many different types of violence and it tends to be acts of violence that have a strong visual impact and can be graphically presented that are most likely to receive extensive media coverage. The very public murder, in May 2013, of off-duty soldier Lee Rigby on a busy London street by two Islamist extremists, captured on CCTV and on footage filmed on witnesses' mobile phones, is a prime example. A video of one of the perpetrators 'justifying' the killing, while still covered in the victim's blood, was carried by ITN's website and was visited so many times that the site crashed. However, while 'spectacular' crimes get a lot of attention because they make good copy and are visually arresting on television, it seems that those crimes which occur in private spheres, or which are not subject to public scrutiny, become even more marginalized, even more invisible. Hence, crimes like domestic violence, child abuse, elder abuse, accidents at work, pollution of the environment, much white collar crime, corporate corruption, state violence and governments' denial or abuse of human rights, all receive comparatively little media attention, despite their arguably greater cost to individuals and society. Similarly, long-term developments, which may be more important than immediate, dramatic incidents in terms of their effects, may not be covered because they cannot be accompanied by dramatic visual imagery.

Furthermore, TV shows like *Big Brother* which blur the line between entertainment and reality and call into question the extent to which people behave 'normally' while being watched on television, might make us question whether court trials should be televised. In some countries, court trials have made celebrities out of lawyers and judges, and led to accusations that they, too, are not immune to playing up for the cameras. In addition, 'real' footage of the kind captured on CCTV or on video cameras by witnesses and bystanders as a criminal event unfolds, is increasingly used in news broadcasts to visually highlight the event's immediacy and 'authenticity'. Such images have graphically and poignantly contributed to the spectacle of crime and violence in the postmodern era. Many of the most shocking events that occurred in the last few years of the 20th century entered the collective consciousness with such horrifying impact precisely because news reports were accompanied by images of the victim at the time of, immediately prior to, or soon after, a serious violent incident. The video footage of black motorist Rodney King being beaten up by four white LA police officers, and the live broadcast of O.J. Simpson being chased for miles down the freeway by police following the brutal double-murder at his home, are examples from the US of graphic imagery being used to heighten the drama of already newsworthy stories.

In the UK, the last moments of the lives of Diana, Princess of Wales leaving the Ritz Hotel in Paris, James Bulger being led out of a Bootle shopping centre, Damilola Taylor skipping down a Peckham street, and Fusilier Lee Rigby crossing a street in Woolwich, only to be mown down by a car and then hacked to death with a meat cleaver in broad daylight and in front of numerous passers-by, are all forcefully etched on the British psyche. Combining the mundane ordinariness of everyday life with the grim inevitability of what is about to unfold, CCTV footage – played out by the media on a seemingly endless loop appeals to the voyeuristic elements in all of us, while at the same time reinforcing our sense of horror, revulsion and powerlessness. Indeed one of the remarkable aspects of Madeleine McCann's abduction (to a UK public at least who have become used to being watched in nearly all public spaces) was that there was no CCTV footage of her being carried away, thus contradicting Haggerty and Ericson's (2000) famous maxim that in today's surveillance-saturated society we have witnessed the 'disappearance of disappearance' (see Chapter 8 for further discussion of CCTV and surveillance).

Children

Writing in 1978, Stuart Hall and his colleagues argued that any crime can be lifted into news visibility if violence becomes associated with it, but three decades later it might be said that any crime can be lifted into news visibility if children are associated with it. In fact, Philip Jenkins (1992) argues precisely this, suggesting that *any* offence, particularly those that deviate from the *moral* consensus, are made eminently more newsworthy if children are involved. This is true whether the children at the centre of the story are victims or offenders, although Jenkins concentrates on child victims who, he says, not only guarantee the newsworthiness of a story, but also can ensure the media's commitment to what might be called 'morality campaigns'. This amounts to

what Jenkins describes as the 'politics of substitution'. In the 1970s, those who wished to denounce and stigmatize homosexuality, the sale of pornography or religious deviation (for example, satanism) found little support in the prevailing moral climate. But the inclusion of children in stories about these activities makes it impossible to condone them within any conventional moral or legal framework. Thus, we have witnessed over the last 50 years a process of escalation whereby morality campaigns are now directed 'not against homosexuality but at paedophilia, not pornography but child pornography, not satanism but ritual child abuse' (Jenkins, 1992: 11). The focus on children means that deviant behaviour automatically crosses a higher threshold of victimization than would have been possible if adults alone had been involved (1992: 11). Nevertheless, despite Jenkins' assertion that the involvement of children guarantees news coverage of a story, this is not necessarily the case. Sexual abuse within the family remains so low down on the media's agenda as to render it virtually invisible, and as we shall see in later chapters, the mass media persist in preserving the image of the ideal family and underplaying or ignoring the fact that sexual violence exists – indeed, is endemic – in *all* communities, and that sexual abuse of children is more likely to occur within the family than at the hands of an 'evil stranger'.

Children who commit crimes have arguably become especially newsworthy since the murder of two-year-old James Bulger by two 10-year-olds in 1993, which was the first case for at least a generation in which the media constructed pre-teenage children as 'demons' rather than as 'innocents'. The case also proved a watershed in terms of criminal justice and crime prevention. The 10-year-olds were tried in an adult court and the case was the impetus for a massive expansion of CCTV equipment in public spaces throughout the country. But at a more fundamental level, it presented a dilemma for the mass media. Childhood is a *social construction*; in other words, it is subject to a continuous process of (re)invention and (re)definition and, even in the modern period, has gone through numerous incarnations from 18th-century romantic portrayals of childhood as a time of innocence, to more recent conceptions of childhood as a potential site of psychological and psychiatric problems. But with the exception of a brief period in the early 19th century when children were viewed as inherently corrupt and in need of overt control and moral guidance (which coincided with a period when child labour was the norm among the working classes, before legislation took children out of factories, mills and mines and relocated them in schools and reformatories), the notion of children being 'evil' has not been prominent.

By and large, childhood has been seen as fundamentally separate from adulthood, and children regarded as requiring nurture and protection, whether by philanthropic reformers, educators, parents, welfare agencies, the medical profession or the law. But with the murder of James Bulger by two older children, the notion of childhood innocence gave way to themes of childhood

horror and evil. Public outrage was fuelled, in part, by sensational and vindictive press reporting which variously described the 10-year-olds as 'brutes', 'monsters', 'animals' and 'the spawn of Satan'. The reasons why children and young people are the usual subjects of such moral panics will be explored in Chapters 3 and 4, but suffice it to say here that the young are frequently used as a kind of measuring stick or social barometer with which to test the health of society more generally. Children and adolescents represent the future, and if they engage in deviant behaviour it is often viewed as symptomatic of a society that is declining ever further into a moral morass. For the media, then, deviant youth is used as a shorthand ascription for a range of gloomy and fatalistic predictions about spiralling levels of crime and amoral behaviour in society at large.

Conservative ideology and political diversion

What all the news values discussed so far have in common is their reliance on a broadly right-wing consensus which, in many news channels (especially the tabloid press), is justified as encapsulating the 'British way of life'. In matters of crime and deviance, this agenda emphasizes deterrence and repression and voices support for more police, more prisons and a tougher criminal justice system. In addition, it appears that we now live in a society where political process and media discourse are indistinguishable and mutually constitutive. The symbiotic relationship between the mass media and politicians is illustrated by the support given by the former to the latter in matters of law and order. For two decades a version of *'populist punitiveness'* has characterized British governments' attitudes to penal policy, a stance which is replicated in the US and in many other countries around the world. There seems little opposition from any political party in the UK to proposals to incarcerate ever younger children, to introduce curfews, to bring in legislation to prevent large 'unauthorized' gatherings, and to introduce new and harsher measures against immigrants, protesters, demonstrators, the homeless and the young unemployed. All these issues are most directly conveyed to the public at large by the mass media.

Of course, the 'British way of life' that is defended most vehemently by newspapers such as the *Sun* and the *Daily Mail* is fiercely nostalgic and may now only be applicable to a minority (ironically usually termed the *moral majority*) of British citizens. Despite claiming to be the voice of the people, the criminalization of certain individuals and activities by these newspapers highlights the general perceived intolerance towards anyone or anything that transgresses an essentially conservative agenda. It is also partial explanation for the vigorous policing and punishment of so-called 'victimless crimes': recreational use of drugs, sexual permissiveness, especially among young people,

public displays of homosexuality and lesbianism, anti-establishment demon-strators exercising their democratic right to protest, and spectacular youth cultures. All are activities which are subject to continuous, and sometimes overblown, repression. At times the generalized climate of hostility to mar-ginal groups and 'unconventional' norms (to the dominant culture of journalists, at least) spills over into racism and xenophobia. The moral con-cerns over mugging in the 1970s was focused on young men of African-Caribbean descent; the inner-city riots of the 1980s were frequently attributed entirely to black youths; and recent media coverage of the immigration into Britain of people from other countries frequently demonstrates a shocking disregard for others' human rights, and the media's inability (or unwillingness) to differenti-ate between political refugees and illegal immigrants. Even people from ethnic and/or religious minorities born and raised in this country may be subjected to overwhelmingly negative press. For example, British-born Muslims first became newsworthy when a *fatwah*, or death threat, was issued against author Salman Rushdie in 1989, resulting in a great deal of unfavourable coverage portraying all Muslims as fanatics and fundamentalists. Since then, Muslims in the UK have continued to be identified in negative contexts, even when cast as victims; a phenomenon that has increased exponentially since the terrorist attacks on the twin towers of the World Trade Center, and the rail systems in Madrid and London.

The concentration of news media on the criminal and deviant activities of people from the lowest socio-economic classes and from religious, ethnic and cultural minorities serves to perpetuate a sense of a stratified, deeply divided and mutually hostile population. Some politicians have been quick to galvanize the support of an anxious and fearful public, and have undoubtedly contributed to negative reporting which has agitated social tensions. By simultaneously focusing attention on hapless victims of serious crime and calling for tougher, more retributive punishment, politicians not only promote an essentially con-servative agenda, but also deflect attention from other serious social problems. Indeed, it could be argued that much of what makes up our newspapers is in fact a mere side-show, a diversionary tactic which removes attention from more serious problems in society, particularly those of a political nature. The media hysteria which has, in recent years, accompanied victims of HIV and AIDS, lone/unmarried parents, teenage and pre-teenage mothers, child abusers, satanic ritual abusers, video nasties, juvenile delinquents, joyriders, ravers, users of cannabis, ecstasy and other recreational drugs, paedophiles, homo-sexual members of parliament (indeed, homosexuals generally), adulterous celebrities, and girl gangs, might all be reasonably argued to constitute part of the overtly sanctimonious moral discourse directed at the institution of the fam-ily, which has characterized the media and political agendas since the 1980s. From John Major's ill-fated 'Back to Basics' campaign and Tony Blair's promo-tion of a 'new moral order' (prompted by studies showing that Britain has the highest rate of teenage pregnancies in Europe), to the Conservatives current characterization of 'broken Britain', successive British politicians have harnessed the mass media to criminalize certain groups of people and divert attention from the systemic social problems of their making; poverty, patriarchy, and an education system that is failing its pupils, among them.

Two examples of newsworthy stories *par excellence*

1. The disappearance of Madeleine McCann

A case that might be described as unprecedented in terms of the global coverage it generated and its perceived newsworthiness was the abduction of three-year-old British girl Madeleine McCann from a holiday resort in Praia da Luz, Portugal, in May 2007. It became an international news story that received saturation coverage through the summer of that year and continues to make the news regularly seven years later, thanks to the efforts of her parents and to the continuing police investigation by officers in the UK and Portugal. Madeleine's abduction provides a case study of how the 12 news values discussed in this chapter (or culturally contingent versions of them) can be applied to any potential news event. The drama of a young child being abducted from her bed while on a family holiday meets the required **threshold** of perceived interest, and the McCann family were extremely skilled at constructing further 'mini' thresholds to keep the story fresh in public minds (praying in the local church, an audience with the Pope, a tour around Europe, a visit to the US, a campaign to introduce a new pan-European 'amber-alert' system to aid police in the hours immediately after a child abduction, and countless others); a grim **predictability** is woven through the account of the crime via recourse to editorials criticizing Madeleine's parents for leaving their children alone in their holiday apartment while they went to eat at a tapas bar, and via references to stories of other child abductions in Portugal and its neighbours; many elements of the story were **simplified** in part of necessity because, under Portuguese law, there was very little information the police could disclose to the waiting world's media; the abduction was constructed as **individual** and random, a cruel act of chance; hence any of us (and our children) are at **risk**; the crimes were explained by reference to **sex** and sexual deviance as rumours circulated that Madeleine had been taken by a paedophile; the McCanns became **celebrities** as they exploited the world's media in order to make audiences in countries beyond the UK and Portugal feel culturally **proximate** to the events unfolding; the **violence** of a child being forcibly taken by a stranger was reinforced by the circulation of **graphic images** of

Madeleine, many taken just hours and days before the abduction, showing her enjoying her family holiday, and by images of her grief-stricken mother forced to confront the cameras on a daily basis to keep the story alive; and the fact that the victim of this heinous crime was an attractive **child** with a 'respectable', middle-class background, made this a cardinal news story. The presence of a **conservative ideology** manifested itself in several ways in the news media. For example, numerous journalists questioned the acceptability of children being left alone at a holiday resort where babysitters were available, and hotly debated the likely guilt or innocence of the only formal suspects named by the police (a British man staying with his mother in a nearby villa, and the McCanns themselves; all of whom were, at times, subjected to extreme vitriol by the press, even though there was no evidence to link them to the child's disappearance). At their xenophobic worst, the British media rounded on the Portuguese police for failing to uncover a credible lead and for not co-operating with English police officers soon enough to make a difference. The dominant theme was that British detectives would have 'solved' the case, while the local officers were lazy, incompetent and corrupt.

2. Anders Behring Breivik and the spree killing of 77 people in Norway

On July 22nd 2011 a bomb exploded in a vehicle outside a Government building in central Oslo, killing eight people inside the building. As news of the blast was being broadcast around the world, the 32-year-old man who had planted the bomb, Anders Behring Breivik, dressed in a police uniform, boarded a ferry to the island of Utøya, 25 miles northwest of Oslo, where 564 young people were attending a Summer Camp organised by the youth wing of the Labour Party. Breivik went on an hour-and-a-half shooting spree, killing 69 people, mostly teenagers, before being arrested by police.

In the UK, the large number of victims and the capture of the gunman alive ensured that the story met the required **threshold** of interest. The publication of his propagandist websites, the discovery of explosives at his house and his subsequent trial created further 'mini' thresholds to keep the story fresh in public minds; a grim **predictability** was woven through the account of the crime via recourse to stories about terrorism (e.g. in London and Madrid) and reports suggesting that his actions bore many of the hallmarks of US school shootings; many elements of the story were **simplified** – he was a 'Nazi', his complex personality disorders were presented as psychosis or schizophrenia; the murders were constructed as **individual** and random, a cruel act of chance; suggesting once again that any of us (or our children) are at **risk** from similar kinds of attack; his crimes were partially explained by reference to **sex** – his sexual frustration, lack of sexual experience and his claims that he'd seen the ravages of promiscuity and venereal disease within his own family. Such is the attention given to mass murderers that inevitably Breivik has become a **celebrity** in his own right. The geographical and culturally **proximity** of Norway to the UK ensured its newsworthiness; in addition, the news media emphasized reported links to English far-right groups and Foreign Secretary William Hague was reported as saying that the UK stood 'shoulder to shoulder' with Norway. The **violence** of the events that day was reinforced by the circulation of **graphic images** of the victims bodies and then again a month after the attacks when news media published images of Breivik re-enacting the murders at Utøya for the benefit of police investigators. The fact that Breivik's victims were mostly young people from 'respectable', middle-class backgrounds made the story even more newsworthy and the press initially suggested that they were even younger than they were (many newspapers stated his crime as 'gunning down children on a holiday island'). The presence of a moralistic **conservative ideology** was most evident in the early reporting as events were still unfolding – initial speculation centred on the possibility of home-grown fundamentalist Muslims being responsible, reflecting a global media preoccupation with the threat of a terrorist attack, a barely disguised 'Islamaphobia' within western media, and a perception of an emerging threat from the extreme right in Europe. These fixations, which are frequently conflated, all contributed to a heightened sense of risk. However, once Breivik was captured, news media hastily sought to distance themselves from his brand of political extremism.

This brief analysis relates to UK media, but this terrible crime has been analysed by Cere, Jewkes and Ugelvik (2013) who use the case to highlight some of the subtle discrepancies underpinning crime news reporting in the UK, Norway and Italy, which themselves reflect broader social, cultural and political differences between the three countries. Among their findings is that in Italy, coverage of the Breivik case was rather subdued at the time of the events, perhaps mindful of the fact that his actions were politically motivated. Right-wing individuals and organizations have left an indelible mark on Italian political and media culture. Memories of bombings in Milan, Brescia and Bologna, and of other crimes, including the killing of two Senegalese immigrants in Florence in 2011 by a right-wing sympathizer, are always in the background of any discussion of right-wing violent actions, and hence the coverage was not only concerned with this particular individual but also with the broader international context of his dramatic actions. Unsurprisingly, Norwegian coverage of the case has been extensive and many of the normal 'rules' of reporting have been broken in this usually sober and ethically conscious nation. For example, while it is illegal to photograph or film defendants in a criminal case, an exception was made by the court in the case of Breivik, and Cere et al. argue that the opposite of simplification occurred in the reporting of the story. Rather, the news media exhausted every possible angle, producing a hugely complex and often confusing melange of contrasting impressions – all of which must be seen within the wider cultural bricolage of stories about acts of terror. Analysing the story from a cultural criminological standpoint, Sandberg et al. (2014) argue that Breivik's crimes followed a cultural script, formed and reformed down years of reporting of campus killings in the US. In a media-saturated world, Breivik's actions on 22 July 2011 constitute an edited and re-edited performance, combining violence, fame-seeking and an extreme form of masculinity. The fact that the attacks were unprecedented in their extent and brutality for a country with little experience of political violence, a low crime rate and just under 35 murders a year on average, made the story all the more shocking, both within Norway and outside it (Berntzen and Sandberg, 2014; Mathiesen, 2013).

News production and consumption in a digital global marketplace: the rise of the citizen journalist

Finally in our analysis of crime news, it is worth mentioning the impact of new media (although in advanced, industrialized nations, satellite and digital media can hardly be called 'new' any more). One of the most profound changes of recent years is that many of us now consume much of our news online and the democratic nature of Internet communication, together with its global penetration and immediacy, have given rise to the *citizen journalist*. '*User-generated content*' or UGC, as it is known in the media industries, encompasses images taken on mobile phone cameras, texts and emails sent by audience members to media outlets, and contributions to Internet sites such as Twitter and YouTube.

Twitter has particularly captured the imaginations of mainstream journalists (see Chapter 9). BBC journalist Rory Cellan-Jones describes the benefits of the micro-blogging service, as 'like a very fast, but not entirely reliable news agency', which he uses to gain immediate notice of breaking stories and file his reports before many of his competitors (www.bbc.co.uk/blogs/technology/). Although now frequently associated with the celebrities who use it, Twitter first came to many people's attention when pictures were posted of a US Airways plane making a forced landing into New York's Hudson river in January 2009. Although not a story about crime, it met most of the news criteria outlined in this chapter, and was notable for the novelty of a major air incident in which every one of the 155 people on board survived. But it was the incredible *images* of Airbus A320 submerged in the freezing water with its passengers standing along its wings that brought home the drama and spectacle of this event. A passenger on a passing ferry took a photo of the stricken airplane on his mobile phone and posted it on Twitter. By the following day, over 97,000 people had viewed the image and its owner was doing interviews with many of the major global news organizations.

Personal, mobile communication technologies have not only added a new dimension to the manufacture of news but, in a few cases, they have had far-reaching consequences for democracy. In May 2008 it was reported that the Chinese Government had responded to the devastation caused by an earthquake in the Sichuan province, in which tens of thousands of people perished, by moderating its control of the Internet. This meant that those affected by the tragedy could use video sharing sites, blogs, chat rooms, instant messaging services and the like to circulate graphic pictures and accounts of their experiences. For these new citizen journalists the Chinese Government's relaxation of its generally tough stance on Internet content brought an unprecedented level of freedom (see Chapter 9). Another example of an event brought to the attention of a global audience by a citizen journalist was the killing of a young Iranian woman, Neda Agha-Soltan, who was shot during an anti-government protest in Tehran on 20 June 2009. A University student, Neda was a bystander watching the protests when she was shot by a man believed to be a member of the pro-government militia (himself later 'identified' when photographs of his ID card were posted on the Internet and then published by newspapers). With journalists forced to stay in their hotel rooms, or even leave the country, these amateur recordings quickly became the only means of getting uncensored news about the protests and the murder of Neda out of Tehran. Within hours of Neda's death, graphic scenes captured by an unknown eyewitness showing her bleeding to death on the street had been posted online and were being published and broadcast in newspapers and bulletins around the world. The shaky video footage even received a Polk Award, one of the highest honours in journalism, representing the first time such a prize had been awarded to an anonymous individual.

Of course what these illustrations from China and Iran also demonstrate is that, although undoubtedly true that major crimes or disasters now generate more material from ordinary eyewitnesses, the extent to which news production and consumption has fundamentally changed can be overemphasized. As Cellan-Jones illustrates, technologically savvy journalists are learning how to access that content and turn it into mainstream media fodder. Furthermore, the relationship between citizen journalism and mainstream media outlets is symbiotic; many of the contributions to Twitter and YouTube are simply regurgitating reports from 24-hour news stations and, while they provide instant information about anything that is happening in the world and are a brilliantly effective way of sharing information, they cannot be relied on to be entirely accurate or impartial. For journalists like Cellan-Jones, that makes the work of mainstream media outlets and professional reporters all the more relevant.

Presenting more of a dilemma for traditional media companies are the forums that encourage the public to express opinions about events in the news.

For example, the assassination of Pakistan's Opposition Leader, Benazir Bhutto in 2007 resulted in several contributions to the BBC news website that were anti-Islam and which prompted discussions at the BBC about whether the 'Have Your Say' facility should be temporarily withdrawn. The issue was not just that the comments might be deemed offensive by some visitors to the site; they also raised questions about their editorial value and how far they should influence the BBC's coverage more widely. In a lecture at Leeds University in January 2008, Director of BBC World Service, Peter Horrocks explained the process of sifting through the vast amount of opinion expressed by ordinary people:

> The top 20 or 30 recommended posts all had variations on the theme, attacking Islam in comprehensive terms. Most of them weren't making distinctions between different aspects of Islam, they were simply damning the religion as a whole. To be honest it was pretty boring wading through them and wouldn't have added much to anyone's understanding of the causes or consequences of the assassination. Buried amongst the comments however... were insights from those who had met Benazir or knew her. And there were valuable eyewitness comments from people who were at the scene in Rawalpindi. Our team that deals with user content sifted through the chaff to find some excellent wheat. (www.bbc.co.uk/blogs/theeditors/2008/01/value_of_citizen_journalism.html)

The right to freedom of speech – even if it prompts views based on some form of hatred – is always going to prove controversial and all media organizations must tread a careful line. It is arguable that forums which encourage audience participation promote a particularly emotive brand of *populism* whereby the views of a small minority who get sufficiently outraged to bother texting or emailing a news organization, radio station or Internet forum, come to represent the editorial line taken by those media outlets. While Horrocks is generally positive about UGC, saying: 'There is no doubt that the stronger voice of the audience is having a beneficial effect on the range of stories and perspectives that journalists cover', he also admits that the average 10,000 emails or posts the BBC receives on its 'Have Your Say' site each day represents fewer than 1 per cent of its users, and he asks rhetorically: 'What organization – a political party, a business, a trades union – would allow its stance to be totally driven by such a small minority?' (ibid.).

What this discussion highlights is that the proliferation of new media – far from encouraging a plurality of news channels – may simply have augmented the dominance of traditional media and forced them to become more competitive. As a senior manager within the BBC, Horrocks gives a fascinating insight into the way that news production has changed since the advent of digital mobile communication technologies. Not only does the BBC have a dedicated User-Generated Content (UGC) Unit working alongside their conventional journalistic resources, dealing solely with information and opinion from the audience – and being able to cope with 'spikes' in such material when a particularly newsworthy event occurs (Horrocks gives the example of a high-school shooting), but the corporation has also invested in personal social media in locations that are difficult to report from:

> In northern Nigeria, for example, we are using mobile phones which we pro-vided to villages. In each village there is one person who is known as 'the keeper of the mobile'. This was a way we learnt about a government confronta-tion with a village about land rights. We looked into that story, and used BBC journalistic rigours to cover that story. (www.guardian.co.uk/media/pda/2010/feb/10/peter-horrocks-social-media)

It would appear, then, that far from being the anarchic, decentralized 'counter-cultural' space we might assume it to be, the Internet replicates the dominance of established media organizations with the BBC, *The Guardian*, *The Times*, *Telegraph*, and *Sun* being the most popular websites for news and public affairs (Curran, 2010). This may not be surprising given the steep costs of establish-ing, maintaining and promoting high-profile sites. However, Pratt suggests that, despite established news organizations being the primary news sources online, their drive to be more attractive to audiences and advertisers has resulted in the picture of crime becoming even more skewed, as they feed audiences an escalating diet of serious, violent, unusual offences and trivia involving celebrities and scandals. In some senses, then, while we might be broadly optimistic about the role of new information technologies in giving ordinary citizens a voice and bringing news from remote corners of the world, we should exercise caution because of the types of crime most likely to be regarded by journalists, editors and directors as newsworthy (Pratt, 2007).

News values and crime news production: some concluding thoughts

While the possibility of a direct causal relationship between media consump-tion and behavioural response (for example, between violent screen images and real-life violence) is downplayed by most media academics in the UK, it is nonetheless widely accepted that those who work in the media do have some degree of influence in terms of what potential stories they select and how they then organize them, defining or amplifying some issues over others. The time and space available for news is not infinite and journalism is, of necessity, a selective account of reality. No story can be told without judge-ments being made about the viability of sending costly resources to film, photograph and report it, or without implicit suppositions being made about the beliefs and values of the people who will be reading, viewing or listening to it.

The desire to accommodate public tastes and interests has prompted some critics to accuse the British media of pandering to what the first Director General of the BBC, Lord Reith, used to call the 'lowest common denominator' of the audience. Since the British media went through a process of deregulation in the late 1980s and early 1990s criticism has intensified, and both broadcast and print media have been accused of 'dumbing down' their news coverage and measuring newsworthiness by the degree of amusement or revulsion a story provokes in the audience. The news values that have been discussed in this chapter seem to support this view. They illustrate that the news media do not cover systemically all forms and expressions of crime and victimization, and that they pander to the most voyeuristic desires of the audience by exaggerating and dramatizing relatively unusual crimes, while ignoring or downplaying the crimes that are most likely to happen to the 'average' person. At the same time, they sympathize with some victims while blaming others.

Moreover, the pressures of having to succeed in such a fast moving, commercial environment might (if one were being generous) help to explain the demise of the best-selling Sunday newspaper, the *News of the World* in 2011, 168 years after it was established. When it – and its daily sister paper the *Sun* – were bought by Rupert Murdoch's News International in 1969, a tabloid or 'red-top' press was created to rival the quality broadsheets and both titles firmly established themselves at the heart of British political and cultural life. However, the enforced closure of *News of the World* followed allegations of extensive phone hacking of high-profile individuals, including murdered schoolgirl Milly Dowler and families of victims of serious crime; a method of news-gathering which, for reporters and editors working on these titles, had the dual benefits of saving huge amounts of time which investigative journalism inevitably involves and satiating a public appetite for immediacy and excess. According to some, this press, with its strong focus on sex, celebrity and sensation, has become the single most detrimental influence on British cultural life and standards; one social commentator, Will Self, describes it as a 'tectonic shift' which is 'eating holes in the British social fabric' (*Guardian,* 11 July 2011). For Self, the following equation follows: 'if anyone can be a celebrity then anyone can be exposed. The hacking into the 7/7 victims' phones, or the relatives of servicemen killed in Afghanistan, or even the phone of a murdered schoolgirl is the only logical continuation of this process' (*Guardian,* 11 July 2011). However, so serious are the allegations concerning phone-hacking by private investigators hired by sections of the press (and prompted by practices uncovered at *News of the World*), that the British Government established a wide-ranging inquiry into press standards, practices and ethics, chaired by Lord Justice Leveson. After more than a year of hearings and considering the evidence,

Leveson concluded 'beyond doubt' that the British press had repeatedly ignored its responsibilities and in doing so had 'damaged the public interest, caused real hardship and, also on occasion, wreaked havoc in the lives of innocent people' (Leveson, 2012). At the time of writing, a criminal investigation of senior personnel at the *News of the World* is still ongoing.

The revelations about phone hacking by journalists represented a nadir in the history of the popular press. Nevertheless, the tabloidization of news (on television and radio as well as in print) is arguably a cultural expression of democratic development, giving voice to new forms of political engagement with issues such as environmentalism, health and sexuality. And while the interests and priorities of the contemporary audience may be regarded as populist and trivial, the fact is that more people consume news today than have at any time previously. Furthermore, there is a valuable investigative tradition in journalism which continues to play an important role, not least in uncovering police or political corruption, miscarriages of justice and, as we will see in Chapter 8, whistleblowing on the extent of state surveillance of private communications.

Summary

- News values are the combined outcome of two different but interrelated factors which together determine the selection and presentation of news. First, news values are shaped by a range of technological, political and economic forces that structure and constrain the form and content of any reported event at the point of news-gathering. Second, news values cater for the perceived interests of the audience and they capture the public mood; a factor usually summed up by news editors as 'giving the public what it wants'.
- Drawing on 'classic' studies by Galtung and Ruge (1965/1973) and Chibnall (1977), which analysed news production in the mid-20th century, this chapter has developed a set of 12 news values appropriate to the new millennium. While faithful to certain news fundamentals that were highlighted in these works, the chapter has suggested that as society has evolved, so too do the cultural and psychological triggers which condition audience responses and, correspondingly, influence the construction of media narratives.
- In addition to the news values discussed in detail, it is taken for granted that crime is inherently highly newsworthy and is usually 'novel' and 'negative' in essence. News values not only shape the production of crime news in the 21st century, but they also aid our understanding of why public perceptions about crime are frequently inaccurate, despite media audiences being more sophisticated and better equipped to see through 'spin' than ever before.
- The emergence of mobile digital forms of communication and the proliferation of Internet sites that permit various forms of 'citizen journalism' have democratized news production, but the news received by the vast majority of audiences still

comes from traditional media organizations who are becoming increasingly adept at weaving user-generated content (UGC) into conventional sources and traditional styles of reporting. The cardinal news values discussed here are as relevant to 'new' media as they are to traditional press and broadcasting.

- The 12 news values discussed in this chapter will be drawn on throughout the remainder of this book in order to demonstrate how types of crime and specific criminal cases are selected and presented according to prevailing cultural assumptions and ideologies.

STUDY QUESTIONS

1. How have news values changed over the last 50 years? Which of the news values identified in this chapter would you say have become most prominent recently? What do these variations tell us about the changing nature of society?

2. As the discussion of Anders Breivik's act of mass murder illustrated, news values, while broadly similar across 'western', industrialized nations, do nonetheless differ in subtle ways, reflecting the particular socio-economic, political and cultural contours of any given country. If you are studying outside the UK, or are an overseas student at a British university, reflect on how news values differ in your country from the ones discussed in this chapter.

3. This chapter has focused mainly on the news values used to set the national news agenda. What news values are most evident in crime reports in your local newspaper, or on your local radio or television news programme? How do they differ from the national and international media?

4. Using international news services accessed via 'new' media technologies, conduct a content analysis of the major crime news stories covered, and draw up a list of the news values prioritized.

5. 'The availability of an image may determine whether or not a story is run. The availability of the right image can help elevate a crime victim or offender to iconic status' (Greer, 2009: 227). What examples can you think of (or find) that bear out this statement?

6. How would each of the theoretical perspectives reviewed in Chapter 1 view the production of crime news?

FURTHER READING

It is still worth returning to the seminal study of press news values produced by J. Galtung and M. Ruge, originally published in 1965, but most easily accessed in S. Cohen and J. Young (eds) (1973) *The Manufacture of News* (Constable). S. Chibnall (1977) *Law and Order News* (Tavistock) also still deserves close

(Continued)

(Continued)

attention. M. Wykes (2001) *News, Crime and Culture* (Pluto) discusses news values in relation to crime and deviance and includes several fascinating case studies. P. Manning (2001) *News and News Sources: A Critical Introduction* (Sage) is a useful introduction to news production more generally. J. Curran and J. Seaton (2010) *Power Without Responsibility: Press, Broadcasting and the Internet in Britain* (Routledge), now in its 7th edition, has been brought up to date with discussions of the impact of the Internet. At 2,000 pages long, the Leveson Report into the Culture, Practices and Ethics of the Press (published on 29 November 2012) is too detailed and too parochial to discuss in this book, which has an international readership. However, it offers a fascinating glimpse into the practices of the popular press and how, for decades, certain news organizations were able to invade the privacy of individuals without any justifiable public interest. The Report can be downloaded at www.official-documents. gov.uk/document/hc1213/hc07/0780/0780.asp.

3

Media and Moral Panics

CHAPTER CONTENTS

The background to the moral panic model   84

How the mass media turn the ordinary into the extraordinary   85

The role of the authorities in the deviancy amplification process   86

Defining moral boundaries and creating consensus   88

Rapid social change – risk   90

Youth   91

Problems with the moral panic model   93

A problem with 'deviance'   93

A problem with 'morality'   95

Problems with 'youth' and 'style'   96

A problem with 'risk'   98

A problem of 'source'   99

A problem with 'audience'   100

**The longevity and legacy of the moral panic model: some
concluding thoughts**   103

Summary   105

Study questions   106

Further reading   106

OVERVIEW

Chapter 3 provides:

- An overview of the well-known but often misinterpreted and misrepresented concept of 'moral panics'.
- An analysis of the pros and cons of the moral panic model as a conceptual tool for understanding public responses to mediated crime and deviance.
- An examination of the five defining features that identify moral panics, as they have traditionally been conceived.
- A discussion of 'deviancy amplification' and the extent to which attempts by authorities to control deviant behaviour actually lead to its increase.
- Brief exploration of the status of paedophilia as a moral panic.

KEY TERMS

- consensus
- demonization
- deviance
- deviancy amplification spiral
- folk devils
- labelling
- mega-cases

- moral panic
- risk
- signal crime
- social reaction
- stigmatizing
- subculture
- youth

'Moral panic' is a familiar term in academic studies of crime, *deviance* and the media. It refers to public and political reactions to minority or marginalized individuals and groups who appear to be some kind of threat to consensual values and interests. The media – usually led by the press – will define a group or act as 'deviant' and focus on it to the exclusion of almost everything else. The concept of *moral panic* originated in British sociology in the 1970s with the publication of Stanley Cohen's (1972/2002) *Folk Devils and Moral Panics: The Creation of the Mods and Rockers*. Although not the first scholar to explore the role of the mass media in *labelling* non-conformist groups and manufacturing crime waves (that was Jock Young in 1971), Cohen has been credited as providing the first *systematic* empirical study of the media amplification of deviancy and subsequent public responses. Since then, the concept of moral panics has been applied, developed, lauded and criticized in equal measure (Hall et al., 1978/2013; Waddington, 1986; Watney, 1987; Jenkins, 1992; Goode and Ben-Yehuda, 1994; Thompson, 1998; Critcher, 2003). In fact, so enshrined is the notion that it is not only found in criminology textbooks, but has also entered the public consciousness and is regularly referred to within the popular media, who have uncritically employed it to describe public reactions to numerous social phenomena from child abusers to flu epidemics and from asylum seekers to bankers.

Yet the field out of which the moral panic thesis emerged and was made famous – sociology – all but abandoned the term within 10 years of its inception and it usually warrants only the briefest of mentions in the best-selling textbooks in the discipline. Further, despite the fact that an understanding of moral panics relies on a working knowledge of the production practices of the media, few university degree courses in media studies pay more than a glancing acknowledgement of the media's alleged power to define and amplify deviance to the level where society experiences a sense of collective panic akin to a disaster mentality. By contrast, the concept was considered to still have sufficient currency within criminology to warrant special issues of *Crime, Media, Culture* in December 2011 and the *British Journal of Criminology* in January 2009. It has also spawned a number of related criminological concepts, including **signal crimes** which posits that media coverage engenders fear of crime, causing long-term modifications in people's behaviour (Innes, 2003, 2004), and **mega-cases** which notes that newspapers engage readers in stories by encouraging them to become 'mediated witnesses' and identify with victims of crime (Peelo, 2006).

This chapter aims to account for the divergences between different disciplines within the social sciences and to consider the pros and cons of the moral panic thesis as a conceptual tool for criminologists. Certainly, in its early formation, the concept of moral panic lent itself to amalgamation with American criminology, which was highly influential in the UK. It is relatively easy to comprehend how the conceptualization of moral panics by Stanley Cohen, Jock Young, Stuart Hall and others found intellectual and empirical compatibility with Lemert's (1951) study of social pathology, Becker's (1963) analysis of the labelling of 'outsiders', and Matza's (1964) study of delinquency and drift. Moreover, it is no coincidence that the emergence of a distinctive British school of subcultural theory accompanied a succession of youth subcultures in the UK, starting with the Teddy boys in the 1950s, followed by mods and rockers and hippies in the 1960s, and skinheads, punks and African–Caribbean groups such as rude boys and Rastafarians in the 1970s. Since that time, British criminologists have continued to test the validity of the moral panic model and it has recently enjoyed a particularly strong revival in relation to the media reporting of child abusers and paedophiles (Jenkins, 1992, 2001, 2009; Silverman and Wilson, 2002; Critcher, 2003; see also Chapter 4).

With this evolution in mind, this chapter considers the background and defining features of the moral panic model as it has traditionally been conceived. The discussion pays particularly close attention to moral panics directed at deviant youth; a theme which will be developed in the following chapter, which explores the confusion and paradoxes that surround contemporary attitudes to children.

The background to the moral panic model

Cohen opens his book with the much-quoted passage:

> Societies appear to be subject, every now and then, to periods of moral panic.
> A condition, episode, person or group of persons emerges to become defined
> as a threat to societal values and interests; its nature is presented in a stylised
> and stereotypical fashion by the mass media; the moral barricades are manned
> by editors, bishops, politicians and other right-thinking people; socially accred-
> ited experts pronounce their diagnoses and solutions; ways of coping are
> evolved or (more often) resorted to; the condition then disappears, submerges
> or deteriorates and becomes more visible. Sometimes the object of the panic
> is quite novel and at other times it is something which has been in existence
> long enough, but suddenly appears in the limelight. Sometimes the panic
> passes over and is forgotten, except in folklore and collective memory; at other
> times it has more serious and long-lasting repercussions and might produce
> such changes as those in legal and social policy or even in the way the society
> conceives itself. (1972/2002: 9)

As Cohen intimates in this extract, threats to societal values and interests are
not *always* personalized (in cases of food scares, health epidemics, NHS
patients dying because of inadequate treatment, environmental concerns and
so on). However, when we are thinking of **subculture** membership there are,
broadly speaking, five types of people who may be the targets of moral outrage: (i) those who commit criminal and anti-social acts (invariably young,
working-class men – and increasingly, women – who can be characterized as
'yobs'); (ii) individuals who commit very serious offences, including sexual
offences against children, violent offences against strangers, and murder;
(iii) those whose behaviour strays from organizational procedures or who
break conventional codes of conduct in the workplace, such as those who take
part in industrial actions and strikes; (iv) those who simply adopt patterns of
behaviour, styles of dress or ways of presenting themselves which are different
to the 'norm', such as mods, rockers, punks, Goths, hippies, skinheads and
urban gang members; and (v) the miscellaneous groups of people who fail to
conform to consensual, conservative ideals, especially concerning the traditional institution of the family. These might include people with Aids (which,
throughout the early 1980s, was coined the 'gay plague' by sections of the
popular press), lone mothers, 'welfare cheats' and those who download pornography from the Internet.

Although these groups are immensely diverse, five distinct but intercon-
nected factors have conventionally been identified in most moral panics (listed
below and then discussed in greater detail). However, this chapter will argue
that the five defining features of moral panics highlighted in traditional conceptualizations are inadequately theorized and that the relationship between

them is more complex than is often suggested. Integral to the discussion, then, will be a consideration of the deficiencies of the moral panic model, and the problems with its application, which have caused some to argue that it has no validity. Waddington (1986) is one such critic. He argues that the notion of moral panics is riddled with value-laden terminology, and he has gone so far as to suggest that the concept should be abandoned altogether. The discussion that follows will attempt to represent both pros and cons of the moral panic model as a conceptual tool, and will assess the extent to which it aids our understanding of public responses to mediated events.

The five defining features of the model are:

1. Moral panics occur when the mass media take a reasonably ordinary event and present it as an extraordinary occurrence.
2. The media set in motion a 'deviancy amplification spiral' in which a moral discourse is established by journalists and various other authorities, opinion leaders and moral entrepreneurs, who collectively demonize the perceived wrong-doers as a source of moral decline and social disintegration.
3. Moral panics clarify the moral boundaries of the society in which they occur, creating consensus and concern.
4. Moral panics occur during periods of rapid social change, and can be said to locate and crystallize wider social anxieties about risk.
5. It is usually young people who are targeted, as they are a metaphor for the future and their behaviour is regarded as a barometer with which to test the health or sickness of a society.

How the mass media turn the ordinary into the extraordinary

The mundanity and sheer 'ordinariness' of the events which gave rise to a moral panic in the seaside town of Clacton in 1964 are beautifully captured by Cohen:

> Easter 1964 was worse than usual. It was cold and wet, and in fact Easter Sunday was the coldest for 80 years. The shopkeepers and stall owners were irritated by the lack of business and the young people had their own boredom and irritation fanned by rumours of café owners and barmen refusing to serve some of them. A few groups started scuffling on the pavements and throwing stones at each other. The Mods and Rockers factions – a division initially based on clothing and life styles, later rigidified, but at that time not fully established – started separating out. Those on bikes and scooters roared up and down, windows were broken, some beach huts were wrecked and one boy fired a starting pistol in the air. (1972/2002: 29)

Although Cohen admits that these two days were 'unpleasant, oppressive and sometimes frightening' (1972/2002: 29), the levels of actual intimidation, conflict and violence in Clacton (and in Brighton where similar incidents occurred during the same period) were relatively low. The media, however, carried headlines such as 'Day of Terror by Scooter Gangs' (*Daily Telegraph*) and 'Youngsters Beat Up Town' (*Daily Express*), and they routinely used phrases such as 'riot', 'orgy of destruction', 'battle', 'siege' and 'screaming mob' to convey an impression of an embattled town from which innocent holidaymakers were fleeing from a rampaging mob. Indeed, the term 'riot' has since become a stock phrase used by journalists to cover *any* emotionally-charged incident involving three or more people (Knopf, 1970).

Like any other newsworthy event, the media construct moral panics according to their criteria of 'news values'. Exaggeration and distortion are thus key elements in the meeting of the required *threshold* to turn a potential news event into an actual story. Moral panics will also frequently involve the news value *predictability*, in the sense of media prognoses that what has happened will inevitably happen again. Even when it does not, a story will still be constructed to that effect, through the reporting of non-events which appear to confirm their predictions. *Simplification* occurs through a process of symbolization whereby names can be made to signify complex ideas and emotions. A word ('mod' or 'youth') becomes symbolic of a status ('deviant') and objects (a particular hairstyle, form of clothing, type of motorbike, or even pet dog) come to signify that status and the negative emotions attached to it. The cumulative effect is that the term ('mod' or 'youth') becomes disassociated with any previously neutral connotations it had and acquires wholly negative meanings. When it comes to political and public responses to these processes, one of Cohen's key findings was that, while the media frequently associate certain minority groups with deviance and condemn their use of *violence*, they nonetheless accept that violence is a legitimate way for the police to deal with problems, and is sometimes a necessary form of retaliation. The media-constructed definitions of the situation are therefore reinforced and all sides behave as 'expected' (Cohen and Young, 1973).

The role of the authorities in the deviancy amplification process

It has been suggested that moral panics have their origins in moral crusades such as the American Prohibition Movement of 1900–20 and, before that, the European witch hunts of the 16th and 17th centuries (Goode and Ben-Yehuda, 1994). The moral crusaders of contemporary society are journalists, newspaper editors, politicians, the police and pressure groups, who combine to set in motion a spiral of events in which the attention given to the deviants leads to their criminalization and marginalization. One version of the moral panic model thus suggests that it is those with vested interests who use the media as a conduit to make a moral statement about a particular individual, group or behaviour (although question of source is by no means straightforward or universally agreed upon, as we shall see shortly). It is argued that those in power label minority groups as subversive with a view to exploiting public fears, and then step in to provide a 'popular' solution to the problem which, in the current rhetoric of populist punitiveness, usually amounts to getting tougher on crime. But not only does increased attention appear to validate the media's initial concern, it may also result in the target group feeling increasingly alienated, particularly when – as often happens – politicians and other 'opinion leaders' enter the fray, demanding tougher action to control and punish the 'deviants' and warning of the possible dangers to society if their activities are not held in check. Such widespread condemnation may lead the group to feel more persecuted and marginalized, resulting in an increase in their deviant activity, so that they appear to become more like the creatures originally created by the media. The continuing deviancy results in greater police attention, more arrests and further media coverage. Thus a *'deviancy amplification spiral'* (Wilkins, 1964) is set in motion (see Figure 3.1). Although a conservative analysis would posit that the spiral demonstrates the media's justification in responding to public interest and rising crime, a more radical account would argue that the hysteria

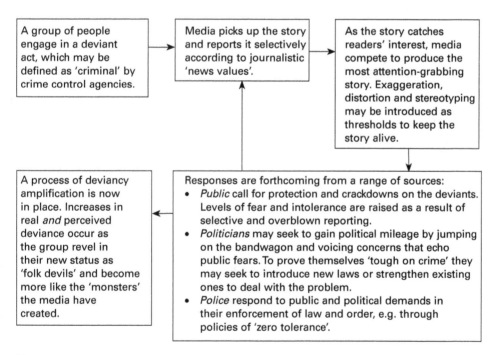

Figure 3.1 Deviancy amplification spiral: the reporting of deviance within a framework of exaggeration, distortion, prediction and symbolization sets into motion a series of interrelated responses

Sources: developed from Wilkins, 1964

generated in this process is an effective way for governments to control their citizens, dissuade people from adopting unconventional lifestyles and coerce them into conforming to society's morés.

The deviancy amplification spiral thus describes what happens when a society outlaws a particular group. As negative *social reaction* escalates and the 'deviants' become increasingly isolated, they become more and more criminally oriented. The spiral of deviancy may go on for weeks or even months, but it never spirals out of control for a number of reasons. Media interest will eventually wane and move on to other issues and, after a period of time, the *'folk devil'* becomes familiar and therefore is perceived as being less of a threat. Ways of coping with the perceived threat are evolved, either as a result of new legislation introduced to minimize or eliminate the problem, or more mundane strategies evolved by the people most affected. Finally, in the case of youth subcultures, the deviant may eventually stop being deviant, grow up and move on.

Defining moral boundaries and creating consensus

In the identification of a group responsible for a perceived threat, a division quickly becomes apparent between 'us' – decent, respectable and moral – and 'them' – deviant, undesirable outsiders. The perception that the threat is real, serious and caused by an identifiable minority does not have to constitute a universal belief, or even be held by a majority, but the national press will report it in such a way as to imply that their condemnation of the threatening behaviour represents a *consensus*. In addressing an imagined national community, newspapers will frequently appeal to a nostalgic conservative ideology, a desire for retribution, and to a much vaunted opinion that 'common sense' should prevail. What these three combined factors amount to is a popular ideological perception that 'thing's aren't what they used to be'. In an echo of mass society theory a century ago (see Chapter 1), many have argued that society is rapidly and inexorably deteriorating due to a decline in religious morality, a growing lack of respect for authority, the disintegration of the traditional nuclear family, the media as provider of role models for the nation's children and – in very recent years – the existence of perverts who prey on our children via the Internet. Moreover, there is a widespread acceptance among politicians and the media that the appropriate response to this sorry state of affairs is to call for tougher action on the part of the police, the courts and the prisons. Take this letter written in the 1950s by a 'family doctor':

> Teddy boys ... are all of unsound mind in the sense that they are all suffering from a form of psychosis. Apart from the birch or the rope, depending on the gravity of their crimes, what they need is rehabilitation in a psychopathic institution. (Brake, 1980: 11)

In the ensuing half century it arguably is not the sentiment that has changed, but the age at which young people are pathologized which has diminished to the level where it is frequently primary school-aged youngsters who are seen to be at risk of turning 'bad'. In addition, the notion of 'troublesome youth' has been emphatically enshrined in political rhetoric and law with a range of policies that *demonize* and criminalize children. The Crime and Disorder Act of 1998 introduced three different types of curfew on children, including 'anti-social behaviour orders' and 'child safety orders', which allow the police and local authorities to act on any child considered to be 'at risk' of behaving in an anti-social manner. The impression conveyed is that children behaving in ways disapproved of by adults is an entirely new phenomenon – a perception that is surely open to challenge from anyone who can remember their own childhood! With the introduction of more and more legislation which seeks to privatize childhood, clearing the streets of young people and criminalizing behaviour that once seemed 'normal' experiences in adolescence (everything from mild sexual experimentation to playing with fireworks), it is no wonder that childhood appears to be in crisis. These moves seem to indicate what Scraton calls the 'sharp end of a continuum of child rejection; a sharp end most accurately described as child-hate, in the same vein as race-hate, misogyny or homophobia' (Scraton, 2003: 15).

However, as we can see from the deviancy amplification spiral in Figure 3.1, it may be that some politicians and opinion leaders are simply seeking to gain political favour from voicing opposition to those whom the media has labelled 'deviant'. With politicians competing to come up with the best soundbite on morality ('moral vacuum', 'moral crisis', etc.) a moral *panic* is virtually guaranteed, and in condemning the actions of a minority, and being seen to be 'tough on crime', politicians are assured of favourable coverage in the majority of the British press. As one commentator bluntly puts it in relation to the death of James Bulger, then Prime Minister Tony Blair 'employed a dead toddler to shift Labour to a hard line on law and order' (N. Cohen, 1999: 84). Within days of James' death there were authoritative calls from politicians, self-proclaimed 'experts' and the press for the greater use of imprisonment for children and young people (Scraton, 2002). The combined assault of law-makers, law-enforcers and the newspapers which purport to reflect the views of their readership serves to widen the chasm between the activities of a few, isolated deviants and the rest of society, and in marginalizing those who are already on the periphery, they give an inner strength to the core. Thus, it might be suggested that not only do moral panics draw together communities in a sense of collective outrage, but they actually make the core feel more complacent in the affirmation of their own morality; when we have defined what is 'evil', we know by implication what is 'good'. Consequently, conventional accounts of moral panics emphasize that they demonstrate that there are limits to how much diversity can be tolerated in a society and they confirm the authority of those who make such judgements (Durkheim, 1895/1964).

Rapid social change – risk

As we saw in our discussion of news values in the previous chapter, over recent years a number of commentators have characterized contemporary Western society as a 'risk' society in which awareness of potential dangers to individual, group and global concerns has overshadowed traditional, more mundane matters. For advocates of the moral panic thesis, they constitute one of the most salient examples of a culture attuned to the possibility of disaster, and the overriding features of a moral panic concerning a deviant group are, in many cases, said to be strikingly similar to those which characterize a natural disaster such as an earthquake or hurricane, or a man-made disaster such as a bombing. In addition to following a sequence of warning–impact–reaction, the concept of moral panics might be said to have further parallels with disaster models in its capacity to expose to the public domain behaviour, attitudes and emotions which are usually confined to the private sphere. But the moral panic thesis has been criticized for its apparent inability to establish a link between the scale of the disaster and the scale of response to it. Not only does it fail to accurately determine public levels of concern, and whether people are motivated by the media to the exclusion of all other influences, but it also makes it impossible to gauge whether the problem is a real one or not. For Goode and Ben-Yehuda (1994) this problem of proportionality is easily solved. Quite simply, problems become the subject of moral panics when they are familiar, close at hand and appear to directly impinge on individuals' lives. Accordingly, future-oriented threats such as the potentially catastrophic effects of the shrinking ozone layer, a rogue meteorite hitting earth, the risk of nuclear war – or even terrorist threats – are unlikely to become the subjects of moral panic. But even this seems too simplistic. Few folk devils have had a direct impact on the lives of more than a handful of people and, as described in Chapter 1, in times of political and social turbulence, even an invasion by Martians can seem a plausible occurrence.

The reasons why a society appears especially susceptible at certain times is debatable. A number of writers have pointed to the transition from a period of modernity to one of postmodernity as explanation for the apparent destabilization of many established aspects of social life. As with any transition from one kind of social order to another, traditional processes and values have been weakened and displaced. Liberal ideologies emphasizing individual choice have combined with advances in technology to produce a greater cultural pluralism, and an increasing awareness of the possibilities of constructing new identities. At the same time, however, the blurring of public and private boundaries has extended to society's institutions, which have sought to regulate social life in ways previously unimaginable (see Chapters 8 and 9). Alternative visions and conflicting points of identification have been formed, which have led to what is often referred to as a 'crisis of identity' whereby media-inspired and consumer-driven aspirations have started to merge and collide with traditional identifications (such as those based on class, race, gender, nationality), resulting in instability and ontological insecurity. The ambivalent and paradoxical nature of this period of late modernity is summed up by Berman:

> To be modern is to find ourselves in an environment that promises us adventure, power, joy, growth, transformation of ourselves and the world – and, at the same time, that threatens to destroy everything we have, everything we know, everything we are ... modernity can be said to unite all mankind. But it is a paradoxical unity, a unity of disunity: it pours us all into a maelstrom of per-petual disintegration and renewal, of struggle and contradiction, of ambiguity and anguish. To be modern is to be part of a universe in which, as Marx said, 'all that is solid melts into air'. (1983: 1)

As described in Chapter 1, America was experiencing such a maelstrom of disintegration and renewal at the time of the 1938 *War of the Worlds* broadcast. But these processes can similarly be detected in the Britain of the mid-1950s: the time of the first modern, media-led moral panic in this country, which was directed at Teddy boys. At this time a number of social trends were converging to challenge and de-centre traditional norms and values. The 'feel good factor' still hung over the nation after victory against Hitler, but for many the celebra-tions were tempered by the trauma of the quarter of a million British deaths and the destruction of homes and workplaces. The war had left the country in a state of economic crisis, yet by the late 1950s a new spirit of optimism emerged and the 1960s became a time of full employment. New social patterns were also radically altering the face of Britain: family relationships changed as legislation was introduced to make divorce easier and more socially acceptable for women; new technologies and the emergence of the service and leisure industries were challenging traditional industrial practices, with semi-professional and professional jobs being created at roughly the same pace as the number of manual workers declined; and migration of British citizens from New Commonwealth countries was taking place. All these factors combined to make many people feel very uncertain and anxious about their lives, and con-cerns about change, instability and the displacement of what went before became consolidated in the group identities of the new youth subcultures.

Youth

The social construction of *youth* as a problem that had bubbled just beneath the surface of British social and political life for many years exploded into the public consciousness in the late 1950s and almost immediately became the subject of sociological enquiry. It is often said that 'youth' came into its own in the post-war era. Before the Second World War, young people tended to model themselves on their parents and their clothes, manners, aspirations and expectations were all characteristic of a previous era. But in the 1950s, young people became seen as a specific social category, distinct from other age groups, and the word 'teenager' was coined for the first time. They rejected their parents' values and interests, and became powerful citizens and consumers in their own right. Traditional class boundaries were also broken down as the media and leisure industries homogenized teenagers into a vibrant, consumer group. Cafés, milk bars and dance halls sprang up, and a range of cultural products were explicitly aimed at a young audience. Hollywood film stars such as Marlon Brando and James Dean, rock-and-roll artists like Buddy Holly and Elvis, pirate radio stations such as Caroline and Luxembourg, and television programmes including *Ready, Steady, Go* and *Juke Box Jury* all heightened the sense of excitement and freedom that was associated with being a teenager in the 1950s and 1960s. Teenagers were more affluent than they had ever been before, and formed a larger section of society than other age groups because of the post-War 'baby boom' years. They had significant purchasing power, and they represented vitality and social mobility to a degree which marked them out from other generations. More than at any time previously youth represented the future and became a powerful metaphor for 'New Britain' in all its vibrant, urban modernity.

However, the combination of rapid social change with distinctive, unconventional and often spectacular styles of physical appearance and behaviour was a heady mixture. If 'youth' represents the future, a future in the hands of these unconventional and unpredictable young people who seemed to be actively resisting authority and rejecting everything that was traditional or conventional, was simply too frightening for many to contemplate. For all the unfettered fun attached to being a teenager in the late 1950s and early 1960s, there was a darker edge; a flipside to the apparently positive traits of youth. Modern life, the expansion of cities, and increased opportunities for leisure were the focus of growing disquiet. Young people represented vitality and social mobility to a degree which marked them out from previous generations, but 'modern' equated to 'brash', being cosmopolitan and classless were inextricably linked to having too much wealth and too little morality, and the homogeneity brought to young people by the growth in consumer industries aimed specifically at them made them thoughtless and selfish in the eyes of many older people. Cohen suggests that this first generation of teenagers symbolized the confused and paradoxical feelings that many held in this period of rapid social transformation:

> They touched the delicate and ambivalent nerves through which post-War social change in Britain was experienced. No one wanted depressions or austerity, but messages about 'never having it so good' were ambivalent in that some people were having it too good and too quickly. (Cohen, 1972/2002: 192)

Young people were thus seen as both a catalyst for change and the guardians of future morality; they personified the desire to move forward, to innovate, to experiment, but were simultaneously the conduits of all the fears in society about change and the unknown. At one and the same time they represented all that was new, shiny and modern, and everything that was transitory, disposable and tacky.

Problems with the moral panic model

The concept of 'moral panics' has been widely criticized for its perceived limitations, yet it is a theory that just refuses to go away. A fundamental difficulty with moral panics is not the concept itself, but the way that it has been embraced by the generations of writers, researchers, journalists and students since its inception in 1971, many of which have created the impression of an outdated model that has outlived its usefulness. There are two common, flawed approaches. One is the failure to go beyond a faithful re-write of the original text and a fawning, unreflective adherence to its theoretical premises. The other is a tendency to overextend the concept of moral panics, stretching it so much that it becomes a catch-all term which encapsulates any public cause for concern from economic crisis to immigration, but tells us nothing meaningful about the interrelationship between the media, social problems, social policy and public opinion in the contemporary world (Hughes et al., 2011). As Kidd-Hewitt and Osborne (1995) point out, media-criminology has become fixed within a pattern of enquiry which frequently relies on 'ritualistic reproductions' or misrepresentations of Cohen's original conceptualization of the term, and *Folk Devils and Moral Panics* left 'such significant and substantial foundation stones that they are constantly mistaken for the final edifice, instead of notable developments to be built upon' (Kidd-Hewitt and Osborne, 1995: 2). So what *are* the shortcomings of the moral panic thesis? Several points of possible ambiguity or contention have already been discussed and it should already be clear that some aspects of the moral panic model are open to several different interpretations. But there remain some fundamental flaws in the idea of moral panics that have yet to be satisfactorily addressed, and it is to these that we now turn.

A problem with 'deviance'

The deviancy amplification spiral is problematic on a number of counts. First, not all folk devils can be said to be vulnerable or *unfairly* maligned (paedophiles provide one such example; the bankers responsible for the recent economic crisis are arguably another), and the accelerating loss of credibility that is implied in the amplification process is not applicable to all groups. Furthermore, there has never been universal agreement about the length of time that public outrage has to be expressed in order to qualify as a moral panic. If we return to Cohen's formulation of the concept we are bound to infer that moral panics are, by their very nature, short-term, sporadic episodes which explode with some volatility on the collective consciousness only to disappear a few weeks or months later. But the origins of some concerns – for example, juvenile delinquency – may go back a considerable length of time and current anxieties about deviant youth have been well rehearsed in this country over several hundred years (Pearson, 1983). Even the current state of heightened anxiety over paedophiles has been sustained since the term was coined in 1996 (see Chapter 4). Further, McRobbie and Thornton (1995) argue that moral panics have ceased to be events that happen 'every now and then' and instead have become the standard way of reporting news in an ever increasing spiral of hyperbole and 'ridiculous rhetoric' designed to grab our attention in a crowded media marketplace. In the current context of 24-hour rolling news and audience participation (via reality television, audience phone-ins, Internet blogs, talk radio, etc.), their observation seems persuasive.

The deviancy amplification spiral has also been criticized for being too rigid and deterministic, grossly oversimplifying the notion of deviancy. There are different levels of what we call 'deviancy', and a theory which accounts for public reactions to cannabis users may not be appropriate in accounting for public outrage over date rapists. Furthermore, the aetiology of deviancy is rarely given the same consideration as the deviant action or behaviour itself. Muncie, echoing Durkheim, comments:

> Moral Panics ... form part of a sensitizing and legitimizing process for solidifying moral boundaries, identifying 'enemies within', strengthening the powers of state control and enabling law and order to be promoted without cognisance of the social divisions and conflicts which produce deviance and political dissent. (Muncie, 2001: 55–6)

In other words, moral panics define for society the moral parameters within which it is acceptable to behave, and marginalize and punish those groups who step outside those parameters, but rarely do they encourage examination of the reasons *why* the group is behaving in that way in the first place. All too often, 'deviance' is simply used as a byword for 'irrationality' (implying mental instability or even animality), 'manipulability' (implying that those involved are passive dupes) or 'unconventionality' (implying that they are weird, alien, uncontrollable). Thus the causes of 'deviance', which in some cases may be entirely legitimate, are seldom considered and are frequently overshadowed by scornful commentaries about the appearance and lifestyle of the groups involved. In addition, the media may resort to conjecture and exaggeration concerning violence or predictions of future violence, or by reference to any sporadic incidents of conflict that occur. As Hall says, 'the tendency is ... to deal with any problem, first by simplifying its causes, second by *stigmatizing* those involved, third by whipping up public feeling and fourth by stamping hard on it from above' (Hall, 1978: 34). This comment is made about football hooliganism, but could equally be said about any other moral panic, from spectacular youth subcultures to the problem of paedophiles.

A problem with 'morality'

A related difficulty with definition is that the 'moral' element in moral panics has either been accepted unproblematically, or otherwise glossed over with little concern for a particular episode's place within a wider structure of morality and in relation to changing forms of moral regulation (Thompson, 1998). In the following chapter we will consider 'morality' as it pertains to the sexualization of children and the age at which young people become sexually active. In brief, we might consider it somewhat hypocritical of society to impose legal sanctions on 'underage' sex (which in the Sexual Offences Bill criminalizes 15-year-olds for all forms of sexual conduct), while at the same time tolerating the overt sexualization of much younger children in other cultural realms – fashion, music, advertising and so on (Jewkes, 2010a). The age of consent was set at 16 in an attempt to thwart the use of children as prostitutes in Victorian England. Prior to 1875, it had been 12. However, in the wake of several cases where 13–15-year-old girls have run away from home with their boyfriends, the debate about the age at which young people become sexually mature has been reignited. It is, however, a debate that is likely to become hijacked by moral crusaders if prior experience is an indicator (a campaign in the 1980s led by Victoria Gillick to stop doctors prescribing contraception to under-16s has been held partially responsible for a simultaneous rise in teenage pregnancies) and it may prove impossible to discuss reasonably and rationally in a culture in which romanticized images of childhood as a time of winsome innocence prevail over a reality that includes child abuse, neglect, exploitation and the highest teenage pregnancy rate in Europe.

Jock Young (1971, 1974) highlights a further aspect of the ambiguity inherent in definitions of morality, suggesting that many of the people who think of themselves as 'moral' and take exception to the *im*morality of deviants, actually have a grudging admiration – envy, even – for those who are seen to be 'breaking the rules'. According to Young (1971), if a person lives by a strict code of conduct which forbids certain pleasures and involves the deferring of gratification in certain areas, it is hardly surprising that they will react strongly against those whom they see to be taking 'short cuts'. For Young, this ambivalence is partial explanation of the vigorous repression against what might be

termed 'crimes without victims': homosexuality, prostitution, drug-taking
and – in the new moral climate – consensual sex among those under 16 years
of age. But in many instances, moral panics appear to contain little or no moral
element at all and the term has become a shorthand description for *any* widespread concern including, most prominently in recent years, health scares,
especially those linking health problems to food and diet.

Problems with 'youth' and 'style'

In much of the moral panic literature, there is a presupposed assumption that
the youth groups or other deviants involved are inevitably economically marginalized and turn to crime and deviance as an anomic means of combating
the boredom and financial hardship associated with being out of work.
Certainly, Cohen suggests that the mods and rockers were driven to violence
as a result of feeling marginalized from the mass consumer culture directed at
young people in the early 1960s. Yet an alternative reading might argue that
the mods and rockers were the products of rising affluence and optimism, and
far from being peripheral to the economic health of the country, they were
largely responsible for making the 1960s swing! Since that time youth fashions
and subcultural affiliations have spawned multi-million pound industries, and
today's young people have on offer a vast range of concurrent subcultures
which may in some cases present the solutions to their subjective socio-economic
problems, but actually in most cases do little more than provide a temporary
sense of 'belonging', a statement of being independent of the parent culture
and a form of conspicuous consumption.

Group identity is thus at least as likely to be a statement of style and status
as it is to be an act of resistance through ritual. All youth cultures require a
relatively high level of financial input, whether they are based on music, fashion, football or some other 'fanship', and as Cohen remarks in his introduction
to the revised second edition of *Folk Devils and Moral Panics*, the delinquent
quickly changed from 'frustrated social climber' to 'cultural innovator and
critic' (Cohen, 1980: iv). Even the punks of the 1970s, who are frequently
characterized as a product of dole-queue despondency (Hebdige, 1979), were
by no means all out of work and lacking economic means. Commitment to the
punk movement was based on political disaffection, rebellion against the parent culture, enjoyment of the music, resistance to conventional codes of dress
and many other varied factors. But it was orchestrated by a music producer
(Malcolm McLaren) and a fashion designer (Vivienne Westwood) and was
essentially a commercial enterprise. Entry into any youth subculture represents a part of the normal transition from childhood to adulthood that most
young people in Western society pass through. But there are few, if any, youth
cultures and styles which are not manufactured by one or more elements of

the consumerist culture industry. Even the gang cultures of the impoverished inner-city ghettos of America and Britain have strong affiliations to particular designer labels.

Furthermore, 'spectacular' youth subcultures – the stock-in-trade of moral panic promoters – are, arguably, not as evident as they once were. Moral panic theory tends to suggest that young people have restricted choices in their statements of style, personality and consumption. But for postmodernist critics, the subject has no fixed or permanent identity, but assumes different identities at different times in an endless act of self-creation. Indeed, a postmodern critique would posit that identity is an 'open slate ... on which persons may inscribe, erase and rewrite' their histories and personalities at will (Gergen, 1991: 228), a phenomenon that has become positively celebrated with the expansion of the Internet. Even sexual identity is seen by some commentators as a reflexively organized endeavour involving an increasing number of choices and possibilities (Jewkes and Sharp, 2003). Thus, in today's multi-media society, young people are able to make the transition from childhood to adulthood via a vast and diverse range of coexistent subcultures, which they may move in and out of at will, thus making their attachments to particular groups only marginal and fleeting. As such, it might be suggested that the notion that moral panics define the limits of how much diversity a society can tolerate is simply not as compelling as it once was, although this is a contested issue. Some would argue that clothing and appearance can still be utilized as symbols of class conflict and social division, and that there remain subcultural styles which are not appropriated by mainstream consumer culture and which are adopted by individuals and groups with the intention of making others feel ill-at-ease. Others would counter that in today's postmodern, technologically advanced, culturally fragmented, pastiche culture, diversity is not only tolerated but is celebrated to the extent where 'street' styles (that is, those emerging from the 'bottom' or margins of society) are often very quickly absorbed into the mainstream fashion industry, a trend that makes the 'deviant' cues of any one group appear less visible and less important in the wider context.

A further difficulty with the construction of youth as a social problem is that it might be suggested that youth now only exists in discourses about crime and deviance. Youth arguably no longer describes a generational category, but instead encapsulates an attitude, a lifestyle not determined by age. The generation gap is shrinking, and unlike 50 years ago when young people were more or less miniature versions of their parents, in contemporary society it is now very often adults who look to their children for style codes. Not only is it more likely that adolescents and their parents will share the same tastes in clothing, music, literature and leisure pursuits than in any previous generation – a trend exemplified by the Harry Potter phenomenon and the widespread, intergenerational adoption of the hooded jacket (or 'hoodie') – but increasingly young people are influencing the political agenda, especially in relation to issues such as animal rights and environmentalism. Collective concerns such as these not only transcend traditional class and ethnic distinctions, but they demonstrate a 'morality' and code of ethics which seem conservative in comparison with the youth subcultures of their parents' and grandparents' generations. Moreover, in a multi-mediated world where global media events vie for public attention, especially among the young, who use interpersonal forms of communication within small groups of friends, the idea of macro-level responses have declined in probability.

A problem with 'risk'

Another weakness with the moral panic model is that the overstated reaction to youth cultures on the part of the 'moral majority' is precipitated by a creeping sense of disorientation and bewilderment at the pace of change in modern life. This argument may underpin many parents' fears about their children's exposure to new and alternative media, including violent computer games and the Internet. But modernity has been a long project. Was there ever a generation which did not feel poised at the edge of something bigger, more exciting and – for some – potentially more frightening? Furedi (1997) has argued that we inhabit a 'culture of fear' in which loss of optimism and a belief in our capacity to change the world for the better has given way to a crippling sense of vulnerability. In a similar vein Carrabine asserts that 'few now dispute that we are living in times of high anxiety and that the mass media provide us with a daily diet of disasters from near and afar to continually remind us that we inhabit a world of crisis, danger and uncertainty' (2008: 162). But while 'high anxiety' might be the goal of the media, in everyday practice it is ontologically unsustainable and it seems overstated to characterize the current epoch as a universal, endlessly cyclical state of 'panickyness' (Sparks, 1992: 65). Indeed, Farrall and Gadd note that, 'few people fear crime frequently'; their research found that fewer than one in ten people (8 per cent) frequently experienced high levels of fear (2004: 127; see Chapter 6). Further, the inference in much writing on the subject that communities in our parents' and grandparents' day were tight-knit, self-policing and prone to spontaneous organization of street parties, while today's media-addicted neighbours are frightened, atomized and unknown to one another, is unproven and untenable. In the second, revised edition of *Folk Devils and Moral Panics*, Cohen himself surmizes that the level and intensity of media activity is sometimes exaggerated by researchers and writers in order to 'fit' their particular illustration of the moral panic thesis at work, and that the material selected as 'proof' of the slide into crisis (newspaper editorials, in the main) does not amount to such monumental proportions (Cohen, 1980).

A problem of 'source'

Although the panics over Teddy boys in the 1950s and mods and rockers in the 1960s meet the criteria of the moral panic thesis in terms of being discrete, transitory incidents that appear to have emerged suddenly and explosively and disappeared equally abruptly some time later, it has been left to later writers (Watney, 1987; McRobbie and Thornton, 1995) to point out that concerns about deviance are much more diffuse than is suggested in many accounts of panic. In other words, the disparate concerns over drugs, sexual permissiveness or perversion, liberal attitudes to marriage, the political re-emergence of the far right, and youth violence, are among the frequently conflicting issues which arise from a number of different sources and are dispersed throughout society. Meanwhile, specific moral panics such as the periodic scares about street crime involving black youth (mugging in the 1970s; the inner-city riots of the 1980s; gang-related knife and gun crime in the 1990s and 2000s) represent a generalized climate of hostility to marginal groups and 'unconventional' or untraditional norms. Far from happening out of the blue, as is sometimes suggested, moral panics may be viewed accordingly as part of the longer-term ideological struggles which are waged right across society and within all fields of public representation (Watney, 1987). As such, the initial targeting of the deviants and the structured responses to them may be regarded as an integral part of the hegemonic function of the media, telling us far more about the nature of the media and their complex relationship with other social institutions than they do simply about the concerns of those in power. For example, a series of 'mega-cases' (Peelo, 2006) which occurred in the first decade of the 21st century not only served to elevate the perceived deviance of a whole category of individuals – young, black men who were on parole – but also inferred that these offences were symptomatic of a wider problem of moral decline and decrepitude in a society in which the professionals charged with protecting the public could no longer be trusted to do so. The opprobrium heaped on the Probation Service at this time was reminiscent of the scorn and criticism that the media have periodically directed at social workers over the last few decades (Jewkes, 2008).

The question of source also problematizes the idea that moral panics are the means by which élite interests become filtered down through society so that they appear to be to everyone's advantage. The term 'moral panic' implies that public reaction is unjustified and, in critical criminological accounts (e.g. Hall et al., 1978/2013), there is a suggestion that moral panics are essentially smokescreens put up by governments to cynically manipulate the media and public agendas. Some critics hang on to the belief that moral panics originate at a macro level and are engineered by a political and cultural élite as a deliberate and conscious effort to generate concern or fear which is actually misplaced. Others maintain that they originate at a more micro level with the general public, and that concerns expressed by the media, politicians, police and so on, are simply an expression or manifestation of wider, grassroots disquiet (a position more in line with Cohen's account and more credible in relation to the paedophile scare). A third model proposes that it is at a *meso* or middle level of society – with social agencies, pressure groups, lobbyists and moral crusaders – that moral panics start. This theory is given credence by those who claim that it is interest groups who stand to gain the most from moral panics. We have already seen this view rehearsed in relation to panics over children viewing violence, where it is often asserted that it is pressure group leaders, academics and politicians who seek to make a name for themselves by jumping on a populist bandwagon. A fourth view of the source of moral panics, and a variation on the meso-level explanation, is that it is journalists themselves who are primarily responsible for generating moral panics, simply as a way of increasing circulation or entertaining their audience (Young, 1974). Despite the fact that we can no longer talk of the 'mass' media in quite the same monolithic sense as we once did, campaigns such as the *News of the World*'s 'naming and shaming' crusade to publicly identify paedophiles living in the community (a campaign originally started by a local paper, the *Bournemouth Echo*) might be said to be a powerful means of gaining readers and satisfying the demands of the market, while paying scant regard for the political consequences of such action (Aldridge, 2003).

A problem with 'audience'

The overriding problem with traditional characterizations of the moral panic model is that they presuppose that in finding **consensus** on certain issues, audiences are gullible and that they privilege mediated knowledge over direct experience; an assumption that is clearly not viable. In fact, more than any other factor, recent cultural and media theorists have resisted the moral panic thesis' implicit supposition that the public are naively trusting of media reports and cannot tell when they are being manipulated. In contrast to this assumption, research concerning the relationship between the media agenda and the public agenda (that is, what the public take from the media and think about or discuss among themselves) stresses that there are many examples of public indifference or resistance to issues that constitute political and/or media crusades. Indeed, studies of advertising demonstrate that the least successful advertising campaigns are those commissioned by social agencies with the intention of changing people's behaviour – for example, anti-drugs campaigns and 'safe sex' messages – while the failure of the general public to take notice of issues which are deemed important by figures in power is evident in the falling numbers of couples in the UK who are marrying, despite the continuing efforts of political and church leaders. Furthermore, both the 1992 American

Republican presidential campaign with its overt moral agenda and the British Prime Minister's 'Back to Basics' campaign of two years later spectacularly failed to interest the voters. Although John Major's agenda was slightly less right-wing than the American 'family values' crusade that openly attacked homosexuality, abortion and divorce, the difference was largely one of style rather than ideology, and both campaigns fizzled out in a tide of public indifference (Goode and Ben-Yehuda, 1994). Quite simply, the **demonization** of those whose lifestyle and beliefs exist outside the political, social or legal norm does not guarantee public – or even media – support. Official attempts to castigate, demonize or ridicule 'deviants' are often resisted, calling into question the notion of a gullible and docile public yielding to the interests of those in power.

There is also a problem in defining what constitutes a moral panic by guessing audience reaction. For example, while generally sceptical about the usefulness and validity of the moral panic model for understanding public responses to crime, I have argued in this volume and elsewhere (Jewkes, 2010a; Jewkes and Wykes, 2012; and see Chapter 4) that paedophilia constitutes the moral panic of our age. That is, if we must use the term at all, then paedophilia would seem to fit the five criteria described earlier. The 'deviancy amplification spiral' set in motion by journalists and various other authorities not only collectively demonizes the paedophile but also silences those who look for alternative explanations. Condemned as wet liberals seeking to make excuses for the worst examples of human depravity, anyone who seeks to go beyond the common sense notion that sexual dangerousness resides in strangers and 'others' who are not like 'us', and highlights the cultural hypocrisy of these attitudes within a society that otherwise fetishises youthful bodies (Jewkes, 2010), also risks moral censure. One of the many troubling aspects of the Jimmy Savile case was the ease with which he – as a popular cultural icon and pioneer of 'youth TV' – managed to gain access to his young victims. It goes without saying that paedophilia marks the moral boundaries of the society: it is the ultimate black-and-white issue with no shades of grey countenanced. Nonetheless, as the countless witnesses who covered up, excused or turned a blind eye to Savile's assaults on children and young people proved, cultural tolerance towards sexual predators has changed over the last few decades. One mother who witnessed her teenage daughter being assaulted by Savile in the 1970s told a newspaper that, at the time, she felt proud that her little girl had been singled out for attention by the celebrity.

In more recent times, the very rapid spread of social media has also led to concerns about technologically proficient paedophiles 'grooming' their young victims online; a doubly dangerous offence frequently held up as representing everything that is wrong with the Internet as well as the risks posed by adults who have a sexual preference for children. For example, in 2009 and 2010, Facebook became the subject of countless reports that appeared intended to instigate moral panic, culminating in calls in some quarters of the British popular press for the site to be closed down after a convicted sex offender was jailed for life for the kidnap, rape and murder of a 17-year-old girl he 'met' on the social networking site. For Jewkes and Wykes (2012) one of the unfortunate outcomes of the media's focus on 'cyber-paeds' is that it has made even more invisible 'real-world' sexual crimes, especially those that occur within private and familial settings. The 'mysterious, invisible, all-pervasive qualities of cyberspace enable all manner of mythologizing' and allow old behaviour to be represented as 'new, more significant threats' (ibid: 945). Countless stories have been reported in recent years involving young people and cyber-bullying, 'trolling', 'sexting' and 'revenge porn' that have, in many instances, had tragic outcomes for the persons involved.

So, it could indeed be arugued that paedophilia constitutes an archetypal moral panic. It fits the model and it has indisputably led to profound changes in behaviour as childhood and adolescence have become increasingly privatized (see Chapters 4 and 9 for wider discussions of childhood and social retreat). But despite the hysterical tone adopted by a media that are happy to peddle overtly sexualized images of young people in other contexts, the issue of Internet-related sexual exploitation of children remains a somewhat hazy and intangible concept in the collective public conscience; we simply do not know what audiences make of it. Philip Jenkins – who once stated that the involvement of children *guarantees* news coverage of a story (see Chapter 2) has more recently contradicted this statement by arguing that child pornography was a *potential* moral panic that 'failed to launch' (Jenkins, 2009). As far as Jenkins is concerned the public have failed to engage with an offence that would appear to have all the requisite components to detonate a panic. The reasons he gives boil down to the institutions which control 'official' information on the subject (the police and, in the United States, the Federal Bureau of Investigation) and their poor grasp of technology (cf. Jewkes and Andrews, 2005), together with journalists' lack of access to the problem itself and the moral and legal embargos on investigating crimes involving the sexual abuse of children. However, Jewkes and Wykes (2012) take issue with Jenkins' analysis, arguing that it is impossible to separate the real-world sexual interest in children from the 'virtual' spaces that bring paedophiles together and gives them a highly effective means of producing and distributing pornographic images. Given the utter ubiquity of the Internet, then, the precise ways in which paedophilia, the Internet and panic interact may be a subject that warrants future research (see Chapters 9 and 10). However, the fact that the paedophile's status as instigator of model panic remains contested may say as much about the usefulness, or otherwise, of the model than about public anxieties concerning paedophilia. Perhaps then we should accept that moral panic is merely a 'polemical rather than an analytic concept' (Waddington, 1986: 258).

The longevity and legacy of the moral panic model: some concluding thoughts

Many of the criticisms levelled at moral panics in this chapter have been confronted by Cohen himself in the Introduction to the third edition of his famous book (1972/2002). Published to celebrate the 30th anniversary of *Folk Devils and Moral Panics*, Cohen addresses some of the problems associated with the concept he popularized (notably, the problems of proportionality, volatility and the value-laden aspect of the term). He also analyses several 'boundary marking' cases (James Bulger, Stephen Lawrence, Leah Betts, the Columbine High School massacre) and considers the extent to which they can be construed as 'successful' moral panics (1972/2002: ix ff.).

As indicated in the introduction to this chapter, it is difficult to explain why criminology – and its related fields – continue to place the moral panic thesis at the heart of studies of deviance and disorder when both sociology and media studies have more or less ignored it for decades. Why the latter subject areas have neglected it for so long is perhaps easier to comprehend. British sociology moved from considerations of structural changes and class-based divisions in the 1970s to the rise of New Right economic policies and ideology in the 1980s. The moral panic thesis seemed less relevant because it appeared to focus on sporadic and discrete episodes making a sudden and dramatic impact, rather than the underlying political-economic trends and their relationship to discourse and ideology; a dilemma already apparent in Hall et al.'s (1978) study of the moral panic over mugging. Media studies, on the other hand, which had whole-heartedly embraced sociological concerns in the 1960s and 1970s had taken a cultural turn by the 1980s. New enquiries in the field emphasized the audience as active makers of meaning or postmodern critics who were well qualified to see through the ideological veils put up by journalists and reporters.

The moral panic thesis was thus regarded by the new vanguard as reactionary, paternalistic and media-centric and the fact that, to a large extent it has been the mediated version of deviance and not the phenomenon itself which has been the focus of attention, is highly problematic for many media researchers. It is for these kinds of reasons that McRobbie and Thornton (1995) have urged us to 'rethink' moral panics in the context of a proliferating and fragmenting media. Following Watney's (1987) study of media responses to HIV and AIDS, they call for a more sophisticated understanding of human motivations for marginalizing certain groups. Certainly, the genuine, deep-seated anxieties at the root of reaction, and the 'outsiders' onto whom these anxieties are displaced, have become secondary concerns amidst all the rhetoric about the persuasive powers of the media. Meanwhile, 'fear of crime' has become a phrase that is widely banded about but seldom fully explained or understood (see Chapter 6), prompting Richard Sparks to observe that mediated lines of influence – or 'effects' – are far more complicated and multi-directional than frequently characterized. His own research (conducted with Evi Girling and Ian Loader) into public perceptions of fear, risk and crime in a middle-English town illustrate the point. It may have become commonplace to regard the media as purveyors of highly emotive and punitive rhetoric exploited by opportunistic politicians to manipulate populist sentiment, but individuals will always make sense of global transitions and transformations, including crime and crime control, from within the context and contours of their local community, and mediated 'fear of crime' becomes substantially more intelligible in the light of a deeper contextual understanding of time and place (Girling et al., 2000). As such, any recourse to the concept of moral panic must be tempered by a knowledge and understanding of blames attributed and solutions sought at a local level (though Sparks counsels against reiterating the usual stand-off between moral panic and 'realism'; that is, fear of crime is either falsely manufactured by the media *or* it is a genuine response based on realistic estimations of likely victimization). Focusing on the local does not mean that some crime stories do not exist on a global plane; some events will always transcend 'crimes' and become representative of much larger social anxieties. But Sparks reminds us that the fact that such cases evoke universally emotional responses neither detracts from the locally constituted lens through which we view them, nor makes the public necessarily gullible, reactionary or punitive.

Above all, as mentioned in Chapter 1, contemporary media research is audience-centred, not media-centred and the emphasis is very much on what people do *with* the media as opposed to what the media do *to* people. But whether the real causes of social problems are 'closer to home' or simply much too complicated to understand (as Connell, 1985, argues) the concentration on symptoms, rather than causes or long-term effects, leads to a somewhat superficial analysis of crime and deviance and frequently negates the fact that those who commit crimes are not 'others', they are 'us' and are of our making. Above all, the construction of crime and deviance as moral panic designed to sell newspapers, signifies a shift from 'hard' news towards the safe territory of sensationalized reporting and public entertainment. As Cohen himself notes, the increasingly desperate measures taken by media organizations to secure a significant audience share results in a hierarchy of newsworthiness whereby a footballer's ankle injury gains more media attention that a political massacre (1972/2002: xxxiii). Moral panics may thus alert us to the shifting sands of audience responses, ranging from significant social reaction at one extreme to disinterest and non-intervention (or even denial) at the other. Ultimately, perhaps, moral panics should be regarded in the way that Cohen intended – as a means of conceptualizing the lines of power in society and the ways in which 'we are manipulated into taking some things too seriously and other things not seriously enough' (1972/2002: xxxv).

David Garland takes up this point, noting that there has been a shift away from moral panics as traditionally conceived, involving a vertical relation between society and a deviant group, towards 'culture wars'; a more horizontal conflict between social groups (Garland, 2008). This not only implies a much more multifaceted and politically attuned approach to understanding the nature of power in society but it also reminds us that, far from bowing under the weight of collective anxiety and endless, cyclical panicky-ness – a state that is ontologically unsustainable – there is some excitement and enjoyment to be had from passionate mass public outrage (cf. Sparks, 1992). Furthermore, strong reaction begets strong reaction. The emotiveness that frames moral panic may account for the amount of criminology students' research carried out on them, and the fact that, in my years as editor of the journal *Crime, Media, Culture*, articles submitted on some or other aspect of moral panic far outstripped those on any other subject. As Cohen himself says, studying moral panics is 'easy and a lot of fun' (Cohen, 1972/2002: xxxv). But implicit in his reflections 30 years on is the caveat that a faithful adherence to the original moral panic thesis may make it impossible to arrive at a balanced and reasonable estimation of the real role of media in people's lives and the true impact of crime on society.

Summary

- Chapter 3 has interrogated the much used but frequently misinterpreted concept of moral panics made famous by Stanley Cohen in 1972. It has discussed both strengths and weaknesses of the term and briefly considered why 'moral panics' are at the heart of much criminological debate about political struggles and cultural reproduction yet, simultaneously, barely feature in contemporary sociology and media studies texts on the subject.
- The discussion has centred on the five defining features of moral panics: the presentation of the ordinary as extraordinary; the amplifying role of authorities; definitions of morality; notions of risk associated with social change; and the salience of youth.
- The chapter has also examined the problems that these five features raise in the context of 40 years of adaptation, adoption, expansion and criticism, some of which has come from Cohen himself (1972/2002: vii ff.).
- We have considered the validity of the model in relation to paedophilia and reflected on whether it constitutes the moral panic of our age or a potential panic that never got off the ground.
- While it has been recognized that there are some fundamental flaws in the way that the term 'moral panic' has been uncritically applied to issues ranging from asylum seekers to dangerous dogs, and from health scares to the music of Marilyn Manson, it has not been suggested that the idea is invalid or unhelpful in conceptualizing social reactions to both immediate, short-term crises and to long-term general reflections on the 'state-of-our-times' (Cohen, 1972/2002: vii). As Cohen

(1972/2002: x–xi) points out, if we accept that moral panics may reflect genuine public anxieties rather than consisting only of media-generated froth, and that not all likely candidates for public outrage actually quite add up to a moral panic (Cohen highlights the example of the racist murder of Stephen Lawrence), then we have a sound conceptual basis for examining the ways that morality and risk are perceived in postmodern society.

STUDY QUESTIONS

1. How convincing is the 'moral panic' thesis in explaining media reporting of, and public responses to, minority and/or deviant groups, in your view?

2. Moral panics have traditionally been directed at male, working-class subcultures and girls and women have been viewed as peripheral to the action. Can you think of any examples where girls or young women have been the recipients of moral outrage? How successful or otherwise has criminological theory been in offering explanations for female subcultural crime?

3. What recent examples of criminal or deviant behaviour can you think of which might be described as 'moral panics'? What is the primary source of the labelling of 'demons' in your chosen cases?

4. What kinds of crime are not the subjects of moral panics, and what effect on public perceptions of crime?

FURTHER READING

Although this chapter has focused on moral panics in the modern era, they are far from a new phenomenon. G. Pearson (1983) *Hooligan: A History of Respectable Fears* (Macmillan) is the 'classic' work on the moral panics that have shaped public anxieties about crime and delinquency through the centuries, but other analyses are emerging including a chapter by Peter King on 'Moral panics and violent street crime 1750–2000' in B. Godfrey, et al. (2003) *Comparative Histories of Crime* (Routledge). It is worth paying close attention to S. Cohen (1972) *Folk Devils and Moral Panics* (McGibbon and Kee), especially the third edition with a new, revised introduction (published in 2002 by Routledge). Of the relatively recent books on media and crime, E. Carrabine (2003) *Crime, Culture and the Media* (Polity) takes a similar approach to that taken in this chapter, insofar as it traces the origins of the moral panic thesis in sociology and highlights some of the problems as it has been revised and reformulated by successive generations of scholars. Of the best attempts to 'revisit' the concept, E. Goode and N. Ben-Yehuda (1994) *Moral Panics: The Social Construction of Deviance* (Blackwell) remains one of the most interesting books on the subject. P. Jenkins (1992) *Intimate Enemies: Moral Panics in Contemporary Great Britain* (Aldine de Gruyter) is also excellent, especially on moral panics over juveniles. In January 2009 a special issue of the *British Journal of Criminology* was devoted to issues as diverse as the shaping of folk devils and moral panics about white-collar crimes, online paedophilia, prostitution in Western Australia and organized crime policing ('Moral panics – 36 years on', *BJC*, Vol. 49: 1). Finally, in December 2011, a special issue of *Crime, Media, Culture: An International Journal* was published with the title 'Moral panics in the contemporary world'. Including some of the last articles written by the key progenitors of the moral panic concept, Stan Cohen and Jock Young, the special issue illustrates how popular and influential the concept of moral panics continues to be, but also how its utility may have been stretched to a point where it is no longer a helpful analytical tool.

4

Media Constructions of Children: 'Evil Monsters' and 'Tragic Victims'

CHAPTER CONTENTS

1993 – Children as 'evil monsters'   111

1996 – Children as 'tragic victims'   116

Guilt, collusion and voyeurism   120

Moral panics and the revival of 'community': some
concluding thoughts   124

Summary   126

Study questions   127

Further reading   128

OVERVIEW

Chapter 4 provides:

- A discussion of the complex and frequently contradictory assumptions made about children in contemporary Britain.
- An analysis of public fears and anxieties surrounding childhood which reached a peak in 1993 with the murder of two-year-old James Bulger by two older children.
- A comparison of media representations of this crime, and other reported incidents that portrayed children as 'persistent offenders', 'evil monsters' and so on, with alternative media accounts representing children as vulnerable innocents who must be protected, not from other children, but from adults who seek to harm and exploit them.
- Evidence that suggests that children killed by strangers are much more likely to receive media attention than those who are killed by close relatives in the home.
- Support for the suggestion (which, in a somewhat crude formulation, under-pins the moral panic thesis) that high-profile crimes involving child victims draw people together and mobilize their feelings of loss and guilt to produce a sense of 'imagined community'.

KEY TERMS

- adultification
- children
- constructionism
- dangerousness
- doli incapax
- evil monsters
- imagined community
- infantilization
- moral majority
- paedophiles
- risk
- social construction
- tragic victims

In the last chapter it was noted that some aspects of the behaviour of contempo-rary British youth which might once have been conceived as normal, natural and an inevitable part of growing up are increasingly becoming subject to moral censure and viewed as symptomatic of a fractured society. Yet, alongside the manufacture of fears about young people and crime, there has been a homogeni-zation of age brackets into aspirational lifestyle categories which has resulted in a blurring of the distinctions between youth and adulthood. It might be argued, then, that the hostility once directed at an age group who were fundamentally different in appearance and aspirations to their parents' generation has, more recently, transmuted into something more confused. *Children* and adolescents are still the subjects of moral panic and public outrage but, as we saw in our discussion of news values in Chapter 2, they are frequently also cast as *tragic victims*. In fact, never have society's attitudes towards young people been as polarized as they are currently. Alongside youth *as* folk devils, we now have children as *the victims of* folk devils. It is precisely this confusion that will be discussed in this chapter. First we will explore changing *social constructions* of childhood, before developing a more detailed critique concerning the paradoxical attitudes to children and young people that emerged in the mid-1990s. In 1993 children became regarded as *evil monsters* capable of committing the most depraved of acts, but by 1996 a counter-construction of children emerged; that of impressionable innocents who must be safeguarded, especially from the new number one demons – *paedophiles*.

1993 – Children as 'evil monsters'

Since the teenage rebellions of the 1950s and 1960s, the age at which young people may be designated folk devils has decreased, and since the early 1990s there have been regular reports about pre-teenage children committing increasingly serious offences ranging from burglary to rape. This trend has only served to reinforce the equivocal attitudes to youth noted by Cohen, to the extent where the precise boundaries of 'youth' and 'adolescence' are now unclear: no one seems to be sure exactly when childhood is left behind or when adulthood is achieved (Muncie, 2009). This problem is compounded by the fact that ideas about the onset of adolescence and the age at which children are deemed to understand the difference between right and wrong are not fixed, but are subject to contestation and change over time. Prior to the mid-19th century when positivism emerged to challenge it, ideas about crime and punishment were dominated by a theoretical perspective known as 'classicism'. A central feature of this approach was that punishment should fit the crime, not the individual offender. As a result, children were seen as equally culpable as adults when they committed an offence and were liable to the same penalties, including incarceration in prisons and prison hulks, and transportation to penal colonies. However, in Victorian society a new conception of childhood emerged out of the dominant cultural, medical and psychological discourses of the time. For the first time in modern history, childhood was thought of as a separate stage of development prior to the independence and responsibility that come with adulthood. Children were seen as requiring nurturing and protection through legislation; it was during this period that compulsory schooling started to be introduced, and laws were passed limiting the number of hours children could work and prohibiting them from working in certain industries.

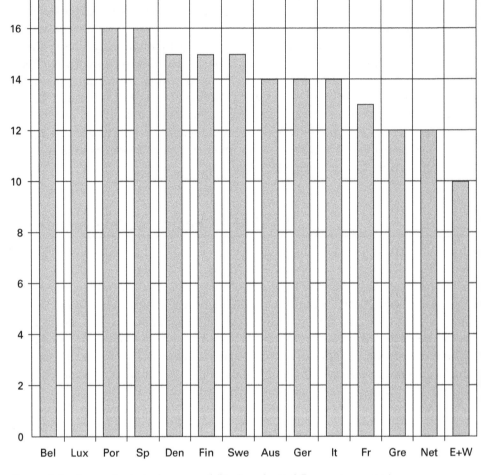

Figure 4.1   Ages of criminal responsibility in selected European countries

Source: Goldson, 2003

Since this time, messages about childhood have been somewhat mixed. For example, in contemporary Britain we have seen the emergence of the *adultified* child, with rises in teenage pregnancies, children being tried in adult courts, children winning the right to 'divorce' their parents and so on. England and Wales not only criminalize children at a much earlier age (see Figure 4.1), but also are by far the most inclined to lock them up. Staggeringly, in England and Wales twice as many children are incarcerated as in Belgium, Portugal, Spain, Denmark, Sweden, Finland, Austria, France and The Netherlands combined (Goldson, 2003). Yet, simultaneously, children are subjected to a greater degree of protective control and regulation which has led to a 'major reorganization of the childhood experience ... [whereby] roaming about with friends or walking to and from school are becoming increasingly rare experiences' (Furedi, 1997: 115). Furthermore, a combination of social, political and economic forces that include a government target of 50 per cent of school leavers in university and a 300 per cent rise in house prices since the mid-1980s in many parts of the country, has resulted in many young people being forced to remain in a state of extended *infantilization*, living with their parents until they are well into their 20s or 30s.

Within criminal justice, the confusion in contemporary ideas about child-hood are exemplified by the case of the two pre-teenage boys tried in an adult court for the murder of two-year-old James Bulger in 1993. As noted in Chapter 2, this case redefined the nature of childhood in almost exclusively negative terms and gave rise to numerous stories about delinquent and danger-ous juvenile offenders. Previously held to be a relatively neutral ascription, the case of Jon Venables and Robert Thompson gave the word 'child' a range of emotive and troubling connotations previously reserved for ascriptions such as 'youth', 'juvenile' and 'adolescence'. Together these terms encompass a series of Lombrosian inferences, ranging from notions of uncontrolled freedom, irre-sponsibility and *dangerousness* to those of moral emptiness and even innate evil. The murder of James Bulger occurred at a time of rising concern about 'persistent young offenders', but this single case has become something of a watershed in the history of youth justice and in our attitudes towards children. Above all, the conviction of two 10-year-olds for the murder of a toddler graphically illustrates how notions of childhood innocence and vulnerability coexist with images of mini-monsters, clearly delineating children as tragic victims and children as evil monsters. The *Daily Mail* of 25 November 1993 encapsulated this contradiction in its headline 'The evil and the innocent' and, while the characterization of blond-haired, blue-eyed James as the epitome of an ideal child needed little reinforcement, the moral decrepitude of the 10-year-old murderers was achieved through interconnecting political, legal and media discourses that sought to prove their guilt via a subtle process of *adultification*.

As others have pointed out, in most European countries evidence would have been heard that was deemed inadmissible in this case – evidence from the boys' 'family backgrounds, their relationships with teachers and peers, their psycho-socio-sexual make-up' and so on (Morrison, 1997: 94). In fact, as Figure 4.1 shows, in most European countries, Venables and Thompson would have been considered too young to be tried at all, let alone tried in an adult court, and there would thus have been no question of guilt or innocence (Muncie, 1999). In English law, however, children between the ages of 10 and 14 can be held accountable for a crime, providing it can be established that they knew they were doing serious wrong, rather than simply being 'naughty', but they will – as a rule – be tried in a 'youth court', which differs in style and approach to adult courts. In March 2010 Children Commissioner Maggie Atkinson rekindled the debate about the ability of children to understand right from wrong (the legal doctrine known as ***doli incapax*** meaning 'incapable of wrong') when she called for the age of criminal responsibility to be raised to 12 and referred to the murder of James Bulger as 'exceptionally unpleasant'; a description described by James' mother, Denise Fergus, as 'twisted and insensitive'. Illustrating the power and authority accorded to 'victims', as discussed in Chapters 2, 6 and 10, Mrs Fergus called for the Commissioner to be sacked and was given pages of press coverage to vent her displeasure. Atkinson was forced to apologize to Mrs Fergus, publicly and privately, and Government Education Minister Ed Balls felt moved to state publicly that, while he supported Atkinson, her comments that the age of criminal responsibility should be raised to 12 had been 'ill-advised'. This was despite the fact that there are few countries which set their age of criminal responsibility at or below this age and most countries set it at 14 or above (16 in several countries including Spain and Japan; 18 in the case of Belgium and Luxembourg).

To return to the original trial in 1993, as Morrison (1997) notes, expert witnesses were called to a Crown Court to give evidence about intellectual maturity, not mental disturbance, and when Venables and Thompson were convicted, it was deemed that they were old enough to understand the difference between right and wrong. Meanwhile, one of the defending barristers showed the jury 247 press cuttings he had assembled which compared the boys to Myra Hindley and Saddam Hussein, a move which probably only served to reinforce the judge's opinion that the murder was an act of 'unparalleled evil and barbarity'. Morrison contemplates the notion of Venables and Thompson being tried before a jury of 10-year-olds, since this would fulfil the role that juries are intended to serve – trial by one's peers. Of course, most people would regard such an idea as preposterous, not least because they would not trust the jurors' maturity, judgement and intelligence. But, as Morrison concludes, these were the very qualities said to be present in the two boys when they killed James Bulger. They are also the kind of qualities that the then Prime Minister imbued them with when he appealed to the British public to condemn rather than understand, a sentiment echoed in his Home Secretary's blunt statement that no excuses could be made for 'a section of the population who are essentially nasty pieces of work' (*The Times*, 22 February 1993). Meanwhile, the *Daily Star* vented feelings of vengeance and rage on behalf of the British public with their headline 'How Do You Feel Now, You Little Bastards' (25 November 1993).

The hypocrisy of an adult society – given its own apparently insatiable appetite for violence, brutality and war (Scraton, 2002) – heaping such ugly sentiments on to the heads of two 10-year-old murderers is an interesting phenomenon. In the aftermath of the Bulger case, the focus of public discourse was not on how two fairly ordinary working-class families with many of the problems and difficulties that beset thousands of similar families across the country, could implode to the degree where two children murder another child. It remained resolutely fixed on the idea that they were a couple of malevolent misfits who came together and spurred each other on along a continuum of offences, starting with bunking off school and stealing from shops, and ending with the murder of a toddler they picked up in a Liverpool shopping centre. The unanimous cry from the British media was that these little boys should be locked up and the key thrown away. By contrast, a similar case in Norway elicited a very different response from the media, politicians and the public. There, the murder of a five-year-old by three children aged six, the year after the Bulger case, was reported as a tragic one-off accident and all four of the children involved were presented as victims who should be reintegrated into society as swiftly as possible (Green, 2008a, 2008b). In another case in 2003, which had sad echoes of the Bulger murder, a 12-year-old boy in Japan was captured on CCTV leading a four-year-old to his death. The older child could not be prosecuted under Japan's Criminal Code, which designates 16 as the age of criminal responsibility and, instead, the boy was placed in a child welfare centre while his needs – and those of his family – were assessed (http://news.bbc.co.uk).

The mediated outrage that shaped every aspect of the case and the court trial extended to reporting of Thompson and Venables while they were in custody. News reports concerning attempts to rehabilitate them were scornful and frequently mentioned the 'injustice' (to James, the Bulger family and the tax-paying public) of the boys being given an education in prison. The cost and quality of the food provided to them was another favourite theme. When, at the age of 18, they were given new identities and released from the secure unit in which they were held, the press responded with more fury – partly because the 'evil monsters' were back in the community and partly because they (the media) were prevented by a court order from publishing any details that might lead to the boys' identification or whereabouts.

The political and media hysteria surrounding the killing of James Bulger already demonstrate some of the paradoxical sentiments with which we view children. Although seen as an aberration, the 'spawn of the devil', no less, according to several tabloid newspapers, Venables and Thompson were nonetheless portrayed as part of a more generalized moral decline:

> The British have sensed for some time that violent crime was gnawing at the edges of the country's social fabric and that those in authority seemed powerless to stop its relentless progress. But it has taken one particular murder to crystallise the country's fears, encapsulate the concern and encourage people to ask out loud what kind of nation we are becoming … It is the world of the video nasty brought to reality. (*Sunday Times*, 21 February 1993)

The fact that the murder of a two-year-old by two 10-year-olds was not viewed as a unique event, but simply the worst example of a much wider phenomenon, indicates a level of concern that statistical measurements of offending and victimization among children simply do not support. As Scraton (2002) observes, in the decade prior to James Bulger's death, just one child under five had been killed per year by a stranger, and none by another child. By contrast, over 70 children under five had been murdered each year by a parent or an adult known to them. Yet the fact that children are more likely to be murdered by their parents or by other family members than by strangers of any age is virtually absent from media and public discourse. Furthermore, it is important to note that, when it comes to the portrayal of children as victims, once again, some children are more 'ideal' victims than others. Consider, by way of example, the case of eight-year-old Victoria Climbié who was tortured and killed by her aunt, Marie Therese Kouao and her aunt's boyfriend, Carl Manning, in 2000. Although her death resulted in a high-profile inquiry by Lord Laming and new legislation designed to protect children (including the appointment of the first Government Minister for Children), the circumstances of Victoria's life and death, her family background and the motivations of her killers have received only a fraction of the media attention and public mourning extended to some of the other cases discussed in this book. Like Damilola Taylor, Victoria had only been in England for a few months (she was sent by her parents from the Ivory Coast 'for a better life') and she was black. But to further ensure her non-newsworthiness, she met her death at the hands of a close relative.

Their unwillingness to report the extent of child abuse and murder within the home is further evidence of the media's obsession with the randomness of **risk** and their overwhelming tendency to locate dangerousness exclusively in the public realm. The net result of this emphasis is that it is paedophiles – including paedophiles who use the Internet to groom online and then commit contact offences with children unrelated to them – who have come to be the recipients of moral outrage in the 21st century. In a tragic postscript to the Bulger case, a 27-year-old Jon Venables was recalled to prison in 2010 following reports that he had committed offences relating to child pornography. The Ministry of Justice refused to specify what the claims being made against him were, but not only did his arrest permit the broadcast and print media to replay and reanalyse the 1993 case all over again (with much the same hysteria and prejudice that accompanied the original coverage), but the nature of the allegations against him served to underline his characterization as an unredeemable and evil person incapable of being reintegrated.

1996 – Children as 'tragic victims'

So embedded is the notion that paedophilia is the most heinous crime of our age that many commentators have suggested that it is the most significant moral panic of the last two decades (Jenkins, 1992, 2001; Silverman and Wilson, 2002; Critcher, 2003). Sex offences have always been newsworthy stories, but the term 'paedophile' first rose to prominence in 1996 when the theme of 'paedophiles in the community' swept across the UK, receiving extensive coverage in both regional and national media (Kitzinger, 1999). There were several catalysts for this sudden eruption of coverage. In the UK there had been a significant increase in public awareness of cases being exposed which involved child sexual abuse in residential child care homes and other institutions where children were supposed to be protected. In Northern Ireland several cases of Catholic priests accused of sexual offences against children made headlines and fuelled accusations of high-level cover-ups within the church (Greer, 2003). Anxiety escalated in the autumn of 1996 when a released paedophile was charged with a series of child murders in Belgium, and again there were accusations of a high-level cover-up, this time involving politicians, the police and civil servants. In the UK, the sexually motivated crimes of Fred and Rose West were uncovered, and 1996 was also the year in which 'Megan's Law' was created in the US following the rape and murder two years earlier of seven-year-old Megan Kanka by a twice-convicted sex offender who lived in the same street in New Jersey. These cases all tapped into existing concerns in the UK where disquiet was already being expressed at the relatively lenient sentences being handed down to some convicted pae-dophiles and their early release from prison. With the introduction of community notification legislation in America (dubbed 'Megan's Law'), lobby-ists in this country were given a powerful new focal point for their campaigns. In response to public pressure and with a general election looming, the Sex Offenders Act was hurriedly introduced in 1997, followed a year later by the Crime and Disorder Act. These acts legislated for a national UK register of convicted or cautioned sex offenders to be held by the police, and for the police to be able to apply to the Magistrates' courts for a sex offender order to prohibit an individual from doing anything which might be deemed to put the public at risk.

In other words, sex offender orders are future-oriented; they require the police to predict an individual's likely future behaviour and make 'an assess-ment in respect of the present risk he [sic] presents' (Crime and Disorder Act, 1998). What is more, the usual civil liberties that would attend the treatment of suspected or past offenders are overridden in the case of sex offenders. In English law, those who have been convicted of a crime and have served a sen-tence then have their civil liberties restored but, in respect to sex offenders, the safety of the public is prioritized over the liberty of the individual (Ashenden, 2002). The individual does not have to have done anything to infringe the law in the present (or even to have a previous conviction for a sexual offence); he or she must simply give the police 'reasonable suspicion' that they might be a risk in the future (2002). For many commentators this is hugely problematic for three reasons (Cowburn and Dominelli, 2001). First, it raises expectations about protection of the vulnerable that cannot be fulfilled on the basis of professional knowledge about sex offenders as it presently stands, and puts faith in the notion that community safety can be achieved by more sophisticated risk assessment methodologies and greater diligence on the part of workers within the criminal justice system. These views are at odds with the opinions of some professionals, including the Association of Chief Officers of Probation (ACOP), who argue that putting the feelings of a community before the needs of individual offenders, or potential offenders, may result in community vigilantism and the driving of offenders underground. Second, future-oriented risk assessments pay little credence to the notion of rehabilitation for sex offenders, especially given the prevailing view that, where children are concerned, there is no risk worth taking. Third, it ignores yet again the much larger problem of women and children who are sexually abused within the private domain and perpetuates the myth of the home as a place of safety. According to the charity Childline, of the 9,857 children who phoned their helplines in 2001/02, 95 per cent knew their abuser (www.childline.org.uk). Meanwhile, it is estimated that between 5–20 per cent of women and 2–7 per cent of men have experienced sexual abuse in the home (Kitzinger, 1999). Yet the invisibility of children abused or killed by members of their family is in sharp contrast to the outrage and near-hysteria that accompanies cases of children murdered by other children or by sexually-motivated adult strangers.

As Kitzinger notes, the second half of the 1990s witnessed a confluence of events which heightened public awareness of the problems associated with releasing convicted sex offenders into communities, and put the popular press and their reading public on 'paedophile alert' (1999: 213). However, it was not until the summer of 2000 that the hysteria over paedophilia reached its zenith with the *News of the World*'s 'naming and shaming' campaign which, itself, was a response to the abduction and murder of eight-year-old Sarah Payne (cf. Ashenden, 2002, for a review of this episode). It is difficult to assess precisely the extent of the media's influence in political–legal discourse and decision making, but certainly the prolonged coverage of the disappearance of Sarah Payne cemented the relationship between 'dangerousness' and 'risk'. Furthermore, the presentation to the British public of an identifiable hate-figure – the 'paedophile' – allowed the popular media to reduce the pervasive problem of sexual violence to a few men whose names and photographs could be printed in the newspapers.

An additional consequence of the media's construction of the problem is that the overriding image of the paedophile is still of a rather grubby, inadequate loner; a misfit who is not 'one of us'. But this image (the inaccuracy of which is self-evident in the reality of sophisticated networks of traders in abusive images of children on the Internet) is not confined to our popular media. The government further entrenches this characterization in its guidance notes to the application of sex offender orders. The Home Office fall back on a well-worn stereotype of the paedophile to illustrate how the orders might work, citing a man with a previous caution for indecent conduct toward a child 'hanging around' outside a school, approaching departing children and offering them sweets (Home Office, 1998: see http://news.bbc.co.uk/1/hi/education/225532.stm). As Ashenden notes, the presentation of an archetype of the paedophile has dual outcomes. First, it makes the topic less uncomfortable as it feeds into a familiar stereotype and enables the public to disassociate themselves from the individual described, and second, it simultaneously maintains the horror of the unknown predator (Ashenden, 2002). Jewkes and Wykes (2012) further argue that stereotypes of sexual offenders (including 'cyber-paeds') divert attention from the fact that most child abuse takes place in the home, perpetrated by a family member of someone known to the victim. At one and the same time, then, the moral panic over paedophilia has perpetuated the notion that sexual dangerousness resides in strangers and that those strangers are not like 'us'. While 'we' are 'normal', morally decent, law-abiding citizens, 'they' lurk at school gates and in playgrounds, preying on innocents in the pursuit of fulfilling their sexual depravities.

As described in the previous chapter, as a 'moral panic', paedophilia certainly fits the criteria. While it cannot be characterized as an 'ordinary' crime, paedophilia is far from extraordinary and the murder of children by strangers has remained remarkably consistent over the last 30 years, with about six such deaths annually. Yet the media persist in portraying it as a growing threat; a risk that could strike at random. Fears over paedophiles using the Internet to stalk or groom their victims may well be partially borne out of their parents' distrust of new computer and information technologies, and their anxieties about the further fragmentation of the family. Other media technologies, from family home-movies to CCTV, have made cases of child abduction by strangers especially fascinating, providing graphic imagery of the last movements of victims to a voyeuristic viewing public who already know their fate. Moreover, like all moral panics paedophilia has acquired a remarkable degree of consensus. There are few issues that have galvanized public reaction more fiercely than that of adults who have a sexual preference for children, and in response to those who act on their desires, procuring children in playgrounds and Internet chat rooms, there is striking unanimity in the condemnation expressed by the media, the Home Office and local communities. It is easy to see, then, why the paedophile has been characterized as the folk devil *par excellence* in contemporary Britain. He (the kind of language and imagery used in popular discourses about paedophiles reinforce the presumption that sex offenders are male) is '*absolute other*' (Greer and Jewkes, 2005); an individual without *any* redeeming qualities, nearly always reduced to a set of sub-human, even bestial, thoughts and urges that are totally alien to right-minded people.

However, like many of the examples mentioned in the previous chapter, the paedophile crisis does not fit all the criteria traditionally associated with the moral panic model, the weaknesses of which should by now be clear. As discussed in Chapter 3, one of the fundamental discrepancies in accounts of moral panics is in explanations of their origins. In the case of paedophilia, the general view is that the process of demonization did not emanate from government (although it might be said that the new sex offender legislation and concomitant public debate had the effect of stigmatizing a large number of men, including those who had actually committed no offence). But most critics would argue on this point that the sex offender legislation was introduced in response to public fears rather than as a means of manufacturing them. Similarly, while it has been argued that public anxieties concerning youth crime generally, and the Bulger case in particular, were a manipulation on the part of the government to construct a 'demonology of deviance' and advance a particular political agenda (Freeman, 1997), most commentators support the theory that the invocation of evil in this case was led by the judiciary and the media (Stokes, 2000). Having said that, we should not overlook the fact that a government does not have to manufacture a crisis in order to benefit from it, and that the construction of social problems as matters of individual wickedness rather than as failures of collective responsibility or social policy, can work to the advantage of governments seeking to diffuse political responsibility (Lacey, 1995; Freeman, 1997).

The 'outing' and persecution of known paedophiles might therefore best be viewed as a meso-level concern. Kitzinger argues that neighbourhood pressure groups, disillusioned by the failure of authorities to prevent child abuse, were already taking direct action as early as the 1990s. These protest groups, consisting mostly of mothers who were outraged at official impotence and scared for their children's safety, provided the impetus for extensive media reports about paedophiles long before the 'watershed' case of Sarah Payne's abduction and murder. Jenkins' (1992) study of the moral panic over satanic child abuse also supports the 'meso' theory of source, albeit from a rather more cynical standpoint. He suggests that the 'exposure' by social workers of a vast and unsuspected prevalence of child abuse fulfilled a number of ideological and professional needs, including providing much needed extra funding for an under-resourced service, and much sought-after credibility – initially, at least – for a relatively low-status profession.

Guilt, collusion and voyeurism

The factors highlighted above reinforce the notion, proposed by left realists, that crime must be taken seriously and not regarded as mediated artifice, but there is another pertinent point to be made, and it is one that is rarely discussed. By reducing serious crimes to moral panics, the media succeed in masking the collective sense of guilt that underpins traumatic events, while at the same time pandering to the voyeur in all of us. In the case of James Bulger a sense of shame and guilt extended beyond the immediate community (primarily the 'Liverpool 38' as the press dubbed them; the people who saw James being dragged to the railway line where he met his death, but who failed to intervene) and seeped into the conscience of the nation as a whole. Subsequent cases such as the abduction and murder of Sarah Payne and Holly Wells and Jessica Chapman, have further shocked a society that effortlessly falls back on notions of 'evil within our midst' while denying its own flaws and colluding in the demonization of offenders as 'others'. In his analysis of the Bulger trial, Morrison (1997) candidly reminds us that most of us experienced events in our youth of which we are now embarrassed or ashamed; after all, children can be cruel, selfish and unconstrained. But at the same time as we recall, and recoil from, our own memories of ourselves as youths, we hang on to the ideal of children as precious innocents who must be protected from the sordid and the spoiled. No wonder that out of such incongruity, when children commit serious crimes, a deep and pervasive cultural unease is borne.

Our failure to protect youngsters from the 'perverts' and 'monsters' in our midst provokes a similar sense of collective anxiety and cultural unease. Yet, again, there are clear paradoxes in our cultural attitudes and legal responses to the sexualization and sexual victimization of young people. One legal anomaly is that the maximum sentence that can be imposed for unlawful sexual intercourse with a girl under the age of 13 is life, yet the maximum sentence for unlawful sex with a girl aged 13 or over is two years. The opportunity for paedophiles to exploit this legal distinction was brought home to the public in June 2003 when a paedophile was given a three-year sentence (subsequently raised to four-and-a-half years when the offender appealed against his sentence in October of that year) for unlawful sex with two girls aged 13. According to prosecutors, he had made contact with one of the girls via a chat room when she was 11 and had 'groomed' her for two years before abusing her shortly after her 13th birthday. Not only does it seem curious that the sexual abuse of a girl a few days before her 13th birthday can carry such a divergent sentence to that which can be imposed for the same crime a week later, but both seem incongruous in the context of an age of consent that is set at 16.

A further illustration of the anomalies that cause confusion over young people's sexuality is evident in the sustained, and frequently salacious, media reporting of teenage 'runaways'. In the aftermath of an intense period of anxiety surrounding the safety of young girls following the disappearances of Sarah Payne, Millie Dowler, Holly Wells and Jessica Chapman, the media spun out the panic through the summer of 2003 by reporting numerous incidents in which girls went missing with male acquaintances. There were several stories involving girls who had been targeted by men on the Internet, including the case of the 12-year-old who disappeared to Europe with a 31-year-old American marine (which will be further discussed in Chapter 8) and the 14-year-old who went on holiday with a 46-year-old 'family friend'. In addition, throughout August and September 2003, much media coverage was devoted to cases involving 14- and 15-year-old girls who went missing with their 16- or 17-year-old boyfriends. While the fact that these young women were all under the age of consent makes the media construction of them as victims somewhat understandable, there was little discussion of the fact that they were all willing partners who left their families under no coercion. The complex issues of morality underpinning these cases (what did the boys and, in some cases, much older men, offer these girls that was otherwise missing from their lives? How would these cases be treated in countries where the age of consent for girls is lower?) was elided in favour of the simple explanation that the girls were the passive victims of male manipulators who tricked them into leaving the safety of their loving families. A similar process is evident in media reports of young people and drugs. Periodic panics that have occurred when young people have died as a result of taking drugs, have been presented as potent images of innocence corrupted by a dangerous and malevolent subculture. As we saw in Chapter 2, the contemporary mediated landscape results in reality being reduced to a set of binary oppositions. Although very young children like Jon Venables and Robert Thompson may be constructed as 'adults', there is simply no place for any discussion of 'adult' behaviour among children who are constructed as victims. For them, childhood innocence is a blank canvas, devoid of sexuality and sexual fantasy, and vulnerable to corruption by the peddlers of drugs and perverse pleasures – invariably sick, older males (Coward, 1990).

While concerns over children's safety in relation to alcohol and drugs have escalated, the agenda on child protection is still largely dominated by a concept laden with very specific ideas and assumptions – the paedophile. Meanwhile, the reluctance on the part of journalists, and the wider public for whom they write, to acknowledge the reality of abuse by men or women within the family – which accounts for more incidents and is arguably more damaging in the long term than assaults by strangers – reflects a powerful emotional and intellectual block. The statistic that 95 per cent of child victims of sexual and physical violence know their abuser was underlined in 2007 when police arrested Timothy Cox who presided over a vast Internet-facilitated paedophile ring. Among the material seized from his computer were clips of fathers abusing their children, and 31 children were identified and rescued, many from their own homes. But these cases did not prompt any further discussion or debate about the subject and in general, incest remains steadfastly un-newsworthy – it is, quite simply, 'a crime too far' (Greer, 2003: 188).

Over the last decade, a few isolated cases of sexual abuse within families *have* been reported, perhaps largely because they were so shocking that they lent themselves to the highly sensationalized agenda of the news media and gave the press a stick with which to beat those who work in social services (one of the most consistently demonized professions over the last 40 years). It is interesting to note, however, that the most well-known case of a father sexually abusing his daughter is that of Austrian Josef Fritzl who abused his daughter over 24 years and fathered her seven children. The details of this story shocked and appalled people around the world and its newsworthiness was guaranteed by the bizarre circumstances in which Fritzl sought to keep his crimes private (he kept his victim in an underground chamber that had no natural daylight). Perhaps the fact that the crimes took place in Austria permitted the British press to distance themselves from the perpetrator and present Fritzl in terms of his 'otherness' which, in turn, allowed them to pore over every gruesome detail, including publishing photographs of the victim (taken before she was kidnapped by her father and moved to the chamber beneath the family home) and pictures and diagrams of the underground prison itself. Far less detail was published about a case in the UK which came to light in 2009 when a 56-year-old man was convicted of raping his two daughters who had 19 pregnancies between them. Legal restrictions prevented the media from naming any of the individuals involved, they had no visual images of the father or his daughters and the offender was simply referred to by all the newspapers as the 'British Josef Fritzl', once again underlining Fritzl's perversely iconic status.

In summary, the fervent, voyeuristic media coverage devoted to cases such as those of Madeleine, James, Sarah, Holly and Jessica, gives them a superordinancy that lifts them above other, equally horrible, crimes. The decisions of those who work within media organizations to select certain stories and present them according to their professional codes and institutional news values can thus secure a powerful symbolic place in the public psyche, while at the same time repressing the collective sense of guilt and denial that such cases provoke. They are directed at events that have sufficient cultural resonance to threaten the fundamental basis of the social order. Yet, in constructing an indefensible, demonized 'other' against a backdrop of taken-for-granted normality, moral panics over children who kill and are killed avoid any real risk to the essential structures of society. Those who look for alternative explanations are silenced or condemned as 'dogooders' seeking to make excuses for the worst examples of human depravity (Stokes, 2000). Not only does this close down further aetiological enquiry, but it also allows the community to remain emotionally and physically intact (cf. Barak, 1994b; Aldridge, 2003).

Moral panics and the revival of 'community': some concluding thoughts

In the previous chapter, we reviewed the concept of moral panics which has traditionally united politics, media and everyday life and in this chapter we have focused on the fear and loathing that is directed at two modern folk devils, offending children and paedophiles, both of whom have been characterized as the 'evil monsters in our midst'. In Chapter 3 it was suggested that the moral panic model is unhelpful and, certainly, it is problematic when applied to paedophilia because it suggests that genuine public fears about the sexual abuse and exploitation of children are unfounded or overstated. Quite simply, Cohen's thesis – or rather, its application by countless acolytes – is open to the criticisms that it reduces serious problems to overblown media reporting, distorts the reality of crime which usually involves victims and often entails human suffering, and can only account for public, spectacular crimes, not the serious offences that take place in private, hidden from the gaze of the media. The reduction of a widespread if largely hidden social problem to 'accessible proportions' (Cowburn and Dominelli, 2001: 403) arguably makes the issues reviewed in this chapter something *other than* or *beyond* moral panic, a term that diminishes incidents such as the murder or sexual abuse of a child to mere media-generated hysteria, negating the very real and rational responses that such crimes provoke (Kitzinger, 1999).

However, there are elements of the moral panic thesis that are interesting to explore further in this context, not least the emphasis it places on the notion of 'community'. As noted in Chapter 3, the tendency to fall back on notions of 'pure evil' are not that surprising; after all, once 'evil' has been defined, the public knows by implication what 'good' is. The labelling of paedophiles as 'enemies within' thus gives the hub of the group (often referred to euphemistically as the '*moral majority*') a sense of their own cultural identity. This is especially apparent in the actions taken by communities in response to the releasing of convicted paedophiles in their towns:

> [I] enjoyed walking up the street with a gang of women, all shouting to get the paedophiles out. I can't help it but this is how I felt. Walking the streets with all the noise, I got a buzz out of it. I know it sounds really childish. But when I came back here and thought 'what have I done' … Now, I think if we have been to innocent people's homes, then I am ashamed. I do think it has got a bit hysterical. And because of what's happened we have been made to look like riff-raff. (*Observer*, 13 August 2000: 4)

This statement recalls the nineteenth-century writings of Gustave Le Bon (1895/1960), who argued that crowds were the beast within, the absolute antithesis of rational citizens, and Charles MacKay who declared that people 'go mad in herds, while they only recover their sense slowly, and one by one' (MacKay, 1841, reprinted 1956: xx). Yet is this coming together in unanimous condemnation of a perceived threat an act of madness or is it, as Pratt (2002) suggests, a rational response to the state's failure to deal with paedophiles in ways that such groups think appropriate; a movement that speaks of resistance and empowerment? As society becomes more fragmented and entire groups of people are excluded on the basis of their look, their style, their behaviour, and even on predictions concerning their potential behaviour (see Chapter 8), people tend to congregate around those issues that offer them a sense of unity, some semblance of community. Through the perception of an identity held in common, each individual member of a group or crowd is able unconsciously to deny his or her feelings of powerlessness in a shared sense of power.

Despite their rarity, then, high-profile criminal cases involving child victims are used in much the same way as other cultural events – coronations, royal weddings, state funerals and assassinations – which become part of a collective memory through mass media. Although late modernity is frequently said to be characterized by fragmentation, surveillance, regulation, dangerousness and risk – all of which are said to mitigate against, if not make redundant the notion of community – individual life histories are structured, shaped and made sense of within frames of reference provided by the mass media. In fact, it may be precisely those 'negative' characteristics of late modernity that fuel people's need for unity and, in a context of uncertainty and insecurity, one of the primary means by which people are afforded a sense of social cohesion and connection with their communities may be via the media. It is therefore no longer only media personalities and celebrities who offer the illusion of intimacy (a phenomenon known in media studies as 'para-social interaction'; Horton and Wohl, 1956), but the victims of violent crimes, and their families, whose circumstances guarantee sufficient 'human interest' to bring people together in public outrage and mourning. It is, however, a climate of public mourning which – while instrumental to the creation and maintenance of an *imagined community* in otherwise fragmented and anonymous circumstances – is on 'our' terms. People want contact and some form of interaction, but *not too much*, and that is why mediated experience can be so much more satisfying than lived experience. Public responses to crimes involving child victims (which range from 'passive' responses such as floral tributes, roadside shrines and books of condolence, to 'active' expressions of violence and vigilantism) are a way of touching a stranger's life without having to endure one's own life being touched back by strangers in any palpable way – save from the fact that we feel better for having taken the time to send the message, sign the book, take part in 'direct action'. These expressions of grief and anger thus correspond with a particular imagination of proximity and closeness (the intimacy of a personal tribute, the primal pleasure of being part of a crowd bent on revenge), but it is an imagination which is largely faceless. Media-orchestrated, publicly articulated responses to serious and violent crime are thus basic components of imagined community, but it is a community that remains tangential and anonymous. Mediated expressions of fear and loathing are thus fundamentally in keeping with the nature of society in late modernity (see Chapter 10 for further discussion).

Summary

Confused attitudes to children

Part of the reason for the elasticity of 'youth' as a concept is that adult society holds contradictory and conflicting views regarding the nature of youth. Views of childhood are paradoxically captured in notions of 'innocence' and 'evil' and are frequently enshrined in law and upheld daily by the popular media. One example of constructions of childhood 'innocence' is encapsulated in the age at which individuals can legally consent to sexual intercourse. When it comes to sex, children are children until they reach 16. Yet, when it comes to youth justice, the Crime and Disorder Act (1998) abolished the presumption of *doli incapax* and structurally reconfigured youth justice in terms of moral understanding and culpability from the age of 10. The inconsistencies that lie at the heart of differing ages of criminal responsibility within the justice system is thus key to the confusing ideas surrounding childhood in contemporary Britain. Moreover, such paradoxes play into the hands of a media which constructs events in terms of binary oppositions and stock stereotypes. The media can position child offenders and victims of crime along a continuum from 'innocence' to 'evil', individualizing their pathology or vulnerability, in order that deeper questions about social structures – the family, education, political institutions and the media industries themselves – need never be asked.

Children as 'evil monsters'

The murder of James Bulger was a watershed in public perceptions of childhood, as well as in English law. As Scraton (2003) argues, James Bulger's death was exploited to the full, first by the Conservatives who, at their party conference in 1993, whipped up fervour with demands for execution, castration and flogging, and then by a New Labour government which rushed through its wide ranging Crime and Disorder Act, 1998 and set about appearing tougher on crime than its Conservative predecessors. And throughout it all, the figures of Robert Thompson and Jon Venables, whose photographs were printed in every paper as soon as the guilty verdicts were reached, were a gift to a media which had squeezed every last drop out of stories about 'persistent young offenders' and the 'yob society', and were now given a new motif for evil with which to provoke respectable fears in the shape of two 10-year-old boys.

Children as 'tragic victims'

The media-orchestrated panic over sex offending focuses attention on the 'paedophile', a social construction which reinforces public fear of 'stranger-danger' and provides the community with an identifiable hate-figure on to whom they can project their anxiety and loathing. At the same time it has brought back to the fore notions of childhood innocence and vulnerability and emphasized the need to manage the threat posed by paedophiles via various 'risk assessment' strategies, while ignoring the reality of danger in the family and home. Mediated constructions of paedophiles and the public responses they shape thus not only present a partial image of the abuse and exploitation of children, but also let the community, in its broadest sense, 'off the hook' (Cowburn and Dominelli, 2001). The impression of random danger is perpetuated, but it is a risk that can be accommodated provided that it is contained within terms which emphasize community. Crimes involving young victims of older or adult offenders are therefore a primary vehicle for expressions of community 'togetherness', ranging from vigilance to vigilantism, and from public sorrow to public vengeance.

STUDY QUESTIONS

1. Why are children and young people frequently perceived to be the crime problem in the UK? What are the problems with this characterization?
2. How do the different theoretical perspectives reviewed in Chapter 1 view young people who commit crime?
3. To what extent, and in what ways, has recent media coverage of paedophilia skewed the picture of sexual abuse in Britain? How do media constructions of the 'paedophile' differ from those of the 'rapist' in an earlier age?
4. How is 'childhood' constructed differently in other countries? Does the paedophile loom as large in the collective conscience of other nations as in the UK?

(Continued)

(Continued)

FURTHER READING

The subject of youth and crime is thoroughly explored by Muncie, J. (2009) *Youth and Crime: A Critical Introduction*, 3rd edition (Sage); in Goldson, B. and Muncie, J. (eds) (2006) *Youth Crime and Justice* (Sage); and in Muncie, J. and Goldson, B. (eds) (2006) *Comparative Youth Justice* (Sage) which, as the title suggests discusses the subject from an international perspective. The murder of James Bulger has been reviewed extensively in both media studies and criminology. See for example Franklin, B. and Petley, J. (1996) 'Killing the age of innocence: newspaper reporting of the death of James Bulger', in J. Pilcher and S. Wagg (eds) *Thatcher's Children? Politics, Childhood and Society in the 1980s and 1990s* (Falmer). More unusually, Morrison, B. (1997) *As If* (Granta) is a semi-autobiographical analysis of the case by a journalist who attended the trial of Thompson and Venables and employed the case to reflect on his own experiences both as a child and as a parent. Finally, David Green has compared coverage of the Bulger murder with that of a very similar case in Norway, and argued that the different cultural constructions of childhood which endure in each country have shaped the responses deemed appropriate for children who commit grave acts: see Green, D. A. (2008a) 'Suitable vehicles: Framing blame and justice when children kill a child' in *Crime, Media, Culture: An International Journal*, Vol. 4 (2): 197–220; and Green, D. A. (2008b) *When Children Kill Children: Penal Populism and Political Culture*. Oxford: Oxford University Press.

5

Media Misogyny: Monstrous Women

CHAPTER CONTENTS	
Psychoanalytic perspectives	131
Feminist perspectives	133
Sexuality and sexual deviance	135
Physical attractiveness	140
Bad wives	141
Bad mothers	143
Mythical monsters	146
Mad cows	148
Evil manipulators	150
Non-agents	152
Honourable fathers vs. monstrous mothers: some concluding thoughts	154
Summary	159
Study questions	160
Further reading	160

OVERVIEW

Chapter 5 provides:

- An exploration – underpinned by psychosocial and feminist approaches – of mediated responses to very serious offending by women, concentrating mainly on women who kill and rape.
- A consideration of whether women are treated more harshly or more leniently by the courts.
- A discussion of whether women who commit violent crimes in partnership with a man are passive victims or active partners who kill through choice.
- An analysis of the standard stories, stereotypes and stock motifs employed by the media to convey deviant women's 'evilness'.
- A consideration of women's 'otherness' and why women who commit very serious crimes are much more newsworthy than men who similarly offend.

KEY TERMS

- agency
- deviance
- difference
- familicide/family annihilation
- feminism
- filicide
- heteropatriarchy

- infanticide
- news values
- otherness
- psychoanalysis
- psychosocial explanations
- spousal homicide
- unconscious

This chapter will consider the public's mediated responses to women who kill and commit other serious offences. As we have already seen, the modern media are highly selective in their constructions of offences, offenders and victims. For a crime to be reported at all, let alone be the subject of the kind of persistent, pervasive coverage which can result in the construction of offenders as folk devils, the prevailing ideological climate must be especially hostile to the offence that has been committed. Something about the juxtaposition of time and place will result in a case standing out as extraordinary or exceptional even in a society where the most horrific of crimes may be presented, if at all, as run-of-the-mill episodes. Often, it is the existence of some kind of mediated representation such as CCTV footage that jolts us out of our cosy stupor and forces us to recognize the reality of serious crime in places we least expect to see it. At the same time, the criminal act, its perpetrator(s) and/or its victim(s) must conform to some of the key journalistic *news values* described in Chapter 2. The synthesis of these two contexts – ideological climate and journalistic assumptions – are instrumental in creating public consensus and in shaping the process by which some individuals are designated 'others' – monsters in our midst. They also determine why some offences (for example, the part played by Myra Hindley in the murders of five children) cast a much longer shadow than others (for example, the murder of at least 150, and possibly as many as 350, adults by Harold Shipman). Following the line taken by many *feminist* critics, it will be argued in this chapter that the media tap into, and magnify, deep-seated public fears about deviant women, while paying much less attention to equally serious male offenders whose profile does not meet the *psychosocial* criteria of '*otherness*'. While many generalized points will be made about women's involvement in certain categories of offending (murder, manslaughter, infanticide and filicide, sexual assault, and rape) specific and, of necessity, selective – though highly newsworthy and notorious – cases will be referred to throughout the chapter as illustrations of media misogyny.

Psychoanalytic perspectives

Contemporary media reflect other socio-political institutions in their attitudes to marriage and the family, which remain curiously embedded in the Victorian age. Notions of the feminine as passive, maternal, married and monogamous co-exist with sentimental ideas about childhood innocence, resulting in any 'other' identities – for example, single mothers and lesbian parents – being subjected to hostile censure (Wykes, 1998). When it comes to constructions of female offending (or, for that matter, female victimization), *difference* is readily constructed as *deviance* by causal association with crime. Despite the fact that women rarely stalk, kill strangers or commit serial murder – in fact they account for only around 10 per cent of convicted violent offenders – those who do so are highly newsworthy because of their novelty. The media, then, are happy to acknowledge that violent or sexually deviant women are relatively uncommon, but concede that they are all the more fascinating and diabolical as a result.

In a psychoanalytic interpretation, 'difference' involves the denial of large parts of ourselves, or the projection of those parts of ourselves which make us feel vulnerable, onto others. Stemming from Freud's conceptualization of the Oedipal conflict which arises when an infant begins to have sexual feelings and desires towards the opposite-sex parent, and at the same time has accompanying feelings of resentment and jealousy towards the same-sex parent, this perspective helps to explain the persecution of the 'other' throughout history. Put simply, in the case of the male child, he has previously seen himself as sharing an identity with his mother, but is suddenly confronted with the reality of her sexual difference. This induces a fear of castration and a masculine identification with the father, not only physically, but also as a source of cultural power and moral authority. In the context of this discovery, culture (that is, the Law of the Father) wins over individual desire, and the child 'succumbs to a destructive unconscious solution' (Minsky, 1998: 83) in which he expels or externalizes the part of himself that he finds intolerable – in other words, the painful 'victim' feelings of humiliation and vulnerability – and projects them onto his newly discovered 'other', his mother. In this way he is able to disown the harmful feelings that interfere with his newly discovered sense of power and project them onto 'woman', who is now defined as 'different and therefore bad' (1998: 84). 'Subsequently, women, femininity or passivity wherever it exists may be deemed contemptible and feared because it represents a despised, castrated part of the self' (1998: 84). Symbolic cultural representations (for example, those which reduce, repress, objectify, silence, humiliate, ridicule or otherwise marginalize women and other 'minorities') are intuitively 'picked up' by individuals, identified with at a psychic level and then played out within social relations, thus reinforcing and reproducing divisions and inequalities.

It is, then, the interplay between **unconscious** fears and culturally reinforced prejudices that defines who, at any given time, is designated 'the scapegoat "other"' against whom we bolster our own individual sense of identity, (Minsky, 1998: 2) and the victimization of feminized 'others' goes beyond gendered relationships and helps to explain not only sexism, but racism, nationalism, tribalism, terrorism, homophobia and religious persecution. Implicit in all these forms of intolerance is the notion of a despised 'other' as the means to maintaining an idealized self. An understanding of 'otherness' helps to explain why identities are often characterized by polarization and by the discursive marking of inclusion and exclusion within oppositional classificatory systems: 'insiders' and 'outsiders'; 'us' and 'them'; men and women; black and white; 'normal' and 'deviant' and so on. Not surprisingly, then, notions of difference and otherness have been put forward as a theory of crime and victimization. As previously noted, media representations of immigrants, political refugees and British-born black and Asian people are frequently underpinned by powerful psychic notions of otherness which frequently find expression in a tendency to see crime perpetrated by non-white people as a product of their ethnicity, while crimes against non-whites are all too frequently constructed in ways that are tantamount to blaming the victims.

The subject of this chapter, however, is the extent to which the relationship between unconscious fears and culturally constructed scapegoats can help to explain mediated responses to women who commit very serious crimes. Psychosocial and feminist theories will underpin the discussion and aid our understanding of the legal, criminological and media discourses surrounding women who seriously offend. Unsurprisingly, given the parameters of this book, it is media rather than legal discourses that will be our focus. However, as Belinda Morrissey argues, the close relationship between legal and media institutions has meant that 'the two function together and their representations ... mostly lend themselves to a single analysis, with dominant media depictions mirroring courtroom portrayals' (2003: 4). Both institutions have a vital role in maintaining notions of feminine wickedness in cases where women offend, just as they preserve ideas of feminine oppression in cases where women are portrayed as victims.

Feminist perspectives

In brief, feminist criminological perspectives emerged in the 1970s to challenge the androcentrism (or male-centredness) of traditional criminology. The first feminist text to make a profound and sustained impact on criminology was Carol Smart's *Women, Crime and Criminology* (1977), which exposed the culturally biased assumptions about women that had underpinned traditional ideas about female criminality since the days of Lombroso over a century before. Smart's pioneering approach led to a number of other influential feminist studies (among them: Heidensohn, 1985; Gelsthorpe and Morris, 1990; Lloyd, 1995) which argued that essentialist assumptions about women's psychological make-up and biological purpose condemned them to differential treatment within law. Women who commit serious offences are judged to have transgressed two sets of laws: criminal laws and the laws of nature. In Ann Lloyd's (1995) memorable phrase, such women are 'doubly deviant and doubly damned'.

There is no single 'feminist criminology', but rather a diverse set of approaches that make different, and often diverging, claims about the intersections of gender, race and class within crime, the criminal justice system and criminology. In their early manifestations, feminist perspectives centred largely on socialization theories and were applied most frequently to constructions of gender in studies of victimization, especially men's violence toward women. However, contemporary interest has broadened to include women offenders and many feminist theorists have sought to understand unconscious as well as conscious processes that might explain both why some women fail to conform to cultural stereotypes of 'femininity' and why legal and media discourses construct and reflect negative public emotions (ranging from antipathy to downright hostility) toward female offenders. Underpinning the discussion that follows, then, are three issues. First is the question of whether women are treated more harshly or more leniently when they come before the courts accused of a serious offence. Second is the question of whether women who commit violent crimes in partnership with a man, or in self-defence against a man, are passive victims of male oppression or active law-breakers acting out of choice and desire. And third, in the light of answers to the previous two questions, how are women who kill and abuse represented in the media?

The question of whether women who offend are treated more harshly or more leniently than men has been hotly debated within feminist criminology, with many critics keen to debunk the so-called 'chivalry hypothesis' which presupposes that women 'get off lightly' in criminal cases because judges and juries extend to them the same kind of gallantry that they would to their female relatives. With regard to 'ordinary' offences, there is still striking disagreement about whether women are treated more or less severely than their male counterparts. Helena Kennedy QC surmizes that women who fulfil society's expectations of the good wife and mother, with all the attendant notions of demure sexuality that these labels imply, are more likely to secure judicial clemency than women who challenge these stereotypes (Kennedy, in Preface to Lloyd, 1995: x). Lloyd further argues that conforming to the stereotype of helpless victim (for example, of an abusive partner) when in the dock 'can work for a woman' (1995: 19), although others have concluded that, while *most* women receive relatively light sentences, *some* female defendants are treated more severely due not only to the woman's perceived conformity to the kind of gender stereotypes already mentioned (marital status, family circumstances and so on), but to other factors such as their class, ethnicity and age (Morris, 1987).

But whatever the fate of 'ordinary' female offenders within the criminal justice system, most feminist commentators assert that when women commit very serious crimes – or commit non-serious offences, but are seen as somehow implicated in their male partners' very serious crimes – they attract more media and public attention, the image created of them is more powerful, and they leave a more long-lasting impression (Heidensohn, 1985; Worrall, 1990; Lloyd, 1995). From Lizzie Borden, who was tried and acquitted of murdering her father and stepmother in Fall River, USA in 1893, to Susan Smith who was convicted of murdering her two young children, after strapping them into their car seats and rolling the vehicle into a lake in South Carolina in 1994, women who are implicated or involved in very serious crimes provide the media with some of their most compelling images of crime and deviance (Heidensohn, 1985). No wonder that in popular discourse the female of the species is said to be more deadly than the male.

In fact, women who commit serious crimes are portrayed in terms very similar to those used to represent children who seriously offend (see Chapter 4). In the absence of any alternative discourse to explain the existence of violence and cruelty in those whom society views as essentially 'good', journalists fall back on stock notions of 'pure evil', which they illustrate with standard stories, motifs and stereotypes. As we shall see through the course of this chapter, these tried-and-tested narratives often keep aspects of the woman's involvement in the crime hidden, or only partially represented, allowing the public to dip into the cultural reservoir of symbolic representations and fill in the gaps as they see fit. Moreover, they combine to render women passive and unstable, lacking in moral agency and somehow not able to act as fully formed, adult, human beings.

The standard narratives used by the media to construct women who commit very serious crimes are:

- sexuality and sexual deviance
- physical attractiveness (absence of)
- bad wives
- bad mothers
- mythical monsters
- mad cows
- evil manipulators
- non-agents.

Sexuality and sexual deviance

In Chapter 2's exploration of journalistic news values, it was noted that the media concentrate on crimes of violence that involve the 'right sort of victims' (those who lend themselves to constructions of innocence and vulnerability), while those from more marginal groups, who cannot so easily be portrayed as blameless or pure, receive significantly less (and certainly less sympathetic) coverage. This preference for particular sorts of victims also extends to offenders, but conversely it is offenders who can be constructed as, in some sense, 'marginal' who are deemed most newsworthy. This makes women who commit serious offences already of news value by virtue of their relative rarity. However, women offenders become even more newsworthy when they can be further marginalized by reference to their sexuality. In line with the binary classification systems within which children are constructed as either tragic victims or evil monsters, women, their behaviour and their crimes are similarly polarized, often via antithetical constructions of their sexuality and sexual histories. In its simplest form, women are categorized as either sexually promiscuous/deviant or sexually inexperienced/frigid, a dichotomy highlighted in the title of a book on the subject, *Virgin or Vamp* (Benedict, 1992).

It is often suggested that, in their general reporting of women in public life, the press are at their most sanctimonious when they can portray a saintly image of a woman as devoted mother or in faithful support of a man. But real women invariably fail to live up to this impossible ideal and, across the whole range of offences, women are sexualized by those who work in the criminal justice system. As a result, women are frequently punished – and further punished symbolically by the media – more harshly. For example, behaviour which would be deemed 'normal' patterns of delinquency in young men is reinterpreted as wayward and amoral in young women, the consequence of which is that the 'offence' is frequently over-dramatized. In fact, non-criminal behaviour such as perceived sexual misconduct is more likely to result in girls being placed in care or through juvenile justice systems, while the courts are excessively punitive toward adult women who deviate from the maternal, monogamous, heterosexual 'norm' (Wilczynski, 1997; cf. Heidensohn, 1985: 47 ff.). According to Chesney-Lind and Eliason (2006) 'bad girls', as they are characterized in the popular media, are thus constructed within a masculinist framework which carries implicit assumptions about crime being the out-come of feminism and equality for women. Meanwhile, cases which could be used by the media to raise questions about the potential dangerousness and culpability of institutions in which we trust (the family, the education system, social services, the police and so on) may be reduced to scintillating titbits reminiscent of a soft porn magazine. During Rose West's trial in October and November 1995, just about every denigratory term applicable to women was thrown at her by journalists:

> She was described variously in the news as: depraved, lesbian, aggressive, vio-lent, menacing, bisexual, likes black men, likes oral sex, kinky, seductive, a pros-titute, over-sexed, a child abuser, nymphomaniac, sordid, monster, she had a four-poster bed with the word c**t [sic] carved on the headboard, posed top-less, exhibitionist, never wore any knickers, liked sex toys, incestuous, who shed tears in silence, no sobs, no sound at all. At puberty she developed, allegedly, an obsession for sex and 'Fred confided, "When Rose was pregnant her lesbian tendencies were at their strongest. I had to go out and get her a girl. She gets urges that have to be satisfied" (*Sun*, 3 November 1995)'. (Wykes, 2001)

Quite simply, when it comes to the reporting of women who commit serious crimes, constructions of deviant sexuality are almost a given and women whose sexual deviance can be alluded to, if not covered by the tabloid press in salacious and slavering detail, represent cardinal folk devils, a contempo-rary incarnation of criminological positivism's 'born female criminal' (Lombroso and Ferrero, 1895). However, it is not just female offenders who are denigrated by a media with lofty expectations about appropriate behaviour for women; female victims are also subjected to reproach if they fail to comply with conventional and rigidly imposed feminine stereotypes. For example, Maggie Wykes highlights the prurient tone that was also adopted by the popu-lar media regarding the victims of Fred and Rose West. The predictability of their fate was suggested by smug assessments of what happens to feckless girls who leave home young and/or accept lifts from strangers. Far from being humanized with details of their lives, family backgrounds and ambitions, they were portrayed as being 'from children's homes; lesbian; illegitimate;

runaways; fostered; students; picked up on the "streets" or hitchhikers' (1998: 238–9). By contrast, there was virtually nothing in the reporting of the West case about the male clients who bought sex (from Fred's 12-year-old daughter, among others) at 25 Cromwell Street, nor about the many policemen who were familiar with the house and its occupants (1998).

Similarly derogatory ascriptions served to dehumanize the victims of 'Yorkshire Ripper' Peter Sutcliffe, the overriding impression of whom remains that they were prostitutes (not only untrue of many of his victims, but suggestive of low-life squalor that elicits little sympathy), with hardly any attention paid to their identities as mothers, daughters, partners, students and so forth. Consider this quote from the Assistant Chief Constable of West Yorkshire Police:

> [The Yorkshire Ripper] has made it clear that he hates prostitutes. Many people do. We as a police force will continue to arrest prostitutes. But the Ripper is now killing innocent girls ... You have made your point. Give yourself up before another innocent woman dies. (Cited in Chadwick and Little, 1987: 267)

The popular press also managed to blame Sutcliffe's wife, Sonia, for his crimes. The *Daily Mirror* (23 May 1981) ran the following quote from a police detective who investigated the case: 'I think that when Sutcliffe attacked his 20 victims he was attacking his wife 20 times in his mind'. According to the article, Sutcliffe worshipped his wife, and she dominated and belittled him. Barrister John Upton comments:

> This was just one of many pieces that put forward Sonia Sutcliffe's failings as a wife – her inadequacies as a sexual partner, her wish not to have children, her mental health difficulties – as the direct cause of his butchery. A woman was expected in the eyes of a prurient, disapproving public not just to stand by her serial killer man but to stand in place of him. (Upton, 2000: 6)

Women's sexual preferences, their enjoyment of sex, or their frigidity, have long been used to demonize them and justify their construction in the pages of the popular press as 'monsters', even when – as in Sonia Sutcliffe's case – the crimes were not hers. However, the ascription 'monster' comes most readily to the minds of journalists if the sexual preference of the woman in question is for other women. Morrissey quotes a newspaper editor (originally cited in Wilson, 1988: 55) who describes his idea of a heaven-sent news story: 'If I could get a story of a beautiful lesbian who mows down children at a kindergarten with a machine gun I would be over the moon' (2003: 18). In fact, 'real life' provided the next best thing in the form of Australian murderer Tracey Wigginton and her three co-accused – not one lesbian killer on the rampage, but four! (Verhoeven, 1993). In our ***heteropatriarchal*** culture, lesbians, prostitutes and women who are deemed sexually promiscuous are archetypal 'outsiders'. Within a group already classified as 'other', they are *even more* other. As victims they are invisible, as offenders they are superordinate.

Millbank further elaborates on the tendency of the media to view lesbian sexuality as a 'cause' of aggressive behaviour. In the cases of two women, Tracey Wigginton who, with three friends, picked up a male stranger in her car in Brisbane, Australia, offered him sex and then murdered him, and Aileen Wuornos who killed seven men in Florida, USA, it is their sexuality that is said to have 'explained' their crimes. They were lesbian, so they hated men. But 'they also hated society and the family – represented by "the father" – so they killed men who were father figures' (Millbank, 1996: 461). Interestingly, in the Wigginton case, of the four women who were accused, only three were convicted. The fourth, who was acquitted, did not conform to cultural stereotypes of lesbians and was portrayed as being not 'properly gay', but rather a straight girl led astray (Morrissey, 2003).

As far as the media are concerned, lesbians represent an 'anomalous' category (Fiske, 1982) positioned precariously on the borderline of maleness and femaleness. Reliant on constructing reality within categories of binary opposition, anomalous beings draw their characteristics from both categories and consequently they have too much meaning, they are conceptually too powerful. In terms derived from cultural anthropology, lesbians 'dirty' the clarity of their boundaries and are subsequently designated taboo (Douglas, 1966; Fiske, 1982). At a psychic level, lesbians represent neither one gender nor the other, but can be superimposed onto the social division between masculinity (as active) and femininity (as passive). Quoting a tabloid, Verhoeven demonstrates the precariousness of such classifications in relation to Wigginton, whose gender was presented literally as shifting between femininity and masculinity:

> At that time [1987 – on meeting her lover Donna] Wigginton rode a motorcycle and took her lover on the pillion. She always exceeded the speed limit. But when Wigginton slipped behind the wheel of the 'loving couple's' Commodore car, her character changed completely – to that of the helpless female who always drove cautiously and never exceeded the speed limit. (*Weekend Truth*, 23 February 1991: 8, cited in Verhoeven, 1993: 114)

The unsubtle Freudian metaphors used in this piece demonstrate the extent to which psychoanalytical themes are part of the currency of popular discourse. As a consequence, women who are (or who are perceived to be) lesbians are more severely punished when they break the law and are subjected to especially damaging representations by the media (Chesney-Lind and Eliason, 2006).

As an anomalous category, lesbianism is often applied to deviant women whatever the evidence (or lack of evidence) regarding their sexuality. The 'natural' harmony between lesbianism and aggression, assumed and reinforced by culture, was epitomized by press coverage of Myra Hindley eight years after her original conviction. Not content with portraying her according to multifarious, and sometimes contradictory, manifestations of evil (as we shall see in this chapter, the only derogatory stereotype the media could not pin on her was that she was 'mad' – and her apparent sanity was held against her), the press alighted on her alleged lesbianism as 'proof' of her ongoing depravity. The catalyst for this new wave of hysteria was the news that Hindley had conspired to escape from prison with the help of a prison officer, who was said to be her lover, and a fellow inmate. Hindley's biographer, ex-*Sun* journalist Jean Ritchie, took the 'jailbreak plot' to be evidence of Hindley's unsavoury promiscuity and power to manipulate others (1988; cited in Birch, 1993). Assumptions about lesbian sexual desire and violent transgression were further reinforced in 1995 when photographs appeared in the popular press showing Myra Hindley and Rose West holding hands in the high-security wing of Durham Prison (Smith, 1997; Wykes, 2001). In a similar example from the United States, Susan Smith, the woman convicted of drowning her two small boys in her car in a South Carolina lake, has been subjected to every single stereotype discussed in this chapter including (hetero)sexual promiscuity (the explanation for the crime being reported as her extra-marital affair with a man who did not want a 'ready-made family') and lesbianism ('Toddler-killing mom Susan Smith "paid off fellow inmate to play guard so she could enjoy lesbian romps with prison girlfriend in cells, closets and even the FREEZER"', according to a *Daily Mail* headline of 2 October 2013).

Another anomalous category for women is that of 'rapist', hence it is one of the most incomprehensible crimes – to the media and public at large – for women to be convicted of. While stories involving men who rape are so commonplace that they do not necessarily make the news agenda (unless, as discussed in Chapter 2, they conform to several cardinal news values), women who rape are already newsworthy, although their relative invisibility is not because they don't exist – 18 women were convicted of rape or of aiding and abetting rape between 1995 and 1999 (http://news.bbc.co.uk/onthisday/low/dates/stories/march/16/newsid_2521000/2521053.stm). Claire Marsh, who at 18 years old is the youngest woman to be convicted of rape in the UK, was not surprisingly subjected to sustained and sensationalized media coverage after she was involved in an attack on a woman in July 2000. Her co-accused, Marvin Edwards, by comparison, was given much less attention and some newspapers and broadcasts did not even name or carry photographs of him. Morrissey (2003) discusses two further cases involving women – Valmae Beck and Karla Homolka – who, with their male lovers, were convicted of abducting, raping and murdering girls. She notes that the crimes of the women were shown to far outweigh those of their partners, and it was they who received most press attention. In addition, while their male partners – Barrie Watts and Paul Bernardo respectively – *were* viewed as dangerous psychopaths, they nonetheless remained comprehensible; their lusts were an extreme manifestation of 'normal' male fantasies. Their wives, on the other hand, were portrayed as sadists whose deviant sexuality stretched the public's concept of malleable femininity beyond comprehension.

If women offenders cannot be constructed as lesbians or sexual sadists, their deviance will be verified with reference to their previous sexual conduct and sexual history. Basically, if a woman can be demonstrated to have loose moral standards, the portrayal of her as manipulative and evil enough to commit a serious crime is much more straightforward. Conversely, men who commit such crimes are often reported in respectful, even romantic terms. Wykes notes how the press referred to the relationship between Fred West and two of his victims (one raped, one murdered) as 'sexual intercourse' and an 'affair'. He was also variously constructed as a good husband, a hard worker and a reliable provider, who was driven by a 'mad and terrible love' for his wife (Wykes, 1998: 238). Before his suicide in prison left Rose to stand trial alone, Fred had declared that he would take all the blame and that her everlasting love was payment enough (Sounes, 1995: 348). Another male murderer whose media portrayal evoked connotations of the 'misguided romantic' was John Tanner who, in 1991, was found guilty of the murder of his girlfriend, Rachel Maclean, a student at Oxford University. The reporting of this incident conveyed the impression that it was a crime of passion ('he loved her to death') and reports of Rachel's alleged promiscuity and infidelity were carried under headlines such as the *Daily Telegraph*'s 'Lover strangled student in jealous rage' and the *Mirror*'s 'Jealous John strangled his unfaithful girlfriend'. The inference, then, was that Tanner was not *entirely* to blame for his actions; his crime was triggered by the infidelity of his girlfriend.

Physical attractiveness

In addition to their sexuality and sexual history, women who kill or who commit other very serious offences are subjected to intense scrutiny regarding their physical appearance and attractiveness; a fact that is entirely in keeping with general life. In contemporary societies, the media are engaged in a very particular construction of gender whereby those aspects of femininity that are valued – youth, slenderness, decorativeness and so on are constructed to suit the 'male gaze' (Wykes and Gunter, 2004). This gendered narrative underpinning media discourses within advertising, women's magazines, tabloid newspapers and so on, extends to news discourses and includes constructions of female criminality. The degree to which media discourses are stuck in a Lombrosian view of female criminality are demonstrated by Australian newspaper reports that portrayed Tracey Wigginton as the epitome of an unfeminine, unnatural woman with 'huge buttocks and thighs' and 'a personality to match her 17-stone frame – big' (Morrissey, 2003: 124). Of her co-accused, the two who were also convicted (and sentenced to life imprisonment and 18 years respectively) were described in turn as 'heavily-built ... her face fixed in a malevolent glare' and 'short and stocky' with a 'dumbfounded' expression (2003: 124). By contrast, the fourth woman who was acquitted was not only regarded as a faux-lesbian, but was described as demure and pretty; the most attractive of the accused. Physical appearance was also a factor in the press reporting of Valmae Beck, who assisted her male partner in the abduction, rape and murder of a 12-year-old girl in Queensland, Australia in 1987. Her motives, apparently, 'lay not in her own sadistic desires, but rather in her insecurity and increasing age' (2003: 151). Morrissey cites the Brisbane *Sunday Mail* (11 February 1990), who claimed that Beck's age and 'frumpish looks' made her terrified of losing her husband to the extent where she would do anything for him. Similarly, in this country, the homely appearance of Rose West inspired the *Daily Mirror* to liken her to a 'toad on a stone' (cited in Smith, 1997).

Yet women, it seems, cannot win. If conventionally attractive they will be presented as *femmes fatales* who ensnare their victims with their good looks, but are cold, detached and morally vacuous. A prime example of this characterization is convicted rapist and murderer Karla Homolka, who was presented by the Canadian media as good-looking but shallow. The media also contrived to portray Homolka in positivist terms, as the epitome of beauty and femininity, yet revealing 'traditionally masculine' traits in her enjoyment of the rapes and of sex generally (Campbell, 1995 cited in Morrissey, 2003). Similarly, British killer Tracie Andrews, who was convicted of the murder of her boyfriend, Lee Harvey, after appearing at a press conference to appeal for his 'road rage murderer' to come forward, was a former model and was, by all conventional standards, an attractive young woman. But the press described her as 'vain' and 'heavily made up' and a headline above photographs of her read 'Looks that could kill' (*Daily Star*, 30 July 1997).

Bad wives

As discussed earlier, the chivalry hypothesis has been most successfully challenged in relation to women who fit popular, mediated images of deviance, either in their dress and appearance or in their behaviour. When women do not conform to Victorian-inspired ideals of femininity and domesticity, and can therefore be judged bad wives and mothers, they are much more likely to confound a judge's idea of appropriate womanhood (Kennedy, 1992; Lloyd, 1995). By contrast, marital status, family background and children have little or no bearing on most cases involving male defendants whose conformity to conventional notions of 'respectability' rely on issues such as employment history rather than factors such as marital status (Lloyd, 1995). Ideally, women should be housewives, content to remain at home, economically and emotionally dependent on their husbands who are busy bestriding the public sphere (Worrall, 1990). Women who transgress these codes of conduct and pursue public lives of their own, are tolerated only if they continue to put their husbands and families before their careers, and occasionally appear beside their husbands as attractive trophies and further evidence of his success.

Little wonder, then, that women who kill their spouse or partner are the epitome of the 'bad wife', almost regardless of the provocation that led to the crime. Sara Thornton, convicted in 1990 of killing her violent, alcoholic husband, Malcolm, is one such case. She says, 'I've been portrayed as a woman who nagged him over his drinking, who didn't always wear knickers and who went off to a conference and left him' (Wykes, 1995). What is perhaps slightly more surprising is that women who are the victims of murder by their spouse or partner are frequently portrayed in a similarly negative light, and put on trial for their own victimization. One infamous example of the 'topsy turvy justice of patriarchal law' (Radford, 1993) concerned Joseph McGrail, who walked free from the courtroom with a two-year suspended sentence for killing his 'nagging' common-law wife. The judge, Mr Justice Popplewell, famously said that the victim would have 'tried the patience of a saint'. Ironically, this verdict came in July 1991; just two days after Sara Thornton appealed against her sentence and lost.

Feminist research has shown that, unlike men for whom there are recognizable patterns of 'lifestyle' violence involving public rituals of heavy drinking and fighting, women's violence is mostly confined to the domestic sphere (Polk, 1993; Heidensohn, 2000). Furthermore, in cases where men murder their female spouses or partners, the crimes are often precipitated by jealousy or depression (for example, when the woman threatens to leave, or leads the offender to believe she is being unfaithful to him). Women, on the other hand, tend to resort to *spousal homicide* as a response to initial violence from their male partner (Browne, 1987; Lloyd, 1995). However, it is interesting to note the extent to which recently there has been a backlash against feminist research and theory. For example, despite all evidence to the contrary, Hornby (1997) concludes that the over-representation of men in the criminal justice system must be evidence of a hugely discriminatory system. He also challenges the notion that men are more likely to be violent than women, with the glib comment that a child is more likely to be hit by its mother than its father. Of course, to say that men are more violent than women is by no means to accept that all men are violent, violence-prone or tolerant of violence, and that all women are non-violent or victims of masculine violence. But in some areas of research, it is arguable that anti-feminist sentiments, such as those that underpin Hornby's views, have clouded the real picture of offending and victimization. One such area is that of domestic violence, a subject which has seen vigorous attempts in recent years to cast men as its victims. But despite the salience of male victims of domestic assault in official and popular discourses, research has shown that victimized men are likely also to be perpetrators of domestic violence, especially in male–female partnerships (Gadd et al., 2003). It is interesting to note that even the most 'reliable' of official figures misrepresent domestic violence. Farrell and Pease (2007) highlight that there is a fundamental misassumption by the British Crime Survey (now split into the Crime Survey for England and Wales, the Scottish Crime and Justice Survey and the Northern Ireland Crime Survey) that people will never be victimized in the same way by the same people more than five times a year. In making this assumption, Farrell and Pease suggest, the Crime Survey is ignoring 3 million crimes a year, including 2.2 million offences against the person. Not only are male 'victims' less likely than female victims to have been repeatedly victimized or seriously injured, but they are more likely to have the financial resources to allow them to leave the abusive relationship (Gadd et al., 2003). Such misrepresentations illustrate Wykes' assertion that media and legal constructions of male and female violence fit within a framework that emphasizes traditional models of family organization and femininity that is commensurate with a 'broader ideological "claw-back" of feminist "gains"' (1998: 234). The consequence of this emphasis is that traditional conservative family and gender relations are endorsed and celebrated, even when the reality of many of the crimes discussed in this chapter indicates families and marriages as sites of (largely masculine) violence, sexual abuse and murder.

Bad mothers

In a Freudian analysis, our psychological make-up means that early dependence on our mothers makes us especially vulnerable to the 'fear that an evil mother in human form can elicit' (Morrissey, 2003: 23). Not only do they kill, hurt or neglect when they are 'supposed' to care and nurture, but they also represent only a tiny fraction of serious criminals, so they frequently have a perceived 'novelty' value that guarantees media interest in them. The 'bad mother' motif is so culturally pervasive that it is ascribed to virtually *all* women, whether victims or offenders, actual mothers or non-mothers, and whether they are involved in the murder of children or commit other crimes but also happen to *be* mothers. In the latter category, Tracie Andrews was widely castigated for committing a crime that carried a life sentence, as this would entail a long separation from her daughter, although in a rare moment of empathy, the *Birmingham Evening Mail* noted that 'this 28-year-old unmarried mother of a little daughter seemed dwarfed by her surroundings ... it was painful to remember that a verdict of guilty would lead to her daughter Karla being deprived of her mother' (29 July 1997). However, we are reminded in the same article that this is no embodiment of the feminine ideal. Illustrating positivist themes already discussed, Tracie is described as a 'bruiser of a woman', a street fighter whose 'bottle blonde hair grew more tawny as the trial progressed ... sometimes obscuring all her features except the heavily-jutting jaw'. More controversially, women who lose their children in terrible circumstances may also be portrayed as bad mothers. One of the most notable cases in this respect is that of Lindy Chamberlain, who was convicted of the murder of her baby daughter in Australia in 1982 despite asserting that she had seen a dingo emerging from the tent where her daughter was sleeping. Sentenced to life imprisonment, Chamberlain had many appeals turned down until, in 1986, in the light of new evidence and mounting public concern, the case was re-examined and Chamberlain was acquitted. A less extreme, but still controversial, example of the media's inclination to portray mothers as 'guilty victims' is Denise Fergus, the mother of James Bulger, who was roundly con-demned by some sections of the popular press for turning her back on her son while paying for shopping in the Bootle mall from which he was abducted. This view was later legitimated by the rather unfortunate comments of Sir David Ramsbotham, then Chief Inspector of Prisons, who informed an inter-viewer that Mrs Fergus would be feeling 'guilt as well as grief'. He went on: 'I don't know, but if I'd left my two-year-old when visiting a shop I'm not sure I'd feel entirely comfortable' (*Independent on Sunday*, 15 July 2001).

But the bad mother motif is most systematically and vengefully applied to female offenders who are involved in the sexual abuse or killing of children. Rose West and Valmae Beck both presented an enigma for the media in so far as they were mothers who were involved in the abuse and murders of children (her own, as well as others', in the case of West). The following pas-sage appeared in an Australian newspaper and is written in response to the sentencing of Beck for her part in the rape and murder of a 12-year-old girl with her partner, Barrie Watts, who was reportedly obsessed with the idea of raping a virgin. Yet it could just as easily have been written about the crimes of Rose West (or for that matter the more recent case of Monique Olivier who went 'hunting for virgins' with her serial killer husband, Michel Fourniret):

> Before this case, how could anyone have believed that a middle-aged mother would be party to such a crime ... what I would like to know is this: If such a plain, ordinary-looking housewife and mother as this one can become physi-cally involved in such a terrifying crime, then how many more ordinary men and women are out there waiting to come under the influence, as she said she was, of an evil swine like her partner in rape, torture and murder? Surely any mother would have enough compassion to be repulsed and in quick succession sicken-ingly enlightened when her husband said he wanted to rape a 12-year-old school-girl? ('Kavanagh on Saturday' in *Courier-Mail*, Brisbane, 10 February 1990, cited in Morrissey, 2003: 148)

In cases where fathers or step-fathers sexually abuse their children, the media frequently contrive to apportion blame, in at least equal measure, on the children's mothers for allegedly colluding with the offences. In most of these cases the women concerned are also the victims of abuse at the hands of their partners and are often too frightened to report it, but this does not prevent judges and juries sentencing them as 'bad' mothers rather than abused women (Morris and Wilczynski, 1993).

More than any other kind of offender, mothers who sexually abuse children and young women embody the 'monstrous maternal' (Morrissey, 2003: 154). When the first edition of this book was published in 2004, I noted that, despite the notoriety of a handful of high-profile female sexual offenders such as West and Beck, society generally was not ready to come to terms with the existence of a group of individuals whose crimes challenge the firmly-held belief that women are incapable of sexual aggression. By 2010, that situation has changed somewhat, partly because the drive to attract audiences and advertisers in a global multi-media environment has resulted in the picture of crime becoming ever more distorted, with atypical offences frequently being used in a sensationalized manner to indicate wider problems in society and endorse political mantras such as 'broken Britain' (see Chapter 2). When Plymouth nursery worker Vanessa George was convicted in 2009 for sexually assaulting and distributing indecent images of children in her care, her role as 'Public Enemy Number One' (*Sun*, 12 June 2009) was underlined by the news that her two teenage children had disowned her. Meanwhile, the man for whom she had produced the images, Colin Blanchard (a man she had encountered on the Internet but never physically met before the court trial), received far less media coverage and public opprobrium.

In some respects the case of Vanessa George recalled that of Beverly Allitt, a nurse who was convicted of murdering four children in her care, of attempting to murder three children, and inflicting grievous bodily harm on six other children. As with George, it was Allitt's chosen profession as well as her gender that was used against her. Not only was she described as the 'angel of death' by many newspapers but an editorial in the *Daily Express* went on:

> Women should nurture, not harm. By and large they do. Even today violence is a male speciality. But nurses are supposed to be the epitome of female care. They are the angels of newspaper headlines. When women do things like this it seems unnatural, evil, a perversion of their own biology. (5 May 1993)

However, the archetypal example of a woman who failed to measure up to the ideals of maternal care perpetuated by a patriarchal media remains Myra Hindley; not because she had children herself (she didn't) but because, as a woman who was convicted of serious (sexual) crimes against children, she was deemed guilty not only of breaking the law, but also of breaking every culturally sanctioned code of femininity and womanhood. Arguably, then, it is women's 'natural' role as mothers and carers that makes it so difficult for society to accept that women can harm children and punish them severely.

Mythical monsters

The images of women that still prevail in media constructions of women who commit serious crimes derive from pagan mythology, Judaeo-Christian theology and classical art and literature. Despite the diversity of these sources, modern constructions of deviant women frequently draw on any or all of these traditions, invoking images of witches, satanists, vampires, harpies, evil temptresses, 'fallen women' and Christian notions of Original Sin, to convey female wickedness. These motifs are often used in tandem with references to lesbianism, and many mythical monsters are similarly anomalous classifications: for example, straddling categories of gods and humans, or the living and the dead. Fitting into neither one category nor the other, but deriving from both, they are invested with too much meaning, which has to be controlled by designating it as taboo (Fiske, 1982).

Two favoured figures from Greek mythology who can be viewed as anomalous are Medea, an enchantress who, when spurned by her lover, murdered her children, and Medusa, the snake-haired monster who turned her victims to stone with a stare. Tabloid newspapers have made ample use of both symbolic figures in their coverage over the last 40 years of Myra Hindley, the reporting of whom is invariably accompanied by the famous police 'mugshot' taken at the time of her arrest in 1965. According to Helen Birch this image, a 'brooding presence' that has held a 'bizarre grip' over the public imagination for four decades, even among those too young to remember the original case, has become detached from its subject (1993: 33). It has become a symbolic representation of the 'horror of femininity perverted from its "natural" course' (1993: 34–5), an icon of female deviance. In homage to Lombroso, many writers have alighted on the peroxide blonde hair and 'hooded eyes', and drawn inferences from these physicalities ranging from haughty indifference to irredeemable evil. An editorial in the *Guardian* hints at the way the image that has become part of the cultural fabric of our country through its constant reproduction in the pages of the popular press, interpellates us via its subtle evocation of mythological monstrosity:

> Myra, Medusa. Medusa, Myra. No matter what she looked like after she was sentenced to life imprisonment in 1966, Myra Hindley was fixed forever in the public eye as the peroxide-haired gorgon of that infamous police snapshot. Look at her defiant, evil eyes, we are meant to say. Spawn of the devil, God knows, she probably had a head of snakes, covered by a blonde wig to fool us, this evil, evil woman. (Glancey, 2002)

Another monstrous motif used in narratives about female killers is that of the vampire. Most notorious in this respect is the representation of the Australian woman Tracey Wigginton who, after killing Edward Baldock in Brisbane in October 1989, was described by the Australian press as the 'lesbian vampire killer'. As several writers have noted, cultural connections have been made between vampirism and lesbianism in film and literature for more than a century, a stereotypical link that is not altogether surprising given that the lust for blood is usually equated with the vampire's role as sexual aggressor (Verhoeven, 1993; Morrissey, 2003). In Tracey Wigginton's case, the vampire appellation came about after her accomplices claimed she killed her victim in order to feast on his blood. Despite psychiatric evidence that they were deluded in this respect, the press began to report the story as fact, revelling in stories of gothic horror, cannibalism and sexual perversion. Although there was *some* speculation in later coverage that her accomplices concocted the 'lesbian vampire' story in order to diminish their own roles in the murder and leave her to face trial on her own (Verhoeven, 1993), in general the vampire motif gave the media a fascinating 'hook' on which to hang a story that might otherwise have elicited little interest. The willingness of the public to believe the (literally) fantastic stories that were concocted about vampirism was not so surprising. As Verhoeven comments, 'if the public could believe a woman would actually kill a man at random, then it was capable of believing anything' (1993: 123–4). This willingness to believe also extended to investigating police officers, who admitted to watching vampire film *The Hunger* in an attempt to find clues as to a motive for the crime (Morrissey, 2003). The vampire motif was stretched almost to the point of incredulity when it was alleged in court that she combed the streets in search of a victim while listening to the strains of the Prince song 'Batdance' (Verhoeven, 1993). Even when psychiatrists declared that she was unfit to stand trial and should be subjected to further psychiatric treatment, their diagnosis was skewed to fit the Gothic narrative. The multiple personality disorder with which Wigginton was diagnosed was taken as further evidence of her vampirism, and subsequently allowed for a re-enactment of other mythical archetypes such as the witch, the siren and Jekyll and Hyde (Morrissey, 2003).

The depiction of female killers as vampires clearly serves to make them less woman than monster. Even the reporting of the Tracie Andrews case was humorously constructed with a nod to vampiric motifs and, echoing Tracey Wigginton's musical tastes, the *Sun* quoted a former boyfriend in the headline 'Tracie was so crazy in bed she made us do it to "Bat Out Of Hell"' (30 July 1997). In fact, most women who commit, or who are complicit in, serious crimes get reported in terms that emphasize their conformity to one or more of these ideological constructions of deviant or monstrous femininity. Lindy Chamberlain was stereotyped as a witch who sacrificed her daughter in a satanic ritual; Aileen Wuornos, nicknamed the 'damsel of death', was a vengeful lesbian prostitute stalking innocent men to fulfil her inhuman lusts; Beverley Allitt was an 'angel of death' who cold-heartedly killed babies and children in her care; Anne Darwin was a 'hideous, lying bitch'; Monique Olivier was the 'Ogress of the Ardennes'; Tracey Wigginton was a 'vampire killer'; Karla Homolka was a beautiful but morally vacuous temptress; like Medusa, Tracie Andrews possessed 'looks that could kill'; Rose West was a kinky Lady Macbeth figure who dominated her husband and was the real instigator of the sordid goings-on within the 'Gloucester house of horrors' – and after her husband's death, Rose became the 'black widow' in mediated discourse; Valmae Beck's confession and court testimony was evidence of her scopophilic desire to watch rape and murder and her sadistic enjoyment in aiding their commission; Joanna Dennehy, who was convicted of killing three men in February 2014, was described by the trial judge as a 'cruel, calculating, selfish and manipulative serial killer' with a 'sexual and sadistic motivation' and 'lust for blood' (*Guardian*, 28 February 2014). As Creed (1996) argues, motifs like these reinforce the notion of female killers as scapegoats for a phallocentric culture. A culture's deepest beliefs and darkest fears about women become entangled with childhood anxieties about supernatural monsters and creatures from the underworld passed down via legend, folklore and myth. Monstrous images of women become so firmly entrenched in the popular consciousness that it becomes almost impossible to view Myra, Rose, Tracey et al. as real women, rather than the grotesque caricatures portrayed in the media. For many feminist commentators this is a problem that is not confined to those women who are constructed via legal and media discourses, but it raises important wider issues concerning attitudes to women: 'The dichotomy between "good" and "bad" women ... serves as a means of patrolling, controlling and reinforcing the boundaries of behaviour considered "appropriate" for *all* women' (Morris and Wilczynski, 1993: 217). This brings us to another set of stereotypes which dominate 'official' discourses on women who offend; namely that *all* women are potentially mad at certain times of their lives (1993: 217).

Mad cows

While folklore and myth have created one collection of motifs of deviant women, another set of images has been supplied by science and medicine (Heidensohn, 1985). Once more, the 'findings' of 19th century male pioneers, from Lombroso to Freud, have been profoundly influential in constructing notions of female pathology as explanation for women's offending. Most women who commit serious offences such as murder or manslaughter are advised by their lawyers to use psychiatric pleas; in other words, to plead guilty on grounds of diminished responsibility or *infanticide* (a crime that applies to women only, referring to the killing of a child under the age of 12 months by its mother when the balance of her mind was disturbed as a result of childbirth). Wilczynski (1997) notes that in cases of *filicide* (the killing of a child by its parent or step-parent), while 30 per cent of men use psychiatric pleas, over 64 per cent of women do so, resulting in women being twice as likely to receive psychiatric or non-custodial sentences (interestingly, filicide is the only type of homicide that women and men commit in approximately equal numbers). Men tend to utilize 'normal' pleas which do not require an 'abnormal' state of mind, for example, involuntary manslaughter, which requires an absence of intent to kill or seriously injure the victim (Wilczynski, 1997). Consequently, men are much more likely to receive a custodial sentence when they kill their children (even in cases where a psychiatric plea has been used). Wilczynski further argues that although men who kill their children are sometimes viewed as 'sad', they are usually regarded as 'bad': their killings are 'less surprising, and they are more in need of punishment and deterrence' (1997: 424).

These findings might, at first glance, suggest that the tendency to 'psychiatrize' women *can* lead to leniency, especially in cases where women commit infanticide or filicide (Morris and Wilczynski, 1993; Wilczynski, 1997). But several commentators are at pains to point out that psychiatric disposals are not necessarily 'lenient' sentences. They can result in women being labelled 'psychotic' or 'psychopathic' for life, and there are many documented cases of women who have been incarcerated in mental hospitals, prisons and other institutions far longer than they might have been had their behaviour not been medicalized and had they not been prescribed drugs on which they became dependent (Lloyd, 1995; Wilczynski, 1997). The casualness with which women's crimes are medicalized is well documented (Dobash et al., 1986; Lloyd, 1995; Wilczynski, 1997) and is typified by the defence's use of Munchausen's syndrome by proxy (MSBP) in the Beverley Allitt trial, an illness that few had heard of prior to this case. In simple terms MSBP – the 'caring disease' – is a condition that affects parents or carers, mostly women, who are driven by a psychological need to gain attention by being involved in the medical care of an infant. In such circumstances it might be assumed that those in the criminal justice system, and in society generally, find it much easier to accept that a woman has committed violent or heinous offences if she can be categorized as a deluded lunatic or unstable hysteric, even if sentences do not necessarily reflect that sentiment. The word 'hysteria' comes from the Greek *husterikos*, meaning 'of the womb', and has long been employed in order to reinforce the notion of women as 'other'. Additional psychopathological states peculiar to women – for example, pregnancy, childbirth and lactation are legally sanctioned explanations of infanticide, while menstruation and menopause are also treated as inherently pathological states which 'explain' female offending (Heidensohn, 2000).

Pathologizing the female reproductive cycle also allows the 'bad mother' motif to be utilized. Treating women who commit infanticide or filicide as hormonally disturbed perpetuates the 'myth of motherhood' (Oakley, 1986) and suggests that 'normal' women are naturally maternal and find motherhood constantly fulfilling and joyful. While this is a dominant construction in mediated discourses, especially advertising, it is an image that is at odds with the stark reality that for many women motherhood can be anything but, for a variety of structural reasons (poverty, lack of support and so on) as well as physiological and psychological ones (Wilczynski, 1997). Most (in)famously, Pollak in his (1950/1961) publication, *The Criminality of Women*, argues that women's 'other' biology not only propels them into crime, but also allows them to conceal their criminality, just as they have, for centuries, concealed menstruation, pregnancy, the fatherhood of their children, menopause and sexual arousal. If women can fake orgasm, Pollack argues, they must be naturally deceitful and are thus better equipped to conceal their deviance. While Pollack has been largely discredited, especially in the feminist literature, the idea that women are ruled by their biology persists in medical, legal and media discourses about crime. The use of pre-menstrual syndrome (PMS) to explain and excuse women's violent offending is the most recent manifestation of a biological determinism that has its origins in Victorian ideas about hysterics (cf. Benn, 1993). Meanwhile, men are regarded as rational agents, ruled by their heads, not their biology. Hormonal imbalance is arguably no more likely to result in women's crime as it is men's, although few criminal cases are defended on the grounds that high testosterone levels might explain male outbursts of violence (notwithstanding that in the 1960s and 1970s some researchers did claim that violent crime was associated with a male chromosome abnormality, dubbed 'supermale syndrome'). The tendency to pathologize women's physiological and 'natural' traits in order to construct them as artful deceivers brings us to the broader stereotype of women as evil manipulators.

Evil manipulators

Many of the individuals mentioned in this chapter – Myra Hindley, Rose West, Karla Homolka, Valmae Beck – did not commit their crimes alone, but in partnership with their male lovers and husbands. Women who form murderous alliances with men are the most problematic for the institutions that seek to understand them and communicate their actions to the rest of society, particularly as their prey are often the archetypal 'innocent' victims – children and young women. These female offenders neither inspire sympathy as victims nor celebration as powerful avengers and, as such, they represent an enigma to mainstream academic and feminist discourses, and offer the least possibility for rehabilitation or redemption as far as the legal and media professions are concerned (Morrissey, 2003).

Women who join with their partners in killing cannot be simplistically constructed as lesbians, even if their victims are girls and young women. The media therefore struggle to employ their standard narrative of lesbianism because their relationships with their male accomplices *insists* on their heterosexuality (although it doesn't stop them from trying, as demonstrated by the image of Rose and Myra holding hands, mentioned earlier). Equally, it is usually not possible to easily construct these women as victims or avengers because rarely is there evidence that suggests either of these defences. Even if there are grounds for constructing them as victims (as in the case of Homolka, who finally went to the police after months of savage abuse at the hands of her co-accused), their involvement in such terrible crimes (in this example, the abduction, drugging, rape and murder of young women, including her 14-year-old sister, Tammy Homolka) makes it impossible for the media to elicit any sympathy for them.

The media's solution to the problem of heterosexual women who appear to be equal partners, or at least to go along unquestioningly with their men's wishes in very serious crime, is to place the burden of guilt on their shoulders. As a consequence, in all the cases mentioned above, the argument runs thus. Ian, Fred, Paul and Barrie were all evil men, capable of extreme cruelty. But without a submissive woman, a sadistic man would never act. It is only together that they become a 'lethal pair' (Morrissey, 2003: 152). It is therefore the woman who is instrumental in unleashing the violence and depravity that the man has thus far contained. Even Maxine Carr, whose crime was essentially providing an alibi for her partner, Ian Huntley, elicited far stronger mediated public reaction than a charge of perverting the course of justice would usually merit. In addition to framing Carr as a modern-day Myra Hindley, and thus implying that she was an accomplice to Huntley's crimes, many newspapers gave more coverage to Carr than to Huntley, including in relation to number and size of the images used to accompany their coverage. As Jones and Wardle (2008) demonstrate, the dual outcomes of reporting Carr using Hindley as their template, and insinuating that she was in some way involved in Huntley's crimes, had an impact far greater than her crime arguably warranted and, on her release from prison in 2004 she was granted an indefinite anonymity order.

The subtle and overt framing of Maxine as the 'new Myra' is illustrative of the Myra and Ian soap opera that continues to play out in the pages of the popular press years after their crimes and even after Hindley's reported death in prison in 2002. Once again, her role in the offences was minor compared to Brady's, but her culpability is somehow greater. In not resisting Brady's sado-masochistic demands, and in failing to intervene to stop his grisly crimes, it was in fact Hindley who let down their victims. As a woman, she should have shown compassion, she could have done more. The betrayal was Myra's. She was the evil manipulator, he the unfortunate bearer of a tormented psyche. This image was reinforced when, in 1985, Ian Brady was transferred from prison to a psychiatric hospital, suffering from paranoid schizophrenia. He went on hunger strike and proclaimed his wish to die. Photographs of a thin, ravaged Brady, 'his body apparently displaying the signs of inner torment' began to appear in the press and provided 'a graphic counterpoint to those of Myra, smiling, in her graduation gown at her degree ceremony, presenting a softer, prettier, happier image' (Birch, 1993: 55). As the decades rolled by, Myra's demonization only intensified, making her a larger-than-life, constantly in-your-face caricature, while Ian Brady literally and metaphorically disappeared.

The motives of women who form partnerships with men who kill, and assist them in their murderous quests, are complex and contested. Some critics argue that, for the most part, these are 'ordinary' women who happen to fall under the influence of a controlling, usually older, man and that without that fateful first meeting they would have gone on to live 'normal', suburban lives (Smith, 1997; Wykes, 1998). Others argue that this conceptualization negates the *agency* and free will of such women, and that they may actually seek out such men because they have similar desires, going along with their partners' murderous plans as a vehicle to their own empowerment (Birch, 1993; Morris and Wilczynski, 1993; Pearson, 1998). For these writers, the unpalatable suggestion that these women may have enjoyed their crimes is the main impediment, not only to the invisibility of their roles in the crimes in media and legal discourses, but also to an adequate feminist consideration of the cases. It is much harder to defend a person who has apparently willingly committed heinous acts of cruelty than one whose actions resulted from duress or oppression and, as such, the actual involvement of these women is 'repressed out of conscious existence' (Morrissey, 2003: 156).

Non-agents

The conclusion of increasing numbers of scholars therefore is that neither academic feminism nor society at large are ready to confront the reality that women can be cruel, sadistic and violent. The simple truth that men are more aggressive than women not only encourages a widespread cultural ignorance of the fact that women have the potential for violence, but it also serves to deny psychically the notion that women can kill *as women*. In general, women are viewed either as big children (which is how they were considered by Lombroso and Ferrero a century ago, and which still permeates clinical discourse; Morris, 1987) or as men (a view endorsed by the many examples of women who are portrayed as 'mannish' lesbians). Stock stereotypes such as vampires and snake-haired medusas also serve to deny women's agency. If a murderess becomes a mythical monster, she loses her humanity and is considered to have acted – but not as a contemporary human woman (Morrissey, 2003).

There are only two crimes for which women may retain their humanity and avoid the ascription of 'evil', but both imply that offending women are nona-gentic. They are 'spousal homicide', where the woman can be seen as acting in self-defence against an abusive partner, and infanticide, where a woman can be viewed as a mixture of 'mad' and 'sad'. In either case, the woman con-cerned can be regarded as a victim who is not responsible for her actions. Morrissey reflects on constructions of victimization and their wider implica-tions for women generally in relation to spousal murder:

> Many portrayals of women who kill depict them as so profoundly victimized that it is difficult to regard them as ever having engaged in an intentional act in their lives … Representations of the murderess as victim, then, function to deny her responsibility, culpability, agency, and often her rationality as well, in their bid to explain her behaviour and secure her sympathetic legal treatment. While unde-niably often successful in securing reduced sentences, the disadvantages of such a strategy outweigh the benefits in terms of improving general societal attitudes to, and challenging negative myths and stereotypes of, women. (Morrissey, 2003: 25)

As discussed earlier, explanations of female criminality that rely on determin-istic assumptions about women's physiology and biology arguably have the most far-reaching implications for deviant and non-deviant women alike, and dominant discourses of madness most incontestably speak to the non-agency of female offenders. While the Beverley Allitt case provoked the majority of the popular media to fall back on stock notions of psychiatric disorder, aug-mented by their discovery of Munchausen's disease, one lone, contradictory voice was reported in the *Telegraph*. Dr David Enoch, a consultant at the Royal Liverpool Hospital and an expert on Munchausen's, argued that popular assumptions about Allitt were incorrect:

> She is not mad, she is not psychotic. When you are psychotic you lose insight and delude yourself, you do not know what you are doing. Those who suffer from Munchausen's know that they are not really ill and have insight into their actions … she would have known what she was doing with the children. (19 May 1993)

Even women who kill their own children may not fall neatly into the category of 'irrational' or 'emotional outburst' that are so often constructed for them. Acts of infanticide and filicide may be perpetrated by women who are highly emotional at the time of the offence, but these acts do not necessarily represent a sudden, irrational loss of control.

The failure of the media to acknowledge the agency of women involved in serious offences is also apparent in terms of the delicacy with which the media side-step the actual details of their offences. Selective reporting is especially evident in cases where women rape and sexually abuse. For example, the crimes of Myra Hindley continue to be held up as perhaps the most heinous ever committed in Britain, yet even many of the journalists who continue using her image in order to sell newspapers are too young to remember her trial in 1966, and may not actually be fully cognisant of her precise role in the sexual torture and murder of the victims. Despite the collective sense of horror and revulsion at her crimes, few of us know what Myra Hindley *actually did*. Similarly, legal and media constructions of Valmae Beck and Karla Homolka glossed over their participation in the sexual assaults they committed. In fact, Homolka was not convicted of sexual abuse because of the temporary absence of incriminating videotapes at the time of her trial and, in the case of Beck who *was* convicted of rape, many newspapers did not mention this important aspect of her crimes (Morrissey, 2003). And, while the media enjoyed slavering over the details of Rose West's sexual predilections, the extent to which she was involved in the sexual abuse and murder of the victims, whose remains were found at Cromwell Street and elsewhere, remains unclear and legally unproved (Smith, 1997; Wykes, 1998). The reticence with which the media confront women's serious sexual crimes is somewhat surprising, especially given the appetite for sex that is often attributed to the popular press and its readership. Morrissey speculates that despite incontrovertible evidence proving women's participation in sex crimes, the media are simply not able to present female protagonists who so clearly deviate from conventional hegemonic, heteropatriarchal conceptions of femininity: 'Apparently, so these news stories say, men rape and murder, women watch and help with the clean up' (2003: 153). Yet, at the same time, the prudish and partial representation of women's involvement in rape and murder encourages the public at large to dip into the cultural reservoir of symbolic representations and 'fill in the gaps'.

Honourable fathers vs. monstrous mothers: some concluding thoughts

Psychosocial approaches to 'otherness' have provided a useful framework within which to study possible explanations for the bigotry and hysteria that characterizes media and legal discourses of offending women, and shed light on the general and deep-seated cultural discomfort generated by women's wickedness. Our inability to view women who commit serious offences as anything other than – well – 'others', may relate to our psychological make-up in so far as early dependence on our mothers makes us especially vulnerable to the fear that evil women can elicit (Morrissey, 2003). Our unconscious fears of feminine evil are then picked up and reinforced by a heteropatriarchal culture that presents any female deviation as intrinsically shocking:

> Those doing the defining, by that very act, are never defined as 'other', but are the norm. Those different from the norm – in this case, women – are thus off-centre, deviant. Man is the norm, the objective standard by which others are measured. Men are perceived to be independent, rational, autonomous and responsible. The ... other, the female is therefore dependent, emotional, not entirely adult and irresponsible. She is defined in reference to men. (Lloyd, 1995: xvii)

'Otherness' is central to the differential media reporting of men who kill and women who kill. Quite simply, when we consider the narratives used to construct mediated stories about serious crimes, women are characterized as bad mothers even when they are non-mothers and/or have killed adults, not children.

Men, on the other hand, are rarely described as 'bad fathers' (although, as with women, stereotypes based on assumptions about class, race, age and family stability, have a bearing on the legal and media discourses constructed around men's offending). Compare the examples of deviant women discussed above with the case of Robert Mochrie who, in July 2000, battered to death his wife and four children before ingesting poison and hanging himself. In a *Cutting Edge* documentary on Channel 4 (29 July 2003), Mochrie was presented as a tragic hero. *'Familicide'* – or *'Family annihilation'* as it has been dubbed by the media – is usually carried out by middle-aged men driven to a violent last resort either by marriage breakdown or by their inability to continue providing for their family in the 'traditional' manner. To some extent, Mochrie was experiencing both: his wife was involved in a relationship with his former business partner, he was regularly visiting prostitutes and, following early retirement, he had made some bad investments and was on the verge of bankruptcy. Despite these factors which might be thought to mitigate against the depiction of a 'typical' middle-class family, the discourse constructed by the Mochries' friends and neighbours and presented uncritically by the television documentary makers, centred entirely around that: their sheer averageness. The words that were repeatedly used to describe Robert Mochrie were 'ordinary', 'normal', 'regular', 'decent'. Cath and Robert Mochrie were 'the perfect couple' and Robert 'adored' his children. Yet in the early hours of 12 July 2000, he 'meticulously', 'calmly' and – according to Cath's best friend – 'gently' bludgeoned each member of his sleeping family to death with a hammer, sent a few text messages, cancelled the milk, and then hanged himself.

As a newspaper editorial following the documentary observed, the sympathy shown toward Robert by friends, while generous and perhaps rather surprising, is not extraordinary. It was probably a brave attempt to square the man they thought they knew with the unknowable man who took six lives, including his own (McLean, 2003). But the collusion of the programme makers is more surprising. Not only did they entirely avoid resorting to stock motifs of monsters and devilry, but they also endorsed the idea of Mochrie as a fundamentally decent man driven to the edge by some sort of heartfelt but misguided heroism. The narrator of the documentary concluded that Mochrie's motivation 'in a strange and terrifying way, was love'. Newspaper columnist Gareth McLean's comment that Mochrie's motivation was more likely to be fear than love brought about by a combination of near-psychotic depression and a 'desperate, sad, proud and defiantly macho inability to ask for help' (2003), once more demonstrates the extent to which psychoanalytic ideas have penetrated popular and media discourses. But of greater interest in the current context is the quietly forgiving response of the community at large to these tragic events. As McLean continues: 'try imagining the tsunami of loathing that would descend upon her were a woman to commit those crimes' (2003).

It is not being suggested here that all men who murder or commit other serious offences are tolerated, ignored, understood or applauded. Most men who commit terrible crimes are not treated with the empathy that was extended to Mochrie, and it is men who are most frequently portrayed by the media as 'monsters' or 'evil beasts'. But the contention is that media and public responses to women who kill and seriously harm are even more exaggerated than they are for men. Male violence is seen to exist on a continuum ranging from the non-violent to the murderous and sexually bizarre, which results in it being viewed only in terms of degrees (Naylor, 2001). Even the criminological literature on masculinity and homicide couch familicide in terms of 'misguided altruism', and as a matter of masculine honour and pride in the face of overwhelming social expectations concerning men's responsibilities for their families' wellbeing (Alder and Polk, 1996). Put simply, violence is viewed as one of the many possible behaviour patterns for men; it is not strikingly unusual, even when extreme. Consequently, when a man kills he can expect that his crime will be both imaginable and possibly – as in the case of Robert Mochrie – even seen as human. Indeed, male crime is intrinsic to the hegemonic masculine ideal. In all spheres of life – political, social, economic and, above all, cultural – masculine violence is articulated, glorified, even fetishized. Men who commit serious crimes are thus normalized to a much greater degree than women who do so, and their crimes tend not to be accompanied by a sense of collective denial. Yet in cases of women who kill, 'vilification operates to displace the offender from her society, to insist on her otherness, thereby avoiding the knowledge that she is produced *by* that society' (Morrissey, 2003: 24). No such expulsion is required when men murder;

indeed, men's crimes might be said to be but one aspect of a prevailing cultural ideology of aggressive macho values that sustains men's crimes and makes them possible (Ward Jouve, 1988).

Two factors were mentioned at the beginning of this chapter that are paramount in securing a female offender's notoriety. One is her conformity to the key journalistic news values outlined in Chapter 2. Women who murder or sexually abuse form a tiny percentage of an already small, though demonized, group of criminals. This immediately guarantees their coverage; their crimes are novel, and they are negative in essence. But in addition they frequently illustrate most or all of the 12 cardinal news values (see Chapter 2). The horror of their crimes meets the required *threshold*; a grim *predictability* is woven through the account of their crimes via the use of stock stories and familiar motifs (lesbian monster, evil manipulator and so on); their histories and motives are reduced to the *simplest* of forms (that is, that they must be 'mad' or 'bad'); their pathology is constructed as *individual* and random, the most meaningless of acts carried out by individuals in whom we are meant to trust – hence any of us (or our children) are at *risk*; their crimes are explained by reference to their *sexuality* or sexual deviance; they frequently achieve a kind of macabre *celebrity*; indeed, some gain iconic status through *graphic imagery*, such as the police mugshot of Myra Hindley, which not only identified her as the 'face of the nation's deepest fears' (Upton, 2000: 6) in the popular media long after the peroxide had grown out and the lines on her face had appeared, but also achieved further immortality in art (e.g. in Marcus Harvey's infamous portrait of her and on covers of *The Smiths* albums); the victimization of *children* in murders by women further cements their newsworthiness, and even when children are not directly involved, the anomaly of women who kill being *potential* mothers is taken as proof enough of their deviation from notions of traditional womanhood, notions that are at the heart of *conservative ideology*. Finally, murderesses become notorious by virtue of their geographical and cultural *proximity*. The generally ethnocentric nature of our media means that those cases which are culturally and geographically meaningful to a home audience – Myra, Rose, Tracie and so on will have every aspect of their lives dissected for an avaricious audience. But many of the women discussed in this chapter who came from Australia, America and Canada (Tracey Wigginton, Aileen Wuornos and Karla Homolka, Susan Smith) – countries all politically, economically and culturally allied to our own – barely rated a mention in the UK media.

The fears of some feminist writers that constructions of women who kill have wider implications for all women are understandable, given the evidence put forward in this chapter. Mediated understandings of deviant women do not exist in a cultural vacuum and negative, potentially damaging stereotypes based on women's appearance, sexuality and behaviour are, of course, not limited to discourses about women who commit very serious crimes. All women who are in the public eye are inclined to become the subjects of narratives that construct them in terms of their willingness, or otherwise, to conform to traditional notions of passive, heterosexual, maternal, compliant femininity. However, many commentators have noted that, when it comes to women who kill – and here, once more, we find echoes of the public response to children who kill – a deep cultural unease is provoked by the uncomfortable reality of the human capacity for depravity. Media reports might blithely attribute women's serious crimes to their *in*humanity and 'otherness', but Smith (1997) argues that society *needs* the figure of the dominant female killer luring her hapless male partner into crimes he might otherwise not have committed, however far from the reality of the cases described in this chapter that depiction might be.

With this thought in mind, it seems fitting to end this chapter with some final reflections on Myra Hindley who has been, for many in this country, a constant, powerful, yet invisible presence throughout our entire lives. Her permanence in the collective consciousness has been assured by a number of high-profile appeals through the courts of Britain and Europe against her natural life tariff. However, her status in the British psyche as this country's number one folk devil has been augmented by a media that has inflicted her with almost every derogatory and damaging stereotype that can be ascribed to women. Hindley has spent nearly 50 years being the focus of society's most profound anxieties. Helena Kennedy (1992) maintains that Hindley became such a symbolic – iconic, even – figure because she was the vessel into which society poured its dark secrets; a reminder of the depths to which human depravity can sink. Fellow barrister John Upton comments: 'she is not merely a woman who has committed a crime; rather, there is an element of criminality inherent in her womanhood' (Upton, 2000: 6). In short, our fascination with Hindley reveals deeply conservative attitudes about the role of women in contemporary culture that are rarely exposed to the light of day. She remains – even in death – the archetypal 'she-devil', a monstrous, mythical, murderess who defies all our conscious and unconscious beliefs about womanhood. Yet her crimes were not unique, far less uniquely evil, as was maintained by Lord Stein during Hindley's final, failed appeal to the House of Lords in 2000. On the continuum of lesbianism, sexual deviancy, depravity and evil, Hindley somehow encompassed all points. Yet her actual participation in sexual assault, rape, torture and murder – what she is actually guilty of – remains overlooked or sidestepped to the point where it is invisible. Women who seriously offend are thus in the curious position of being held aloft as the most depraved examples of humanity by a public who are largely unaware of their actual deviations. Such women become symbolically detached from their crimes; crimes from which we all derive a moral certainty. Myra Hindley was irredeemably evil, no further discussion is necessary. But we have to ask ourselves whether this is an appropriate response by the media, the legal, political and justice systems, or by society at large? Is the curious mixture of public apathy and outrage in the interests of anyone, not least the victims and bereaved families? The other factor noted at the start of the chapter which secures criminal notoriety is the prevailing cultural climate in which an incident occurs. In the case of women who kill and sexually abuse, it is unlikely that there will ever be a climate of opinion which views these crimes as mundane or humdrum, even in the cynical and crime-saturated times in which we live.

Summary

- This chapter has located psychological and sociological concerns with identity and difference within criminological discourses of responses to crime in an attempt to understand the origins of, and reasons for, the fear and loathing that is directed (arguably disproportionately) at a particular group of deviant 'others' – women who kill and rape.
- The cultural inclination to view women's deviance as a manifestation of their 'otherness' is compounded by its newsworthiness, which is unquestionable, and the proposition that there may never be a prevailing ideological climate that tolerates women who deviate from cultural expectations of 'appropriate' feminine behaviour.
- It has been argued that, in common with wider media and cultural constructions, women who kill are subject to intense scrutiny – both in legal and media institutions – regarding their sexual proclivities and history, and are frequently judged on their body size, shape and sexual attractiveness. Paradoxically, conventional constructions of both beauty and ugliness can be used as evidence of a woman's inherent badness, and the media borrow from a range of classical literature and mythology to evoke images of monstrous women. Women who kill (especially those who kill children and young women) are the diabolical antithesis to the myth of the good mother, and much media discourse is constructed around 'essentialist' notions of women; in other words, they presuppose that the 'essence' of women is different from that of men, and that women are biologically predisposed to be caring and nurturing. Women's crimes against children are especially inexplicable and 'unreal'. Unless an offence can be accounted for in terms of a 'sickness' that is compatible with the essential 'nature' of womanhood, it will be regarded as 'unnatural' and evil (Worrall, 1990). A degree of biological essentialism is also evident in the common theme that women who commit serious crimes – especially when they do so in partnership with a man – are the prime movers in these relationships and are, in essence, evil manipulators.
- If a woman's serious offending cannot be explained as 'madness' but appears to be a lucid and rational act, it becomes symbolically disturbing. Women who claim that they acted in an autonomous and calculated manner (as Myra Hindley did) are so transgressive of societal notions of 'proper' (that is, non-agentic) womanhood that the details of their offences are glossed over in legal and media discourses and explanations for their crimes are curiously absent from feminist readings.

- The discussion has demonstrated that psychosocial and feminist perspectives are far from incompatible, drawing on psychoanalytically informed ways of understanding gendered identities. In the cases discussed in this chapter, psychoanalytic concepts have been used in conjunction with sociologically-informed ideas from media studies and cultural studies in order to explore exactly why it is that some individuals generate a level of hysteria and vilification that is arguably disproportionate to their actual offences. In addition, it has been argued that the media have consistently represented the abuse perpetuated on women and children as extraordinary rather than as the worst outcomes of the institutions of marriage and the family which historically have enshrined unequal relations between men, women and children.

STUDY QUESTIONS

Study a range of newspapers and pay close attention to stories involving women offenders.

1. What evidence can you find for the proposition that women are constructed according to their perceived 'otherness'? What kinds of motifs and stereotypes are apparent in your chosen news report?
2. To what extent do Lombrosian ideas about 'born female criminals', whose deviance is indicated by their very physiology, permeate contemporary discourses concerning women and crime?
3. What sorts of women conform to mediated ideas about 'ideal' victims and which women are invisible in media discourses about victimization?
4. The unwillingness of media, legal and academic discourses to recognize the possibility of women's agency has arguably resulted in other 'omissions' in our understanding of female offending. Explanations which centre on women's lust, greed, revenge or sheer entrepreneurism are curiously absent from criminological enquiries (Davies, 2003). What examples of 'invisible crimes' can you think of which illustrate this observation?

FURTHER READING

There is now quite a substantial literature within criminology concerning gender and violence, and much of it draws on media representations to illustrate the circulation of ideas concerning both women's violence and victimization. Frances Heidensohn has written extensively on feminist approaches to sex and violence; see, for example, Heidensohn, F. (2000) *Sexual Politics and Social Control* (Open University Press). Maggie Wykes (1995) has written about specific cases in her chapters in Dobash, R., Dobash, R. and Noaks, L. *Gender and Crime* (University of Wales Press) and in Carter et al. (see below). So has Joan Smith in the 1997 publication *Different For Girls* (Chatto and Windus). Helen Birch's (1993) *Moving Targets: Women, Murder and Representation* (Virago) is an edited collection which includes chapters on Myra Hindley, Hollywood representations of female killers, mothers who kill their children and female serial killers. Cynthia Carter et al.'s (1998) *News, Gender and Power* (Routledge) is another edited collection which covers some of the same ground, but from the perspective of gendered institutional working practices in newsrooms. Belinda Morrissey's (2003) *When Women Kill* (Routledge) is a more theoretically advanced book, and she discusses many of the cases featured in this chapter (for example, Homolka, Beck, Wigginton and Wuornos), which she interprets through a psychoanalytic lens. Philip Jenkins (1994) discusses serial killers, including female serial killers, in *Using Murder: The Social Construction of Serial Homicide* (Aldine de Gruyter).

6

Police, Offenders and Victims in the Media

CHAPTER CONTENTS

The mass media and fear of crime   165

The role of the police   170

The role of mobile and social media in policing   175

Tactical responses to crime and investigation   175

Image management   176

Crimewatch UK   179

Crimewatching victims   183

Crimewatching offenders   185

Crimewatching the police   186

Crimewatching crime: some concluding thoughts   188

Summary   189

Study questions   190

Further reading   191

OVERVIEW

Chapter 6 provides:

- A discussion of the relationship between the media and public fears about crime, and the rationality or irrationality of such fears.
- A comparison between 'critical criminological' and 'left realist' perspectives on fear of crime.
- A consideration of the changing role of the police and of the powerfully symbolic place of the community police officer in the British psyche, exemplified by the fictional television character *Dixon of Dock Green*.
- A discussion of the symbiotic relationship between the police and the media.
- An analysis of the origins and genre conventions of long-running 'reality' BBC series Crimewatch UK and its constructions of victims, offenders and the police.

KEY TERMS

- critical criminology
- fear of crime
- left realism
- legitimacy

- police and policing
- rationality/irrationality
- representation/misrepresentation
- victimization

Recorded crime is falling year-on-year. The Crime Survey for England & Wales, published in April 2014 by the Office for National Statistics showed that overall crime rates fell by 15 per cent in 2013, and violent crime dropped by 22 per cent. Yet many people believe that crime is rising inexorably and that personal safety is in decline. Politicians and senior police personnel have charged the police service with closing such 'perception gaps' via measures designed to reassure the public, including high-visibility policing and enhanced police communications strategies (Mawby, 2010; Lee and McGovern, 2014). This chapter will explore the proposition that media *representations* of crime make certain individuals and groups feel more vulnerable than their likelihood of actual *victimization* suggests they should be, and it will discuss the relationship between the police and the media, including dramatized images of policing. We will consider the ways in which the media and the police have become accustomed to working together, a partnership that serves to legitimate the police's power and authority, but which has been put under pressure by events including the transmission in 2003 of an undercover documentary disclosing racism among police recruits, footage filmed by 'citizen journalists' in 2009 of heavy-handed police tactics during a G20 protest in London, which resulted in the death of a protester, and the police shooting and killing of a 29-year-old man in Tottenham in 2011 which sparked the worst street riots that Britain had seen for twenty years. We will consider the implications of these events and the police service's attempts to counter the negative publicity and bolster its image through its own use of mobile and social media. Finally, the chapter will discuss public fears of crime in relation to *Crimewatch UK* which consistently over-reports the most serious but statistically uncommon offences, constructs particular and polarized views of victims and offenders, and portrays the police as calm and efficient crime fighters who are unwavering in their commitment to bring criminals to justice.

The mass media and fear of crime

Numerous writers have examined the proposition that the media present crime stories (both factual and fictional) in ways which selectively distort and manipulate public perceptions, creating a false picture of crime which promotes stereotyping, bias, prejudice and gross oversimplification of the facts. Their conclusion is that it is not just official statistics that misrepresent the picture of crime, but that the media are also guilty of manipulation and fuelling public fears. Studies carried out in the UK and US indicate that crime reporting in the press is more prevalent than ever before, and that interpersonal crimes, particularly violent and sexual crimes, are consistently over-reported in relation to official statistics. Some studies have also found that newspaper readers overestimate the proportion of crimes solved, and that the police sometimes reinforce journalistically produced concerns about a 'crime wave' by feeding reporters stories based on previously reported incidents. This can sometimes provoke fear of a crime surge at a time when statistically incidents of that crime are on the decrease (Schlesinger and Tumber, 1994). The reasons for the media's preoccupation with certain types of crime may be largely pragmatic and economic (they are, after all, in the business of selling newspapers and gaining audience ratings), but the dual outcomes of their portrayals of crime and violence are heightened public anxieties and a greater public mandate for increasingly punitive punishments.

Within criminology, discussions of public fears about crime tend to be polarized along theoretical lines. Marxist-inspired *critical criminologists* argue that politicians, the media and the criminal justice system set the agenda for public debate about crime and the implementation of criminal justice, and collude in perpetuating notions of 'enemies within'. These agendas then shape public perceptions, not only about their likelihood of being a victim of crime, but also about who they should fear. Steven Box (1983) suggests that the picture of crime that the public receive is manipulated by those in power, and that there is an over-concentration on the crimes of the young, the black, the working class and the unemployed, and an under-awareness of the crimes of the well-educated upper and middle classes, the socially privileged and those in power. He argues that the processes by which the public receive information about crime via the mass media result in perceptions about criminal justice being determined by very narrow legal definitions that tolerate, accept or even applaud the crimes of the privileged, while criminalizing the disadvantaged (see also Tombs and Whyte, 2007; Walters, 2010). Signorielli (1990) goes further, claiming that the way the media constructs crime and violence encourage populations to accept increasingly repressive forms of social control: 'fearful people are more dependent, more easily manipulated ... more susceptible to deceptively simple, strong, tough measures and hard-line postures ... they may accept and even welcome repression if it promises to relieve their insecurities and other anxieties' (1990: 102). In all these expressions, crime is viewed as an ideological construct; it protects the powerful and further marginalizes the powerless.

However, there is an implicit assumption in this proposal that *fear of crime* is *irrational* and unreasonable – that it is a kind of false consciousness produced by those in authority. *Left realist* criminologists hotly dispute this suggestion, arguing that there is a *rational* core to images of crime and to the public concerns they generate. Young, for example, claims that popular perceptions of crime and justice are largely 'constructed out of the material experiences of people rather than fantasies impressed upon them by the mass media or agencies of the State' (1987: 337). Crawford et al. concur, arguing that 'in inner city areas mass media coverage of crime tends to reinforce what people already know' (1990: 76). Of course, these are valid observations, and left realist criminologists have been right to point out that it is not just the media who are to blame for instilling fear of crime. Actual risk of **victimization**, previous experience of victimization, environmental conditions, ethnicity and confidence in the police and the criminal justice system are among many of the factors interacting through complex processes to influence public anxiety about crime. And as we have already seen in Chapter 1, the notion of passive audiences soaking up media influences in isolation of their lived experience is regarded as reductive and untenable.

Our interpretation of statistics on fear of crime may thus have to go beyond their face value. For example, crime survey findings that fear of crime greatly outweighs likelihood of actually being a victim is sometimes associated with wider insecurities that are provoked during prolonged periods of economic recession. Furthermore, the fact that the readers of popular newspapers (that is, those that report crime in a sensationalized and salient fashion) have the highest levels of fear of crime may simply reflect their actual risk of victimization. Put simply, readers of tabloid newspapers are concentrated in the lower socio-economic strata of society, and are more likely to live in areas, and behave in ways, that expose them to greater levels of risk of crime and greater surveillance by the police.

But while a *specific* media effect may be difficult to isolate in a world that is increasingly characterized as 'media-saturated', we should not dismiss the idea that the media play some part in the distribution of fear. Media use, while not reducible to crude 'effects', is centrally implicated in the routines and practices of everyday life and is inextricably interwoven into people's biographies and the stories they tell about themselves. It is impossible to separate situated experience from mediated experience and so, while women and older people may have genuine grounds for being fearful of male violence, their anxiety is constantly and pervasively reinforced by a media that recognizes and perpetuates the newsworthiness of violent crimes against women and the elderly. Quite simply, media coverage of crime and deviance is rarely grounded in fact. Crime has been exploited as commercial entertainment since the earliest days of cinema and remains the most salient theme in television dramas and 'reality' shows, which enthusiastically mix fact, fiction and titillation. Meanwhile, as we have seen in Chapter 2, news about crime and deviance has a strong social control element – 'watch and beware'. Consequently, media images of crime perpetually reinforce people's anxieties: we are, at one and the same time, fascinated by representations of crime and alarmed by them. It is little wonder, then, that those groups who become most over-sensitized to their risk of victimization are the same people whose victimization is over-reported and over-sensationalized.

Interestingly, children and young people's fears about crime are rarely discussed, although parents' fears for their offspring are part of the currency of everyday media discourse. For many decades, television was regarded as a multi-coloured narcotic, depriving children of more healthy forms of interaction and making them vulnerable to ideological manipulation. Music has also been seen as a bad influence since Elvis Presley made his first record and periodic concerns about musicians – the Rolling Stones, Beastie Boys, Eminem, Marilyn Manson, Lady Gaga and Miley Cyrus, to name just a few – have always made the headlines. In the second decade of the 21st century, rarely a day goes by without some new scare-story about young people's use of mobile technologies and social media. But rarely is media content discussed in relation to youngsters' anxieties about real-world crime. In 1998, Bok suggested that a growing trend in the US for news reporting of child abduction, kidnapping and murder was responsible for creating a climate of fear linked to an increase in child depression and suicide (cited in Keating, 2002). In both the US and the UK, concerns have been expressed about forms of music which glorify gun and drug cultures and promote homophobic and misogynist attitudes. But any link between gang-related offences and wider cultural statements legitimating or glamorizing gang life and gun crime has not yet been adequately researched.

Fear is notoriously difficult to define. Often conceptualized as a tangible quantity which we possess in smaller or greater amounts, fear may be more accurately thought of as a mode of perception consisting of a range of diffuse anxieties about one's position and identity in the world (Sparks, 1992). Furthermore, it is very difficult to generalize about 'fear of crime "effects"'. A high-profile crime might cause people to modify their behaviour for as long as the offence is newsworthy, but this amplification of anxiety may be periodic, short-lived and confined to the environs where the crime took place. On the other hand, the relationship between fear and the media might be best conceptualized in more subtle and pervasive terms as contributing to a cultural climate which normalizes male violence and reinforces notions of female submissiveness. Ultimately, the long-term effects of exposure to mediated images of crime are virtually impossible to gauge. But as already noted, while we should be cautious when making statements about the media 'causing' fear (Sparks, 1992), it is also worth bearing in mind that fear of crime is a much more widely experienced phenomenon than victimization. Although victims of crime will probably become more fearful about the likelihood of future victimization as a result of their experiences, many more individuals will experience fear as a result of indirect contact with crime. These vicarious experiences of crime will encompass personal observations, private conversations with victims, second-, third- and fourth-hand accounts passed down through multifarious flows of communication; and, of course, the media. Attempts to measure the impact of media reporting on public fears about crime are notoriously problematic. Historically, the majority of people have attributed their knowledge of the risk of crime to information received from television and newspapers (Williams and Dickinson, 1993; Surette, 1998). In a 1995 MORI poll, 66 per cent of people interviewed said they got their information from television, and 33 per cent claimed their fears about crime are increased by news and documentary coverage of crime (Keating, 2002). Now, of course, the Internet and social media give us continual access to news which can be constantly updated and, in this frenetic news hypermarket, even traditional news organizations such as the BBC will report news stories in an exaggerated and potentially anxiety-inducing manner, in an effort to grab audience attention. As Lee (2007: 165) comments, fear of crime can, perversely, be *attractive* to audiences, if it is 'invoked with just the right editorial zeal'.

According to British Crime Surveys, peaks in 'worry about crime' often coincide with falls in recorded crimes. Using data from the 1996 BCS, Hough and Roberts (1998) found that, when asked how much crime involves violence, 78 per cent of those surveyed replied 30 per cent or more – Home Office statistics recorded it at just 6 per cent. Conversely, substantial underestimates were routinely made about the extent to which the courts use custodial sentences for convicted offenders. Relying on statistical measurements to gauge the extent of crime is in itself a problematic endeavour, but the key point is that public perceptions reflect the view propagated by much of the media, that is, of a continually spiralling crime rate and an over-lenient criminal justice system. Neither view is accurate and Hough and Roberts blame the media for such public misunderstanding:

> Media news values militate against balanced coverage. Erratic court sentences make news and sensible ones do not. As a result, large segments of the population are exposed to a steady stream of unrepresentative stories about sentencing incompetence. (1998: x)

While the media frequently focus on relatively uncommon issues and report them in a sensationalized, overblown manner with demands for harsher and more uncompromising punishments, local responses to anxieties about crime are often much more immediate and micro in orientation. Two examples serve to illustrate the point. In the immediate days following the murder of Damilola Taylor, the demand of local people in the area of Peckham where he lived was on community policing – an appeal for more visible patrol officers to allay people's fears. A similar response was forthcoming following the murder of Sarah Payne. Although the *News of the World*'s 'Name and Shame' campaign reported that the majority of people (76 per cent of those questioned) wanted to know if there was a convicted paedophile living in their neighbourhood, a closer look at the MORI poll on which the newspaper's campaign was based reveals a rather different picture:

> Asked what could be done to improve the safety of children in their local area, 24 per cent said more policing, 23 per cent suggested speed restrictions and 16 per cent more safe areas for children to play in. Only three per cent offered the public naming of paedophiles as a solution, the same proportion who felt more parking wardens were part of the answer. (Garside, 2001: 32–3)

The issue of community policing remains at the heart of debates about fear of crime and the public appetite for more 'bobbies on the beat' is unflagging, despite a general decline in respect and faith in the police. Although criminological studies have repeatedly shown that providing more police officers on the streets is unlikely to reduce offending, the perception that community police officers patrolling the streets are a highly visible deterrent persists in the public imagination. It has become a key issue over which politicians fight to prove their 'tough on crime' credentials and is one of those powerfully emotive 'common sense' subjects over which it is almost impossible to publicly debate. The lazy and misinformed link that is popularly made between police officers on foot patrol and reductions in crime reflects the journalistic priorities that shape news reporting and the more general limitations of 'fear of crime' debates. As Downes remarks:

> That the 'fear of crime' … remains most developed in relation to certain forms of street crime is probably more to do with collective representations of unpredictable violence than that which more frequently occurs in the home,

or that which is normalized as accidental, or where victimization is indirect and dispersed, as with corporate crime. (1988: 182)

Public demands for bobbies on the beat may be linked to unconscious fears of 'others', including immigrants, political refugees, people from ethnic minority backgrounds, Gypsies, Roma and travellers, and the homeless. It may be a more widespread manifestation of the 'fortress mentality' visible in many modern cities where some areas have been turned into fenced, guarded, middle-class ghettos (see Chapter 8). This would certainly help to explain why fear of crime is disproportionately felt in the relatively comfortable, low-crime areas of 'middle England' (Girling et al., 2000, 2002). Public support for beat officers might also be taken as evidence of the critical criminological proposition that citizens are likely to support more visible and repressive forms of social control if they soothe their anxieties and insecurities about crime (Signorielli, 1990). Public demands for visible police patrols may further reflect a lack of faith in the bureaucratization of the police service. In 1990 a report was published that looked at the weakening in public confidence in the police and at Home Office plans to impose new efficiency targets. The Operational Policing Review was commissioned by the police and it was essentially designed to consider the fundamental tension that was – and still remains – at the heart of the relationship between the police and the public whom they serve, namely that the police are chasing the elusive goals of economy and efficiency, while the public are demanding more community policing, which is costly and inefficient.

The role of the police

One aspect of the Operational Policing Review was that both individual police officers and members of the public were asked to choose between two mediated ideals: a *Dixon of Dock Green* character called PC Jones, who spent most of his time working with local people in communities to prevent and solve crime, and a PC Smith who was at the time characterized as a *Sweeney* style cop but would be more familiar to us now as Gene Hunt from *Life on Mars* and *Ashes to Ashes*, who believed in the strong arm of the law and spent his time chasing round in fast cars arresting major criminals. It hardly needs revealing that the public favoured PC Jones, while the officers preferred to see themselves in the mould of PC Smith. But the fact that the researchers used readily-identifiable television characters to assess attitudes towards the police is interesting, if not surprising. The police are by far the most widely covered profession on television in both factual and fictional representations, and many senior police officers are aware that fictionalized media representations of the police go beyond mere entertainment. In an age when the police have been accused of institutional racism, incompetent murder investigations and recurring corruption, dramatic portrayals of police work, and of the nature of crime and criminal justice, perform an important symbolic function and help to perpetuate a 'mythology of policing' (Manning, 1997).

For this reason, it is worth just briefly considering the role of *Dixon of Dock Green*. In recent years a surfeit of studies about media representations of the police have emerged and, for that reason, a detailed chronological analysis of media images of policing is not included here (although see suggestions for further reading at the end of this chapter). Instead, the focus will remain on the responses of public and police to mediated representations of *police* generally and the extent to which media portrayals inform perceptions of the police and produce a sense of public *legitimacy* for the institution of *policing*. But Dixon is worth mentioning on two accounts. The first is that he played a key role in shaping cultural perceptions of policing in the mid- to late-20th century and remains a looming presence in the British psyche. He first appeared in *The Blue Lamp* in 1950, an Ealing film that spawned the 20-year-long series *Dixon of Dock Green* (1955–76) on BBC1. Since that time the police have been a source of endless fascination for television producers and public alike and the ghost of Dixon continues to overshadow debates about public attitudes towards the police. In fact, despite not being a regular presence on our screens for 40 years, he is still constantly evoked by politicians, the media and the police themselves. Yet, public trust and confidence in the police is, and arguably always has been, very fragile and there has *never* been a time when the police have been universally loved and respected, nor a time when the police have conformed to the gentle, benevolent, 'firm but fair' characterization that George Dixon embodied.

The Blue Lamp, and the television series it inspired, were explicitly produced as extended tributes to the Metropolitan force and were made with their co-operation at a time when the police were feared to be losing public confidence and respect (Reiner, 2000). In fact, *The Blue Lamp* tells us much about post-war attitudes to crime, criminals and the police (anticipating our discussion in the next chapter on film) and illustrates many of the themes already discussed in this book. The remnants of mass society theory, anxieties about brash and immoral 'teenagers', fears about certain types of crime, namely juvenile crime and offences committed by armed gangs, and a desire to seek moral certainty in figures of authority, are all to be found in this black-and-white cinematic classic. Released at a time of heightened public anxieties over juvenile delinquency following the disruption of war, the loss of fathers, a relaxing of moral standards and so on, the film is a conventional morality tale of good versus evil. PC Dixon is portrayed as a kindly, avuncular figure who takes his role of keeping the public safe from harm very seriously. However, he lasts only 20 minutes into the film, dying after being shot during an armed robbery at a cinema by a baby-faced petty criminal played by Dirk Bogarde. The shock waves created by the depiction of the violent death of a policeman at the hands of an adolescent tearaway are hard to comprehend half a century on, but the shooting of Dixon had a wider resonance as a representation of the death of order. In other words, this plot device was entirely consistent with moral panics about youth and change in the rapidly moving society of the late 1950s (see Chapter 3). Young delinquents were regarded as a new breed of criminal who, according to a voice-over narration, lacked 'the code, experience and self-discipline of the professional thief'. They were from 'broken homes', 'a class apart' and 'all the more dangerous for their immaturity' – so unstable that they were even rejected by the established criminal underworld. Even the fact that the murder of PC Dixon takes place in a cinema is significant. In the film, cinema is contrasted with a nostalgic reference to music hall, a more traditional form of popular culture. We see a young couple on a date, quarrelling as they leave – hence the impression is reinforced that it is an appropriate place for the young delinquent with all his connotations of sex and violence (Geraghty, n.d.). Following the shooting, the film becomes a conventional thriller as the police pursue the feckless young villain. The audience witness Bogarde's character descending into a morass of fear and paranoia until finally he takes refuge in a greyhound stadium. The tacit understanding between the police and the criminal underworld (the decent, respectable, 'gentleman' crooks) works to track him down and together they corner him. The crowd (signifying 'the community'), who have gathered at the stadium, then close in on him and sweep him up into arms of the police, symbolically communicating society's intolerance of young offenders and their commitment to delivering criminals up to the law.

The television series *Dixon of Dock Green* continued the cosy, paternalistic and highly idealized view of the police that was established in *The Blue Lamp*, but by the time it was decommissioned in 1976 the age of innocence portrayed by Dixon was looking even more incongruous and irrelevant than it had 20 years earlier. Policing had become increasingly politicized, crime rates were rising and public concerns were escalating in the wake of a number of high-profile crimes involving notorious villains, widely publicized escapes from prisons, and the abolition of the death penalty. Within this context police series became more realistic and hard-hitting and there began a procession of police officers who were portrayed not as gentlemen or heroes, but as ordinary people doing a difficult job. From *Z Cars* (BBC, 1962–78) through *The Sweeney* (ITV, 1974–78) to *The Bill* (ITV, 1984–2010), the police have been depicted on British television with all the human flaws and vices that any other section of the population would have. Once again, the *BBC* series *Life on Mars* and *Ashes to Ashes* (first broadcast in 2006), comic-dramas about policing in the 1970s and 1980s respectively, have succeeded in exposing these flaws and vices in an honest, if arguably caricatured way. Meanwhile, shows ranging from *Juliet Bravo* (first shown in 1980) and *Heartbeat* (1979) to *Prime Suspect* (1991) and

Between the Lines (1992) have offered diverse and sometimes contradictory images of policing. Officers have variously been portrayed as caring, controlling, corrupting and corrupted (Reiner, 2000; Leishman and Mason, 2003). In contemporary police dramas more divergent and previously neglected 'types' of officers have been introduced, including high-ranking female and ethnic minority officers and openly gay officers (ironically, such 'minority' groups are probably more represented in police dramas than in real-life policing). The discourse of equal opportunities can thus be seen to operate in both fictional representations and real policing, even if much progress is still to be made in both domains (O'Leary, 2003).

Interestingly, the politically incorrect (though ironically so) *Life on Mars* probably generated more public debate about the nature of policing than any other cultural form since *Dixon*. Based on the implausible premise of a police officer from the 21st century (DCI Sam Tyler, played by John Simm) being transported back in time to 1970s Manchester and partnered with an unreconstructed throwback from the *Sweeney*, DCI Gene Hunt (played by Phillip Glenister), the series is a postmodern pastiche that pits the methods and morals of contemporary policing against those of 1970s crime fighting – and it is 'the Gene Genie's' world that ultimately appears to win the contest (Leishman, 2008). The statement by a former Chief Constable that in Dixon's era the police force, far from being benevolent and cosy was 'brutal, authoritarian and corrupt' (Hellawell, 2002: 40) is brought to life in *Life on Mars*. However, in addition to reminding us about some of the problems with 1970s law enforcement, *Life on Mars* also highlights the politically correct, performance-driven, paperwork-saturated and intelligence-led service of the 21st century; a scenario that DCI Tyler ultimately rejected to return to the more colourful and intuitive policing environment of the 1970s.

Throughout the last four decades the police have also become increasingly visible in the factual news media, and dramatic portrayals of the police have to some extent reflected 'real life' events (many of which have been 'negative' in essence). Significant milestones in the recent, mediated history of the police – many of which were referenced in *Life on Mars* and *Ashes to Ashes* – include stories of police corruption (most notoriously within the West Midlands Serious Crime Squad in the 1970s, which resulted in the wrongful conviction of the 'Birmingham Six'); the inner city riots of the early 1980s, which led to a transformation in public order policing from inexperienced officers trying to protect themselves with dustbin lids to trained and 'tooled up' professionals – dubbed 'Robocops' by the media; the bungled investigation of the Yorkshire Ripper case, during which the police were led up a blind alley by a hoaxer with a north-east accent; the murder of WPC Yvonne Fletcher at the Libyan Embassy in London in 1984; the Miners' Strike of 1984 in which the police were involved in bloody clashes and mocked as 'Maggie's boys' by miners protesting at the closure of their pits by a government led by Margaret

Thatcher; and the inquiry into the death of black teenager, Stephen Lawrence in 1999, in which the Met were found to be 'institutionally racist'.

There has been very little research on the extent to which media representations inform public opinions about the police, and even less about the impact that media have on the police. For example, Leishman and Mason (2003: 21) note that a 'question rarely asked ... concerns the "effects" that media images may have on the police themselves', but they do not develop this point or draw any conclusions themselves. In a small-scale study involving interviews with 12 serving police officers, Nicola O'Leary found that positive and negative media images of the police were influential in their decisions to join the police service. The younger, male officers talked of their 'positive' expectations of the police based on their mediated perceptions of excitement, glamour and car chases, while the older males remembered (with a rose-tinted hue) joining a *Dixon of Dock Green* style force in which their colleagues were men of pride and principle. Perhaps most surprisingly, the two female officers interviewed cited negative media portrayals as reasons for joining the police. Following damaging portrayals in documentaries which showed police officers in a poor light (for example, as racist), they decided that the service needed people, like them, 'joining with the right attitude' (O'Leary, 2003: 31).

This research is undeniably limited in scope – largely because the researcher (a postgraduate student) faced difficulties in access when she told her target police force the subject matter on which she wished to interview respondents; an indication of the sensitivity felt by the police regarding media representations of their work, even three months prior to the transmission of the infamous BBC documentary uncovering racism among recruits. It cannot, therefore, be said to be conclusive in its findings. However, the study does raise important questions about the symbiotic relationship between police and media. The younger officers interviewed cited fictional portrayals of the police which they enjoyed; in line with previous studies, O'Leary found that *The Bill* is still viewed as one of the most accurate reflections of police work although their perception is somewhat undermined by Mason's (1992) finding that the detection rate at Sun Hill Police Station was 78 per cent; more than double the real average for England and Wales which, at the time was 34 per cent. Generally, O'Leary found that her respondents were dismissive of factual representations and were suspicious of the motives of journalists. Young male officers hinted at a combative relationship between themselves and the media, viewing their own role as that of 'gatekeepers', preventing the media from getting 'what they want'. They also saw themselves as 'easy targets' for a critical and scandal hunting media in contrast to 'the criminals who don't have to play by the same rules' (O'Leary, 2003: 33; cf. Graef, 1989; Reiner, 2000). Senior officers were more positive in their views, regarding the relationship as one of interdependency, mutual benefits and 'trust' rather than 'power'. They were more inclined to talk of the media as an effective tool to be used by the police (O'Leary, 2003: 33).

Over the decade since this research was conducted, police forces around the world have seen their relationship with traditional media change somewhat. They have also embraced mobile and social media as effective tools in image management, as well as in tactical responses to crime and investigation, as the following section will describe.

The role of mobile and social media in policing

Tactical responses to crime and investigation

The use of mobile and social media in crime investigations covers many aspects of police work. Most obviously, platforms like Facebook and Twitter are helpful in publicizing details of a case and responsibilizing the public, for example in circumstances where someone has gone missing and their description, photo and last known whereabouts can be shared or re-tweeted (Lee and McGovern, 2014). Facebook has even developed a tool to assist law enforcement agencies to harness their potential in social media, 'Building your presence with Facebook Pages: A Guide for Police Departments' https:// developers.facebook.com/attachment/PagesGuide_Police.pdf. In addition, social media platforms are used for: alerting people to crimes or crime waves that may be ongoing; for disseminating details of crime prevention pro- grammes; monitoring suspects; gathering intelligence; obtaining information for tactical purposes about threats of mob violence, riots, or isolated criminal activity during otherwise lawful gatherings and demonstrations; identifying associates and acquaintances affiliated with persons of interest; understand- ing criminal networks; gleaning information to back up application for a search warrant; and liaising with police colleagues in different forces and jurisdictions. To take a few examples highlighted by a report in the US com- missioned by Lexis Nexis (2012), YouTube aided police in an investigation into the recruitment of gang members and promotion of gang violence, with a video that had known gang members rapping about shooting named offic- ers, which allowed the suspects to be identified, located and arrested; while sites like Facebook are frequently used by offenders to brag about their criminal exploits. In one case, an officer says that he requested a suspected drugs offender as a 'friend' from a fictitious profile, which was accepted. The officer reports: 'he kept "checking in" everywhere he went so I was able to track him down very easily' (2012: 14).

Meanwhile, a branch of the US Department of Justice that has come up with a name that enables itself to be known by the acronym COPS (Community Oriented Policing Services) has produced a joint report with the Police

Executive Research Forum (PERF) on policing and social media in the US, Canada and the UK. Summing up one of the most salient applications of social media, the report notes:

> Social media has now given protesters the ability to informally and very quickly organize and communicate with each other in real time. Police must know how to monitor these types of communications in order to gauge the mood of a crowd, assess whether threats of criminal activity are developing, and stay apprised of any plans by large groups of people to move to other locations.
>
> Similarly, in the aftermath of an incident of mob violence, police can 'mine' social networking sites to identify victims, witnesses, and perpetrators. Witnesses to crime—and even perpetrators—often post photographs, videos, and other information about an incident that can be used as investigative leads or evidence. (2013: 1)

The report also notes something that Boston police and the FBI may have felt when investigating the 2013 marathon bombings, discussed in the Introduction to this volume: that the strategic challenges of monitoring social networks and transforming huge amounts of data into actionable intelligence is a daunting task for police agencies, with one one official describing it as 'like trying to take a sip from a fire hydrant' (ibid.).

Image management

In addition to being harnessed as a 'push' mechanism to facilitate the solving of crimes, as described above, social media are also now embraced by police forces to facilitate dialogue between the public and the police, to 'demystify' the work they do and to try and increase their popularity (Lee and McGovern, 2014). Of course, the police are supported by a raft of employees including press officers, marketing professionals, public relations officers and corporate identity specialists, all engaged in the business of 'image work' on behalf of the police (Mawby, 2002). As Lee and McGovern (2014) highlight, the police press release has become a powerful tool for communicating the service's preferred message, while making it easier for journalists to write audience-satisfying stories about crime and policing. But when combined with the complex mix of 'traditional' mediums and social media platforms now at their disposal, the police are succeeding in managing their image in such a way that frequently bypasses journalists altogether. However, according to Mawby, while the police are under pressure to communicate openly with diverse communities, there is a danger that 'image work' can also be deployed for improper motives; for example, *misrepresentation* to mask malpractice, deflect responsibility or simply to protect themselves from outside scrutiny (Mawby, 2002;

2010). In support of this, Green (2009) criticizes some police forces in the UK for over-controlling their publicity machines and diverting attention from cases that represent negative public relations. Green claims that serious crimes such as sexual assaults and stabbings are sometimes selectively communicated in police press releases, or not communicated at all, in order that they do not get reported in the media and create an unfavourable impression of policing.

Notwithstanding such accusations, it is not surprising that the police have seized on new communications tools in the pursuit of legitimacy, as well as efficiency and control of image (Lee and McGovern, 2014). However, it is still arguably the case that PR success stories remain buried on local forces' websites and Twitter feeds, while their PR disasters go viral and make national and international news. For example, the Metropolitan Police's image management strategy came to the fore when a man died during G20 protests in London in 2009. The Met came in for criticism for issuing a press release suggesting that 47-year-old Ian Tomlinson had died of a heart attack as he walked home from the protest. The statement failed to include a vital part of the picture, which was that Mr Tomlinson had been struck and pushed to the ground by a police officer. As a result, there were six days of substantially false media coverage about the incident which the Met failed to contradict. It was only the evidence of ordinary people with mobile phone/camera footage of the protest that led to questions about the police's version of events and it later emerged that the press release had been the subject of intense argument in the police press bureau, with an earlier draft having been rejected (Davies, 2009).

The crucial role that mobile media and CCTV can play in cases where police accounts and the testimony of witnesses contradict each other is frequently underlined when these media technologies are absent. On 4 August 2011, officers of the Specialist Firearms Command Unit of the Metropolitan Police stopped a minicab, containing a passenger, 29-year-old Mark Duggan, who tried to run from the scene. Police shot him twice and he died. The actual events that unfolded in these few minutes are complex, disputed and subject to highly contradictory versions and interpretations (but see http://www.the-guardian.com/uk-news/2014/jan/08/mark-duggan-death-london-riots for a useful overview and LSE's *Reading the Riots*; eprints.lse.ac.uk). Without CCTV footage or mobile phone images, the actual sequence of events can never be known for sure and, despite hearing from a witness that Mark Duggan was not holding a gun, as the officers had thought, but a mobile phone, and that when he tried to run away, he was shot by an officer within five to seven steps of him – despite appearing 'trapped', 'baffled' and holding his arms up as if to surrender – the jury decided that the killing was 'lawful' (http://m.bbc.co.uk/news/uk-england-london-25321711). Despite this verdict, revelations of highly controversial decisions by the Met and the Independent Police Complaints Commission (IPCC), which investigates police shootings, severely damaged public confidence. The *Guardian* quotes one 'informed Met source': 'It was death by a thousand fuckups' (http://www.theguardian.com/uk-news/2014/jan/08/mark-duggan-death-london-riots). As a result of the poor policing decisions, which included the driving away of the taxi (thus compromising or destroying valuable forensic evidence), there was anger and frustration among sections of the community in Tottenham and, two days after the killing, riots began on the streets of London which then spread to many other cities, constituting the worst civil unrest in a generation.

These tragic cases support the view that the police may be giving an impression of democratic accountable policing, while simultaneously sustaining the restricted interests of the police service (Mawby, 2002). It could even be said that the main lesson learned by police in the wake of the milestone events mentioned above is that they must exert greater control over the conditions where brutality or failure occurs, an argument put by Monahan (2006) in response to the LA police beating of Rodney King. Nevertheless, the language of 'openness' remains embedded in police image work and police forces espouse 'open' communications and transparency as they seek to secure public 'trust' and 'confidence'. But the police service is unlikely to be grateful for the emergence of citizen journalism and is responding with more informal communication strategies of its own. ACPO (Association of Chief Police Officers) rhetoric continues to suggest that the police are very happy to allow the media and the wider public to be informed about their work, but the fact that the police are increasingly sidestepping traditional media altogether and communicating directly with the public via blogs, Twitter and the like, suggests otherwise (Mawby, 2010). And while the police may publicly congratulate themselves on their openness and accountability, they regularly seem to fall foul of outside attempts to highlight their ongoing, internal, structural deficiencies.

In October 2003 a documentary broadcast on BBC1, *The Secret Policeman*, proved to be a public relations disaster for the police service. The programme showed the results of secret filming by an undercover journalist posing as a trainee police officer over a period of seven months at a national police training centre. In an eerie echo of a simulated racist attack by the young men suspected of murdering Stephen Lawrence (also filmed covertly), rookie police officers were shown voicing extreme racist opinions, and one was seen wearing a makeshift Ku Klux Klan hood. The police's PR nightmare began a month before transmission when a senior civil servant in the Home Office wrote to the BBC chairman accusing the corporation of deceit and demanding that they withdraw the programme from the schedules (*Observer*, 26 October 2003). Subsequently, in the days before the broadcast, the Chief Constable of Greater Manchester Police (GMP), one of the forces concerned, and the Home Office, issued defiant statements, criticizing the BBC for its methods and for going ahead with the broadcast. The day after the broadcast, however, senior officers and the Home Secretary were competing for media airtime in which to condemn the officers filmed, perhaps having had time to ingest the horror and revulsion felt by many viewers at the scenes they had witnessed. Among the most surprising aspects of the exposé was that racial awareness training for new recruits appeared to consist of them being told the *four* racially offensive words they must not use!

To this extent, while superficially the programme might be interpreted as reinforcing the notion of a 'few bad apples', it actually hinted at more disturbing, widespread, structural problems at the heart of the police. This impression was not helped by Chief Constable Mike Todd, who threatened the BBC with a 'Hutton-style inquiry' if the programme went ahead. Perhaps unsurprisingly, given the BBC's revelations, police forces have started 'cyber-vetting' potential employees; that is, evaluating job candidates' online presence and reputation before shortlisting them. As the aforementioned report by COPS (2013) states, candidates may be deemed unsuitable if they have posted comments or other content on social media sites that is perceived as damaging to the trust that a police department must earn with the public. For example, obscene, racist, or reckless comments made by a job candidate on Facebook or Twitter can disqualify candidates or raise serious questions about their judgement and character. Establishing and maintaining a sense of legitimacy is central to a police service's role in any democracy as the following discussion about *Crimewatch UK* will further underline. Fifteen years ago Richard Osborne wrote: 'The fear of crime is greater than the fear of an inadequate police force and as long as the police can win the media war through programmes like *Crimewatch UK* their control of the news flow is guaranteed' (1995: 39). Ironic, then, that in his efforts to get *The Secret Policeman* withdrawn, Chief Constable Todd's most petulant shot across the bows was the threat that the police would withdraw their co-operation from the BBC's *Crimewatch UK* (*Observer*, 26 October 2003).

Crimewatch UK

The threat of the police retracting their support for *Crimewatch UK* was deemed significantly shocking to make headline news in the week following the transmission of *The Secret Policeman*, attesting to the place of *Crimewatch* in the television establishment and in the cultural identity of Britain. Still – after 30 years of transmission – pulling in audience shares of 17–18 per cent (around 4 million viewers), the show uses both dramatic reconstructions and surveillance footage of crimes to try to gain information from the public. *Crimewatch* is frequently singled out as being a significant contributor to false ideas about offending and victimization, and its format adheres closely to the 'news values' (discussed in Chapter 2) which skew public ideas about crime.

This final section of this chapter will explore this proposition, paying particular attention to the programme's constructions of offenders, victims and the police.

Crimewatch UK was one of the forerunners of 'reality television' and although shot conventionally in a television studio, was one of the first television programmes to include dramatic reconstructions of crimes and footage from CCTV, and also among the first to rely on audience participation. The series, which is broadcast monthly for 10 months of the year, began on BBC1 in 1984, a time of increasing political focus on issues of law and order, and mounting public concern that victims of crime were getting a raw deal (Schlesinger and Tumber, 1994). *Crimewatch* itself became the subject of media attention when, in 1999, its presenter, Jill Dando, was violently murdered on the doorstep of her home. The show's producers took a concept that already existed in the form of *Police Five* (an ITV show that ran from 1962–90) and added the 'magic ingredient' of audience participation (Schlesinger and Tumber, 1994: 253). They looked to the phenomenally successful *America's Most Wanted* but rejected the overt dramatization favoured in this show, where reconstructions of crimes were filmed in slow motion and accompanied by dramatic music in order to heighten viewers' sense of suspense and excitement. They also studied the German programme *Aktenzeichen XY ... Ungelost* (*Case XY ... Unsolved*), which had already been running for 17 years, but decided against the German method of filming reconstructions from the perspective of the offender, especially in relation to sexual offences such as rape (1994: 253).

The formula of *Crimewatch UK* has remained virtually unaltered since it first aired in 1984. There are three or four reconstructions, usually of very serious crimes such as murder, armed robbery or rape; a segment which reveals CCTV footage of offenders with an appeal to anyone who can identify them to come forward; photographs of suspects whose names are known, but whose whereabouts are not; and updates on cases previously featured – a device that has the three-fold purposes of congratulating the audience for helping to secure convictions, making them feel absolutely integral to the show, and further giving the (inaccurate) impression that *Crimewatch* is largely responsible for solving serious crimes in the UK. There have been only three significant changes in content since the first broadcast nearly three decades ago. First, the show has come to rely increasingly on CCTV footage, which is more common and of better quality than was the case in the 1980s. Accordingly, stills and moving images from CCTV cameras form a much greater part of each programme, sometimes being used to supplement dramatic reconstructions of a crime, as well as being used as free-standing items in other sections of the show. The second major new innovation is in DNA testing, which has enabled the police to reopen old files and work with the producers of *Crimewatch UK* in reconstructing cases that might otherwise have been consigned to history.

Reconstructions of crimes from the 1960s and 1970s have added an interesting new element to the programme, requiring *Crimewatch* researchers to reflect the period in which the offence occurred with authentic cars, fashions and hairstyles, which also have the benefit of appealing to audiences through discourses of memory, nostalgia and loss. The third innovation since the very earliest days is that the programme is now supported by a website (http://www.bbc.co.uk/crimewatch/) which carries details of the cases covered and facilitates audience response. Otherwise, the only variations in the programme's content have reflected commensurate changes in patterns of offending, with decreasing numbers of armed robberies on banks and building societies featured and an increase in appeals for information about terrorists and paedophiles.

Dramatized reconstructions are the trademark of *Crimewatch UK* and are the elements that have drawn most vehement criticism. The writing and filming of crime reconstructions are governed by guidelines intended to guard against them being used to attract, entertain or disturb audiences and to minimize the potential distress caused to victims of crime and their relatives. As we shall see through the remainder of this chapter, these guidelines are interpreted somewhat loosely by the producers of *Crimewatch UK*. The tension between information and entertainment that lies at the heart of *Crimewatch*'s audience appeal is a source of anguish for the programme's producers – or so they claim. Angela Holdsworth, former editor of the show, says that crime is kept in context:

> We don't only focus on violent crime, but we are trying to help the police catch the more serious criminals, and a lot of serious crime involves violence. We agonise over everything we put in. We don't choose items for their entertainment value. But clearly we couldn't do something where television wouldn't help, where there's nothing to film. A journalistic sense must come into it.
> (*Guardian*, 3 September 1990)

But it is precisely this 'journalistic sense' that concerns many. Schlesinger and Tumber reflect on the fine line between documentary and drama that the programme makers have to tread, and the remarks of the show's original producer, Peter Chafer, that the emphasis is firmly on the former rather than the latter are arguably not as true in 2010 as they were in 1984 (Schlesinger and Tumber, 1994). For example, in an episode broadcast in October 2003, a reconstruction of what is described in the voice-over as an 'unprovoked ambush on a woman which could easily have killed her' starts with the sound of high-pitched screams which are then revealed to emanate from a group of women enjoying a hen party at a house in Blackpool, but a grisly impression has already been conveyed and the audience's appetite for vicarious violence has been whetted. As Sparks (1992: 156) notes, it is no coincidence that these 'crime scarers' employ the 'same syntax of depiction, narration and editing as crime fictions do', and excitement, suspense and fear are the intended objectives of these techniques. In fact, it could be argued that the success of *Crimewatch* is dependent on its very capacity to frighten its audience and to give them a visceral thrill as they watch a serious crime unfolding.

Although intentionally dramatic, the crime reconstructions are defended by the programme makers and the BBC on public service grounds. Schlesinger and Tumber (1994) observe that, by featuring human-interest-based tales of misfortune, *Crimewatch UK* has much in common with the popular press, and indeed nearly all the crimes selected will conform to journalistic news values. Like the popular media more generally, then, *Crimewatch* prioritizes crimes of violence and may amplify public fears that crime is spontaneous, random and indiscriminate. One of the unfortunate consequences of a television programme that relies on audience ratings, not only for its commercial success, but also to justify its self-proclaimed role in the business of crime detection, is that the producers actively seek out stories that will capture the public imagination and prick the consciences of any potential informants sufficiently to encourage them to pass on information. According to the Executive Producer in charge of BBC crime programmes (cited in Weaver, 1998), this justifies their steadfast adherence to a tried-and-tested formula that concentrates on the most violent and serious crimes, such as murder and rape, perpetrated on the most vulnerable victims; young women, girls and elderly women.

The preoccupation with danger, risk, fear, reassurance and retribution which underpins the reconstructed cases on *Crimewatch UK*, and the pleasure with which those emotions are experienced by the audience, inevitably raises ethical questions regarding victims' rights and the feelings of bereaved families. Actors' dialogue is frequently used to convey a sense of reality and encourage the viewing public to empathize with the victim, but it might be construed as titillating and taking unnecessary liberties with the truth. The BBC is a public service broadcasting company, but it still operates in a commercial environment and must produce attention-grabbing television in order to attract audiences. Barry Irving, then Director of the Police Foundation, alluded to this tension when he remarked:

> A show like Crimewatch is too attractive to programme makers to be evaluated properly. It has everything. It panders to the British taste for a modicum of violence and nefarious activity, it's cheap to make, it promotes a whizz-bang action view of the police and encourages viewer participation. And over it all is a halo, because it is so evidently A Good Thing (*Guardian*, 3 September 1990).

Crimewatch UK is also viewed as A Good Thing because it has become a flagship for the BBC; an integral part of the broadcasting establishment, snuggling alongside *The Antiques Roadshow* and *Eastenders* in terms of longevity and audience familiarity. The possibility that it could start to be seen as 'cosy' and 'safe' may have encouraged its producers to 'up the ante' with increasing use of ploys designed to encourage viewers' inquisitiveness and maximize their loyalty. One favourite tactic to try and keep viewers watching this thirty-year-old programme is to include 'new' information about ongoing, unsolved but highly newsworthy crimes. For instance, in 2014, both the Madeleine McCann inquiry and the ongoing investigation into the disappearance of York University chef, Claudia Lawrence, have been featured on *Crimewatch*, seven years and five years respectively after they went missing. On the days following each broadcast, the new revelations brought to us by the *Crimewatch* team were, themselves, headline news items (e.g. 'Claudia Lawrence: Crimewatch appeal leads to "hugely significant" lead in hunt for missing chef', *Mirror*, 20 March 2014.

Crimewatching victims

Another innovation is the use of home video footage, showing the victim in 'happier times'. Like all photographic images, video footage speaks of a moment frozen in time, but may be all the more compelling because – to borrow a phrase from Paul Willis (1982: 78) it gives us 'real, solid, warm, *moving*, and *acting* bodies in actual situations'. Moving images of murder victims in the prime of life, smiling, laughing, fooling around for the camera, are a particularly poignant reminder of the fragility of life. A common device used to convey the wider impact of fatal crimes is the 'triangulation' of presenter, victim and victim's close relative (Jermyn, 2003: 185). In an openly emotional interview a bereaved partner or parent will be interviewed in the studio with a large photograph of the victim positioned in the background, between them. As the interview progresses the camera cuts back several times to a close up on the image of the victim, while the presenter describes them as primarily a good wife and mother, or loving son and father. Victims are seen at weddings, birthday parties, on holidays and at graduation ceremonies – all quintessentially 'family' occasions. By allowing us into aspects of a life usually kept private, *Crimewatch* invites us not only to relate to the victim and their family, but also to imagine ourselves in their tragic circumstances. The privileging of familial ties also underlines the conservative ideological framework that is at the heart of assumptions about a case's 'newsworthiness' and reinforces cultural stereotypes about 'deserving' and 'undeserving' victims (see Chapter 2). As Jermyn states: 'It is difficult to imagine a *Crimewatch* victim outside of the parameters of the family: to not be in a family would be to not be a proper victim' (2003: 185).

However, even 'deserving' victims who are portrayed within a loving family context are also open to censure, which implies that they were partly to blame for their victimization. In cases of sexually motivated murders of young women – one of the most commonly featured crimes on the programme despite its relative infrequency in real life – there is often implicit criticism of the victim's behaviour in both the reconstruction and narration by the studio presenter. Furthermore, despite strenuous claims to the contrary by those responsible for making the programme, the reconstructed crimes are frequently presented in a graphic and sensationalized manner, and female victims are sexualized unnecessarily. C. K. Weaver (1998) describes in detail one *Crimewatch* reconstruction of the sexual assault and murder of a 17-year-old female hitchhiker in which the victim, played by an actor, is shown lying on a sunbed at a friend's house in her underwear. Its invitation to voyeurism is reinforced by the fact that the frame is shot from above with the viewer's gaze bearing down on her. The scene has no relevance to the case and does not in any sense move the plot forward, yet is pivotal in conveying to the audience an impression of the victim. Allusions to the girl's culpability in her violent end are made throughout the reconstruction: she refused a lift home from her mother, failed to contact her boyfriend who spent the evening searching for her on his motorbike, resorted to hitchhiking home from her friend's house after dark and accepted a lift from a stranger in a van. All these examples of her recklessness are crystallized in the scene where she lies on the sunbed in her bra and pants, giggling with her friend. Here we see connections graphically made between feminine vanity, the desire for an attractive body to solicit attention on her forthcoming beach holiday, and risk-taking behaviour as the audience already knows that she met her death when she left her friend without arranging transport home (Weaver, 1998).

According to Kidd-Hewitt (1995), *Crimewatch* is guilty of locking certain sections of the audience into a terrorizing world of fear reinforcement, a belief supported by Weaver who conducted focus group interviews with women who were shown the reconstruction of the hitchhiker's murder. A common response was that taking a lift in a car may have been preferable to walking all the way home in the dark – the 'lesser of two evils', as one participant put it (Weaver, 1998: 256). Respondents also praised the reconstruction for raising awareness of the dangers facing women who go out alone in the evening, and even the sunbed scene was endorsed by some who felt that its 'watch and beware' tone justified its titillating nature. Although Weaver's study illustrates the polysemic nature of media texts with several different, and often competing, interpretations of the reconstruction being offered by her interviewees, the overwhelming response from the women interviewed is an unproblematic acceptance of *Crimewatch*'s warning to other women against hitchhiking. Most welcomed the 'public service' element of the show and ingested the programme's implicit criticism of the victim for engaging in irresponsible behaviour. Few questioned the belief that it is women's individual responsibility to restrict and censure their behaviour in order to avoid being the victim of crime, and none criticized *Crimewatch* for failing to provide any alternative means of imagining how violent attacks on women could be prevented. Weaver concludes that her interviewees' unquestioning absorption of this gendered narrative suggests that women accept that they must live in fear and can never expect to achieve the personal freedom and independence of men (Weaver, 1998: 262).

The extent to which *Crimewatch UK* amplifies fear among its viewers – especially those least likely to be victims of serious crimes – has been a central theme of both media studies and criminology literature on the subject. Schlesinger and Tumber (1994) note that research carried out by the Independent Broadcasting Authority found that one in three viewers thought that *Crimewatch* had made them, and probably other viewers, feel more afraid of being a potential victim of crime. The BBC's own research claimed that fear was largely confined to female viewers, especially those living alone. A particularly unfortunate monologue by then presenter Nick Ross in the March 2003 broadcast followed the reconstruction of the sexually motivated murder of 17-year-old 'A'-Level student, Hannah Foster:

> Murders of young women like Hannah make headline news for the very reason that they're pretty unusual. Two-thirds of Britain's murder victims are male and six times more people are killed each year in road accidents than in homicides. But of course there is something especially upsetting about the murders of women and these are the appeals that tend to get the biggest response from Crimewatch viewers.

Ross then proceeds to give updates on four similar yet unconnected murder cases, all of which occurred in the capital or surrounding area within a 12-month period. Despite apparently trying to reassure viewers, Ross's decision to then bring together reports on five young women murdered by strangers in unconnected, unprovoked, seemingly motiveless attacks, created the impression of a terrifying crime wave and made his cheery advice at the end of the show – 'Don't have nightmares, do sleep well!' – seem rather hollow. Furthermore, by its very nature, *Crimewatch UK* may amplify audience fears because it only reconstructs crimes that are unsolved; crimes, in fact, where the police have no significant leads and have reached the end of an investigative cul-de-sac. Hence, the viewer is denied a sense of closure – the murderer/rapist/ thief is still 'out there' and ready to strike again.

Crimewatching offenders

A further problem that has been identified in relation to *Crimewatch UK*, and one which it shares with the media more widely, is that it may generate fear of, or hostility towards, particular groups such as people from ethnic minorities. *Crimewatch* tends to over-represent crimes involving black offenders and under-represent black victims, especially males in both categories. For example, of the six 'Wanted faces' featured in March 2014, five were black men (www.bbc.co.uk/programmes/b006ppmq/profiles/wanted-currentyear). The programme also frequently fails to distinguish between different ethnic and national groups, homogenizing offenders' 'otherness' with phrases like 'North African appearance', 'Mediterranean appearance' or 'Kosovan appearance'.

Female 'serious' offenders are rarely included and women more commonly feature as perpetrators of fraud and other financial crimes.

While victims are firmly located within family structures and are thus 'legit-imized' as innocent and undeserving casualties, the same contextualization is never extended to offenders (Jermyn, 2003). Constructions of offenders are the antithesis to those of victims. While victims are shown within their family contexts, affirming their 'normality' and 'typicality', offenders are invariably anonymous, constructed as individuals and existing in isolation of social and familial ties. Because *Crimewatch* can show only cases where there are no sig-nificant leads or suspects (for fear of prejudicing a trial), the offender is frequently not seen in the reconstruction at all, or may be represented only symbolically as a figure in extreme long-shot, either walking or running near the scene of the crime or as a shadowy figure at the wheel of a vehicle. These representations-from-a-distance reinforce the impression of the offender as 'outsider' with no ties to domesticity or 'normality'. This is an important point in relation to public constructions of criminals, and contrasts with other televi-sion genres where knowledge about the background of offenders and the context of their crimes, elicits a very different response. For example, Gillespie and McLaughlin (2002) conducted a study which showed that, in group discus-sions of media narratives, respondents displayed shifts in opinion regarding offenders depending on what television genre was being discussed. In conver-sations about soap operas the overtly punitive opinions that many had previously expressed about offenders were challenged, and ultimately reconfig-ured, in line with what they 'knew' about the character. In accordance with early media studies which proposed that media content had a more significant impact on audience members if they could, in some way 'identify' with the character being portrayed, Gillespie and McLaughlin found that where respondents could empathize with the offender on the basis of what they knew about him or her, a less punitive attitude was adopted. This 'deeper knowledge' of the background of the offender and the crime is precisely what is missing from *Crimewatch UK* where sympathy, empathy or understanding are simply not options. In presenting offenders as 'others' and their crimes as senseless and random, programmes like *Crimewatch* stimulate sentiments of revulsion and repugnance towards offenders and reinforce populist ideas about punish-ment (Gillespie and McLaughlin, 2002).

Crimewatching the police

When the police were first approached about co-operating with the show's producers they were initially suspicious of the idea. However, *Crimewatch UK* has proved to be one of the most effective public relations exercises at the police's disposal. In fact, the benefits to them in terms of the warm feelings induced by watching the police and public working together to solve crimes arguably outweighs all other benefits of the programme. This is a fact clearly understood by the police, despite the threat by Greater Manchester Chief Constable to boycott the show. The producers of *Crimewatch UK* are at pains to point out that they maintain their autonomy from the police (although ironically one of the current presenters, Rav Wilding, is himself an ex-police officer) but one of the main criticisms levelled at the programme is that they do not seek information from any other source and that the police have too much say in what gets broadcast. While this means that the production team have unique access to every detail of an investigation, and are privy to aspects of a case that may not have been revealed publicly, the flipside is that the police can determine the conditions under which knowledge is used. Each broadcast of *Crimewatch* includes around 30 police officers from all over the UK who appear on the programme in support of their respective cases. Typically, these will include senior investigating officers who will usually take part in a live interview with one of the main presenters. These personnel represent the human face of the police service and are there to inspire confidence in potential witnesses or informants to telephone the incident room. In this respect the programme is undoubtedly successful, although of the calls that come in during and after each broadcast (an average of around 1,000 according to the programme's website) only two or three may be of use.

In essence, then, editorial control is a trade-off between the police, who recognize that *Crimewatch* gives them unparalleled access to potential sources of information, and the programme makers who are in the business of entertaining their audience – however voyeuristically that might be achieved. It is the alliance between the media and the police that is the key to the programme's longevity. *Crimewatch* is a safe haven for the police: unlike other media genres they are not going to be criticized or challenged here. The success of the partnership is measured in arrests. Between 1984 and 2000, the *Crimewatch* team claimed there were 582 arrests as a direct result of the programme (cited in Leishman and Mason, 2003: 115) and they point to several 'mega-cases' that were solved after being covered on *Crimewatch*. While undoubtedly impressive, quantitative claims are impossible to substantiate: many of these arrests may have occurred anyway. Nonetheless, the programme functions as a vehicle for reinforcing the police's role as successful crime fighters and both *Crimewatch* and its spin-off *Crimewatch Solved* which, as the title indicates, reconstructs investigations that have resulted in a positive outcome and justice done, could hardly be more laudatory and less challenging in their portrayal of the police as heroic crime fighters (O'Leary, 2003).

Crimewatching crime: some concluding thoughts

It is increasingly recognized that the medium of television is situated within, and fully interwoven with, many other social practices, to the extent where crime, criminals and criminal justice cannot be separated from their representations on television (Sparks, 1992; Ferrell, 2001). While we cannot make sweeping claims about media 'effects' or the media being responsible for 'causing' fear of crime, we can look at the ways in which media in general, and television in particular, are integral to the processes of meaning making by which we make sense of our everyday lives. For example, although this chapter has deliberately avoided discussion of the many TV series concerning forensic- science-based detection, the phrase 'CSI Effect' has become commonly used to describe phenomena including jury members' expectations of criminal cases and the rising popularity of degrees in criminology! Media may also contribute to fears about crime: if, as Sparks (1992) contends, fear of crime is more likely to be governed by uncertainties than known probabilities, the issue of fear must be inextricably linked to issues of representation, interpretation and meaning. Misrepresentations concerning the extent of certain types of crime, the likelihood of victimization, and the locations in which crime commonly occurs, are bound to create a skewed picture of the 'problem of crime' in this country.

One of the central aims of the makers of *Crimewatch UK* is to vary the cases featured on the show, but the programme as a whole fails to diverge far from its tried-and-tested formula of representing a limited range of very serious crimes perpetrated against a restricted category of victims. A *Crimewatch* producer's comment that the programme strives for a mixture and balance of items – which he illustrates with the evidence that in one show they included a sexual assault and murder of a woman in Tonbridge Wells and then did a reconstruction/report into the Notting Hill rapist – is unlikely to convince many that *Crimewatch* represents a cross-section of crimes in Britain (cited in Schlesinger and Tumber, 1994: 261). To put it bluntly, incidents most likely to feature on *Crimewatch* are crimes against the person in which a high level of violence is involved, and crimes of a sexual nature, especially in cases involving young women and girls. Much less likely to be included are white-collar crimes, corporate or state crimes, and crimes in which the police have bungled the investigation. Also unlikely to be featured is any useful advice concerning crime prevention. In all these respects, *Crimewatch* reproduces the values and genre conventions of most other media, including news. Not only is the programme emblematic of wider trends in media output, adhering closely to the twelve cardinal news values outlined in Chapter 2, but it also upholds the patriarchal structures and stratifications highlighted elsewhere in this volume. These observations raise important questions about where the public service/entertainment balance lies – not only of *Crimewatch,* but also of factual news-based programming more broadly.

Summary

- The media are not solely to blame for inciting fear of crime. Actual risk of victimization, previous experience of victimization, environmental conditions, ethnicity and previous contact with the police and criminal justice system are among many factors interacting through complex mediated processes to influence public anxiety about crime. As Richard Sparks comments: 'the reception by people of media stories about crime and punishment is best grasped … in situ, in which case many public responses that are commonly deprecated by criminologists and others as "irrational" or "hysterical" tend to become substantially more intelligible' (2001: 197).
- However, the media might be said to play an important role in creating a cultural climate in which certain types of criminal behaviour are portrayed more frequently, and with greater intensity, than others. This distortion may cultivate fears among certain sections of the audience, and exaggerate their risk of victimization. Given that the British Crime Survey (now the Crime Survey for England and Wales) shows that fear of crime has an inverse relationship with statistical occurrence, the media may be partially responsible, in so far as crimes against the most 'fearful' but least likely to be victimized members of society – especially young women and elderly people – are over-reported and over-sensationalized.
- Some critics argue that, as a consequence of the media's tendency to concentrate on the most atypical crimes and present them in a sensationalistic and voyeuristic manner, women and the elderly are socialized into fear and become over-sensitized to their own roles in avoiding becoming victims of crime. Research shows that programmes like *Crimewatch* encourage women to think of themselves as potential victims and that most female viewers uncritically accept their 'at risk' status and modify their behaviour accordingly.
- The genre conventions employed by *Crimewatch UK* are very similar to those found in other media, including news and cinema. They not only result in an overwhelming emphasis on violent and sexual crimes perpetrated mostly on women (invariably constructed as 'tragic victims'), but they also serve to construct offenders and crime scenes in particular ways. Crimes featured on the show are usually committed by non-white, male strangers ('others'); in either the victim's home (a particular violation, and indicative of their vulnerability) or in public places (usually 'the streets'); which results in not just the victimization of the individual, but of their entire family who have been 'robbed' of their loved one. Like other examples discussed in this book, this structuring of events means that traditional conservative family and gender relations are endorsed and celebrated, even when the reality of sexual and violent crime suggests that the home is frequently a site of (largely masculine) violence, sexual abuse and murder. Corporate crimes are almost entirely invisible in *Crimewatch UK*, just as they are in other media genres.
- *Crimewatch UK* is also a prime example of the collaborative relationship between the police and the media. The issue of policing has increasingly come to be understood not simply in its political or social context, but as a set of semiotic practices enmeshed with mediated culture (Ferrell, 2001). 'Image work' is central to a police service that is increasingly coming to recognize that policing is as much about symbolism as it is about substance (Mawby, 2002).

- Both traditional media and 'new' social media have changed the way that the police do their work and communicate with the public. Platforms such as Facebook and Twitter have a myriad of benefits to the police, from allowing recruitment personnel to covertly check on a candidate's suitability to join the police force, through to gathering intelligence and responsibilizing the public. But as we have seen, new media have a democratizing role to play on occasions where the police (or individual officers) act inappropriately. During protest events such as demonstrations or riots, the battle to control the 'virtual' version of events on Twitter can be every bit as important as what occurs on the ground.

- Thanks to programmes like *Crimewatch*, appeals from families, crime reconstructions and interviews with senior detectives requesting help from the public are now familiar communicative formats across a range of media genres. The images and language of such communications are carefully crafted and chosen by the police in an attempt to persuade potential witnesses, offenders or people who suspect someone of the offence to come forward with their information. In this respect, we have seen a return to the kindly benevolent, consensual policing epitomized by the fictional *Dixon of Dock Green*. Unfortunately, since PC Dixon walked the beat, the relationship between the police and the media has often been characterized as difficult and mutually hostile. In recent years the police have sought to embrace and exploit the media in pursuit of a positive image and an impression of legitimacy and accountability. However, the bond of trust formed between the two institutions is still fragile, as witnessed by periodic media exposés of racism and sexism within the police service.

STUDY QUESTIONS

1. It has been said that PC George Dixon has been 'exhumed and laid to rest more times than some care to remember' (Greer, 2004). What accounts for the enduring popularity of Dixon and why is his image still evoked so long after *Dixon of Dock Green* was taken off air?

2. Lee and McGovern (2014: 213) claim that Facebook and Twitter are simply the new Neighbourhood Watch and Crimestoppers: 'traditional policing reframed... through new technologies'. Do you agree with this assessment? What can social media enable the police to do which they could not by traditional means?

3. Conduct your own analysis of an edition of *Crimewatch UK*. To what extent does it follow the conventions of news reporting (that is, 'news values') in the popular press and broadcast media? In your own experience as a viewer, does *Crimewatch* amplify fears about certain types of crime and victimization? If so, are its effects long-term and diffuse or short-term and based on geographical and cultural proximity?

4. In addition to the example of *The Secret Policeman*, there have been a number of other cases where individuals (especially celebrities) have been covertly filmed engaging in criminal and deviant behaviour, such as accepting money

to rig sporting events and dealing in, or buying, drugs. Frequently, as in the case of the BBC documentary, the individuals are set up by journalists in what amounts to entrapment. Are undercover investigation methods by journalists justified in cases where issues such as sexism, racism, corruption and crime might otherwise not be revealed?

FURTHER READING

Robert Reiner has written extensively on police and the media, including in Reiner, R. (2010) *The Politics of the Police,* 4th edition (Oxford University Press). An excellent analysis of the subject is provided by Leishman, F. and Mason, P. (2003) *Policing and the Media: Facts, Fictions and Factions* (Willan/Routledge). The classic text on policing, crime, public disorder and moral panics remains Hall, S. et al.'s (1978) *Policing the Crisis: Mugging, the State and Law and Order.* In 2013, a 35th anniversary edition was published, containing two new chapters that explore the book's continued significance, with a new Preface and Afterword, in which each of the authors takes up a specific theme from the original book and interrogate it in the light of current events and contexts. Mawby, R. (2002) *Policing Images: Policing, Communication and Legitimacy* (Willan/Routledge) was an early contribution on the 'image work' that the police now have to engage in and Lee, M. and McGovern, A. (2014) *Policing and Media: Public Relations, Simulations and Communications* (Routledge) provides an up-to-date analysis. Murray Lee has also written about *Inventing Fear of Crime: Criminology and the Politics of Anxiety* (Willan/Routledge, 2007). Given the relationship between fear of crime and issues of policing, this chapter has deliberately concentrated on a single element of the criminal justice system – the police. However, that is not to say that fears about crime are not implicitly related to other aspects of criminal justice, for example courts (especially when sentences are passed that are perceived as erratic or too light) and prisons (which might be perceived as overcrowded because of the dangerous and volatile nature of contemporary society). These other aspects of criminal justice, and their representations in the media, are explored in Jewkes, Y. (2004) 'Media Representations of Criminal Justice' in Muncie, J. and Wilson, D. (eds.) *Student Handbook of Criminology and Criminal Justice* (Cavendish). The best introductory analysis of *Crimewatch* remains that in Schlesinger, P. and Tumber, H. (1994) *Reporting Crime* (Clarendon).

7

Crime Films and Prison Films

CHAPTER CONTENTS

The appeal of crime films	195
The crime film: masculinity, autonomy, the city	197
The 'prison film'	201
The prison film and the power to reform?	203
The documentary	205
Documentary as ethnography	206
The remake	210
The Taking of Pelham One Two Three and The Taking of Pelham 123	211
Discussion	214
Concluding thoughts	216
Summary	218
Study questions	218
Further reading	219

OVERVIEW

Chapter 7 provides:

- A consideration of the enduring appeal of crime films.
- A discussion of some of the most popular crime film genres including cop films, private eye movies, the Western, pirate films, gangster movies and the gritty British crime film.
- An analysis of some of the main themes which commonly emerge within these genres, with a particular focus on the various forms of masculinity represented in crime films.
- A discussion of the prison in cinema, its role as allegory and its relationship to penal reform.
- A consideration of the documentary film.
- An exploration of what 'remakes' of classic crime films can tell us about changing cultural attitudes to crime and justice, using *The Taking of Pelham 123* as a case study.

KEY TERMS

- audience
- catharsis
- crime film
- documentary
- film noir
- genre

- masculinity
- narrative arc
- prison film
- realism
- remakes

The *crime film* is arguably the most enduring of all cinematic *genres* which makes writing this chapter somewhat daunting. Where does one start and finish with a subject as vast as 'crime film'? What to include and what to miss out? How to condense into a single chapter movies as diverse as *Bullitt* (1968) and *Batman* (1989), *Murder on the Orient Express* (1974) and *Midnight Express* (1978), *Some Like It Hot* (1959) and *Heat* (1995), *Tightrope* (1984) and *Man On Wire* (2008), or *Pirates of the Caribbean: the Curse of the Black Pearl* (2003) and *Captain Phillips* (2013)? The answer is that it is impossible. The 'crime film' incorporates and underpins an array of better-known genres including cops-and-robbers, the gangster film, the pirate movie, the Western, the private eye film, the classic 'whodunnit', the heist movie, anime and *film noir* and, ultimately, all this chapter can do is to introduce the reader to a few ideas and encourage further reading and watching. The chapter discusses crime films, *prison films*, documentaries and *'remakes'*, and will largely focus on those films that have enjoyed significant commercial success. This highly selective and deliberately populist stance is in contrast to other criminological treatments of film which aim to cover 'the best and most important crime films and avoid the worst and most trivial' (Rafter, 2000: 7), and/or which try to say *something* (however pithy) about every film that can be included within a particular genre for fear that some pedant will shout 'but what about ...?'. This chapter simply hopes to raise some interesting but exploratory issues about a handful of somewhat randomly selected films which tie in to some of the themes raised elsewhere in this volume.

The appeal of crime films

First of all, though, it is instructive to ask the question: what accounts for the enduring popularity of the crime film? Generally such movies will centre on a criminal, a victim and an avenger (Leitch, 2002) and the similarities, differences and interactions between these adversaries usually constitute an exciting and tension-building dynamic. Another possible reason for their attraction is that they incorporate elements which appeal to the audience's own antisocial or deviant tendencies or to their ambivalence toward the police and other authorities; hence the number of incompetent or corrupt cops and judges we encounter in movies. We sometimes find ourselves empathizing with the villain rather than the good guy and even the most depraved offenders can be attractive and charismatic in the movie world (Anthony Hopkins' portrayal of serial killer Hannibal Lecter in the 1991 film *The Silence of the Lambs*, for example). In cinema, activities which in real life are often grubby, mundane or quite administrative – such as organized crime – are given an aura of mystery, glamour and recklessness. Some film-makers and critics maintain that crime film is cathartic; it allows audiences to live out their normally suppressed deviant fantasies in a vicarious but harmless manner and gives them a glimpse of other worlds (from the old-fashioned casino to the courtroom) that may be unknown to them in the real world. In some cases, film may illuminate worlds that are not just unknown but unknowable to many viewers. Films about prisons and the Mafia are two examples of subjects that are surrounded in myth; hidden societies that fascinate and intrigue. Curiously, then, the mediated version of these worlds is better known to most people than the reality, and many individuals who do enter these realms may have expectations of them that come straight from the movies – and may even adopt personas or modes of behaviour in imitation of characters from films (Jewkes, 2002; Larke, 2003; Fiddler, 2007; Parker, 2009b).

Audiences may also achieve *catharsis* through the conversion of potentially unbearable social anxieties into entertainment, as latent moral panics are scaled down from the global to the subcultural and threats as diverse as terrorism, invading aliens and natural disasters are vanquished by charismatic heroes within the comfortably generic lines of the crime film (Leitch, 2002). Alternatively, as noted in Chapter 1, the media's inclination to make all audience members equal in their potential 'victimness', may result in an obsessive fascination with such narratives. Consequently, like all other media, films may represent an hysterical replaying of the possibility of being a victim and staving it off (Osborne, 1995). Or perhaps crime films appeal simply because they permit closure: they reassure us that criminal behaviours *can* be explained and that serious offences *can* be solved. They offer immutable definitions of the 'crime problem' and guide our emotional responses to it (Rafter, 2007).

While much of the appeal lies in the thrill inherent in most crime film genres – the pursuit of the 'baddie', the high-speed car chase, the casual violence, the clever build-up of tension, or whatever – these scenes are often little more than set pieces which would leave the audience disappointed and unfulfilled if left out. Many crime films have a limited **narrative arc** and are relatively predictable in terms of their structure, storyline and dialogue. For example, the 23-part *James Bond* series succeeds in being a multi-million dollar global franchise, as well as a very British institution, partly by virtue of its sheer formulaic-ness. While Daniel Craig's 007 is a darker and more violent character than Bond as played by Pierce Brosnan or Roger Moore, it is only his new-found sensitivity to (some) women – and, much to some fans' chagrin, his blond hair – that differentiate him from the first incarnation of Bond played by Sean Connery in 1962. While the production team behind Bond have had to respond to the rapid-fire camerawork and impressive stunts that showcase Jason Bourne, the decision to continue with the tried-and-tested formula of 007 movies also suggests that the franchise is impervious to the ideas of different directors (there have been ten directors so far). Both Steven Spielberg and Quentin Tarantino are reported to have wanted to direct a Bond film, perhaps thinking they could bring something fresh and personal to the franchise. They may have been rejected precisely because something new is not considered desirable.

To take another example, gangster or 'mob' movies usually have a structure formed, in part, by the obsession with rules that is fundamental to the genre. Based on unquestioning loyalty to the 'family', honouring one's debts to each other, and regarding the 'godfather' or gang leader with a mixture of fear and respect, the group is constituted as the supreme social authority and, while the rules are frequently broken, with double-crossing and dealing providing much of the pace and anticipation of the genre (as well as underlining the message that crime doesn't pay), the social structure and unshakeable authority of the gangster family remains intact. Moreover, there is a strong, recognizable lineage that takes us from the gangster movies of the 1920s and 1930s through *The Godfather Trilogy* (1972, 1974, 1990) and *Goodfellas* (1990) to Guy Ritchie's parodic *Lock,*

Stock and Two Smoking Barrels (1998) and Quentin Tarantino's even more stylized pastiches of gangsterdom in *Reservoir Dogs* (1991) and *Pulp Fiction* (1994). We understand each by reference to the others and it is partly the audience's assured familiarity with the codes and conventions of the genre that accounts for their continuing success (Langford, 2005). Finally, the message that crime doesn't pay also frequently underpins movies based on real-life stories – for example *Blow* (2001), *The Krays* (1990) and *Goodfellas* (1990) – even if they have spent the best part of two hours demonstrating quite graphically that it does.

The crime film: masculinity, autonomy, the city

The pleasing familiarity of a formula also extends to cinematic themes. Indeed, what strikes me as I start to reflect on the topic is that there are a small number of key premises and characterizations that shape many crime movies. One theme that appears to run through all crime genres is a particular type of 'manliness'; a rugged *masculinity* that combines with heroic agency (Sparks, 1996) to form a self-confident and self-reliant protagonist. The 'tough guy' has been a staple of cinema since the first gangster movies were produced in the late 1920s and early 1930s. Exemplified by characters such as Tony Camonte in *Scarface* (1932; remade in 1983) and Tom Powers in *The Public Enemy* (1931), strong heroes (even if engaged in illegal activities) held huge appeal for American audiences in the Depression era who were disenchanted by authority and wanted to take control of their lives (Leitch, 2002).

Since that time, crime films have presented an archetype of individualistic masculinity set against larger forces, whether the wide expanse of the high seas or cattle plains (and the primitives who inhabit these territories), or the formal, occupational organizations and structures that contain and curtail their individual autonomy and maverick tendencies. For example, *cop films* (let us use *Dirty Harry* as an archetype) are dominated by the loner who battles against the bureaucracy and incompetence of their own police department, or at least refuses to play by the rules (Carrabine, 2009). In addition to being obsessive and isolated at work, the American cop usually has a private life which is deviant, dysfunctional or nonexistent and his lonely isolation has been described as 'the most immutable of all the genre's conventions' (Leitch, 2002: 222). The *gangster movie* reveals the 'fantasy of a secret society with masculine rituals' (Larke, 2003: 128) and the 'Godfather' is surely the alpha male of the film world. The *pirate film* – from the swashbuckling epics of the first half of the 20th century that showcased matinee idols such as Errol Flynn and Tyrone Power, to the recent *Pirates of the Caribbean* series starring Johnny Depp – has been characterized as 'a man fighting for the right in a world that does not understand the right as he sees it' (Parish, 1995: 3, cited in Parker, 2009a: 174). The freedom, solitude and resourcefulness evoked in the *Western* appears to have a near universal appeal to men and boys: 'it's fair to say that in the minds of many men, even if only for fleeting moments, there's a hankering to be as free and rugged, as engaging and boisterous, as hardworking, daring and independent, as truly American, as the cowboy' (Hassrick 1974: 139; cited in Parker, 2011). The *heist movie* is about the masculine pursuit of professionalism and perfection – the 'perfect crime' – at the expense of domestic and familial ties (Rayner, 2003). More complex is the *film noir*, which may be read as a definition and defence of masculinity as the hard-boiled hero grapples with 'the dangers represented by the feminine – not just women in themselves but also any non-"tough" potentiality of his own identity as a man' (Leitch, 2002: 72; see also Krutnik, 1991). In short, the hero embodies a charismatic, self-contained, hyper-masculinity. He may be unusual, unpleasant even, but he is always a 'complete man' (Chandler, 1944: cited in Sparks, 1996).

The private eye – who often appears in film noir – is sometimes described as the urban cowboy of the screen and, once again masculinity is a defining feature:

> The popular image of the private eye has less to do with his idealized, often obsessive professionalism, however, than with his masculinity. Far more than films about police detectives or amateur detectives, [private eye] films regard detective work as a test of what Frank Krutnik calls the private eye's 'self-sufficient phallic potency'. This convention is so deeply ingrained in private eye films that it is hard to appreciate how arbitrary and strange it is ... there is no reason to assume that testosterone ought to be a prerequisite for the job. (Leitch, 2002: 197)

Leitch goes on to explain that the genre's celebration of masculinity is exemplified by *The Maltese Falcon* (1941) in which the private eye hero, Sam Spade, is pitched against a voracious femme fatale and three men clearly characterized as homosexuals. Spade is thus 'admirably, heroically masculine' precisely because he is not female and not gay: hence the private eye's manliness must constantly be confirmed through conflicts with asexual or bisexual characters – or more often with female or gay male characters – whom the film leaves 'demystified, disempowered, defeated and dehumanized' (Leitch, 2002: 198).

That is not to say that all cinematic heroes are the same or even that their (hetero)sexuality is as clearly defined as Leitch's description suggests; crime films permit a wide variety of masculinities within a diverse array of settings and narratives (Sparks, 1996). In fact Davies and Smith (1997: 19) go so far as to suggest that since the late 1980s representations of white males as domesticated, feminized or paternal have dominated film genres to such a degree that it is only in the films of Quentin Tarantino that 'macho masculinity' (which we might characterize as violent and uncompromising, although always underpinned by wit and humour) remains intact. This seems an overstatement and one that overlooks both that even 'macho masculinity' can have many facets. It is also worth remembering that some of Tarantino's regular cast members have taken a Tarantino-esque version of masculinity into other roles, as the discussion below of John Travolta's character in *The Taking of Pelham 123* will illustrate. Furthermore, hyperbolized representations of masculinity may be cyclical: Sparks observes that the exaggerated muscularity of Schwarzenegger, Stallone, and their ilk in the cinema of the late 1980s and 1990s may have been in reaction to instabilities in notions of masculine gender identities at the time, i.e. the domesticated, feminized and paternal roles that Davies and Smith refer to. But since that time we have seen a new type of hero emerge, personified by *The Bourne Identity* (2002) and its sequels. While undeniably an action hero, actor Matt Damon has said of his character; 'Bourne is about authenticity, not fashion, frippery and style. He's about essence and, unlike Bond, you'd never see him watching a girl coming out of the sea with a bikini on. There's none of those old-fashioned macho attitudes' (*Telegraph*, 11 August 2007).

Ironically, Bourne might not be directing his gaze at the near-naked female form but it seems that it is not just representations of women which are erotically charged in mainstream cinema. The appeal – to men rather than women – of the muscular physiques of Stallone and Schwarzenegger are summed up by Sparks, following Laura Mulvey, as a 'narcissisitic identification of the male spectator with images of mastery and omnipotence' (Sparks, 1996: 352). To these former action heroes we might add Daniel Craig as James Bond in *Casino Royale* (2006) emerging from the sea in his swimming trunks in a pastiche of the iconic moment in *Dr No* (1962) where Ursula Andress steps from the sea in a white bikini, and Johnny Depp as camp pirate Jack Sparrow in the *Pirates of the Caribbean* series who embodies the male beauty and joyous love of adventure that marked the classic pre-war films about outlaws and pirates and was intended to appeal to men and women equally (Parker, 2009a).

It is also not the case that there is no female counterpart to the masculine hero; there are, of course, examples of women leads in Westerns (*Calamity Jane*, 1953), cop films (*Blue Steel*, 1989; *Fargo*, 1996), assassin movies (*Nikita*, 1990; *Kill Bill Vols. I and II*, 2003 and 2004), films about serial killers (*Monster*, 2003), pirate films (*Cutthroat Island*, 1995), films about outlaws (*Bonnie and Clyde*, 1967), buddy/road movies (*Thelma and Louise*, 1991), and 'girls-with-guns' (for example in countless Japanese anime films – and films starring Angelina Jolie), but they are anomalies. For Martin Parker, these heroines are interesting, and might be celebrated as examples of a feminist politics, but this is largely because there are so few examples of women in these genres, and he notes that, in the main, women are still portrayed in fairly predictable ways:

> The suffering housewife, the raped hostage, the accomplice in love, the golden hearted prostitute and so on. Women usually only make sense in relation to men,

and are found in homes, towns and gardens, looking after men, yearning for men, being wounded by men. The Western director Budd Boetticher put it neatly (though without any obvious irony) when he suggested that a woman's job ... is to react. 'In herself she has no significance whatsoever'. (Parker, 2009a)

Bob Connell – who popularized the term 'hegemonic masculinity' – concurs, arguing that while there is 'a bewildering variety of traits considered characteristic of women' (1987: 183), there is no superordinate version of femininity which is deemed more structurally powerful than others. *All* versions of femininity are subordinate to the patriarchal power of men.

Although hard to pin down as a 'genre' there is a particular type of crime film which has emerged since the mid-1990s (but whose lineage can be traced right back to films like the 1947 classic *Brighton Rock*), which combines masculinity, violence, class, race and nostalgia in a form that is immediately recognizable and unmistakeably British. Tending to lack the gloss, the special effects and (not unrelatedly) the big budget of their Hollywood counterparts, the 'crimes' in these crime films include heroin use (*Trainspotting*), football hooliganism (*The Firm; The Football Factory*), gangster violence (*Lock, Stock and Two Smoking Barrels; Sexy Beast*) and crimes too complex to describe in a few words (*Shallow Grave*). What they have in common is a dark humour, a grittiness, and a presupposition that the audience will have – or at least recognize – shared popular cultural experiences. Although the violence may be casual and brutal ('more potent than sex and drugs put together', as the four male leads in *The Football Factory* put it) it is usually set against a backdrop and soundtrack designed to elicit pangs of nostalgia in the audience. To take an example, *This is England* (2006), is set in Margaret Thatcher's Britain of 1983, and is largely based on the director Shane Meadows' own experiences as a youngster. Facing the prospect of a long and lonely summer break from school, 12-year-old Shaun (Thomas Turgoose) runs into a group of amiable skinheads, one of whom – Woody – takes Shaun under his wing and introduces him to the wonders of Ben Sherman shirts, Doc Martin boots, Ska music, male friendship and girls. With skinhead uniform and newly shaved head, Shaun enjoys the feeling of belonging that the group provides; that is, until Combo comes out of prison and returns to the gang. Older than the others, Combo is a racist, militant psychotic who divides the group and draws the young Shaun into a murky world of nationalism and racist violence which eventually leads to the savage beating of Milky, the only black skinhead in the gang. The film is set against a backdrop of the Falklands War in which Shaun's soldier father was killed, and reflects a time of mass unemployment and casual racism that is becoming politicized and organized. The pain of losing the father he idolized and the exhilaration of being part of a gang and feeling accepted by older and more knowing peers is sensitively handled by the director and cast. *This is England* manages, at one and the same time, to be gritty *and* romantic.

In most of the British films mentioned, location is important in conveying the inner emotions and motivations of the characters. For Shaun in *This is England*, the grimness of growing up in a coastal town in the north of England is captured in the brutal architecture of the estate on which he lives and the bleakness of the North Sea where, in disillusionment, he throws the Union Flag at the end of the film. Both *Trainspotting* and *Shallow Grave* are set in Edinburgh but largely filmed in Glasgow, where the rather austere Georgian architecture lends both films a mordant quality perfectly suited to the graphic scenes that unfold. Hollywood has also produced numerous films where the location is an important signifier of the dark motives of the characters. The 1990s saw the emergence of postmodern fables offering a nightmare vision of middle America. Epitomised by David Lynch's *Blue Velvet* (1986), these portrayals 'mingled cloyingly saccharine glimpses' of small-town America with 'horrific revelations about its psychosexual underside' (Leitch, 2002: 48). In some films the location becomes almost a character in itself; for example the director of *Trainspotting* and *Shallow Grave* was Danny Boyle, who went on to make *Slumdog Millionaire* (2008) where the city of Mumbai is used to dazzling, if controversial effect (some politicians and film-makers in India condemned it as 'poverty pornography').

The most famous city on film, however, must surely be New York which feels well known even to those who have never visited through its depiction in the movies (and TV programmes and song lyrics). Once known as a city with a particularly bad record of violent crime, New York has been used as a backdrop for countless crime films and its streets and subways, courtrooms and police department (NYPD) are familiar to audiences around the world. While Los Angeles and Chicago are also iconic settings (particularly for private eye/film noir and mob films respectively) no other city comes close to NYC for its number of instantly recognizable locations and landmarks. Films that used the twin towers of the World Trade Center as a location now have a particular poignancy – none more so than *Man On Wire* (2008) the Oscar-winning documentary about Frenchman Philippe Petit's daring tightrope walk (described variously as a 'real-life heist' and 'the artistic crime of the century') between the twin towers in August 1974. Since the very first gangster 'talkie' was produced in 1928, *The Lights of New York*, to contemporary films such as *The Taking of Pelham 123* (2009) which is discussed below, New York has lent vividness, thrill and menace to the movies.

The 'prison film'

The inclusion of the 'prison film' in a book entitled 'Media & Crime' might seem controversial. Crime and punishment are, after all, quite different entities. My reasons for discussing prison films are twofold. First, the prison does not feature much elsewhere in this volume; and second, prison films arguably must be included because of their sheer popularity, both among the cinema-going public and with academic scholars (see, for example, Nellis and Hale, 1982; Rafter, 2000; Jarvis, 2004; Wilson and O'Sullivan, 2004; Mason, 2006). As Nellis (1982: 6) observes, 'no other type of crime film – the gangster movie, the police procedural movie and the characteristically English murder-mystery – has claimed such impressive credentials in its bid for genre status'. The author of several publications on the prison film genre, Paul Mason (2008), concurs, commenting that most people could probably name several films about prison and he speculates that most lists would feature *The Birdman of Alcatraz* (1962), *Cool Hand Luke* (1967), *Papillon* (1973), *Midnight Express* (1978), *Brubaker* (1980), *McVicar* (1980), *Scum* (1983), *The Green Mile* (1999) and, indisputably *The Shawshank Redemption* (1994) which, nearly two decades after its original release, still tops many viewers' polls of their favourite films of all time. Among academic treatments of the genre, *I am a Fugitive from a Chain Gang* (1932) and *The Big House* (1931) are commonly discussed and, although unlikely to have been seen by the majority of this book's readers, many of the themes they deal with – the banality and repetitiveness of the prison regime, the limited movement afforded prisoners, the brutality of the chain gang, and so on – are familiar to modern audiences.

However, many 'prison films' are not really about prison at all but could actually be set in any number of other environments. Like the mob or gangster movie, the prison lends itself to being used allegorically; and like those genres, a staggering number of American prison films were made in the 1930s – the decade of the economic depression – in part because the prison offered filmmakers a metaphor for the disempowerment, injustice and isolation felt by the masses (Mason, 2008; and see Chapter 1 of this volume for a discussion of 'mass society'). Incarceration has also commonly been used as a backdrop for tales about individual perseverance and the indomitable human spirit, whereby the viewer is encouraged to empathize with the convicted offender and share in the highs and lows of their journey of self discovery. The central protagonist may have been wrongfully convicted, as Andy Dufresne (played by Tim Robbins) was in *The Shawshank Redemption*, but even when this is not the case, prisoners are often portrayed as old-style romantic heroes struggling to beat (or at least survive) the system.

One of the reasons for the popularity of the prison film is that the prison is a highly ordered, repetitive and restrictive institution and it therefore can give a film an immediate structure and rhythm. Mason (2003) characterizes the cinematic prison as a dehumanizing 'machine' with an impenetrable set of rules and regulations which grind on relentlessly, and he notes that the convention of prison films to continually repeat shots of inmates doing the same tasks – whether it is walking the landings, tramping around the exercise yard, queuing for and eating the unappetizing food presented to them in the food hall, or breaking rocks – is a powerful visual reminder to the audience of the mundane and monotonous routine inside prison. For Mason, the representation of the prison as a machine is fundamental to the prison film for it is from this metaphor that other themes flow: 'escape from the machine, riot against the machine, the role of the machine in processing and rehabilitating inmates, and entering the machine from the free world as a new inmate' (2003b: 291).

Like 'crime films' more generally, there are a very limited number of plots to be found in prison films – Nellis (1982) suggests no more than a dozen – and for the audience there is a certain gratification to be had from this awareness and recognition of character traits and plot devices. Images of rock breaking chain gangs, depictions of admissions into prison, pyjama-style prison uniforms consisting of broad black-and-white stripes or black arrows on a light background, and scenes of solitary confinement are part and parcel of most people's understanding of imprisonment and have become iconic symbols associated with loss of liberty. Jewkes (2013) goes further, arguing that the prison must be understood through a Dante-esque lens of darkness and lightness and Heaven and Hell, and that these metaphors – which underpin numerous cinematic portrayals – serve to justify and authorize the prison as infernal hell-hole. Of course, prison films also lend themselves to the commercially winning themes of sex and violence, with violent assaults, riots and rapes far more common in cinematic jails than they are in most real-life prisons. It also goes without saying that prison films are by and large about men.[1]

The prison film and the power to reform?

That the prison is frequently depicted as a brutal institution which punishes, degrades and humiliates might be said to present opportunities for those concerned with prison reform to initiate public debates about the futility and inhumanity of incarceration. However, Mason (2008) argues that a closer reading of most prison films reveals not only a reluctance to challenge the existing penal system, but also a voyeuristic obsession with interpersonal violence. Even when the audience is encouraged to empathize with the prisoner protagonist, this is achieved by representing the rest of the prison population as dehumanized monsters and animals: 'while the prison hero/ine is afforded character, emotional development and agency, the rest of the jail is mere cardboard cut-out and cliché. Consequently, prison is constructed as necessary to keep such psychotic deviants caged and incapacitated and the public safe' (Mason, 2008).

An example that illustrates this point well is the 1997 film *Con Air*, which is about prisoners, if not set in a prison, and stars Nicholas Cage as the 'prisoner-good-guy', formerly a highly decorated United States Army Ranger who accidentally killed a thug who was attacking his pregnant wife. After seven years in a Federal Penitentiary, our hero implausibly finds himself on a plane transporting some of America's most violent criminals to a maximum security prison. Predictably enough the cons take over the aircraft, killing the prison guards and diverting the plane to Las Vegas. Led by Cyrus 'The Virus' Grissom (played by John Malkovich), who charmingly claims to have 'killed more people than cancer', this motley bunch of serial killers, drug smugglers, kidnappers and rapists do nothing to challenge stereotypes of the prison population as inhuman 'others'. Indeed, in persisting in portraying 'the vilest aspects of prison life' (Cheatwood, 1998: 210), the movie industry might be said to be endorsing the view that penal reform is undesirable and unachievable.

It is arguable, then, that cardboard cut-out and clichéd portrayals of prisoners as brutal, violent and ultimately stupid thugs has a role in making prison population growth acceptable to – or at least unquestioned by – the public; in fact Thomas Mathiesen (2001) argues just this. For Mathiesen, the problem is not simply that the public turn a blind eye to dramatically rising global prison populations, but that the picture they *do* receive of imprisonment is grossly misrepresented. Some commentators have suggested that, given most of us will never even see a prison at first hand (it is probably the least visible part of the penal system), the prison film stands in for the real thing (Fiddler, 2007) and, in celebrating prison violence and encouraging voyeuristic participation among the audience, the prison film even has echoes of the spectacle of public executions described by Foucault (1977) in the *ancien regime*, with the film-viewing audience replacing the crowd at the gallows (Sparks, 1992; Mason, 2003; Jarvis, 2004). Furthermore, films which are set in the future – *Fortress* (1992), *Face/Off* (1997) and *Minority Report* (2002), among others – may be an accurate barometer with which to gauge the direction in which punishment is going. The prison of the (near) future is automated, dehumanized and secret, and it is run by sadistic and corrupt wardens working for faceless global corporations. Welcome to the dystopian world of 'Technocorrections' (Nellis, 2006: 226).

Of course, some might say 'why *should* cinema have a reforming agenda?' There are many reasons why audiences are drawn to particular films, not least because of the quality or celebrity status of the actors appearing in them, and the notion of being educated at the cinema may not have mass appeal. In the end, films are primarily about entertainment and even when film producers do try to make a case for prison reform their efforts may be open to misinterpretation (Nellis, 1982). Further, any inherent messages that movies may carry about the inappropriateness of certain aspects of punishment in a civilized society must compete with other media portrayals which Mason characterizes as: 'bottom-up pressure from an angry public, driven onwards by screaming red-top headlines, demands [for] more displays of repressive punishment:

longer prison sentences, boot camps, ASBOS...' (2006: 1). This is why, despite the considerable quantity of prison films made over the last 100 years, few (if any) have done anything to challenge the institution of the prison. Indeed, as film-making has become more sophisticated, able to show ever more graphic scenes designed to shock and titillate, so society has accepted – demanded, even – crueller, more retributive and more humiliating forms of punishment (Jewkes, 2013). For many observers it is of little surprise, then, that for most of the last century, the production and popularity of prison cinema has grown in line with actual incarceration rates. It is also why – despite the harrowing portrayals of capital punishment in movies as diverse as *Let Him Have It* (1991) which is based on the case of Derek Bentley, a British teenager who was hanged in 1953 for allegedly urging his 16-year-old friend to shoot a police officer in the course of a burglary (and posthumously pardoned in the 1990s), and *Dead Man Walking* (1995), a relatively unsentimental Hollywood movie about a convicted murderer on Death Row – mediated and sensationalized real-life offences are frequently greeted by politicians, commentators and newspaper readers in the UK with calls for the return of the death penalty and in the US with demands for its greater use.

The documentary

Before closing this section on crime films and prison films and going on to discuss the 'remake', it is worth considering a genre that has a more explicit agenda in bringing to public attention the social contexts of crime and the realities of the experience of imprisonment – the ***documentary***. Usually made for television rather than cinema release, there has been a long tradition of post-war television documentaries, especially in the UK and Australia, which aim to narrate social history from below. One of the most influential was the classic documentary series that started with *Seven Up!* about a group of seven-year-old children, first broadcast on commercial television in the UK in 1964. The man behind the series is Michael Apted who also directed such blockbusters as the Bond film, *The World Is Not Enough* (1999) and the spy thriller, *Gorky Park* (1983). Although not originally planned to have a follow-up, one of the production team had the idea of returning to film the children aged 14 and the series is still going strong, revisiting the participants every seven years.[2] The *Up!* series is essentially a longitudinal study of social class comprised of in-depth, open-ended interviews recorded on film, and might justifiably be regarded as a precursor to reality television (Burawoy, 2009) or, at the very least, the first example of 'Quality Tabloid TV' (Willis, 2009: 351). The subjects numbered 14 in all and they were from different areas of the country and selected from all points on the socio-economic scale. The idea behind the series was to examine the proposition that the class system in the UK is so embedded that a person's life path is predestined and fixed. While there were a few cases of upward mobility among the 14 participants, one scholar has commented that at the extremes of the spectrum, i.e. the individuals from the upper classes and the very poor, 'the accuracy of the children's personal predictions for their own class trajectories is shocking in its precision' (Burawoy, 2009: 319). Although seen almost entirely through the lens of class and thus perhaps a very British take on individuals' lifecourses, the Jesuit maxim which inspired the series, 'Give me a child until he is seven and I will give you the man', has universal resonance and the programme has spawned imitators in many other countries, including the US, Russia, South Africa and Japan.

Documentary as ethnography

Documentaries resonate with the work of ethnographic researchers who revisit the field, seek to create coherent narratives from an excess of material, and who confront ethical dilemmas as they investigate the private lives of subjects (Thorne, 2009). Like an ethnographer, documentary makers usually end up with a surplus of material: in *42 Up* Apted says that he uses about 1/30th of the footage gathered. While the documentary genre appears to offer transparency and honesty, it is of course within the power of the director to control, manipulate or exploit the medium. Like any sociological analysis, the most interesting variable can be applied retrospectively to make sense of the whole or to give the data a particular slant. Duneier (2009) cites the case of Nicholas, who grew up on a farm and had little structured activity to occupy him. 'The world of the seven-year-old can be primitive, even violent,' the narrator says as Nicholas discusses his enjoyment of fighting. For Duneier, Nicholas' lack of discipline makes him the same as the East End working-class children in an orphanage who were portrayed as having too much freedom and not enough structure and discipline, but because he went on to study physics at Oxford and became a university professor the focus moves to him at age seven saying that when he grew up he wanted to understand the moon, and as an adult saying he was always interested in technical and scientific things (Duneier, 2009).

Apted acknowledges the manipulative possibilities of a genre that purports to tell the truth, and confesses that during the making of *21 Up* he believed Tony (who at seven was at an East End primary school and dreamed of being a jockey) would soon be in prison, so he filmed him around dangerous looking areas for use in later films:

He lived in a pretty violent environment, and was making quite a lot of cash running bets at an East London greyhound-racing track for some pretty unsavoury looking characters. It didn't look like the future held much promise, so I had him take me round all of the crime hot-spots in anticipation of shooting 28 Up! in one of Her Majesty's prisons. I was wrong and embarrassed. Tony married Debbie, they had children, and his life took a different course. Tony was decent about it and let me off the hook: 'Don't judge a book by its cover, Michael', he told me. (Apted, 2009: 362)

Nonetheless some critics have found it difficult to move away from a Marxist interpretation of the series. Paul Willis laments 'Class still matters to me' (Willis, 2009: 349), and he talks of the 'achingness I pick up in Michael's subjects [which] continues to relate to the structured exercise of power, the costs of domination and the pains of subordination' (ibid.).

The prison documentary brings the exercise of power and pains of subordination into particularly sharp relief. Given our earlier discussion of the failure of prison films to have any positive impact on prison reform, it seems a bold assertion to say that the prison documentary may be one of the few types of prison film that can claim to have made any difference at all to perceptions of prisons and prisoners but, given Michael Apted's belief that 'empathy is at the heart of most documentaries' (2009: 360), there may be a case for the suggestion. Of course, some prison documentaries are simply voyeuristic and pander to stereotypes: *America's Most Deadly Prison Gangs* and *Louis Theroux: Behind Bars* (filmed at San Quentin prison in California) are two examples which apparently set out to demonstrate that US jails really are like their Hollywood depictions.

By contrast there have been several thoughtful and challenging prison documentaries and series broadcast on British television which may genuinely be able to claim some influence; although, in the case of *Feltham Sings* (2002) a Channel 4 documentary musical filmed inside the biggest young offenders' prison in Europe and co-produced by well-regarded film-maker and academic Roger Graef, the notion of inmates expressing their thoughts and lives to reggae, R&B and hip hop beats did not precipitate a more enlightened attitude to prison arts. Despite the endorsement of Graef who is quoted as saying: 'The arts – especially music that links with their experience – can reach those parts that no other form of rehabilitation does' (http://tinyurl.com/yehnwx4), the programme pre-empted an announcement by the Justice Minister that arts in prison were to be curtailed. Embarrassed by a newspaper report that inmates at a high-security prison were offered courses in stand-up comedy, the Minister's directive to prison governors that they must consider how activities 'might be perceived by the public and victims' was interpreted by the course teacher rather differently: 'I wouldn't mind if it was a new idea, but we've been doing this programme for 10 years now. I'm trying to understand what other areas of criminal justice the *Sun* gets to decide' (quoted in the *Independent*, 25 January 2009). In fact, the public at large may not be as punitive as the Minister assumes: prison documentaries are generally commercial as well as critical successes and it is unlikely that all viewers are tuning in to be disgusted and outraged at how cushy prisons are. For example, the first part of an ITV series about the women's prison *Holloway*, which focused on a teenage girl who self-harms, won the prime time slot with 4.2 million viewers, or a 17.9 per cent share of the 9pm to 10pm audience (www.guardian.co.uk/media/2009/mar/18/tv-ratings-holloway). Moreover, several newspaper TV critics confessed that they tuned in with certain preconceptions largely based on their viewing of *Bad Girls* or *Cell Block H*, but watched instead with sadness or distress.

The Executive Producer of *Holloway*, Paul Hamann, has made several other documentaries about criminal justice, including *Fourteen Days in May* (1987), a film covering the last two weeks in the life of Edward Earl Johnson who became only the second man to be executed in Mississippi after the national hiatus in capital punishment was ended in 1977. *Fourteen Days in May* charts the build up to the execution; the preparations of the gas chamber, the media coverage and the legal challenges, led by the Human Rights lawyer Clive Stafford Smith. Commenting on the film, Jamie Bennett (2009) says that the film is given 'an unusual moral depth' by virtue of the fact that it raises specific concerns about the validity of Johnson's conviction, including an alibi witness who came forward who was refused access to the court. As the execution approached, Hamann became increasingly disturbed by events and started not only to openly sympathize with Johnson, but also raise his concerns with those in authority. The difficulties – and indeed, undesirability – of impartiality on the part of the documentary film-maker are articulated by Hamann in an interview with Bennett:

> I felt I was in a strange nightmare because it became clear off camera that the prison psychiatrist, the warden, the death row staff, all felt he did not commit the crime he was convicted of. At that moment I stopped being the objective BBC journalist and started doing everything I could to stop the execution ... In the end it didn't work. The last week of making that film was really horrible, I didn't want to be making it, but morally we had to. Afterwards, myself and Clive Stafford Smith ... made a follow up film called The Journey where we tracked down the man who everyone thought had really carried out the murder ... the film did prove that Edward Earl Johnson should not have been executed. It was a film made a year too late. (Bennett, 2009: 47)

In the same interview Hamann says that he was greatly influenced by the work of Fred Wiseman, an American pioneer of documentary film-making in the tradition of cinéma vérité and by the British documentary film-maker Rex Bloomstein, particularly his eight-part series *Strangeways* about life inside

HMP Manchester. As someone who has shown his work in prisons and lectured at criminological departments, and is a recipient of two British Academy Film and Television Arts (BAFTA) awards, Bloomstein has to a large degree built his reputation on exposing the realities of prison life and addressing aspects of the British penal system that are usually closed to public scrutiny. Employing apparently simple (though in fact highly sophisticated) film-making techniques that eschew background music and narrated voice-overs in favour of a more direct focus capturing genuine, spontaneous emotions (sometimes known as 'fly-on-the-wall' filming), Bloomstein is widely appreciated for humanizing his subjects, while still conveying the complexities of their personalities, motives and circumstances; a process he has called 'undermining the simplicities' (Bloomstein, 2008; cf. Bennett, 2006a).

Perhaps the most profoundly affecting of Bloomstein's subjects was Steve, who was interviewed twice; first for *Lifer*, a two-hour documentary made for ITV in 1982 and, 21 years later for the follow-up, *Lifer – Living With Murder*, which was broadcast on Channel 4. In the first film Steve is serving a life sentence for kicking a man to death at the age of 17. Twelve years into his sentence he is cocky, athletic-looking, restless and resistant. Prone to responding violently to provocation, he describes how his anger has led him to trash his cell and cause damage to the prison wing on several occasions. He speaks contemptuously of the prison officers who restrain him physically and with drugs. But 21 years later we see the effects that the 'liquid cosh' has had on Steve. Bloated, dulled and his speech so slurred that the interview has to be accompanied by subtitles, the effects of 32 years in custody are dramatically conveyed. Now held in the secure wing of a psychiatric hospital and reduced to a shell of his former self, there can be no more graphic or moving illustration of a life inside.

With a prolific back catalogue that includes *The Sentence* (1976), *Release* (1976), *Prisoners' Wives* (1977), *Parole* (1979), *Strangeways* (1980), *Lifer* (1983), *Lifers* (1984), *Strangeways Revisited* (2000), *Lifer: Living With Murder* (2003) and *Kids Behind Bars* (2005), Bloomstein has arguably done more than any other single individual to reveal the experience of imprisonment and its effects on inmates and their families. He has also influenced those who work within the Prison Service, including its senior personnel. The most published author on Bloomstein's work, Jamie Bennett (see, for example, Bennett, 2004, 2006a, 2006b) is also a serving prison Governor, while former Director General of the Prison Service, Martin Narey, has cited *Strangeways* as the primary inspiration for his decision to join the service (Narey, 2002).

The question remains, however, whether the powerful, reflective and raw films created by Graef, Hamann, Bloomstein and others have the ability to challenge public attitudes to prisoners. Rex Bloomstein firmly believes that documentaries do have the ability to alter entrenched attitudes and he counsels against underestimating the potential for a change in public attitudes, if the complexity of criminal conduct is allowed to be developed in documentary form (Bloomstein, 2010, personal correspondence). Conversely, the empathy inherent in the documentary process may only be felt by those viewers who already share the narrative's perspective and have pre-existing sympathies with its subjects. While prison documentaries such as those described here unquestionably create a profoundly important media space for more considered and thoughtful reflection (Bennett, 2006), the audience may inevitably view them – like any other media text – through the lens of their pre-existing cultural resources, experiences and prejudices.

The remake

There is nothing that divides film-goers more than a remake of a much-loved 'classic'. While there have been some notable critical and commercial successes (*The Departed; The Thomas Crown Affair; Ocean's 11*) other remakes have been met with indifference, mirth or even outrage (*The Italian Job; The Wicker Man; Psycho*). The most successful remakes are probably those that stay broadly true to their predecessor (perhaps with some oblique references to the original for those in the know) yet which also add something new. If a story is compelling, yet would benefit from a modern treatment or change of context, so much the better. Some film buffs will always argue that remakes are inferior, but that doesn't mean that the majority of current cinema goers won't prefer them. In part, the attraction of a remake to modern audiences lies in the quickened pace of action, the special effects and computer generated wizardry, and the inclusion of familiar A-list stars. But what can remakes of classic crime films tell us about changing social attitudes to crime over the decades?

At a fairly superficial level they may tell us that film-goers have a greater appetite for violence (including sexual violence) and verbal profanity than their forebears; and they certainly indicate more relaxed censorship laws than in previous eras. The remake usually highlights that ours truly is a celebrity culture and that sometimes movies become vehicles for high-profile stars even if some critics question the appropriateness of a particular actor in a role. Equally, stars are now more able to move between quite diverse roles as heroes, anti-heroes or downright villains and are more willing to play psychopaths, killers and characters who have few, if any, redeeming features. Hollywood movies fully exploit all the technological tools at the film-maker's disposal, creating spectacular, eye-popping, explosive action and underlining the fact that the film industry is a multi-billion dollar enterprise. But can movies help us chart deeper historical transitions; for example, changing social fears and anxieties? Let us consider one film, *The Taking of Pelham One Two*

Three (1974), and its remake, *The Taking of Pelham 123* (2009) to see if it can shed light on this interesting proposition.[3]

The Taking of Pelham One Two Three and The Taking of Pelham 123

The Taking of Pelham 123 (directed by Tony Scott, 2009) stars John Travolta as Ryder, a sociopath and leader of a kidnap gang who take over a train on the New York subway, but also (somewhat implausibly) a former financier on Wall Street who was convicted of fraud and has come out of prison with comic-book prisoner characterizations: shaved head, poor complexion, a handlebar moustache and a lot of tattoos. His demands are succinct: he wants $10 million in 60 minutes or he'll start killing the hostages (18 passengers and a conductor) one-by-one. His adversary is Walter Garber (Denzel Washington); a train dispatcher who happens to be on duty at the time and becomes an unwitting hostage negotiator. As the film unfolds, we learn that the quiet, modest and well-meaning Garber has a back-story which Ryder learns of. He has been demoted while an investigation is conducted into allegations that he took a bribe (which, later, he is forced to confess when Ryder threatens to kill a young man onboard the train – his defence is that it was to pay for his kids' college education). The focus of the film is the relationship formed by Ryder and Garber, as they engage in a psychological chess-game.

In the 1974 original (directed by Joseph Sargent), the villain's adversary and 'avenger' was not a train dispatcher but a policeman, Lieutenant Zachary Garber, played by Walter Matthau (Zach Garber became Walter Garber in the remake, in homage to Matthau). A natural curmudgeon, Matthau's character is terse, cynical and 'hard-boiled' in the classic tradition of cinematic cops and private eyes who have seen it all before. The fact that modern cinema audiences bring to their viewing ambivalent, even hostile, attitudes to law enforcers might be partial explanation for the decision to make Garber a train dispatcher in the remake. In contrast to Matthau's character, Denzel Washington's Garber is a much softer, more sensitive character; presumably intended to elicit sympathy, but universally panned by film critics for being far less interesting than his predecessor. As the *Independent*'s movie reviewer, Geoffrey Macnab, put it:

> We are lumbered with details about his private life: we hear him promising his wife he'll pick up some milk before he gets home in the evening and we learn how he may have had his hand in the till to pay for his daughter's college fees. The remake creaks under the weight of its sentimentality. (*Independent*, 12 June 2009)

The 'villain' also diverged quite considerably between the 1974 film and its 2009 successor. Most critics who compared the two films suggested that, despite Travolta's cartoonish Hells Angel appearance and expletive-ridden dialogue (both of which owe debts to the character he played in Tarantino's *Pulp Fiction*), the urbane Robert Shaw was much more successful in conveying quiet menace and a cold-blooded and calculating attitude toward the hostages. Travolta's frenetic characterization suits the faster pace of the action. Where Shaw was quietly chilling, Travolta is a loose cannon 'willing to kill innocents not out of necessity but out of spite' (*San Francisco Chronicle*, 7 June 2009), perhaps reflecting contemporary fears that violent crime is random and indiscriminatory. Although writing several years before *The Taking of Pelham 123* was made, Thomas Leitch might have been talking about the film when he said that violence was becoming 'more and more successful, and more and more in demand, in selling movies to a generation of teenagers who had grown up with remote controls that had sharpened their impatience, discouraged the deferred gratifications of slow-moving films, and reintroduced...[the] principle of slapstick comedy' (Leitch, 2002: 45–6). In the original movie, all the gang members are dressed conservatively and alike; all wear large framed glasses and false moustaches as disguise; and all go under colour-coded monikers, copied to similarly creepy effect by Quentin Tarantino in *Reservoir Dogs* 20 years later (Shaw is 'Mr Blue'; his accomplices Messrs. Green, Brown and Grey). The original movie thus follows the more common convention of the time of setting up relatively clear-cut distinctions between 'evil' and 'good' (personified by Blue and Lt. Garber). By the time of the remake, it was more usual to find distinctions blurred between 'good' people and 'bad' people and adversaries were frequently portrayed as mirror images or similarly morally ambiguous (*You're just like me!* says Ryder to Garber).

An immediate and obvious difference between the 1974 film and the 2009 version are the cultural attitudes towards 'minorities' and the use of language to express intolerance. While today's cinema audiences are more tolerant of frequent use of the 'f-word' (which does appear in the original but with far less frequency and to much more shocking effect), they are less broadminded about language that reveals socio-political motivated hatred of others. The original film was a very 1970s production, containing casual misogyny (*I gotta watch my language just because they let a few broads in?*), racism (*shut your mouth, nigger*) and xenophobia (a supposedly comic scene has Matthau referring to Japanese visitors as 'Chinamen' and 'monkeys' to their faces, unaware that they speak perfect English). Another area where the remake noticeably differs from its predecessor is in the use of technology; both in the cinematography and in the plotline. The hostage-takers set up a wi-fi booster to enable Ryder to access his laptop underground and monitor the Dow Jones Index (he has short-sold the market and invested in gold, earning him a profit far larger than the ransom money). But unknown to the kidnappers, a young male passenger has an active laptop with a webcam, which has been knocked to the floor but is facing the interior of the carriage with a decent view of the action. It reconnects using the same wi-fi link, re-establishing a previously used videochat to his girlfriend's PC. When she realizes what she's witnessing via the webcam she alerts – and provides a feed to – the local television station, thus providing a perfect example of synopticism, to titillate, terrify and panic the TV audience watching at home (Mathiesen, 1997).

Some critics felt that the producer of the remake employed technical trickery simply because it was available and to cover up for a much thinner plot than in the original (hectic camera action, high colour contrast levels and frenetic editing and are the hallmarks of Tony Scott's films). The more mundane plot devices of the earlier film are also preferred by many:

> It's all in the sneeze. If you want to know why 1970s thrillers are so much better than their counterparts today, you just need to pay attention to the part that flu and coughing play in the original … The film-makers don't rely on the visual pyrotechnics that characterise Scott's movie, in which the camera never seems able to stay still for more than a moment. Instead, key plot points are conveyed in far more subtle fashion. Who needs a line of dialogue or a final-reel shootout when you can have a character giving himself away by blowing into a handkerchief? What better way to depict a corrupt and ineffectual mayor than to show him in bed with flu, being scolded by a nurse? (Macnab, *Independent,* 12 June 2009)

In 2009, the conflict takes place in the control room between Garber, his boss and a professional hostage negotiator, but in the original movie, all the conflict occurs within the gang and on board the train as Mr Blue fights to control dissent and disharmony among his men. In 1974, the gang are portrayed as a disparate band of thieves but by 2009 they reflect the *zeitgeist* by initially appearing as terrorists and then being revealed as the new enemies of the people; bankers and hedge fund operators (French, *Observer,* 2 August 2009).

Terror striking on an underground train retains some currency as a modern urban nightmare. One only has to think of the incident on the Tokyo subway in 1995 when the deadly virus SARIN was released on several lines killing 12 people, or the suicide bombings on the London underground in July 2005 which killed the four bombers and 52 others, to be reminded of the threats that a subterranean transport system can harbour. Nevertheless, in a post- 9/11 world, the train no longer has quite the same potency as the passenger plane as a source of fear. Added to that, the remake of *The Taking of Pelham 123* remains faithful to the 1974 original's simple plot device of having the hijackers fool the authorities into believing they are still aboard the train when they have in fact escaped. Employing the same, relatively low-tech method, they lock the driving lever in the full-speed position, bypassing the 'dead man's switch'; a supposedly fail-safe system that automatically comes into operation if the driver of the train becomes incapacitated. Even the energetic pace that is maintained throughout Scott's version and the obligatory high-speed chase at the end of the film (a new addition since the 1974 version) do not prevent the remake from having a rather quaint, old-fashioned feel. Most surprising of all is that Scott's film makes no reference to 9/11 itself:

> Tony Scott's version of *The Taking of Pelham 123* makes one very curious omission. It doesn't foreground at all the event that changed everything – the September 11, 2001 attacks on the World Trade Center. This gives the film's portrayal of New York a time-warp feel. The hijackers and the cops alike both seem to be playing by old-fashioned rules. We're not in the realm of suicide bombing or apocalyptic destruction. The robbers want a ransom, not necessarily to bring western democracy tumbling down. (Macnab, *Independent*, 12 June 2009)

This omission is especially puzzling because, although much of the action takes place beneath New York, *The Taking of Pelham 123*, like so many other films, is in part a fable about the city itself. As the *Independent* film critic implies, the character of the city mayor is an allegory for the state of the city itself. In the original film, the mayor is a neurotic, bloated and sickly figure who can be read semiotically as a symbol of the bureaucratic mess that New York was in, and of the US's political vulnerabilities following the Vietnam War and Watergate scandal. The original screenplay is rife with references to the instabilities troubling New Yorkers (*We don't want another Attica do we?*, in reference to the most serious prison riot in US history which occurred in 1971; *There's another strike taking place; The city is broke*). According to Macnab (2009), New York was a city 'coming apart at the seams', it had 'something apocalyptic about it'; a sense of urban unease later captured in extreme form in *Escape From New York* (1981) in which the whole city becomes a maximum-security prison. In the remake of *The Taking of Pelham 123* the mayor (played by James Gandolfini of *Sopranos* fame) has become a slick, sardonic, financially savvy figure in control of his technologically sophisticated multi-media environment, and New York is similarly clean-cut and efficient (even the train carriages are remarkably free of graffiti). The final shots when the action moves above ground are unashamedly sentimental and are perhaps the most telling – if still somewhat oblique – reference to the legacy of 9/11. Flying in a helicopter over the beautifully-lit Manhattan skyline at sunset, the official hostage negotiator remarks to Garber that the city's beauty reminds him of what he's fighting to preserve.

Discussion

The analysis above has highlighted some of the differences between two versions of a film separated by 35 years, and what they have to tell us about changing perceptions of, fears about, and attitudes to, crime. To broaden this discussion and generalize somewhat, the films of the 1960s were about art burglars, jewel thieves, bank robbers or Cold War spies, and the individuals that perpetrated them were essentially gentleman (usually English) who played by the rules. Crime was cool and the movies of this period were filled with dashing heroes, dastardly villains and glamorous but merely decorative women. However, by 1970, fears about violent, inter-personal crime were increasing and the shock of rising urban crime rates in the US was hitting home – literally. In 1969 the murder of Sharon Tate (an American actress and wife of film director Roman Polanski who was heavily pregnant at the time of her death) and four others at Tate's home and then, two days later, the equally brutal murder of Rosemary and Leno LaBianca in their home, stunned and repulsed the American public. It was reported that the gang that committed the crimes – Charles Manson and his 'family' of followers – had precipitated the murders by breaking into several homes; sometimes stealing items, but sometimes simply moving them around in what they called 'creepy crawlies'. The violation of the domestic space – particularly these homes in attractive, suburban, affluent neighbourhoods – have since become the theme of countless crime and horror movies (*The Last House on the Left*, 1972, remade in 2009; *Funny Games*, 1997, remade 2007 and *Panic Room*, 2002) (Simon, 2009; cf. Lowenstein, 2005).

As discussed elsewhere in this chapter, the 1970s also gave rise to several cop and private eye movies concerning a lone man taking on conspiracies and corruption by state, municipal and police organizations (*Dirty Harry*, 1971; *Chinatown*, 1974). By the 1980s the maverick police officer was still around but by now he had morphed into an all action hero with an excessive physique to make up for his limited dialogue. It is somewhat ironic that the US state which has chosen to pursue the most emotive, passionate and retributive approach to crime control (Barker, 2009) is California, the home of the movie industry and the state governed by Arnold Schwarzenegger who once played *The Terminator* (1984). Another iconic cop film of this period, cited in many policy documents, academic studies and media reports, is *Robocop*. Released in 1987, *Robocop* summed up the changes in policing that many felt were overdue. In the UK, a series of civil disturbances had demonstrated how ill-equipped police officers were to deal with large-scale disorder (they infamously faced rioters in Brixton, London in 1981 armed only with truncheons and dustbin lids) and there were growing demands for the police to get 'tooled-up'. As riot shields, full-face helmets, rubber bullets and tear gas were introduced and the term 'zero tolerance policing' was imported from the United States, many commentators made comparisons between law enforcers and the police cyborg of the film. The motif still retains sufficient currency for documentary maker Roger Graef to observe in 2009 (following a public demonstration which the police were accused of handling with undue force; analysed in Graef's Channel 4 film *Dispatches: Ready for a Riot*) that 'Police dressed up as Robocop act like him too' (*Independent*, 18 October 2009).

The early 1990s saw the rise of the serial killer movie (*Silence of the Lambs*, 1991; *American Psycho*, 1991; *Se7en*, 1995) which Jarvis (2007) argues was closely linked to the rise of a voracious consumer culture: society's greed and vanity in this period was transmuted into themes of cannibalistic consumption, orgiastic gluttony and fetishism in the movies. The decade also brought another kind of 'excess' – computer-generated imagery (CGI) – to most films, although the decade closed with an exceedingly low-budget riposte to CGI – *The Blair Witch Project* (1999) – a horror film made to look like a grainy, home movie and seeking to emulate the **realism** of documentaries. Since then, movies (at least movies aimed exclusively at adults – we'll leave aside the pirates and magicians who have conquered the box office in recent years) have been dominated by technology, terrorists, military combat, environmental disasters and other apocalyptic global threats to the human race.

To an extent, this is simply art imitating life and life imitating art. Stories in cinema run parallel to stories in the news and film-makers are merely picking up on the issues that audiences will recognize and which provoke the strongest reactions. Hence, many of the themes that have been highlighted in this chapter – drama; predictable storylines and themes; a simple narrative arc; masculine individualism, autonomy and lack of normative social ties; the risk of random, violent (and sexual) crime; the importance of A-list celebrity actors, etc. – all spectacularly and graphically portrayed thanks to the technological tool-box at directors' disposal – are precisely the values that news journalists use to structure their reporting of crime (see Chapter 2). It is not surprising that the spate of films about children being left unsupervised by their parents (most famously, *Home Alone*, 1990) coincided with several real-life 'home alone' cases, or that recent cinema releases have reflected contemporary moral panics, including a sensitively-handled movie about the rape and murder of a little girl by a paedophile neighbour (*The Lovely Bones*, 2009) and a film about a four-year-old child abducted from her apartment, the release of which was postponed when Madeleine McCann disappeared (*Gone Baby Gone*, 2007).

Concluding thoughts

The question of what makes a film a crime film is a tricky one and this chapter – by including pirate movies, Westerns, prison films and documentaries – has pushed the definition about as far as is possible. But the truth is that there are few films which contain zero visual references to crime, deviance, anti-social behaviour, policing, punishment, justice, or any number of other criminological themes. Is *Superman* a crime film? Or *Some Like It Hot*? What about *The Truman Show*?

While academics attempt to address the thorny question of why people become criminals via recourse to competing theories such as 'rational choice', disadvantageous life chances, genetic predispositions, environmental factors, and so on, crime films offer a similarly diverse range of motivations for criminal behaviour. Gangster, pirate and outlaw movies link crime to a sociopathic alienation from a remote or uncaring society combined with excessive vanity or megalomania. Private eye and classic cop films blame institutional corruption or a malfunctioning system. Modern police films link criminal behaviour to psychopathy. Heist movies and kidnap films peg it on simple greed. Film noir blames sexual victimization by a predatory femme fatale. British films use class, and sometimes race, to explore how the disenchantment of those who are economically and culturally at the margins of society can turn into aggression and violence. For the criminologist the themes of crime films may overlap with their academic interests but, equally, their appeal might be that they deal with matters beyond the range of academic criminology:

> Philosophically, [crime films] raise questions concerning the nature of good and evil. Psychologically, they encourage viewers to identify with victims and offenders – even serial killers – whose sexualities, vulnerabilities and moralities may be totally unfamiliar. Ethically, they take passionate moral positions that would be out of place in academic analyses. Crime films constitute a type of discourse different from academic criminology, one with its own types of truth and its own constraints. (Rafter, 2007)

In fact, part of the appeal of writing scholarly treatments of crime movies may also be that they permit more passion and moral positioning than most 'criminological' subjects; certainly, academic analyses of film usually betray the personal predilections of the author. All of which leaves me slightly puzzled as I realize that I have come to the end of this chapter without mentioning my own favourite crime film: *Battle Royale* (2000). Directed by Kinji Fukasaku, the movie is a kitsch Japanese take on teenage delinquency which contains cartoonish, bloody brutality similar to that seen in Quentin Tarantino's movies (Tarantino has discussed in many interviews his debt to Fukasaku and his son, Kenta Fukasaku, who wrote the screenplay). The film has a simple plot. While on a school field trip, 42 students are taken hostage and find themselves on a remote island where they must play a fascist government sponsored game called Battle Royale. Each is made to wear a collar which will explode, killing them instantly, if they break any rules, and each is randomly assigned a different weapon and told that they must fight each other to the death. They have three days to kill each other until one survives – or they all die. The film has a quality which is part video-game and part reality TV. What does *Battle Royale* tell us about its socio-political context and about public attitudes to crime in the 21st century? Must it be viewed differently in the light of the ghastly events on Utøya island in July 2011, described in Chapter 2? These are discussions that will have to wait for another time ...

Summary

- This chapter has attempted to account for the enduring appeal of crime and prison films, both to scholars of media criminology and to the wider public. It has offered several possible explanations for their attraction to audiences, ranging from an appeal to everyone's innate desire to be deviant, to a cathartic satisfaction in seeing offenders get their just deserts.
- It has been argued that a relatively small number of generic themes dominate crime film. This chapter has chosen to focus on three: masculinity, autonomy and the city, all of which are examined via some of the most popular sub-genres including: the Western, the gangster movie, the pirate film, the spy franchises, the classic American cop movie, the private eye or film noir, and gritty British cinematic realism.
- The 'prison film' has been included because of its sheer popularity and longevity. It has been noted that, while most academic scholars are content to analyse crime films without going much beyond their entertainment value, there have historically been greater demands of prison films to educate and influence the public on matters of penal reform. It is generally recognized, however, that prison films have on the whole not succeeded in this endeavour and have instead continued to create and perpetuate stereotypes of prisoners as a dangerous and violent underclass.
- The documentary has arguably had more success in informing the viewing public about the pains of imprisonment, although its claims to realism may be compromised, as the discussion of Apted's 'Up' films has demonstrated. Like other forms of ethnography, the documentary cannot be separated from the beliefs, motives and agenda of its originator; and, like all other media content, the documentary also has a mission to entertain.
- The cinematic remake has much to tell us about changing socio-political climates and attitudes to crime and punishment over the decades. Our discussion of two versions of *The Taking of Pelham 123*, made three decades apart, illustrates the ways in which audience's perceptions of offenders, crime, the police and other authorities, have evolved; the different entertainment imperatives that viewers bring with them; and the sentimental affection with which New York is held, especially since 9/11.

STUDY QUESTIONS

1. Reflect on some of your own favourite crime and prison films and why it is that you enjoy them. In what ways do you think your responses might be different to those of your parents' and grandparents' generation?
2. Write a review comparing an original crime film and its remake. From this comparative analysis, what can you observe about emerging social anxieties and

changing attitudes to crime and justice over the years covered by the two films you have reviewed?

3. Given this volume's earlier discussions about media influence and effects (and the problems with making causal links between screen violence and real-life offending behaviours) how would you characterize the relationship between crime movies and criminals?

4. Why have prison movies, despite their popularity, failed to inform penal reform agendas? Do you agree with Rex Bloomstein that documentaries such as those he produces have greater potential to change public perceptions of prisoners and lead to less punitive attitudes more widely?

FURTHER READING

Just as there are a vast amount of crime films to choose from, there seems to be an almost equally daunting array of academic commentaries on them, making any particular recommendations appear highly subjective. However, since first writing this chapter, one excellent book has been published which I would thoroughly recommend: Rafter, N. and Brown, M. (2011) *Criminology Goes to the Movies: Crime Theory and Popular Culture* (New York University Press). In this, the authors base each chapter on a criminological theory and apply it to a famous Hollywood movie, so, for example: Strain Theories and *Traffic*; Feminist Criminology and *Thelma and Louise*. Although, like this chapter, inevitably highly selective in the films they discuss, Rafter and Brown provide an inventive and very readable treatment of many of the theories discussed in Chapter 1 of this volume. Other than that, I will limit my suggestions to the two books I found especially useful: Leitch, T. (2002) *Crime Films* (Cambridge University Press); and Mason, P. (ed.) (2006) *Captured By the Media: Prison Discourse in Popular Culture* (Willan/Routledge). In addition, I would urge readers to follow up the references to some of the criminologists mentioned here who have written about film, among them, Mike Nellis, Jamie Bennett, Michael Fiddler, Richard Sparks, Eamonn Carrabine, Michelle Brown and Nicole Rafter; and some of the media/cultural theorists who are interested in crime movies, including Martin Parker, Steve Chibnall and Brian Jarvis.

Notes

1. The titles of many prison films about women give an indication of their agenda, among them: *Girls in Prison* (1956), *Women in Cages* (1971), *The Big Doll's House* (1971) and *Chicks in Chains* (1982). There are, however, exceptions, including *Yield to the Night* (1957) which starred Diana Dors as the

condemned murderess, Mary Hilton, and which Steve Chibnall (2006) credits with making a crucial contribution to the abolition of the death penalty almost a decade later.

2. The most recent instalment with the original participants was *49 Up,* broadcast in 2005, and *56 Up* is currently planned to be shown in 2011/12. A new version of *7 Up* was started in 2000, continuing with *14 Up 2000* in 2007.

3. Both films adapt their basic plot from John Godey's 1973 novel. There was an additional made-for-TV version in 1998.

8

Crime and the Surveillance Culture

CHAPTER CONTENTS	
NSA, GCHQ and the new age of surveillance	222
Panopticism	224
The surveillant assemblage	226
Control of the body	228
Governance and governmentality	230
Security and 'cybersurveillance'	232
Profit	236
Voyeurism and entertainment	239
From the panopticon to surveillant assemblage and back again	242
'Big Brother' or 'Brave New World'?: some concluding thoughts	243
Summary	248
Study questions	248
Further reading	249

OVERVIEW

Chapter 8 provides:

- An overview of recent revelations concerning the covert surveillance and spying activities of government agencies in the US and UK over their own citizens and the citizens of numerous other countries
- A consideration of the dominance of the panopticon as a metaphor for contemporary surveillance techniques.
- A discussion of the extent to which surveillance technologies and systems are linked to form carceral networks of disciplinary power.
- An exploration of the institutional rationales and motivations that have led to a dramatic expansion of surveillance over the last two decades.
- An analysis of the ways in which media and popular culture have helped us to conceptualize various forms of surveillance through their representation in newspapers, television, films, music, art and so on, and how the 'viewer society' that traditional and 'new' media have given rise to, synthesize panoptic and synoptic models of surveillance.

KEY TERMS

- carceral society
- control of the body
- cybersurveillance
- governmentality
- panopticon and panopticism

- profit
- security
- surveillant assemblage
- synopticism
- voyeurism

NSA, GCHQ and the new age of surveillance

Vodafone reveals existence of secret wires that allow state surveillance

Vodafone, one of the world's largest mobile phone groups, has revealed the existence of secret wires that allow government agencies to listen to all conversations on its networks, saying they are widely used in some of the 29 countries in which it operates in Europe and beyond.

(*Guardian*, 6 June 2014)

Everyone is under surveillance now, says whistleblower Edward Snowden

People's privacy is violated without any suspicion of wrongdoing, former National Security Agency contractor claims.

The US intelligence whistleblower Edward Snowden has warned that entire populations, rather than just individuals, now live under constant surveillance.

"It's no longer based on the traditional practice of targeted taps based on some individual suspicion of wrongdoing," he said. "It covers phone calls, emails, texts, search history, what you buy, who your friends are, where you go, who you love."

(*Guardian*, 3 May 2014)

Over the last 30 years, Western societies have experienced a rapid growth in the use of surveillance, to the extent where most citizens have come to take for granted that they are observed, monitored, classified and controlled in almost every aspect of their public lives. Such has been the volume of news about state surveillance and counter-surveillance in the form of whistle blowing by activists, military personnel, computer experts and former security employees, that such stories seem to have been circulating for a very long time. Indeed, it might appear scarcely believable that WikiLeaks, the online organisation that publishes 'secret', sensitive and classified information, only came to many people's attention in 2010 when the extent of war crimes committed by coalition troops in Afghanistan was published. Nonetheless, revelations such as those reported by the *Guardian* above, are shocking for the level of personal, intimate intrusion they claim is occurring. The disclosure by Vodafone that government agencies have been using its network to snoop on the conversations of its customers, represents the first time such an organization has publicly admitted both to initial complicity in surveillance and subsequent resistance to governments' demands for access to user data (*Guardian*, 6 June 2014).

The *Guardian* has been at the forefront of bringing revelations about the US's National Security Agency (NSA) surveillance activities to a global audience. In June 2013, Edward Snowden, a former systems administrator for the Central Intelligence Agency (CIA) and Defense Intelligence Agency (DIA), and then a contractor working for an intelligence and security company in Hawaii, allegedly downloaded 1.5 million secret files about the NSA's covert and highly controversial practices, before flying to Hong Kong to meet journalists. He then flew on to Moscow where he has been granted asylum while, in his absence, the US Department of Justice charged him with violating the Espionage Act, an offence punishable by 30 years in custody. Among Snowden's revelations were that the NSA, together with the British Intelligence Agency at GCHQ, collected the phone records of millions of citizens, accessed and collected data from Google and Facebook accounts via a program called Prism, mined personal data from smartphone apps such as 'Angry Birds', hacked computers, intercepted phone and internet communications (including those of foreign politicians attending G20 meetings), carried out offensive cyber-attacks and infected more than 50,000 computer networks worldwide with malware designed to steal sensitive information, shared raw intelligence data with Israel in an information-sharing agreement, bugged offices of the European Union, spied on at least 38 foreign embassies using a variety of electronic surveillance methods, tapped the private phone of German Chancellor Angela Merkel, sifted through vast amounts of email and text communications of its own citizens and those of many other countries, and harvested millions of faces from web images for use in a previously undisclosed facial recognition database (www.businessinsider.com/snowden-leaks-timeline-2014-6). While these examples are fairly wide-ranging, they merely represent the tip of the iceberg (see website above for a full list of 'Everything we've learned in one year of unprecedented top-secret leaks'). Snowden's fate remains uncertain but, while the US Government have branded him a traitor and criminal, his alter-ego as patriot and hero have been under-lined by his appointment, in February 2014, as Rector of Glasgow University.

At the time of writing, the scale of the US and UK Governments' surveillance programmes is still unfolding with new revelations being reported on a near-daily basis. A decade ago most academic scholarship in the field of surveillance was concerned with closed circuit television (CCTV), and experts could scarcely have envisaged how pervasive and invasive surveillance was actually becoming. Nonetheless, CCTV continues to ignite heated debate, perhaps largely because it was introduced on a rapid and grand scale in the UK with little or no public discussion. With the oft-cited estimation that the average person living and working in a major city could be filmed up to 300 times a day, surveillance became a cornerstone of the literature on 'target hardening', 'defensible space' and victimization. Some studies examined whether visual surveillance technologies such as CCTV were effective in cutting crime or whether they simply displace it to surrounding areas (with contradictory findings). Others focused on the capacity for visual surveillance systems to reduce public fears about personal safety. On the basis that these issues are dealt with at length in other books (for example Coleman and McCahill, 2010), this chapter will take a different approach and will discuss some of the key motivations behind the rapid expansion of surveillance and its potential for social classification and social control. The chapter will also attempt to blend voices from criminology with those of the most prominent writers in the fields of sociology and cultural studies. But first let us consider the primary motif that unites debates about surveillance across all academic disciplines: the Panopticon.

Panopticism

In the popular consciousness, many forms of surveillance are dominated by the figure of 'Big Brother', George Orwell's creation of an all-seeing, all-knowing, invisible super-power. In academic discussions of surveillance, however, the dominant metaphor has been that of the *panopticon*, an image that lends itself especially well to discussions of surveillance technologies which allow some individuals to monitor the behaviour of others. The panopticon, developed by 18th-century reformer Jeremy Bentham, was an architectural design that could be used for prisons, schools, factories, workhouses and any other social institutions that required the management of large groups of people by a small number of individuals with authority over them. While Bentham's vision was essentially a benign one, the panopticon became a motif for punitive prison regimes, and although it is often written that Bentham's model was never realized, several prisons have been and continue to be constructed according to the broad principles of *panopticism*. In brief, Bentham's design consisted of a circular building with individual cells built around its entire circumference, and a central watchtower in which the activities of the prisoners could be constantly watched. A system of lighting that illuminated the cells but kept the inspection tower in darkness made it possible for just one person to monitor many inmates, each of whom knew they were under surveillance, but did not know exactly when. They were therefore obliged to behave as if they were being monitored at all times, and conformity and passivity were assured. The mental state of being seen without being able to see the watcher induced a fear that eliminated the need for visible deterrents or overt force.

Writing about the plague at the end of the 17th century, Foucault (1977) describes how certain areas of a town were cordoned off and kept under continuous vigil with guards inspecting every part of the town to ensure that no-one escaped to spread the disease further. Consequently, like the inmates in Bentham's prison, the town's population were not simply observed; the surveillance of them was designed to act as a deterrent, a caution to encourage them to behave in a certain way. Thus, for Foucault, Bentham's architectural design was not only a blueprint for future surveillance technologies which would allow a small, unseen few to observe the lives of the masses, it was also a means of dispersing control over a conforming, docile population.

The panopticon was subsequently appropriated by others following Foucault's example, who took the ideological concept behind the design and used it to demonstrate the potential of new communication and information technologies. Most notably, Stan Cohen (1985) has considered numerous manifestations of surveillance, including community penalties, neighbourhood watch, private security, and the use of public surveillance cameras, and argued that they have enabled the 'dispersal' of social control. Among the consequences of dispersal are the move to informal, private and communal controls which 'widen the net' of the formal system by bringing about 'an increase in the total number of deviants getting into the system in the first place' (Cohen, 1985: 44). At the same time there is a 'thinning of the mesh' which increases 'the overall level of intervention, with old and new deviants being subject to levels of intervention (including traditional institutionalization) which they might not have previously received' (ibid.). In short, surveillance has a tendency to disperse and become operative in a wide range of social settings not merely found *within* the criminal justice state but also *alongside* it, and to subject a large number of individuals and groups to criminalization or being labelled as deviants who formerly would not have been (cf. Coleman and McCahill, 2010).

The surveillant assemblage

The pertinence of the panoptic model is obvious in relation to the widespread surveillance of private data and communications by governments as revealed by Ed Snowden. Panopticism has also been evoked to explain the insidious presence of CCTV although, as Norris and Armstrong (1999) demonstrate, the panoptic effects of CCTV systems are limited. Three shortcomings are highlighted. First, CCTV systems that operate in public spaces, such as streets, are impossible to monitor continuously and it is relatively easy for those intent on behaving deviantly to disguise their appearance or move outside of the camera's gaze. Second, even when deviance is observed, the ability to mobilize a rapid response is constrained. In most cases, CCTV operators themselves are not authorized to deal with incidents, and neither are they in a position to demand swift intervention by the police. Third, the disciplinary power of CCTV is only complete when one-way total surveillance is combined with additional information about the individual being monitored. Norris (2003) suggests that despite the massive expansion of CCTV surveillance in Britain, its operators' inability to routinely link a person's image to any more detailed knowledge or information about them, places a severe limitation on CCTV as a Panopticon; such surveillance is, as Haggerty and Ericson note, 'often a mile wide but only an inch deep' (2000: 618). To put it in its simplest terms, there is not much the police can do with a recorded image of an offence that has already taken place unless further data can be gathered about the offender – name, whereabouts, address, previous convictions and so on – hence the use that the police make of television programmes like *Crimewatch UK* in appealing to the public to 'fill in the blanks'.

However, depth, or intensity, of surveillance can also be achieved via the connection of different technologies (for example, digitized CCTV systems and computer databases) and institutions (such as the police and private security companies). In the second decade of the 21st century, social media profiles have become one of the primary sources of information about both offenders and victims and few criminal cases are reported without recourse to the self-revelations posted by the individual concerned on Facebook and Twitter. Haggerty and Ericson refer to this convergence of once discrete surveillance systems as a *'surveillant assemblage'* and argue that we have witnessed the 'disappearance of disappearance' (2000: 619). This raises the interesting question of whether our electronic identities have taken precedence over our 'real' identities. Once information (be it visual or textual) about a person is entered onto a linked surveillance system, their identity is 'fixed' even if it is 'false'. In much the same way as a person's legal identity is constructed from a mass of facts taken from the beginning to the end of life – birth certificate, passport, employment histories, medical and dental records, criminal record, post mortem, and so on – a cumulative mass of documents that captures and fixes them (Finch, 2003, 2007; cf. Foucault, 1977), so an individual can be captured in a web of non-documentary, visual surveillance.

Writing well before the advent of social media, Mark Poster was prophetic when he noted that, increasingly, in any major serious crime investigation both the victim(s) and the suspect will have their movements, consumption patterns, reading tastes, personal contacts, sexual histories and various other aspects of their private lives compiled into a detailed 'dossier that reflects the history of his [sic.] deviation from the norm' (Poster, 1990: 91). But even before the ubiquitous Facebook was invented, information was coalesced and then made public knowledge via the mainstream media. For example, following the murder of *Crimewatch UK* presenter Jill Dando on the doorstep of her London home in April 1999, it was revealed that 14,000 emails were examined, 486 names in her Filofax were investigated, and 2,400 statements were taken. Stories about Dando's relationship with her fiancé and several of her previous boyfriends appeared in the tabloid press. Further depth of knowledge was achieved by means of additional layers of surveillance. For example, after CCTV footage showed a blue Range Rover speeding south of the murder scene shortly after the killing, 1,200 cars were traced (the result of which was that seven months later the murder team arrested a man on suspicion of the theft of such a vehicle). In the week following her death, police released CCTV footage of her shopping in Hammersmith on the morning of her murder, and also revealed that their 'prime suspect' had made his getaway on a number 74 bus, speaking on a mobile phone before disembarking at Putney Bridge. A year after her murder, on 25 May 2000, Barry George (who ultimately was found not guilty of the crime and was released from prison after eight years) was arrested following a period of intensive surveillance of his home.

Another early example that illustrates the depth of information which can be achieved when fragments of data are coalesced is the police hunt for 12-year-old Shevaun Pennington, who disappeared with a 31-year-old American in July 2003 after 'meeting' him in an Internet chat room. Following Shevaun's safe return home it was reported that, despite her family's pleas for information about their missing child and her abductor, the police had known their whereabouts all along, thanks to a GPS (global positioning satellite) system picking up the suspect's mobile phone transmissions. Not only did this allow the police to triangulate the phone's location to within a few metres, but they were reportedly able to activate the phone even when it was switched off. In addition, the police alerted credit card companies so that an alarm was automatically triggered when the suspect used his credit card to buy airline tickets. Meanwhile, police in his home town were examining his personal computer where they found downloaded child pornography, and his criminal records which revealed that he had previously been charged with molesting a 12-year-old child in the US. In Wigan, Shevaun's computer was also examined, and it was discovered that, unbeknown to her parents, she had been in communication with the American for over a year. Perhaps most bizarrely, it was reported that the former marine had planned the abduction with military precision. Forensic analysis of his computer apparently revealed that his rendezvous and escape with Shevaun 'smacked of special forces "in-hit-out" tactics' (2003).

These are just two examples demonstrating that surveillance is far from a unitary technology and hasn't always relied on social media. They happen to be two high-profile criminal cases, but even when we confine our discussion to the mundane monitoring of 'ordinary' citizens by government agencies, as discussed previously in relation to the NSA and GCHQ, we are in fact referring to a nexus of computers, telecommunications and people. Taken together, these networks are said to constitute a *'carceral society'* (Foucault, 1977), whereby more and more aspects of life are becoming subject to the kind of disciplinary power that we usually associate with the prison. Moreover, these systems of discipline and domination are driven by a common set of motives and desires on the part of those who instigate and operate them. In a slight modification of Haggerty and Ericson's (2000) typology, these rationales for surveillance will be further explored in this chapter under the following headings: *control of the body*, governance and governmentality, *security* and *cybersurveillance*, *profit*, and *voyeurism* and entertainment.

Control of the body

A great deal of surveillance is directed towards monitoring, codifying and controlling the human body. Surveillance of specifically targeted groups can be achieved via an interface of technology and corporeality that can range from direct physical contact between flesh and technological device, to more oblique or covert methods of producing information (Haggerty and Ericson, 2000). The former would include the various forms of 'electronic tagging' that are now commonplace, such as securing an electronic tag round newborn babies' wrists or ankles in hospital which not only contains personal information about the child and its medical condition, but also triggers an alarm if the infant is moved beyond a secure area. The electronic monitoring of offenders and those on probation, and the use of microchips inserted under the skin of pets to monitor their whereabouts, are also examples of the diversity of applications which exploit the flesh-technology-information amalgam. Less direct forms of surveillance that rely on distanciated monitoring of corporeality include the computer monitoring of keystrokes to assess output and efficiency in offices and the visual surveillance of shop workers' body language to ensure that they are conveying the customer service ethos of their employer.

When it comes to techniques of identification, body surveillance extends beyond individuals and discrete groups to entire populations. In this respect, identity verification is achieved by means of 'biometrics', which are identification techniques based on physical attributes – fingerprints, palm scans, retina identification, body fluids and so on. In the global surveillance society, one is no longer identified by what one has (for example, a passport or credit card), or by what one knows (for example, a personal identification number or PIN), but increasingly by what one *is* – a collection of unique body parts (Aas, 2005). Ironically we have returned to the anthropometric preoccupations of the positivist school of criminology with their measurements of the body, skull and so on – albeit in a more sophisticated guise. There is, then, nothing intrinsically new about the 'informization of the body' (van der Ploeg, 2003: 58). Primitive forms of biometric identification have existed for centuries, and advancements in photography and fingerprinting at the end of the 19th century coincided with the centralization and bureaucratization of administration and record-keeping. In fact, fingerprinting is a good example of a form of surveillance that has lost a great deal of its stigma through familiarity and diversity of use. Once used uniquely by law enforcement agents to identify suspected criminals, with all the negative connotations that such an application would evoke, the use of fingerprinting has expanded to include privileged cardholders, frequent flyers, club members and library users (van der Ploeg, 2003). What *is* new is that information has 'lost' its body (Aas, 2005). Again, to take the example of forensic crime investigations, traditional fingerprinting is being superseded by 'genetic fingerprinting', otherwise known as DNA testing. Many criminal cases that had been consigned to police files years or even decades ago have been belatedly solved by recourse to DNA tests on items of clothing, weapons or other items touched by a suspect and which have been stored by investigators. But despite the fact that DNA provides a unique identifier that cannot be transferred between individuals, no system is foolproof. Even if an effective form of everyday personal identification incorporating DNA could be found, as with other technological advancements it is likely that the professional criminal and terrorist would remain one step ahead of the police (Jewkes, 2003a, 2003b). DNA can be cloned, 'planted' or, in the case of suicide bombers and terrorist 'martyrs', rendered irrelevant.

Governance and governmentality

A salient theme in the criminological literature on surveillance has been its contextualization within an 'actuarial' discourse. In other words, surveillance occupies a central role in a broad strategy of social control that has moved from being 'reactive' (that is, only activated when rules are violated) towards one that is 'proactive' (that is, tries to predict rule violations before they happen). Visual surveillance systems are thus seen as just one element within a raft of risk-calculating crime control strategies which also embrace risk assessments of 'dangerousness' in relation to prisoners and those on probation, a national register for sex offenders and the notification of communities about paedophiles in their midst, community safety partnerships undertaking local crime audits, and attempts to 'design out' crime in architecture and town planning (O'Malley, 2001; Stenson, 2001). Not only do surveillance systems underpin correctional policies, then; they have created a new mode of governance. The 'rehabilitative ideal' with its promise of 'treating' the sickness that causes individuals to offend, and its evocation of a benevolent state concerned to eradicate poverty, deprivation and hardship, dominated criminological discourse throughout much of the 20th century (McCahill and Norris, 2002). But in recent years, as concerns about crime and the perceived failures of the criminal justice system have intensified, those in power have retreated from any pretence of liberalism and adopted the language of authoritarian populism, using phrases like 'prison works', 'zero tolerance' and 'tough on crime' (Stenson, 2001).

The new discourse of governance is also reflected in the re-emergence of 'Classical' criminological theories that view crime as opportunistic and 'normal'; in other words, requiring no particular maladjustment on the part of the offender. The salience of these theoretical perspectives in recent years has been accompanied by a shift from policies directed at the individual offender to those aimed at 'criminogenic situations' including car parks, city centres at night, run-down neighbourhoods, poorly lit streets, subways, schools and colleges, shopping centres and football stadia. While one objective of the new *governmentality* is to develop methods of situational crime control, a related aim is to single out those who do not 'belong' in these environments and take pre-emptive action to exclude them. Thus, rather than attempting to tolerate, understand and rehabilitate the different and the dangerous, there has been an ideological shift towards the less expensive and simpler task of displacing them from particular locations and from opportunities to obtain goods and services; of restricting mobility and behaviour; and of managing them rather than changing them. These shifting attitudes are increasingly being seen not simply as attempts to govern crime but also to involve 'government through crime'; a new 'governmentality' (Simon, 1997). According to Stenson, it is targeted disproportionately at poor whites and ethnic minorities who are being increasingly segregated into ghettoized spaces that function as 'human garbage dumps, where survival, excitement and success and opportunities for entrepreneurship depend increasingly on involvement in illegal economies' (Stenson, 2001: 18; cf. Ferrell, 2002). Davis, writing specifically about Los Angeles, detects a similar segregation of new core business zones from the ghetto areas, a process of sequestration which, he observes, carries 'ominous racial overtones' (1994: 4).

The move to render populations quantifiable through identification, classification and differentiation is achieved through a complex network of strategies to manage danger and predict risk transformation, and it is not difficult to see how surveillance technologies have played a crucial part. As more and more of contemporary society's ills are represented as problems of 'criminality', individuals and organizations are being encouraged to view themselves as potential victims and actively respond to the risks facing them. Government of crime is thus practised not only by police and criminal justice professionals, but also by the insurance industry, communities, employers, retail managers and so on (O'Malley, 2001). Often justified in terms of their ability to monitor 'risk' groups, who pose a significant threat to economic stability or social order, the surveillance measures adopted by these diverse bodies can quickly lead to a much broader definition of dangerousness being adopted. For example, to the concern of civil liberties groups the police in England and Wales have for several years been able to take a DNA sample from anyone they arrested for, or even a witness to, a recordable offence and have been able to keep it indefinitely. The European Court of Human Rights has criticized the UK Government and ruled out the 'blanket and indiscriminate' policy of permanent retention, so there are now proposals to retain permanently the DNA profiles of offenders, but those of innocent people – arrested once, but never convicted of anything – will be destroyed after six years.

There are few issues which divide people to the extent that a national DNA database does. Many people feel inherently uncomfortable with the fact that a society governed by calculations of risk makes everyone a legitimate target for surveillance (McCahill and Norris, 2002). Another of the concerns raised by critics is that DNA does more than establish identity; it provides a complete genetic profile. The issue of race is a particularly contentious one: because young black men are disproportionately targeted by the police, it has been estimated that 40 per cent of all black men in the UK are on the database, compared with just 9 per cent of white men. Professor Sir Alec Jeffreys, the University of Leicester scientist who discovered DNA, has publicly criticized the way it is being used, likening the database to creating a 'presumption of likely future guilt' (http://news.bbc.co.uk/1/hi/uk/7532856.stm).

The growing body of research into how specific genes can predict future substance addiction, sexual orientation, and criminal and violent tendencies is also of concern to many, who argue that DNA profiling could lead to the stratification of society, creating a Brave New World based upon genetic élitism (Finch, 2003). In the other camp are those who believe that if you have nothing to hide, you have nothing to fear, and that DNA has been proved to be a powerful tool for assisting the police to catch individuals who have committed very serious crimes; sometimes many years ago. However, the suspicion of many critics that the authorities target 'low-hanging fruit' may be borne out by the admission from the Home Office in February 2010 that, while the DNA database contains samples from almost one million innocent people, they have failed to collect samples from thousands of convicted prisoners (http://www.guardian.co.uk/politics/2010/feb/18/prisoners-dna-database). In addition, while DNA-assisted convictions frequently garner the newspaper headlines and may give the impression that DNA is a miracle weapon in the fight against crime, ACPO has admitted that only 33,000 of the 4.9 million crimes the police recorded in 2009 were solved as a result of a match on the national DNA database, a statistic that prompted one MP to describe as 'negligible' the rate of DNA detections (http://www.guardian.co.uk/politics/2010/jan/05/dna-database-crime-police-vaz).

Security and 'cybersurveillance'

There are two aspects of security commonly discussed in the criminological literature on surveillance: personal safety against crime (e.g. from assault by a stranger) and security against an act of terror. In relation to the former, one of the outcomes of the processes of governance and capitalism outlined above is that, as urban space has become progressively fragmented and fortified, the population that inhabits that space become subject to feelings of insecurity and paranoia. Despite the unwanted and undesirable being left in the spaces *between* the controlled urban spaces, there is a tendency for those who occupy the newly privatized public realm to nonetheless demonize them (Graham and Clarke, 2002). As discussed elsewhere in this volume, when difference and diversity are not tolerated, far less celebrated, the inclination to regard some people as 'other' and fear them as a result becomes more pronounced. In such a climate, visible surveillance technologies may further increase public anxieties and contribute to the image of public spaces as dangerous places. Paradoxically, the solution most frequently put forward to counter the public insecurity that is, in part, generated by the prevalence of surveillance systems is to introduce yet more surveillance systems. Hence, a greater level of exclusion is created and a 'fortress mentality' of segregation and ghettoization is reinforced. For example, personal and home security devices, including do-it-yourself CCTV systems, are increasingly commonplace in urban and rural areas alike. Architects and planners in Britain are following the American example of fortified 'gated communities', offering security to residents with high walls, ID-protected gates and 24-hour surveillance systems. Meanwhile, the 2002 film *Panic Room* reflected a growing demand among affluent homeowners for indoor bunkers capable of withstanding biological, chemical and armed attack. These rooms contain a panic button to alert police, and internal CCTV monitors to allow the homeowner to view the rest of the property without risk. Although mostly found in the US, the *Observer* reports that in the UK demand is growing from businessmen, celebrities and diplomats who hail from politically volatile countries (Townsend, 2003).

There is little doubt that surveillance technologies have radically destabilized the public/private boundary, and no other issue has generated public disquiet about surveillance to the extent that fears about loss of privacy have (Lyon, 2001). Yet anxieties about acts of terror have altered people's tolerance to surveillance and, in the wake of the terrorist attacks on America in September 2001, the climate of political and public acceptability appears to have became more accepting of the idea of being monitored. For example, in the UK, as elsewhere, identity cards have been presented by government as a panacea to the problems of illegal immigration, crime and terrorism. 'Smart' ID cards hold a wide range of coded data, and can incorporate national identity card, driver's licence, health details, passport information and e-cash applications as well as eye scans or thumbprints. It is often assumed that technological progress has made it much more difficult for those with 'spoiled' (that is, criminal or illegal) identities to hide the unfavourable elements of their past, and that identity cards would ensure that goods and services would be allocated on the basis of entitlement (Finch, 2003, 2007).

However, two somewhat contradictory issues must be borne in mind. First, it has never been easier to 'fabricate a more acceptable self' (Finch, 2003: 93). Identity theft has become a growing problem, exacerbated by the ease with which it can be achieved via the Internet (Finch, 2003, 2007; Jewkes, 2003b; Aas, 2013). As Finch notes, the 'carceral network' of documentation 'fixing' the identity of the individual is, in some senses, subverted by the Internet which offers the identity thief a 'plethora of "new" identities to "try on"' (2003: 96). Furthermore, a relatively high-integrity identity can be constructed by accumulating a collection of relatively low-integrity documentation (Finch, 2003; Stalder and Lyon, 2003). Many forms of identification can be bought via the Internet, including fake passports, driving licences, birth certificates, electronic PINs and credit card numbers and, as Stalder and Lyon observe, no matter how sophisticated an ID card is, it is only as reliable as the document on which it is based. Administrative identity may be established by reference to a series of documents, but the reliability of the final document, the ID card, will be defined by the weakest link in this chain of references. If a person possesses a convincing counterfeit birth certificate, they can acquire an ID card which will duplicate whatever information happens to be on this certificate.

In addition, the scope for bribing officials to issue a genuine document in the knowledge that it contains incorrect information makes these systems much more vulnerable than their 'high-tech dazzle might suggest' (Stalder and Lyon, 2003: 84).

The second point to be considered is that not all criminals and terrorists have spoiled identities. Even a relatively sophisticated ID system could not have prevented the terrorist attacks on the Pentagon and World Trade Center from taking place in September 2001:

> Most of the 'terrorists' had valid visas and no criminal record of any sort. All three checks that ID cards can perform – verifying the legitimacy of the document, verifying the link between the person, and conducting a quick background check against a list of suspects – would have turned up negative because the documents were legitimate and most of the individuals were not on suspect lists. Terrorists, particularly the ones willing to kill themselves in the attack, belong to a special class of criminal. They rarely have prior convictions, thus background checks are rarely revealing. There are no repeat suicide bombers. (Stalder and Lyon, 2003: 85)

Moreover, the overwhelming tendency, fuelled by the popular media, to assume that all terrorists are Muslim and affiliated to networks such as al Qaeda, means that so-called, 'home-grown', 'lone wolf' perpetrators sometimes operate beneath or beyond the carceral net. Thomas Mathiesen cites a Europol report that notes that of 174 prevented and successful terrorist attacks in Europe in 2011 (of which 63 per cent were caused by separatists from France and Spain), 'no al-Qaeda affiliated or inspired attacks were carried out in EU Member States' (TE-SAT, 2012; cited Mathiesen, 2013: 72). It was in that year, however, that Anders Breivik, a right-wing, anti-Islamist extremist, killed 77 people in Norway. As Mathiesen shows, this case raises numerous important questions, not least how this man was unknown to police in the years during which he was plotting the massacre, and why it took police so long to act on intelligence received during Breivik's murderous spree on 22 July 2011, when they could possibly have saved lives. In part, he suggests, Breivik was allowed to slip under the radar precisely because he was a white, blond-haired Norwegian, dressed on the day in question in a police officer's uniform. He didn't 'look' like a terrorist, and in the months leading up to the attacks, the only thing the police had registered was that he had legally bought large amounts of fertilizer online (to make bombs), which did not alert undue suspicion as he lived on a farm.

These shortcomings have done nothing to thwart the seemingly relentless drive by governments to oversee and regulate the activities of their citizens, as the revelations by Edward Snowden have demonstrated, and it is state surveillance that remains of greatest concern to many commentators. While current fears about terrorism may have mollified the general public into accepting a greater degree of surveillance (and there is no convincing evidence that this is the case), many political commentators, human rights campaigners and civil liberties organizations have expressed extreme disquiet about the licence that governments take in unstable times. In fact, remote monitoring is no longer the exclusive privilege of state authorities and, as long ago as 2002, there was a political furore when the British Home Secretary announced plans to permit every local council and a number of other public bodies access to phone, email and Internet data; powers that previously had been uniquely held by the police, M15, M16, GCHQ, Customs and Excise and the Inland Revenue. The fact that the Government was forced to withdraw the plan in favour of one that allows for the retention of data by Internet Service Providers, has done little to allay the fears of those who believe that the Regulation of Investigatory Powers Act 2000 (RIPA) already makes Britain the most surveilled country in Europe (see Edwards et al., 2010; and Walden, 2010, for discussions of RIPA and its implications).

In the States, the principal legislative response to 9/11 was the legislation entitled 'Uniting and Strengthening of America to Provide Appropriate Tools Required to Intercept and Obstruct Terrorism Act of 2001' (USA PATRIOT Act), hastened into law the month after the attacks on New York and Washington. This act expanded powers to require businesses to turn over records to the FBI and Internet Service Providers (ISPs) to preserve all data specific to a client for a specified period of time. The Act also included proposals that require college and university administrators to provide authorities with any information on foreign students suspected of being involved in terrorism and proposals to make medical records of suspects available to investigators (Coleman and McCahill, 2010). Not everyone feels secure in the knowledge that state authorities have this level of power to monitor the communications and movements of individuals, not least because they frequently fail to identify and act on a known threat, for example the Boston Marathon bomber, Tamerlan Tsarneav, who had previously been investigated by the FBI at the request of officials in the Russian Federation. More worrying for many in the aftermath of the 'War on Terror' is that American governments have a long and troubled history of defining deviants, miscreants and people displaying the 'wrong kind' of patriotism, and post-9/11 fears that persons with 'Arab' or 'Muslim' backgrounds are among the primary targets of intensive surveillance at airports or border checkpoints (Lyon, 2003) have not receded. Dissenters claim that the sweeping legislation brought in by governments around the world in response to the fear of terrorist attack is applied indiscriminately – or indeed applied very discriminately and knowingly to individuals and contexts that pose no terrorist threat but are being surveilled for other reasons. For example, in Spain, anti-globalization protestors have complained of monitoring by security forces who equate them with 'terrorists' (Coleman and McCahill, 2010). The US intelligent search agent 'Echelon', which intercepts and monitors traffic on commercial communications satellites and is essentially a sophisticated 'eavesdropping' device, was justified on grounds of terrorism and crime, but has been found to routinely intercept valuable private commercial data (Hamelink, 2000).

Of course, surveillance does not necessarily rely on technology. The disciplinary and repressive character of the Panopticon was exemplified by its ability to influence behaviour and transform selves. Using only a fairly primitive lighting system the panoptic prison engendered a climate of fear and paranoia. History shows that the most oppressive political regimes do not necessarily require high-tech methods to achieve the same aim. For example, the Romanian dictator Nicolae Ceausescu (who ruled between 1965 and 1989, when he and his wife were overthrown and executed) and the former leader of Iraq, Saddam Hussein, both created a low-tech climate of fear based on a culture of enforced eavesdropping that effectively amounted to a total surveillance society, with secret police mandated to employ rudimentary forms of torture to ensure that self-imposed censorship was upheld. But the Internet has taken whispering campaigns to a new and potentially dangerous level – described by Valier as 'transnational vengeful networks' (2004: 103) – as the man mistaken for child killer Jon Venables found when a Facebook page was created urging vigilantes to kill him. Moreover, the monitoring of communications by governments in the West might be seen as no more lawful, for all its high-tech gloss and covert methods, than the practices of Ceaucescu and Saddam. As communications intelligence has moved its operations from narcotics trafficking, money laundering and terrorism to intercepting 'ordinary' citizens' personal and commercial telex messages, mobile phone communications, e-mails and Internet traffic, notions of what is 'acceptable' in the interests of security are once again under scrutiny.

Profit

One of the most significant drives behind the expansion of surveillance comes from the companies who manufacture the hardware and software, many of which were once suppliers of military equipment, but have adapted to a changing global market. As the technology becomes more sophisticated, the commercial market for surveillance equipment sets to grow even further, with manufacturers of biometric access controls and facial recognition software among the most profitable. CCTV systems are themselves big business: in the period of rapid expansion of CCTV in the 1990s the UK Government invested 75 per cent of its crime prevention budget in CCTV schemes and in the 10 years to 2002 committed over a quarter of a billion pounds of public money to its expansion through the City Challenge Competition and Crime Reduction Programmes (Norris, 2003). In total around £500 million has been invested in CCTV in the UK, which makes it the single most heavily-funded crime prevention measure operating outside the criminal justice system (Welsh and Farrington, 2008). Sadly, its impact on offending has been described as 'modest'; it is only in car parks that it has had any significant effect (ibid.). But while car thefts and break-ins may have declined as a result of CCTV, motorists are likely to be victimized (or criminalized, depending on your point of view) by other kinds of camera. According to one insurance company, 2 million drivers are caught speeding each year on roads (an increase of 328 per cent over a decade) and the fines generated from these cameras exceed £114 million every year (www.swiftcover.com/about/press/speed_cameras_cost/).

The desire for profit has interesting social implications. When Foucault (1977) developed his vision of surveillance as a form of hierarchical social control, he emphasized the power that panoptic surveillance techniques had over the masses, stating that surveillance did more than observe and monitor people. For Foucault, panoptic surveillance targets the soul, disciplining the working populace into a form of self-regulation designed to meet the requirements of the developing factory system (Haggerty and Ericson, 2000). However, Bauman (1992) argues that surveillance is becoming less about discipline and repression, and more to do with classifying individuals according to their conspicuous wealth and consumption patterns, seducing those deemed 'desirable' into the market economy. With the advent of networks of computers 'data mining' has become operational through the extraction of information about individual citizens and can be used to classify high and low value customers for corporations, in just the same way that it can be used to assess and rank 'high' or 'low' risk groups in relation to criminal behaviour (Coleman and Norris, 2000). There are three potential outcomes of this process. First, surveillance can be used to construct and monitor consumption patterns in order that detailed consumer profiles can be put together. Second, these profiles can then be used to predict future behaviour or consumption habits, lure customers to a rival organization, or even encourage people to buy items they may not otherwise have purchased, on the basis that they fit in with a pre-existing aspect of their lives. This increases potential profits for corporations based on knowledge of consumer behaviour in the name of 'efficiency' (Coleman and McCahill, 2010). Third, surveillance can be used to differentiate between populations, limiting the movements of some on the basis of their identity profiles, consumption habits or spending power. The meeting of certain criteria by desirable (i.e. relatively affluent) consumers might then determine anything from preferential credit ratings to rapid movement through customs and airports (Haggerty and Ericson, 2000).

These processes combine to create what Gandy (1993) terms the 'panoptic sort'; a situation in which *all* individuals are continuously identified, assessed and sorted into hierarchies which are then used to manage and control their access to goods and services. Furthermore, they have taken place against a backdrop of changes which have resulted in the supremacy of conspicuous consumption and the commodification of the city. No longer are Western cities characterized by industrialization and an emphasis on welfare. Now big budgets are made available for advertising the virtues of cities, and the role of CCTV has been recast as not simply a means of deterring criminals, but also as a friendly eye in the sky promoting the 'feel good factor' for those who work, visit or are at leisure there (McCahill and Norris, 2002). Shopping centres or malls have become the cathedrals of the age but were, from the start, designed with a darker touch of the panoptic prison where visibility and surveillance prevailed (Langman, 1992). The mall's primary defining characteristic is that it is an enclosed aggregation more or less isolated from the larger environment. Moreover, within its boundaries, everything, from temperature to the movement of people and the shop displays, is rigorously controlled to permit consumption of an unending stream of spectacles. But within these cathedrals of capitalism, the weak create their own 'spaces', inflicting damage on the strategic interests of the powerful. De Certeau (1984) uses the language of warfare, arguing that subordinates are like guerrillas, appropriating space as a means of resistance; an apt metaphor for the 'mall rats' who gather in shopping centres. Presdee also elaborates on this subject in his study of unemployed youth in a South Australian town, 80 per cent of whom visit the local shopping mall at least once a week, aggressively 'invading the space' of those with a legitimate right to be there (Presdee, 1986: 13). These 'outsiders' are tricking the system, consuming images, warmth and places of consumerism, without any intention of buying its commodities. At the same time, they offend 'real' consumers and security personnel by asserting their difference within, and different use of, the glittering palaces (Presdee, 1986; Fiske, 1989). Presdee's research details the various ways in which the young unemployed appropriate the space for subversive performance and resistance, including illegal drinking, provoking security guards and crowding round shop windows, preventing 'real' customers from seeing the displays or entering the stores. Little wonder, then, that the 'policing' of malls has become progressively more rigid and uncompromising in recent years, as witnessed by the ban on young people wearing 'hoodies' in many retail outlets. The desire to remove 'undesirables' is an economic one: 'the malls are there to make profits, to sell goods and services, not to provide environments for "deviants" who refuse to spend or who cannot afford to spend' (Bocock, 1993: 107).

The drive to exclude some individuals from certain public spaces raises questions about the kind of society that is left as a result. There is a danger that the moral engineer has replaced the social engineer (Stenson, 2001) as 'difference' is eliminated and those who do not conform are displaced to the dark, and often dangerous, corners of the city where their capacity to 'convey a negative image' is less material (Norris and Armstrong, 1999: 45). Numerous writers have drawn on themes of cleanliness and dirt in attempting to characterize the ordering of contemporary public spaces. For example, Mulgan (1989) describes how CCTV is used to purify space of the homeless and alcoholics in order to create a convivial atmosphere for those who conform to the demands of the consumerist environment. Lyon (2003: 22) further notes that the poor are 'cleaned away' from cities for tourism. Meanwhile Bauman (1997: 14) refers to the 'new impure' who are prevented from responding to the entice-ments of the consumer market and are thus dismissed as 'the dirt of post-modern purity'. These analogies recall the work of anthropologist Mary Douglas, who argues that the elimination of 'dirt' is a positive effort to organ-ize the environment; dirt invites social control because it is perceived as a threat to order. There has also been, in recent years, a more literal manifesta-tion of this idea, with restrictions in many city centres on litter dropping, alcohol consumption, smoking and traffic. McCahill further notes that in the city centre shopping mall he observed, banned activities included walking a dog, pushing a bicycle, eating, sitting on the floor and lying down. When CCTV operatives observed these kinds of behaviours, a patrol guard would be deployed to request that the miscreant 'position their body in a way conducive to the commercial image of the mall' (McCahill, 2002: 128). In this respect, the flawed consumers who come under surveillance in shopping malls are, quite simply, 'matter out of place' (Douglas, 1966: 2).

Voyeurism and entertainment

While many commentators argue that recent developments in systems of sur-veillance and social control have augmented an intensification of panopticism (where the few observe the many), an emerging theme in the sociological and criminological literature on surveillance has been that of *'synopticism'*, where the many observe the few (Mathiesen, 1997). Synopticism has been acceler-ated by the proliferation of mobile phone cameras, which have led to a number of instances where members of the public have filmed events that were not 'meant' to be seen, or have simply arrived on the scene before jour-nalists, and either posted the footage online or sold it to national television networks for broadcast around the world. For some, this is the essence of synopticism's appeal: 'surveillance footage represents one of the crudest satis-factions of the scopophilic drive, a sense of power at being privileged to see that which was meant to remain unseen: the point at which the private ... goes public' (Dovey, 1996: 127).

In fact, the drive is not only to look, but to be looked at. In the 21st century, to be watched elicits a positive as well as a negative response, a synoptic devel-opment which suggests that CCTV, video and webcam footage is as much about entertainment as it is control. The popularity of social networking sites such as Facebook, Instagram, Snapchat, LinkedIn and Twitter are testament to the desire to see and be seen. In addition, the 'reality TV' genre that surveillance, home movie equipment and mobile phone cameras have given rise to has revolutionized television. Where television documentaries and news-based programmes were once 'normal, safe, middle class and secure', surveillance footage of serious and spectacular crimes as they happen have taken these formats into the realm of the extraordinary, the 'raw' and the dangerous (Dovey, 1996: 129). And inevitably, they are not only shown on local and national television stations but are available to a global population via YouTube.

Other media genres similarly exploit the information and entertainment potential of surveillance technologies. As we saw in Chapter 6, CCTV clips are an integral component of news broadcasts and interactive programmes like *Crimewatch UK*, as well as light entertainment programmes that show the police and emergency services at work, or which expose 'rogue traders', deviants and criminals. In the postmodern quest for the hyperreal, the desire to be part of the 'action' may be satisfied by the ability to see it played out as it was caught on camera. Although clearly a more secondhand experience than actually being there, it may constitute the 'next best thing'; or arguably the 'best thing' in so far as one can 'witness' a criminal, dangerous or spectacular event from the safety of one's home. Not only do news programmes, documentaries and populist entertainment shows routinely make use of both CCTV and domestic video footage of everything from high-speed police car chases to air disasters, but there is a burgeoning trade for such material on the Internet. Newspapers also use stories involving CCTV footage to fill their pages. In a study of three British newspapers, McCahill (2003) finds that CCTV constitutes a 'good news story' because it illustrates many of the key journalistic news criteria and 'adds value' to already newsworthy stories. As we saw in Chapter 2 the mainstream media frequently deal in binary oppositions, and McCahill reports that this is no less true in the reporting of CCTV-related stories than any other news event. He discovers that the central discursive reporting strategy is that of a polarization between 'respectable' or 'powerful' targets of CCTV and deviant 'others'. The press have thus created an 'us' and 'them' divide, with 'us' embodied by the figure of the modern motorist at the mercy of the most expansive network of speed cameras in Europe and being hammered unfairly by a revenue-hungry government, and 'them' being the legitimate targets for surveillance; muggers, robbers, terrorists and the like.

So, surveillance is a common theme in mediated culture. Indeed, we find that art, science fiction, comic books, jokes and cartoons, film, advertising and popular music have all anticipated and even inspired surveillance systems and their applications (the *James Bond* films, *Star Trek* and *Spider-Man* being just a few of examples). Gary Marx (1995) suggests that these cultural materials can further help us understand surveillance by providing an alternative language of visual metaphors (for example, Sting's 'classic' pop song 'Every Breath You Take' offers a plethora of metaphors for omnipresent and omnipotent surveillance; 1995: 114). They remind us that the meaning of surveillance is contested and is often about power (Charlie Chaplin's 1927 film *Modern Times* contains surveillance themes to illustrate the relationship between controller and controlled, manager and worker). Many cultural artefacts convey the profound ambivalence of our culture toward surveillance technologies which can both protect and violate (take two Bob Dylan songs – 'Subterranean Home Sick Blues' and 'Talkin' John Birch Paranoid Blues' – by way of example). Yet we can often see that the meaning is not in the object but in the context and in how it is interpreted (most people would agree that the song 'Santa Claus is Coming to Town' – Santa knows where you are sleeping, he knows when you're awake, he knows if you've been bad or good, so be good for goodness sake' – is an illustration of benign panopticism). There is, as several commentators have observed, nothing inherently threatening or sinister in the technology itself. Finally, cultural material raises new questions for social research, such as: what is the effect of popular media creating an environment that welcomes, tolerates or opposes new surveillance? Does constant media exposure normalize, routinize, domesticate or trivialize surveillance? (Marx, 1995: 106ff).

Marx reminds us that cultural material must be viewed against the backdrop of the times, and a detailed analysis such as his can tell us much about technological evolution and public attitudes to surveillance. For example, Hitchcock's dark depiction of voyeuristic surveillance, *Rear Window* (1954), was released at the height of the Cold War when a climate of suspicion prevailed and people distrusted even their neighbours. The television series *The Prisoner* (1967) was broadcast at a time when fears about technological progression collided with the ubiquity of the gadget-laden secret agent in popular fiction, television and cinema. Following the period of McCarthyism when political attention was directed toward the enemy within, as opposed to the enemy without, *The Prisoner* both reflected this theme and anticipated the impending Watergate scandal, perfectly encapsulating the escalating conspiracy theories of the period. More recently, films such as Spielberg's *Minority Report* (2002) reflect current developments in face and eye recognition techniques, as well as underlying concerns about the potential applications of new surveillance technologies. Set in a police state, circa 2054, *Minority Report* seamlessly combines current allegiances to proactive crime strategies with an equally contemporary faith in 'new age' prescience to raise questions about the ethics of taking predictions as 'facts' (a point that brings to mind the newly-proposed charge of 'grooming', which is causing concern among civil liberties groups because it is designed to target adults who meet a child after contact has been made on the Internet but *before* any offence has taken place; this 'real life' example raises the same question as Spielberg's movie, that is, whether *thinking* about criminal acts is the same as committing them).

In short, perhaps what Marx's analysis demonstrates most forcefully is that over the last century, surveillance has been consistently viewed, at best, with ambivalence, and at worst with paranoia and hostility; indeed, all the examples discussed link oppression and exploitation with technologies of seeing. Surveillance technologies and their uses may have evolved to an extent that George Orwell could only have nightmares about, but the sentiments with which they are viewed by society at large show a significant degree of cultural continuity (Marx, 2002).

From the panopticon to surveillant assemblage and back again

Of course, these categories – control of the body, governance, security, profit and entertainment – are far from mutually exclusive. A brief consideration of recent developments in workplace surveillance serves to illustrate the constitutive nature of surveillance rationales. Originally justified by the fear of external threats, surveillance technologies have inevitably been turned inwards, and workers in a wide range of employment sectors now come under the scrutiny of their managers. The notion of trust – once regarded as an essential element of the management–staff relationship – has arguably been displaced by surveillance systems which are now in regular use to deter theft, monitor areas that were previously the responsibility of supervisors, assess training needs, ensure that the correct organizational procedures are followed, monitor compliance with health and safety regulations, check that goods are not being damaged during loading and unloading procedures, observe workers taking unauthorized breaks, and encourage punctual time-keeping (cf. McCahill, 2002: 153ff.). In all these practices, the governance–security–profit alliance can be discerned in various guises and formations. Moreover, it is not just employees, but also *potential* employees who are vulnerable to forms of surveillance. As I discuss elsewhere (Jewkes, 2003a), there exists software capable of sifting through any written communication and spotting when the writer is lying or confused about the facts. One of the potential applications of this high-tech lie detector is for companies to recognize embellished or false CVs, which they can then reject on principles very closely aligned to the governance–security–profit motives discussed above. On the other hand, many employers may prefer the cheaper and simpler method of checking out applicants' profiles on their social networking sites to make judgements about their suitability for employment.

But it is arguably surveillance that targets the body as an object to be monitored and controlled that is most alarming to the majority of employees. Examples of surveillance technologies that are being introduced in work environments around the world are toilet bowls that automatically check for drugs and CCTV cameras in cubicles that then film the people who test positive, sensors monitoring whether workers wash their hands after visiting the washroom, smart badges that track employees' movements, high-tech clocking-on procedures, and various 'Big Brother' systems that check the performance quality of staff in call centres and other telephone-based work environments – including the number of calls taken and the number of calls with a 'successful' outcome in a given time period (Hamelink, 2000; Jewkes, 2003a). Even more insidious are the workplace surveillance systems that monitor employees' presentation of self; for example, ensuring that service industry workers are always smiling and using appropriate body language. In these circumstances, the employee becomes the 'bearer of their own surveillance' and the panoptic model is once again recalled:

> In the enclosed and controlled setting of the workplace CCTV can easily become an instrument of disciplinary power exercised through the architecture of the panopticon, allowing management to see everything without ever being seen themselves ... In the name of 'customer service' employees' gestures, facial expressions and body language all become subject to the disciplinary gaze ... The anticipatory conformity that this induces in employees who recognize that they are always potentially under surveillance presents management with an extremely powerful managerial tool. (McCahill, 2002: 162–3)

And if there seems little voyeuristic entertainment value in these workplace examples, consider the case in 1996 of the Australian police officers caught on camera having sex, drinking alcohol and taking drugs while at work, a series of misdemeanours made more embarrassing by the fact that they were subsequently broadcast on several television networks in Australia and round the world. Or closer to home is the case of Claire Swire who, in July 2001, was severely reprimanded by her employer when she sent a risqué message from her work email address to her boyfriend at a different company. In a short space of time the offending email was forwarded to an estimated 10 million people, several of whom were themselves disciplined or suspended from work; a series of personal misfortunes that inspired a BBC television series called *E-mails You Wish You'd Never Sent*.

'Big Brother' or 'Brave New World'?: some concluding thoughts

Much of this chapter has been concerned with the ways in which surveillance systems are bound up with wider relations of power and discipline, reinforcing existing inequalities along traditional lines of class, gender, ethnicity and age. This stance is in line with most critical criminologists who have been generally sceptical (if not downright hostile) to the idea that surveillance technologies liberate, empower and comfort the general citizenry. The panoptic model of top-down scrutiny is exemplified by Coleman and Sim's (2000) analysis of CCTV in Liverpool city centre, in which the authors argue that the surveillant gaze is turned almost continuously downward on those who are already disenfranchised. By contrast, they say, there is a virtual absence of 'upward' surveillance of the powerful, 'whose often socially detrimental and harmful activities remain effectively beyond scrutiny and regulation' (2000: 637). However, several commentators have taken exception to the idea that the powerful are exempt from the watchful gaze and argue that power does not entirely reside in the hands of those at or near the top of social and occupational hierarchies. There are numerous examples that could be offered which support this; not least the whistleblowers who expose wrongdoing by those in power. While WikiLeaks source, Chelsea (formerly Bradley) Manning, and Ed Snowden, are the most high-profile whistle-blowers of recent years – together with the journalists they co-operated with to bring their disclosures to a global audience – good old-fashioned investigative journalism remains a cornerstone of the fourth, and indeed, fifth estate, as the *Telegraph*'s exposure of the MP's expenses scandal in 2009 illustrated. Further, as Haggerty and Ericson (2006) comment, and as Snowden's disclosures about the extent of government snooping appear to bear out, contemporary surveillance transforms traditional social hierarchies because people from all social backgrounds are now under surveillance in many aspects of their everyday lives. Indeed, those most subject to surveillance are likely to be the relatively privileged and most affluent who use regularly use credit cards, mobile phones and computers.

Haggerty and Ericson (2000: 617) concede that the targeting of surveillance *is* differential, but assert that it has nonetheless 'transformed hierarchies of observation', allowing for the scrutiny of the powerful by both institutions and the general population. Examples of 'bottom-up' surveillance include the introduction of CCTV systems into police custody suites and cells, allowing the activities of custody officers to come under just as much scrutiny as those of the inmates (Newburn and Hayman, 2001), and the global proliferation of video cameras that has resulted in numerous recordings of police brutality and government abuses of human rights (Dovey, 1996). In addition, it has been suggested that surveillance contributes to 'the political pluralism central to democracy by making ... [its] tools ... widely available so that citizens and competing groups can *use them against each other*, as well as government, to enhance accountability' (Marx, 2002: 22, emphasis added). Dovey (1996: 126) expands on this notion of 'lateral, intrasocial surveillance', noting that police issue members of Neighbourhood Watch groups with camcorders, neighbours film each other's anti-social behaviour to use as evidence in court, and parents surveil their kids for drug abuse. Returning to a familiar theme, he says: 'here's a panopticon where the warders in the all-seeing tower can go home, safe in the knowledge that the inmates are all busy trying to record each other's misdemeanours on video tape' (1996: 126).

It is not just bottom-up or lateral surveillance that may enhance due process, fairness and legitimacy (Marx, 2002). Those who operate conventional top-down CCTV systems have also been known to resist the 'higher' authority of the police in a show of solidarity with their subjects. McCahill notes that many of the security personnel in the shopping centre he observed were from the same part of town as the people they spent their days observing and monitoring; they went to school together, played on the same football team, knew each other's families. This degree of familiarity between the observers and the observed is interesting for three reasons. First, it endorses Gillespie and McLaughlin's (2002) findings that a less punitive attitude to 'offenders' is adopted when a 'deeper knowledge' of their background is known. Second, it challenges the notion implicit in the moral panic thesis that exaggerated public responses to deviants are magnified when the perceived threat is 'close to home'. Third, the fact that watchers and watched are known to each other inevitably places limits on the disciplinary potential of the surveillance systems:

> [Some] security officers are not always willing to co-operate with the police. For instance, the local beat officer has given the security personnel a list of 'wanted' persons and asked them to give him a ring ... if they see any of these suspects on camera. However, whether or not this information reaches the beat officer depends upon the degree of familiarity between the security officers and the local 'surveilled' population ... Recall, for example, the security officer who said, 'I wouldn't grass ... on Tommo 'cause he's all right, he's never given me any bother'. (McCahill, 2002: 199)

Even in the workplace, the notion of surveillance as panopticism is not universally endorsed. Zureik (2003: 44ff.) summarizes several studies that challenge the view that all surveillance by managers of workers is exploitative and disempowering. One report, by Mason et al. (2000), provides evidence from several work environments to support their argument that both workers and unions generally accept surveillance as an extension of traditional monitoring in the workplace, and have no problems with it as long as it is transparent, based on collective agreement, and does not contravene the law (cited in Zureik, 2003). In fact, many workers welcome the 'electronic supervisor' because it provides protection against unfair work distribution, violence and bullying, and accusations of negligence or poor productivity. On the whole, though, a distinction is drawn between surveillance of work, and surveillance of the worker, with only the former being deemed acceptable. For example, a report from the Office of the Data Protection Commissioner (2000: 28) recommends that monitoring should not violate trust nor be excessive and 'should not intrude unnecessarily on employees' privacy and autonomy' (cited in

Zureik, 2003). Marx believes that this recommendation is not being heeded by many employers, and that the 'information-gathering net' is constantly expanding to encompass aspects of workers' private lives, personal characteristics, appearance and so on. Genetic testing and screening are being introduced into the workplace to allow employers to assess the behavioural dispositions of potential employees and their propensity to certain illnesses. Because they claim to rely on precise scientific evidence, they have been characterized as 'total surveillance' (Regan, 1996: 23); a feature that makes these forms of surveillance qualitatively different to the CCTV cameras and their operators in McCahill's English shopping centre.

It might be argued, then, that discussions of surveillance have a tendency to flatten the terrain of power, control and the role of individuals in social systems, and that a more finely nuanced approach is required. The Panopticon has been a useful metaphor for the notion of surveillance as social control and has given rise to several theoretical developments of the original concept: synopticism (Mathiesen, 1997), 'super-panopticism' (Poster, 1990) and 'post-panopticism' (Boyne, 2000) to name a few. But the main limitation of the panoptic thesis is that it overstates the power of systems, institutions and processes and underplays the importance of the individual actor. The human element is often forgotten or ignored (a response known as 'technological determinism'), but as Lyon reminds us, socio-technical surveillance systems are affected by people complying with, negotiating, or resisting surveillance (Lyon, 2003, 2007). One of the foremost commentators on surveillance and social sorting, Lyon has always argued that surveillance is ambiguous and that technologies which permit surveillance can be positive and beneficial, enabling new levels of mobility, efficiency, productivity, convenience and comfort. In the contemporary everyday world of telephone transactions, Internet surfing, affordable domestic as well as international air travel, street-level security and work, the metaphors of Big Brother and the Panopticon may indeed seem increasingly less relevant. What is more, a general ethos of self-surveillance is encouraged by the availability of home testing kits and do-it-yourself health checks, allowing people to test for alcohol level, pregnancy, AIDS and hereditary or potentially fatal medical conditions (Marx, 2002). Such innovations empower people and offer them personal choice (for example, whether to have a child if there is risk of it being born with a congenital illness) on an unprecedented scale.

The subject of surveillance thus remains contradictory and contested. In the pursuit of the goals discussed in this chapter – control, governance, security, profit and voyeuristic entertainment – surveillance would seem to go hand in hand with suspicion and segregation. But several commentators have highlighted the extent to which surveillance can be played with and used for fun, seduction, narcissism, even exhibitionism. Perhaps more significant than any other development is the centrality of mobile phones and social networking sites to the ways in which we communicate with and 'keep tabs' on each other. Online social networking has taken Mathiesen's 'viewer society' to a completely new level and created scopophiles of us all. The increasing numbers of (especially) young women willing to expose intimate details of their private thoughts, lives and bodies through online diaries and blogs, reality TV shows and bedroom-based webcams challenges the idea of 'panopticism' with its rather threatening implications of authoritarian control (Koskela, 2006; see also Chapter 9). But the fact that we've become a culture that enjoys watching and being watched 'socially' may make us more inured to other forms of surveillance, for example those introduced in the name of 'security'. Younger generations in particular may be so accustomed to the Internet and increased social visibility that they do not think, let alone protest, about the erosion of civil liberties: quite simply, 'the general tide of surveillance washes over us all' (Haggerty and Ericson, 2000: 609).

However, while most of us barely notice the extent to which we are at the centre of a surveillance society, so easily have we internalized the changes in our conduct (using swipe cards instead of keys to access our workplaces, banking online rather than 'in person', keeping in touch with our friends using mobile phones, email and social networking sites, and so on), there can be no doubt that the Internet has also changed the ways in which 'private' information is shared, controlled and compromised. Now when *any* serious crime occurs (or, for that matter other stories, such as suicides and fatal accidents) the first port of call for journalists is the social network site of each of the individuals involved and the millions of users who regularly upload personal information into cyberspace with relatively little control over how it may eventually be used and abused may end up regretting their self-disclosures, as Amanda Knox and Raffaele Sollecito surely must. Convicted of the sexual assault and murder of Leeds University student, Meredith Kercher, in Perugia, Italy in November 2007, they found aspects of their characters exposed to a global media audience when – before they were even formally charged – the press reproduced text and images from their social media pages (including pictures of them individually posing with weapons) and linked this content to the police allegations against them (see Chapter 2).

Like any technological innovation, then, surveillance must be viewed as part of a network of systems that operate within a wider context of political, cultural, technological and economic shifts. For Lyon (2006), the conundrum at the heart of surveillance is that the more stringent and rigorous the panoptic regime – for example, compulsory biometric ID cards – the more it generates active resistance, whereas the more soft and subtle the panoptic strategies – for example, social networking sites – the more it produces docile subjects. Dystopia or utopia? In the words of the other (Channel 4) *Big Brother* – you decide!

Summary

- Advances in technology have resulted in the disciplinary gaze being extended beyond the confines of closed and controlled environments, such as the prison or the factory, to encompass society as a whole. The exponential growth of surveillance techniques in most areas of contemporary life have led some commentators to suggest that the primary advantage of technological advancement is the potential that arises for risk management at a distance. Discussions of surveillance have been dominated by pessimistic images of 'Big Brother' and the panopticon, metaphors that have helped to perpetuate the notion that surveillance technologies are linked to insidious and repressive forms of regulation and social control. However, in recent years the idea of the 'synopticon' has emerged to challenge this cynical and despairing view. Views of surveillance systems are now split between those who hold that technologies such as CCTV constrain people's activities, restrict their behaviour, and are used to regulate demonized 'others', and those who characterize surveillance as essentially liberating and democratizing.
- It has been suggested that we are increasingly witnessing the convergence of once disconnected systems to the point that we can now speak of a 'surveillant assemblage' (Haggerty and Ericson, 2000). The systems of discipline and domination that make up this convergence of once discrete systems are driven by five principal motives: control of the body, governance, security, profit and entertainment, all of which have significant social and cultural implications. An analysis of surveillance in the workplace has served to illustrate these motives in situ, and has demonstrated the arguments for and against the regulation and monitoring of individuals.
- The subject of surveillance remains an ideological battleground, but whatever view one takes of its purposes and outcomes, it must be remembered that technologies such as CCTV do not exist in a cultural vacuum, and are inextricably entwined with the human motives, values and behaviour of both observers and observed.

STUDY QUESTIONS

1. Due to limitations of space this chapter has only discussed in detail a few of the systems and practices that can broadly be defined as 'surveillance'. How many other applications of surveillance (in both its guises as coded data collection and visual monitoring) can you identify in contemporary Britain?

2. Gary Marx (1995) demonstrates that surveillance motifs are pervasive in popular culture. They range from themes of erotic fantasy (of secret watching) to political paranoia about the 'enemy within'. What are the impacts of the widespread cultural treatment of surveillance as entertainment on the public at large? Do they help to 'normalize' surveillance and make it acceptable, or do they increase public fears and anxieties about crime?

3. For all their benign appearance, are sites like Facebook and Twitter simply the most instant and global means of surveillance on the planet? Are they just the most effective way of keeping in touch or do they legitimize people spying on each other and make the notion of privacy (and indeed friendship) a thing of the past?

4. The UK DNA database currently stores over two million profiles, but there are frequent discussions about whether it should be extended, even to the entire population of the UK (though such suggestions are currently being held in check by the European Court of Human Rights). What are the pros and cons of keeping samples taken from the entire population on a national DNA database? Would such a move reduce discrimination or might it create 'at risk' categories which reinforce racial and ethnic stereotypes (Nelkin and Andrews, 2003)?

5. From your reading of this subject, would you say that on the whole, surveillance systems empower or constrain?

FURTHER READING

So vast has the subject of surveillance now become, and so expansive is the criminological literature on the subject, that this chapter has been able to do no more than scratch the surface. By including discussions of surveillance as entertainment, and the surveillant properties of Internet sites like Facebook, it has selectively picked out some themes which strike a chord with discussions throughout *Media & Crime*. Inevitably, however, this has been at the expense of more detailed analyses of the surveillance-governance-security nexus, which is more commonly addressed in criminological circles. The most comprehensive and up-to-date overviews of surveillance are: Coleman, R. and McCahill, M. (2010) *Surveillance and Crime* (Sage), and Mathiesen, T. (2013) *Towards a Surveillant Society* (Waterside Press). Also excellent are: B. Goold and D. Neyland (eds) (2009) *New Directions in Surveillance and Privacy* (Willan/Routledge); K. F. Aas, H. O. Gundhus and H. M. Lomell (eds) (2008) *Technologies of InSecurity: The Surveillance of Everyday Life* (Routledge); and K. Haggerty and R. Ericson (eds) (2006) *The New Politics of Surveillance and Visibility* (Toronto University Press). David Lyon has been prolific on the subject of surveillance and all his books are worth a look, including his published 'conversation' with Zygmunt Bauman, *Liquid Surveillance* (2012, Polity). There is an excellent e-journal devoted to surveillance – *Surveillance & Society* – which can be accessed at http://www.surveillance-and-society.org/ojs/index.php/journal, and *Crime, Media, Culture: An International Journal* also embraces new research on surveillance technologies as well as other 'new' and alternative media: http://cmc.sagepub.com. Finally, it is worth reading the *Guardian*'s reports on the Snowden revelations and their repercussions: www.theguardian.com/world/series/the-snowden-files

9

The Role of the Internet in Crime and Deviance

CHAPTER CONTENTS

Redefining deviance and democratization: developing
nations and the case of China   254

Cyber-warfare and cyber-terrorism   257

'Ordinary' cybercrimes   259

Electronic theft and abuse of intellectual property rights   259

Hate crime   260

Invasion of privacy, defamation and identity theft   262

eBay fraud   264

Hacking and loss of sensitive data   265

Child pornography and online grooming   267

Childhood, cyberspace and social retreat   268

Concluding thoughts   271

Summary   272

Study questions   273

Further reading   273

OVERVIEW

Chapter 9 provides:

- A brief overview of the ways in which linked, mobile, digital technologies have revolutionized the ways in which (especially young) people communicate and interact with each other.

- Discussion of the 'digital divide' and an analysis of the ways in which the Internet and World Wide Web are shaping the development of China as it moves from totalitarianism to 'market authoritarianism' and partial democracy.

- A description of some of the 'ordinary' cybercrimes that most frequently appear in the news.

- Reflection on the ways in which the Internet is transforming, not only young people's leisure and pleasure habits, but specifically and explicitly their sexual development.

KEY TERMS

- content
- cybercrime
- cyberspace
- cybersurveillance
- cyber-terrorism
- cyber-warfare

- democratization
- digital divide
- Internet
- user-generated content
- World Wide Web

Over the last two decades take-up of the **Internet** has resulted in radical and far-reaching changes in both industrialized nations and, increasingly, in the 'developing world'. Even in the period since the first edition of this book was published (in 2004, just as Mark Zuckerberg was setting up Facebook as a local-ized college directory and messaging service at Harvard University), most people's working, shopping, financial and leisure patterns have altered dramatically as a result of linked, mobile, digital technologies and the **World Wide Web.** At the vanguard of profound social, cultural, political and economic changes, Facebook had, as of the end of 2013, 1.23 billion active users, was worth $135 billion, and is accessed by 556 million people every day (*Guardian*, 4 February 2014).

While social networking sites are used by people of all ages, they have par-ticularly revolutionized the ways in which young people communicate, compete and interact. We may have seen the emergence of the 'kidult', as the media have termed adults who enjoy a prolonged (or permanent!) state of adolescence, but young people use new communications technologies differently to their parents' generation. By way of example, in July 2009, a story broke that had the UK media all of a Twitter. Matthew Robson, a 15-year-old schoolboy on work experience within the Media and Internet Research Team at global financial services company Morgan Stanley wrote his placement report on *How Teenagers Consume Media*. In it, Matthew describes a mediascape which has become a great deal more confusing and complicated in some respects, and considerably easier, more mobile and more accessible in others. The report reveals that teenagers do not listen to the radio, preferring to use their PCs and phones to access online streaming sites which are free of adverts and allow users to choose the songs they want instead of listening to what the radio presenter chooses. They rarely purchase music; most have never bought a CD but do download tracks and albums illegally, using iPods if they are from higher income families and mobile phones if from lower income families. No-one in their mid- to late teenage years, according to the report, regularly reads a newspaper, as most do not have the time and cannot be bothered to read pages and pages of text when they could view a short summary of the news on the Internet or on TV. Teenagers have also stopped going to the cinema by the time they reach 15 because they have to pay the adult price and, besides, it is possible to buy a pirated DVD of the film at the time of cinema release. The report further informs us that nearly all young people are registered with Facebook, that girls are a lot more prone to spend their time on social networking sites than boys but that, unlike their male counterparts who spend the majority of their free time gaming, 'only about one in fifty' girls plays console games, though the dominance of the Nintendo Wii is put down to girl gamers and its status as a console that the whole family can enjoy. Most widely and sensationally reported by the media was Matthew's observation that young people don't use Twitter. As he drily observes, Twitter is 'pointless', 'strictly for the elderly' and its chief advocate, Stephen Fry (a man in his late fifties known principally for appearing on TV and radio and being very clever), 'is not particularly cool' among British youth.

What is abundantly clear from these brief details of Matthew Robson's report is that the continuing development of networked computer technologies have transformed how we communicate and consume, work and play, and engage with others across the spheres of economic, political, cultural and social life. So embedded have these technologies become that it is easy to forget just how profound the changes have been and how rapidly new forms of social action and interaction have become normalized, taken-for-granted, even mundane. eBay (established in 1995), Google (1998), Wikipedia (2001), YouTube (2005), Facebook (2006) and Twitter (2007) are among the most ubiquitous brands in contemporary life. Yet it is worth remembering that 25 years ago the Internet was unheard of among the general populace, and was known only to a small and specialized community largely confined to academic and scientific institutions. From this position of marginality, the subsequent expansion of the Internet has been exponential (Jewkes and Yar, 2010).

Redefining deviance and democratization: developing nations and the case of China

While there have been far-reaching developments in the rise of 'new' media technologies in the West, the transformations that are taking place in some parts of the developing world are arguably even more profound. Having said that, we should not lose sight of the continuing global *'digital divide'* which, as Miller (2010) explains, means that the move to the digital age is greatly enhancing the position of the advanced, industrialized economies over those of the developing world, allowing them to play by a fundamentally different set of economic rules. Start-up costs of Internet access are still prohibitively high for the poorest people in the world, where many do not even have access to a telephone service. Moreover, regional growth in Internet use is not always smooth and continuous, but may be disrupted by war, disaster or displacement. For Miller it is quite simply the case that, without some form of intervention, developed countries will benefit from increased access to knowledge, increased economic flexibility, and increased communication efficiency, while developing nations are at risk of being ever more victimized and marginalized by these trends. The optimism that once accompanied the Internet revolution has begun to fade in light of the realization that our culture has transformed the Internet more than the Internet has transformed our culture (Miller, 2010).

To illustrate further the digital divide, usage statistics now put the global Internet population at 2,405,518,376 or 34.3 per cent penetration (up from 23.8 per cent penetration in 2009; www.internetworldstats.com/stats.htm). Leading the world table is North America where 78.6 per cent of the population are online. At the other end of the scale, just 15.6 per cent of Africa's population has Internet access – although this is triple what it was five years ago. Of the total world Internet users by region, 44.8 per cent are in Asia; 21.5 per cent are in Europe; 11.4 per cent are in North America; 10.4 per cent are in Latin America and the Caribbean; 7.0 per cent in Africa; 3.7 per cent in the Middle East; and 1.0 per cent in Australasia/Oceania. In terms of languages, 536.6 million Internet users communicate in English, closely followed (and rapidly being caught up) by Chinese language speakers at 444.9 million (www. internetworldstats.com/stats.htm).

China provides a fascinating case study because it illustrates in dramatic ways how digital technologies are implicated in social, political and economic change. Use of the Internet in China grew from 22 million in 2000 to 162 million at the beginning of 2007 (www.internetworldstats.com/asia/cn.htm). By 2010 that figure had risen again to 420 million and, in 2014, the China Internet Network Information Center estimate that 618 million Chinese people use the Internet, and 281 million use popular microblogging sites known collectively as Weibo (www1.cnnic.cn). The biggest distributor of online video is Yukou Tudou, which has overtaken YouTube with over 1bn megabytes of data transfers every day. The Mandarin search engine Baidu has more hits than Google, and Chinese entrepreneur Jack Ma has set up Taobao to compete with eBay.

These examples are all the more remarkable given the Chinese authorities' fears about the potential uses of the Internet by 'subversives'. Over the last two decades China has undergone immensely important economic reforms which have given rise to tensions involving the Chinese media industries. With a population of nearly 1.4 billion and an increasingly important role to play in the global political economy, the Chinese media have been described as being in transition between totalitarianism and market authoritarianism (Winfield and Peng, 2005). Nowhere is the dual role that Chinese media play – simultaneously commodities in the market and ideological apparatuses – more apparent than in relation to new information and communication technologies; in particular, Internet restriction and censorship. A study conducted in 2002 found that of approximately 200,000 websites to which access was attempted, 19,032 sites accessible from the US were inaccessible from China on multiple occasions, suggesting that even allowing for temporary technological glitches, the vast majority of these sites were deliberately blocked via government-maintained web filtering systems (Zittrain and Edelman, 2003). In 2004 an Amnesty International report revealed that the Chinese Government was becoming increasingly heavy-handed with people using the Internet to circulate anti-government beliefs. All Chinese Internet Service Providers (ISPs) have to register with the police and all Internet users must sign a declaration that they will not visit forbidden sites. Among those routinely blocked are news, health and education sites, although pornography sites are virtually unregulated (http://web.amnesty.org/web/content.nsf/pages/gbr_china_internet). In January 2010, Google declared that it was no longer going to censor search results on Google China and two months later the company announced that it was moving its Chinese operation from the mainland to Hong Kong to avoid the rules and restrictions imposed by the authorities in Beijing such as the blocking of results for searches using sensitive words and phrases, for example 'Tiananmen Square 1989'. In 2014, as the 25th anniversary of Tiananmen approached, many Western news agencies reported that the Chinese Government had further cracked down on access to information about the unrest of 4 June 1989, when troops shot dead hundreds of pro-democracy protesters gathered in central Beijing. The Chinese authorities have never publicly admitted how many people were killed and many people born in China after these events maybe unaware that it ever happened (www.bbc.co.uk/news/technology-18321548).

As the *Guardian* (22 March 2010) noted: 'The furore highlighted the challenges of doing business in China for western companies and drew a line under the era of unfettered optimism about the Internet's ability to change the country'. For all its reputation as a wild frontier, then, the truth is that the Net can be used as just another means of constraint by those governments around the world who wish to discourage free thought, speech and action. Nevertheless, there has been some softening in attitudes on the part of Beijing in recent years, even if benevolence is somewhat inconsistently applied. In May 2008 it was reported that the Chinese Government had responded to the devastation caused by an earthquake in the Sichuan province in which tens of thousands of people perished by moderating its control of the Internet. This meant that those affected by the tragedy could use video sharing sites, blogs, chat rooms, instant messaging services and the like to circulate graphic pic- tures and accounts of their experiences. For these new citizen journalists the Government's relaxation of its generally tough stance on Internet content brought an unprecedented level of freedom and, as noted in Chapter 2, citizen journalism has changed the relationship between traditional news producers and audiences and taken the 'immediacy' of news and its synoptic power to a new level. *User-generated content* is particularly powerful when produced by ordinary people in regions where professional journalists and cameramen have been unable to get to the scene quickly enough or where reporters are banned for political or military reasons.

China has also become the home of much activity that criminologists usu- ally refer to by the shorthand term '*cybercrime*'; a word that encompasses both 'computer assisted' and 'computer oriented' crimes. The former refers to those offences which, while pre-dating Internet technology and having an existence independent of it, find a new lease of life online. For example, falling into this category are: certain types of fraud, such as selling non-existent, defective, sub-standard, or counterfeit goods; theft of monies through credit card and bank fraud; investment frauds such as pyramid schemes and fake stocks and shares; intellectual property offences, including the unauthorized sharing of copyrighted *content* such as movies, music, digitized books, images, and computer software; posting, sharing and selling obscene and prohibited sexual representations; and harassment, 'stalking', bullying, sexual predation and forms of hateful or defamatory speech. These offending behaviours are not unique to the online world (having long-established terrestrial counter- parts), and have thus been described as 'old wine in new bottles' (Grabosky, 2001). However, if we stick with this analogy, we can certainly appreciate that we are dealing with *an awful lot of wine* in very many, differently shaped and capacious bottles (Jewkes and Yar, 2010). This point is illustrated by the fact that the first cybercrime in China took place in the mid-1980s, which was two decades later than the first active digital crime in the West, when the Chinese banking system was defrauded. Throughout the 1980s and 1990s the growth of cybercrime in China was slow and steady, but today cybercrime in China is a vast self-perpetuating criminal industry and is proliferating partly because current law is wholly inadequate to deal with it (Qi et al., 2009).

In addition to 'computer assisted' crimes we have those which are 'computer oriented'. This category of offence takes as its target the electronic infrastructure (both hardware and software) that comprises the 'fabric' of the Internet itself. Examples include various forms of 'malicious software' (viruses, worms, Trojans) that corrupt files and hard drives; 'denial of service attacks' that overload server capacity and effectively 'crash' websites; and various forms of 'defacement' through which web content is manipulated, changed and/or deleted without permission or authorization. Again, to take the example of China, it was the emergence of a hitherto unknown phenomenon, a computer virus in the form of a malware program known as 'Ping Pong' that first drew cybercrime to the attention of the Chinese public. According to a Symantec report at the end of 2006, Beijing is now home to the world's largest collection of malware-infected computers (nearly 5 per cent of the world's total) and research by the security company Sophos showed that China has overtaken the US in hosting Web pages that secretly install malicious programs on computers to steal private information or send spam e-mails (http://www.msnbc.msn.com/id/19789995/).

Cyber-warfare and cyber-terrorism

The decision by Google to pull out of China is said to have followed a cyber-attack it believes was aimed at gathering information on Chinese human rights activists. Most recently attention has been directed, in the post-September 11 context of the 'War on Terror', toward the possibility of attacks upon computer infrastructure by terrorist groups (so-called *'cyber-terrorism'*). For example, Dorothy Denning (2010) has outlined six areas of terrorist practice that have been substantially altered or enhanced by the Internet and the Web: media operations, attacks, recruitment, learning, finance, and security. However, while most commentators have focused on the specific threats from named terrorist cells and networks such as al Qaeda, state-authorized and government-sponsored attacks also appear to be on the rise and, again, China has suddenly appeared alongside nations that are more usually identified as posing a threat. *The Military Balance 2010* is an annual study published by the International Institute for Strategic Studies (IISS) and is an assessment of global military capabilities which now includes analysis of cyber-terrorism and *cyber-warfare* (http://www.iiss.org/publications/military-balance/). A news report about *The Military Balance* illustrates the complexity of understanding where the battle lines are drawn in a cyber-society:

> In December the South Korean government reported an attack in which it said North Korean hackers may have stolen secret defence plans outlining the South Korean and US strategy in the event of war on the Korean peninsula. Last July,

espionage protection agents in Germany said the country faced extremely sophisticated Chinese and Russian internet spying operations targeting industrial secrets and critical infrastructure such as Germany's power grid.

One of the most notorious cyber-warfare offensives to date took place in Estonia in 2007 when more than 1 million computers were used to jam government, business and media websites. The attacks, widely believed to have originated in Russia, coincided with a period of heightened bilateral political tension. They inflicted damage estimated in the tens of millions of euros. China last week accused the Obama administration of waging 'online warfare' against Iran by recruiting a 'hacker brigade' and manipulating social media such as Twitter and YouTube to stir up anti-government agitation. (www.guardian.co.uk/technol ogy/2010/feb/03/cyber-warfare-growing-threat)

According to IISS terrorism and warfare in *cyberspace* may be used to disable a country's infrastructure, meddle with the integrity of another country's internal military data, confuse its financial transactions or to accomplish any number of other possibly crippling aims (ibid.). In June 2009 the Pentagon created US Cyber Command and in Britain it was announced that a cyber-security operations centre would be established at GCHQ in Cheltenham. Yet governments and national defence establishments at present have only limited ability to tell when they were under attack, by whom, and how they might respond (ibid.).

While these measures might give cause for alarm and seem to be in response to threats that might come from a Hollywood movie (almost certainly starring Bruce Willis) we should not overstate the threat of cybercrime, cyber-terrorism or cyber-warfare. Further, it has not been my intention here to paint China as a particular problem; rather, it has been presented as a fascinating case study illustrating the speed and scope of Internet penetration and the consequent shifts in local and global power that occur. However, we must retain a healthy scepticism about claims made in the West regarding the threats posed by rapidly developing nations such as China. Put bluntly, media commentators, politicians, criminal justice actors and security professionals in countries like the UK and US may have strong vested interests in overplaying the risks presented. As Majid Yar (2010) has intimated, much of the debate about Internet regulation and censorship appears to be based on speculative notions of the anti-social and harmful impacts it may have at some point in the future rather than actual, current levels of victimization. Some of the concern expressed by authorities in the West about China as a source of cybercrime, cyber-terror and cyber-warfare therefore might reasonably be said to emanate from economic and political fears about Chinese growth and dominance in arenas and markets that other countries (particularly the US) have owned for many decades. Maggie Wykes (with Daniel Harcus, 2010) concurs, and suggests that the media has been instrumental in heightening public fears about the possibility of terrorist attack. It is her view that since

9/11 the media have consistently reported that terrorist groups use Internet technologies to organize and plan both terrestrial and cyber-attacks, and that these accounts have supported the concept of an ever-present global threat and underwritten policy from the US and its allies regarding the 'War on Terror'. Wykes suggests that the meaning of terrorism in the 21st century has been reconstructed and allied to the Internet through hyper-realistic criminal-izing practices and fear-inducing discourses which have legitimated policies, alliances, laws, actions and – as we saw in Chapter 8 – invasive surveillance methods, with profound implications for netizens, citizens and the exercise of power (Wykes with Harcus, 2010).

Although global acts of cyber-facilitated warfare and terrorism are certainly possible, and their consequences terrifying to contemplate, it is the more mun-dane, 'ordinary' cybercrimes that affect millions of people worldwide that are of most concern to most of us, so let us take a brief overview of some of the offences that come under the heading of 'cybercrime'.

'Ordinary' cybercrimes

Electronic theft and abuse of intellectual property rights

One of the most obvious consequences of the new information and communi-cations revolution is its creation and distribution of unimaginably more information-based products which force us to re-evaluate traditionally held ideas about crime and criminality. For example, theft has commonly involved one person taking something belonging to another person without his or her permission – the result being that the first party no longer has possession of the property taken. Investigation of this type of offence is usually relatively straightforward in so far as it involves property that is tangible, visible and atom based (Goodman, 1997). But in a virtual context, it is quite possible for one person to take something that belongs to another person without permis-sion and, in some cases, make a perfect copy of the item, the result being that the original owner still has the property even though the thief now has a ver-sion as well. Intellectual property can take a number of recognized forms – patents, trademarks, trade secrets, industrial designs and copyright. Such acts chal-lenge conventional and legal definitions of offences and render traditional copyright laws irrelevant (Wall and Yar, 2010).

Electronic reproduction of data can take many forms. One of the most com-mon is 'peer-to-peer' (or P2P) file-sharing, which has arguably returned to the Internet a sense of the liberal, collective ethos and benign anarchy that charac-terized its early days in the 1960s and 1970s. But for the film and music industries who are losing millions of dollars in lost sales, this form of 'digital piracy' taking place in teenagers' bedrooms the world over is every bit as unlawful as the knowing and criminal use of the Internet to market or distribute copyrighted software (Yar, 2006). Moreover, it is not just young people who believe that it is morally acceptable to illegally download movies, music and software: in the US a survey found that only 26 per cent of professionals oppose piracy (Yar, 2010). The industry has been slow to respond to the problem of file-sharing, and broadband technology has made it even quicker and easier to download music and movies illegally. However, some CDs are now being manufactured in such a way as to make it impossible to play them (and copy them) on a PC. Meanwhile, the Record Industry Association of America (RIAA) is taking legal action against individuals it alleges offer file-swapping services on university campuses, and the Movie Picture Association of America is attempting to close down sites that distribute films online. But many believe that big corporations are being forced into playing cat-and-mouse games they can't possibly hope to win because – as the RIAA's infamous closure of Napster demonstrated – when the illegal business of one outfit is terminated, numerous others will appear in its wake. Most recently, legal controversy has arisen around the Sweden-based website 'Pirate Bay', which directs searchers to media files available across the Internet, but does not store or offer any content itself, as a way of circumventing anti-piracy laws. While copyright-holders claim it is a major source for piracy, its operators claim they are acting within the law, and the case remains ongoing.

Hate crime

Hate crime may be racist, religiously motivated, homophobic, gendered, disablist (Chakraborti and Garland, 2009) or, as we shall see, simply a violent reaction to a particular offender who has been in the news. The promotion of hatred is widespread and the Internet is a relatively cheap and accessible means of connecting similarly minded people across the world and coalescing their belief systems. The Net is also a sophisticated tool for recruitment and unification, providing links between hate movements that were previously diverse and fractured, and facilitating the creation of a collective identity and empowering sense of community (Perry, 2001). In fact, while the potential of the Internet as a weapon of warfare has already been discussed, it must also be remembered that the Internet has increased the global reach of terrorist groups, such as al Qaeda, who can use computer and telecommunication links, email, cellular and radio networks to conduct operations over long distances while dispensing with the need for fixed physical presence. Coleman and McCahill (2010) note that a former radical Muslim claimed that more than half of young Saudis who had embraced a radical ideology were recruited through the Internet. In Europe arious groups on the political far right – neo-Nazis, skinheads and groups with ties to the Ku Klux Klan – use the Net to target a youthful and impressionable audience with racist, anti-semitic and homophobic propaganda with little fear of the kind of legal sanction that might accompany the circulation of such material in more 'traditional' forms. Although Germany and many other European countries have criminalized the publication and distribution of hate propaganda, the Internet remains largely unregulated and there is little the police can do unless a specific crime is reported. Moreover, the constitutional protection afforded to 'free speech' in the USA makes it difficult to challenge the global dissemination of messages of hate.

Although often targeted at broad demographic groups, religions and so on, hate crime is increasingly taking the form of vigilantism against individuals. Two examples from recent years demonstrate how unregulatable the Internet can be and how linked technologies can create 'viral' chains of communication in a very short space of time. In November 2008 the case of 'Baby P' or 'Baby Peter', a two-year-old tortured and killed by his mother's boyfriend, shocked the British public. Breaching two separate legal orders, several Internet sites revealed the child's identity and posted photographs of his mother and stepfather along with their names, address, and other personal details. Several social networking sites had to take swift action to remove pages with the mother's profile on after online vigilantes began a campaign calling for violent retribution against them, and the court trial itself had to be postponed for several months (with the cause of the delay being cited as 'legal reasons'). In March 2010, following the recall to prison of Jon Venables on suspected child pornography offences, an entirely different individual, David Calvert, was mistakenly identified as the man who, as a child, had murdered James Bulger. Within a few days more than 2,370 people had joined a group on the site asking whether Calvert was in fact Venables (this despite the fact that Venables was in prison and Calvert was at home). The group was removed after complaints to Facebook, but the rumours persist on other sites such as Yahoo Answers, with people claiming to have learned his identity via text messages. Calvert is said to have endured a torrent of abuse and had to produce family photo albums to prove his identity to doubters. So severe was the reaction against him by some parts of the community that a panic button was installed at his home (*Guardian*, 9 March 2010).

It was in fact Jon Venables and his co-accused Robert Thompson who led to a change in the law governing blame attributable to Internet Service Providers (ISPs). In July 2001 ISP Demon won a change to the injunction protecting the two boys when they were released from custody and given new identities. The original form of the injunction, designed to prevent the mainstream media from publishing or broadcasting details of the offenders or their whereabouts, was deemed 'inappropriate' for the Internet because of the risks of a service provider inadvertently providing access to material about the pair and consequently being found in contempt of court. ISPs are now compelled to take all reasonable measures to prevent this from happening. A similar order was imposed on behalf of Maxine Carr following her release from prison in 2005 (the first time a lifetime injunction to protect identity has been awarded to someone not convicted of murder). Her QC made the case for his client's anonymity on the basis of serious threats and allegations made in Internet chat rooms and their linking to unfounded press reports about her (*Guardian*, 25 February 2005).

More legally ambiguous are 'hate' behaviours that might be termed 'cyber-bullying' or 'trolling'. As we shall see later in this chapter, some bullying among children and young people is linked to sexual behaviour but, much like traditional bullying it may range from name-calling to serious threats of assault and blackmail. Like its 'real-life' equivalent, cyber-bullying behaviours may be covered by legislation (such as the 1997 Harassment Act) but much of it consists of low-level abuse, gossip and rumour which, while potentially very upsetting to the recipient, is not usually a criminal offence. 'Trolling' on the other hand is usually associated with more serious behaviour. Formerly known as 'flaming', trolling has become associated with the worst displays of hatred, misogyny, racism and homophobia, usually on public Internet forums and has, in several cases, resulted in the victim taking their own life. Trolls can be prosecuted in the UK under the Malicious Communications Act, introduced in 1988 and updated in 2003 to make it an offence to make improper use of a public electronic communications network such as grossly offensive, indecent, obscene, menacing or annoying phone calls and emails. There have been numerous reported cases involving celebrity victims; for example, a young man who used Twitter to send Olympic diver Tom Daley offensive tweets during the London 2012 Games was arrested and issued a formal harassment warning. Several offenders have been sentenced to prison sentences for trolling.

Invasion of privacy, defamation and identity theft

The entitlement to security of person is regarded as a fundamental human right, yet the scope and pervasiveness of digital technologies open up new areas of social vulnerability. Invasion of privacy takes many forms from 'spamming' to online defamation, stalking and violence. Spamming has thus far been considered little more than an extension of conventional junk mail, although it is increasingly being recognized as an insidious and frequently illegal activity. It can encompass electronic chain letters, links to pornographic sites, scams claiming that there are extensive funds – for example, from over-invoiced business contracts or a deceased relative's will – available for immediate transfer into the target's bank account, fraudulent pyramid investment schemes, phoney cancer cures and bogus test kits for anthrax.

One increasingly prevalent crime, originating particularly in countries in West Africa, and targeting women in Europe and the US, is online dating scams, whereby fraudsters post bogus photographs and establish relationships with vulnerable victims (sometimes over several months) before persuading them to send them money. In addition, the past few years has seen a massive rise in incidents of so-called 'phishing', in which communications purporting to come from legitimate organizations such as banks and building societies target Internet users, inducing them to voluntarily surrender sensitive financial information which can then be used to defraud them. The extent of such fraud solicitation has reached such levels that the EU has recently launched the Consumer Protection Cooperation Network in an attempt to tackle cross-border Internet scams (Espiner, 2007).

The law also offers protection to individuals whose reputation is slurred by defamatory Internet content. Teachers and lecturers seem particularly vulnerable to such attacks. In 2000, Demon paid over £230,000 to a British university lecturer who claimed that the ISP had failed to remove two anonymous Internet postings defaming him, while in America a 'teacher review' site set up by students at the City College of San Francisco resulted in one teacher filing a lawsuit against the site, denouncing it as a 'disgusting, lie-filled, destructive force' (Curzon-Brown 2000: 91). Since Facebook became the primary mode of communication for many young people, the site has had to respond to many requests from teachers, lecturers and other professionals for unkind and potentially libellous material to be removed.

In providing a forum for discussion among discrete groups (such as the present and past students of a particular teacher) the Internet inevitably makes public what might be assumed to be private, as some students have discovered when fined by their universities for 'breaking the rules' on post-exam celebrations and posting photographic 'evidence' on Facebook. In addition, staff at several universities have reportedly checked personal profiles on networking sites to make decisions about whether or not to admit individual students. Teachers themselves have to be cautious when they make public what they assume might be relatively private statements. In 2006, a former Conservative Party politician successfully sued Tracy Williams, a college lecturer, who had accused him of being a 'Nazi' in an online discussion forum relating to the Iraq war; Williams was ordered to pay at total of £17,200 in damages and costs (Gibson, 2006). Even email is subject to public scrutiny as a case at the Climatic Research Unit at the University of East Anglia in 2009 demonstrated. Following suspicions that leading scientists had misled politicians and the public on aspects of climate change and devised 'tricks' to combat the arguments of climate change sceptics, the Freedom of Information Act (FOI) was used to gain access to thousands of university email communications and other documents.

Another cybercrime related to privacy is the theft of personal identity, a practice that has dramatically increased in the last few years. In 2007, the US

Federal Trade Commission reported that 8.3 million Americans had been victims of identity theft over a 12-month period. Meanwhile, the UK credit-checking agency Experian reported a 69 per cent increase in identity theft over the same period. According to UK government figures, identity theft now costs the British economy £1.7 billion per annum (Home Office, 2006, see http://www.identitytheft.org.uk). Identity theft encompasses a full range of offences from the appropriation and use of credit card numbers to the wholesale adoption of someone else's persona. It can be mundane and opportunistic; for example, many identity thieves rummage through dustbins for discarded credit card statements or pick up receipts left at bank ATMs. However, more high-tech versions include hacking into an individual's personal computer in order to steal his or her bank and credit card details, using software programs designed to work out or randomly generate PIN numbers, and 'skimming' credit cards in shops and restaurants to produce a near perfect copy of the original card. Apart from financial fraud, identity theft has come to be viewed as an important 'precursor' enabling a range of further offences, including illegal immigration and human trafficking using stolen identities (see http://www.met.police.uk/op_maxim/).

Concern over the growth of identity theft has inspired initiatives such as the UK Government's Identity Fraud Steering Committee, which brings together police, government and financial bodies in an attempt to develop a coordinated response. Meanwhile, financial services providers such as banks and credit card companies now routinely offer customers 'identity theft insurance' intended to protect individuals against the consequences of having their identity stolen and used to defraud them. There may be a generational divide in levels of public anxiety, however. On the whole, fears about possible identity theft appear to be more strongly experienced by older people (illustrated, perhaps by the fact that in 2004 sales of shredders increased by 50 per cent at one international supplies company, with 1.3 million units sold in a single year; Jewkes and Yar, 2010). But as Smith (2010) points out, although young people may be more cavalier about their potential for victimization, the expansion in social networking sites has left young people at greater risk of identity crime. By way of example, he notes that one in seven users on Facebook log into their profile virtually all the time during office hours, rendering both themselves and their organizations open to criminal activity.

eBay fraud

Identity theft clearly can be a prelude to fraud, but fraud can be perpetrated via the Internet without recourse to stealing someone else's bank account details, credit card number, or other aspects of their documentary identities. A growing number of criminal offences are facilitated via online auction site eBay, including the sale of knives and other weapons, metabolic steroids, hard-core pornography and abusive images of children. More mundanely, however, it is goods that are counterfeit, or which breach intellectual copyright laws or are knowingly stolen, faulty or damaged that make up the bulk of the criminal transactions that occur on eBay. Most individual consumers do not pursue legal action when the 'designer' goods they purchase arrive and are clearly not genuine. But the global corporations that trade on their luxury brand names have the finance and motivations to act when they feel their brand has been damaged. In a landmark legal ruling in 2008 a French court ordered eBay to pay 19.28 million to Louis Vuitton Malletier and 17.3 million to its sister company Christian Dior Couture for damage to their brand images and for causing 'moral harm'. Damages were sought over two issues: first it was argued that eBay had committed 'serious errors' by not doing enough to pre-vent the sales of fake goods, including Louis Vuitton bags; second, it was argued that eBay had allowed unauthorized sales of perfume brands owned by the group. The company's view was that, whether the perfumes are real or fake, an offence has been committed because the sale of real goods and per-fumes on eBay violates the company's authorized distribution network which only allows sales through specialist dealers (*Guardian*, 1 July 2008).

While these kinds of offences can cost luxury brand companies millions, more pervasive in terms of perpetration and victimization, are offences involving han-dling stolen goods, financial fraud, obtaining property by deception or instances where sellers simply fail to provide goods to buyers. According to newspaper reports, the police in England and Wales investigate one alleged eBay scam every hour, some of which have moved beyond the cyber-realm and precipitated 'real world' crimes including burglary, assault, possession of firearms offences, civil disputes, harassment and an arson attack (*Daily Mail*, 8 October 2008). Users of the auction website reported an estimated total of more than 8,000 crimes in 2007 prompting eBay to respond by offering training to 2,000 police officers to tackle suspected Internet fraud. Cases that came to court in 2007 included that of a woman in South Wales who made more than £13,000 from photographs bearing forged signatures of celebrities and was given a 42-week suspended jail term, and a man from Yorkshire who was given a 26-week suspended sentence and 180 hours community service after selling £40,000 worth of fake *Take That* tickets to 270 victims on eBay (*Daily Mail*, 8 October 2008).

Hacking and loss of sensitive data

eBay has also been the target of hackers. In May 2014 the auction site was forced to ask 145 million users to change their passwords when it was revealed that hackers had stolen email addresses, birth dates and other identity infor-mation in a significant data breach. As this book goes to press, there appear to be numerous stories circulating about the potential threat of cyber-attack; reports that hackers in Russia are infiltrating people's Apple devices, blocking them, and demanding payment from their owners to unblock them; that Chinese hackers have targeted US defence and European security industries and stolen data relating to satellite, aerospace and communications; and that the Bank of England 'is to let hackers loose on Britain's biggest banks to test their defences against cyber-attacks' (*Independent*, 10 June 2014)

Hackers can be driven by a wide range of motives. In addition to the acts of 'cyber-terrorism' and 'cyber-warfare' described earlier, hacking can emanate from a relatively benign belief in freedom of access to information for all or, even, simply, a desire for mastery for its own sake (Taylor, 2003). There are, then, inherent complexities in the term 'hacking', some of which will be perceived by society at large as more legitimate than others. Indeed, 'hacking from the moral high ground', as Furnell (2010) puts it, is a fascinating subject and hacking is one of very few cybercrimes that can elicit social tolerance and even a grudging admiration for its audacity and the technical skill required. The authorities of most countries take a different view, however, especially the United States post-9/11. Gary McKinnon, a 42-year-old Briton accused of breaking into Pentagon computers and raiding US army, navy and NASA networks in 2001 and 2002 is facing the full wrath of the American criminal justice system. At the time of writing, he is facing extradition and up to 70 years in an American prison under terrorist charges, despite support from several high-profile British politicians, academics and celebrities who claim that, as a man with Asperger's Syndrome, McKinnon should be tried, not as a terrorist but as a man with a social disability.

The penetration of any security system may be damaging enough, but the Pentagon – Headquarters of the US Department of Defense – may be regarded as one of the greatest prizes by hackers around the world. Yet what is striking about the story of Gary McKinnon is how easily he accessed potentially sensitive data. As Ronson (2009) rather colourfully puts it: 'He spent between five and seven years roaming the corridors of power like the Invisible Man, wandering into Pentagon offices, rifling through files'. When he was eventually arrested in November 2002, British arresting officers told him to expect a few months' community service. But they underestimated how draconian the US administration had become in the aftermath of the War on Terror and Ronson notes that 'US prosecutors saw him not as a north London nerd who had allowed his addictive actions to escalate stupidly, but as the man who had committed the biggest military computer hack of all time' (ibid.). According to a statement from the US attorney general's office made to a press conference, McKinnon had:

> intentionally hacked into 97 protected computer systems. He stole computer files and obtained secrets that might have been useful to an enemy. He has done

enormous damage to the computer systems of the United States government, and in so doing he has threatened the safety of every single American citizen. In the immediate aftermath of the September 11 terrorist attacks, McKinnon intentionally caused a network in the Washington DC area to shut down, resulting in the total loss of internet access and email service to approximately 2,000 users for three days at a cost of $900,000 (£544,000)... (cited ibid.)

McKinnon admitted the hacking, but strenuously denied having malevolent motives of the kind suspected by the US authorities. Described by Ronson as 'essentially an idiotic but harmless conspiracy theorist who spent far too long on the internet because he was too nerdy to make it on the outside' Gary McKinnon may be simply a 'social type US prosecutors don't recognize' (ibid.).

Another illustration of the vulnerability of supposedly secure systems is the data lost or stolen from various government departments that is said to be worth billions to potential criminals. More than 1,000 laptops have gone missing from UK Government departments according to figures released in 2007, including 13 from the Cabinet Office. One of the most notorious and newsworthy cases was reported in 2007 when HM Revenue and Customs mislaid two CDs containing the Child Benefit database on which the names, addresses, dates of birth, National Insurance numbers and bank account details of 25 million people were stored. As if this were not shocking enough, it was revealed that the discs also contained the real names and new identities of up to 350 people who had been placed on the witness protection scheme after giving evidence against serious criminals.

Child pornography and online grooming

Pornography is a subject that provokes fear and fascination in equal measure and, while online porn (depicting adults and children) was the force that propelled the rapid growth of the Internet and demonstrated its commercial potential, equally it was child pornography that precipitated the establishment of some of the most high-profile organizations which police the Net. 'Adult' cyber-porn has *democratized* sexual gratification and provided greater freedom of access to women, as well as its traditional customers, men (Jewkes and Sharp, 2003), yet at the same time it has reignited debates about the exploitation of women and the relationship between pornography and sexual assault, and provoked a significant degree of technological determinism whereby blame is attributed to the Internet itself. The death of music teacher Jane Longhurst, who was sexually assaulted and murdered by an acquaintance who reportedly downloaded images and accounts of necrophilia and asphyxiation to fuel his deviant sexual desires, was reported in the UK under the sensational headline 'Killed by the Internet' (*Daily Mirror*, 4 February 2004; see Jewkes, 2007).

Characterized by Yar (2010) as a 'signal crime', the mediated public outcry following this case led to legislation criminalizing the possession of 'violent pornography' which is now punishable by up to three years imprisonment.

Despite such alarmism, which invariably reinvigorates debates about greater self-regulation, tougher legislation, and even censorship of the Internet, reported cases involving adult victims are extremely rare and the most intensive focus continues to fall upon pornography featuring children. It has been argued elsewhere in this volume that paedophilia constitutes *the* moral panic of our age (although that ascription has also been problematized) with all the attendant implications that moral panics tend to have on government and policing priorities. In common with broader news values, the issue is largely kept in the public eye through cases involving high-profile 'offenders' including celebrities and newsworthy 'victims'.

Many believe that the police have taken too long to address the problem of online child sexual abuse and have, for many years been playing catch-up with online offenders. Limited resources, lack of technological expertise, a tendency to target 'low hanging fruit' and an occupational culture resistant to new challenges are among the impediments to successfully policing online abuse of children (Jewkes and Andrews, 2005; Jewkes, 2010a) but, thankfully law enforcement is now beginning to reflect the changing technological and cultural landscape. The launch of the Child Exploitation and Online Protection (CEOP) Centre in 2006 underlines the UK police's commitment to stemming the global Internet trade in child pornography. One of their achievements has been to develop a pro-active strategy based on specialist intelligence. An initiative that has proved reasonably successful is the employment of undercover officers posing as children on fake websites and in chat rooms to lure paedophiles, although investigators are hampered somewhat by the law. However, the charge of 'grooming' has caused concern among civil liberties groups because it is designed to target adults who meet a child after contact has been made on the Internet but *before* any offence has taken place, raising the question of whether *thinking* about sexual acts is the same as committing them. Even if a case reaches court, proving intent is notoriously difficult for the police and prosecutors. This legislation enables the police to carry out 'sting' operations by posing as children in Internet chat rooms and then arranging to meet the unsuspecting groomers at a 'real' location, but they are not legally entitled to entrap a suspect.

Childhood, cyberspace and social retreat

Interestingly, anxieties about crime and safety, especially of children, have been significant factors in many aspects of life becoming isolated and atomized activities. Numerous forms of 'social retreat' have become commonplace, including the growing numbers of gated communities, ownership of four wheel drive vehicles, the popularity of home leisure systems including social gaming platforms, and many others. For young people new social trends including the all-pervasiveness of the Internet and the tendency for parents to accompany their children in every public sphere constitute profound changes in the way that identities are shaped and social skills learned. At the same time – and partly as a consequence – of this privatization of social discourse and interaction, the Internet has become something of a scapegoat for a myriad of deviant human behaviours and conditions from sexual aggression and homicidal urges to attention deficit disorder and obesity. Unsurprisingly, it is children and young people who are considered most vulnerable to the potentially harmful effects of 'new' media technologies and most likely to be victims of predators wishing to exploit or abuse them.

As noted in Chapters 3 and 4 childhood has been transformed, especially since the paedophile emerged to haunt our collective imagination in the mid-1990s. In the 21st century adventure is for many children a virtual pleasure; competitiveness is honed at the games console rather than on the sports field; and sexual development occurs in chat rooms, on social networking sites and via mobile phones (Jewkes, 2010a). Unfortunately this means that some children and young people put themselves at risk of victimization and engage in more 'extreme' behaviours online than they would in the 'real' world. Among the 'risky' behaviours to emerge in recent years is 'sexting', where an individual sends nude or suggestive photos of themselves over their mobile phone. While such pictures are usually sent by young women to their boyfriends, Kent police report that predatory adults are taking advantage of the willingness of young people to experiment with their sexuality over the Net by engaging in sexually explicit chat and by exposing their bodies in front of a webcam (http://tinyurl.com/agfq2j). In the United States, a survey carried out by the National Campaign to Prevent Teen and Unplanned Pregnancy found that one in five teenagers had sent or posted online nude or semi-nude pictures of themselves and 39 per cent had sent or posted sexually suggestive messages (http://uk.reuters.com). So widely reported has 'sexting' since become (including stories of young celebrities who have found their 'private' photos posted online) that Australia's state government of New South Wales launched an education campaign in May 2009 to try to educate young people about the dangers of the practice and warn them of the consequences which can include bullying, harassment, sexual assault and, in one case in Cincinnati, USA, the suicide of an 18-year-old woman following months of taunting and bullying after nude images of herself that she had sent to her boyfriend were circulated, first across her high school and subsequently far beyond.

The 'normality' of *cybersurveillance* and the apparent willingness of children to take risks with their online activities, and to flaunt their emerging sexuality within a forum that they mistakenly believe to be private is illustrated by the case of a sexual assault on a 13-year-old girl in Nuneaton. Investigating police said they were exploring whether there was a connection between the attack and the fact that she described herself on her webpage as a 'Bebo whore' (*Sunday Mercury*, 14 April 2008), although that line of inquiry probably ended as soon as they realized the routine frequency with which girls describe themselves as whores to indicate their attachment to social networking sites. Similarly, research conducted by an educational sociologist found that more than 25,000 users of Bebo (a former Facebook rival) had 'slut' in their usernames (Ringrose, cited in the *Times*, 5 August 2009); again, illustrating to each other (if not to any paedophiles viewing their sites) that there has been a cultural shift in the meaning of such terms. Koskela (2006) suggests that some young women who charge people to view their home pages may not have grasped that they are effectively turning images of themselves into pornography. New communications technologies also have reportedly facilitated novel kinds of aggressive and sexually aggressive behaviours among children and young people, including sexual cyber-bullying. For example, Devon and Cornwall police report that children as young as 10 are posing as predatory paedophiles on Internet networking sites to frighten other children they have fallen out with (*Guardian*, 9 January 2009) and, in 2007, a 16-year-old schoolboy was charged with sexually assaulting a 14-year-old girl, and another was charged for filming the attack and distributing the pictures on his mobile phone (*Sunday Times*, 4 February 2007). In a 2002 survey, 25 per cent of young people between the ages of 11 and 19 years reported that they had been threatened or bullied via their computers or mobile telephones, including death threats (http://tinyurl.com/oabfem).

It is ironic, then, that as childhood has been privatized the private sphere has itself become a source of anxiety, so inextricably is domestic space now intertwined with cyberspace. Hardly a week goes by without some new moral panic being generated about Facebook (which, once again, may say as much about its economic presence as its social and cultural importance). But long before the development of the Internet, children bullied, and their sexual experimentation has always, on occasion, had a dark side. In his partially autobiographical account of the Bulger case, Blake Morrison (1997) recalls the rape of a 14-year-old girl at a party he attended when he was 15. He uses the story to illustrate that most of us experienced events in our youth of which we are now embarrassed or ashamed; after all, children can be promiscuous and unimpeded by perceptions of risk. Perhaps social networking sites and mobile phones simply offer a new means and a new lexicon with which to explore their identities, including their psycho-socio-sexual make-up, and to exert power over their peers. The *Sunday Mercury* perceptively notes that, for young people, the virtual realm represents a space for teenage rebellion: 'children see MySpace literally as their own space away from parents' (*Sunday Mercury*, 14

April 2008; available at http://tinyurl.com/qs2ejt). Despite the age restrictions imposed on many social networking sites, children may simply lie about their age to gain access. Girls, in particular, use the Net to express their sexuality:

> A trawl of social network sites revealed the shocking, highly personal content youngsters are uploading for all to see. They include a 15-year-old girl whose profile picture, which can be viewed by anyone, focuses on her breasts. Another 15-year-old is pictured sitting provocatively, exposing her breasts and bare legs up to her thigh. And we found one 16-year-old girl who is seen posing in her underwear in dozens of photographs. (*Sunday Mercury*, 14 April 2008; available at http://tinyurl.com/qs2ejt; cf. Koskela, 2006; Jewkes, 2010a)

The pervasiveness of images of young women asserting their sexual agency on networking sites and on YouTube may be unsettling but it is arguable that they are simply using a new channel to express what is essentially 'normal' adolescent behaviour, especially in a culture which increasingly attaches more emphasis on the desire to look, to be watched, and less stigma to nudity, intimate confession and explicit material in published diaries and blogs. The open displays of sexuality by young women that one encounters on social networking sites are arguably the inevitable consequence of a surveillance-rich and surveillance-tolerant society (as discussed in Chapter 8). In today's 'celebrity culture' women are urged to live up to prevalent feminine codes regarding their domestic roles, body shape, dietary habits, dress sense, sexuality and sexual performance. While, for some, this imposed self-surveillance may result in negative responses including disgust and shame at their failure to live up to these ideals, for others, the ability to make public their private bodies via webcams, phone cameras and social networking sites may constitute empowerment, albeit nonetheless a form of 'obedience to patriarchy' underpinned by a 'pervasive feeling of bodily deficiency' (Bartky, 1988: 81–2; cf. Coleman and McCahill, 2010).

Concluding thoughts

This chapter has discussed a range of 'cybercrimes' and included more detailed discussion of two very different case studies. At the beginning of the chapter, we considered the role that the Internet is playing in the development of China as an economic and cultural super-power, briefly dwelling on issues as diverse as cyber-warfare and citizen journalism. In the latter part of the chapter we reflected on young people's sexual experimentation online; the freedoms it affords them that they may be denied in other spheres of life, and the deviant and criminal consequences that can result. These examples illustrate the extent to which the evolution of the Internet may be characterized as a 'chronicle of contradiction' (Curran, 2010). From its military origins and the massive investment put into its development by a US government seeking military and technological superiority over the Soviet Union during the Cold War, to the 'hippy', liberal counter-culture in which the World Wide Web was conceived in the 1980s, and the era of deregulated media in the 1990s which allowed the newly commercialized Internet to flourish, the history of the Internet has combined paradoxical influences and outcomes. In its post-military phase, it amalgamated the values of academic science, American counterculture and European public service ideals. But having come to public life as a profoundly democratic concern it eventually had to offer itself to commercial interests and, then, to private and state bodies who wanted to use it for surveillance of populations (Curran, 2010). Vestiges of the counter-culture ethos remain intact and arguably are evident in the sexual and political freedoms afforded to users, as described in this chapter. But it is also true that the liberty and democracy that many of us take for granted have more negative, even sinister, connotations.

Summary

- This chapter has discussed two examples of online activity that raise urgent social, cultural and political questions and illustrate some of the complexities and paradoxes inherent in our uses of the Internet in the 21st century: namely, its facilitation of democracy and freedom on the one hand, and repression and risk on the other. Our focus could have been any number of online behaviours that would illustrate the contradiction and dilemmas thrown up by the Internet, but the two chosen – its role as a conduit of power within China and between China and the West; and its radical reformulation of the ways in which children and young people communicate, interact and negotiate sexual relations – are in keeping with broader themes that underpin this entire book.
- Like so many other issues examined throughout this volume, the Internet crystallizes social attitudes towards youthful deviance, and highlights both the ambiguous status occupied by adolescents (simultaneously infantilized and adultified) and also the paradoxical relationship between young people as victims and, conversely, as offenders or deviants.
- Chapter 9 has also offered a broad introduction to the types of activities that may be described as 'cybercrimes'; including electronic theft and abuse of intellectual property rights; hate crime, invasion of privacy, defamation and identity theft; eBay fraud; hacking and loss of sensitive data; child pornography and online grooming.

STUDY QUESTIONS

1. Do you, or have you ever behaved online or using any form of digital/mobile technology in ways that you would not risk in 'real' life? Why do you think that sometimes different rules and moral codes apply in cyberspace?

2. Both this chapter and the preceding one have highlighted that we live in a scopophilic, synoptic society. What are the social messages underpinning this 'mass looking exercise' (Coleman and McCahill, 2010)? Exactly what is being looked at and with what social consequences?

3. What do you understand by the term 'digital divide'? Can it be applied in local as well as global contexts?

4. Are there negative consequences of the democratization of access to information that the Internet has brought?

5. How newsworthy is cybercrime? Give reasons for your answer.

FURTHER READING

There are now a number of useful collections that discuss many kinds of 'cybercrime', some of which I have edited: Y. Jewkes and M. Yar (eds) (2009) *Handbook of Internet Crime* (Willan/Routledge); Y. Jewkes (ed.) (2007) *Crime Online* (Willan/Routledge); and Y. Jewkes (ed.) (2003) *Dot.cons: Crime, Deviance and Identity on the Internet* (Willan/Routledge). See also: M. Yar (2013) *Cybercrime and Society* 2nd edition (Sage) and Jewkes, Y. and Yar, M. (2008) 'Policing cybercrime: emerging trends and future challenges' in T. Newburn's *Handbook of Policing*, 2nd edition (Willan/Routledge). Covering many of the issues raised both in this chapter and the previous one is: K. F. Aas (2013) *Globalization and Crime* 2nd edition (Sage); especially Chapter 8 on 'Controlling cyberspace?'. David Wall has also written extensively on cybercrime including: Wall, D.S. (2007) *Cybercrime: The Transformation of Crime in the Information Age* (Polity). Finally, McGuire, M. (2007) *Hypercrime: The New Geometry of Harm* (Routledge) is a more theoretically advanced treatment of the subject.

10

(Re)Conceptualizing the Relationship between Media and Crime

CHAPTER CONTENTS

Doing media-crime research   276

The importance of the visual   280

Taking media-crime research seriously   281

Stigmatization, sentimentalization and sanctification: the
'othering' of victims and offenders   282

Summary   291

Study questions   292

Further reading   292

OVERVIEW

Chapter 10 provides:

- Some thoughts on how an interest in media criminology might extend to conducting research.
- Criticisms of existing scholarship in the field, particularly in relation to the methodologies employed.
- A bringing together of the main themes of the book.
- An examination of the significance of 'mega-cases'.

KEY TERMS

- audiences
- folk devil
- images
- media criminology
- mega-cases
- methodologies

- organizations
- otherness
- qualitative vs. quantitative
- research
- texts

In this final chapter, I want to reflect on what this book has been about and offer some concluding thoughts about how some of the primary themes that have emerged might help us to better understand the complex relationship between media and crime. First though, it is likely that many of the readers of *Media & Crime* will be students planning to write an undergraduate or postgraduate dissertation in this area, so it is worth dwelling briefly on how the study of the field may be approached. The chapter will be divided into two parts; it will end with some thoughts on what we have learned from our discussions so far, but first we will consider the business of doing media-crime *research*.

Doing media-crime research

Researching the kinds of issues discussed throughout this volume is an exciting prospect but conducting studies that aim to enhance our understanding of any aspect of the relationship between media and crime should not be undertaken lightly; the very best studies in the field have not compromised on theoretical depth or methodological rigour. For example, Cohen's (1972/2002) model of moral panics has proved impressively enduring and many followers have sought o emulate, explain or advance it. It is more easily understood than many media theories; it is more tangible than some subjects (e.g. those which appear to belong in the 'virtual' world of cyberspace); and it seems relatively easy to research. However, despite its continuing popularity, it is frequently misrepresented or cannibalized in contemporary scholarship, and even established academics may cherry-pick the bits of it that make their point, while ignoring much of its theoretical substance and empirical exactitude. Few research studies since Cohen's famous analysis have come close to the empirical rigour and diversity of methods with which he approached his subject. Cohen's documentary sources included national and local press cuttings from the entire two-and-a-half year research period; tape recordings of most radio and television news bulletins over the Bank Holiday weekends during which the incidents took place; local publications with restricted circulation (parish newsletters, council minutes and the like); Hansard reports; and letters received by the National Council for Civil Liberties alleging police malpractice. In addition to these secondary sources, Cohen administered questionnaires to trainee probation officers; interviewed news editors; held informal discussions with local hotel owners, shop assistants, taxi drivers, etc.; interviewed 65 members of the public who had witnessed the clashes between the mods and rockers; wrote letters to MPs and other public officials, some of which were followed up with interviews; talked to local action groups; and participated as a volunteer worker for a youth project in one of the seaside towns in which conflict had occurred (Cohen, 1972/2002: 173–7). It is perhaps precisely this methodological thoroughness that helps to explain both why this kind of empirical research is now so rare and why many contemporary studies of moral panic are hackneyed and unconvincing.

Although today's students may not be able to devote the time and resources to a project of this scope (apart from PhD students, that is, which Cohen was when he conducted the *Folk Devils and Moral Panics* study) that does not mean that they should compromise on theoretical and empirical robustness, or that doing any kind of media research should be viewed as an easy option. Chris Greer has voiced his concern about 'the types of research that appear increasingly to be defining the field' and he urges new scholars to engage in 'more fully interdisciplinary, theoretically and methodologically rigorous, *qualitative* engagement with the crime-media nexus' (2009: 1). Implicit in his critique is an appeal to students of media and crime to take risks and push the boundaries of existing knowledge. Explicit is his criticism that *media criminology* sometimes seeks to shed light on the role of media in society without any grounding in sociology or, sometimes even, any reference to the vast literature that has been borne out of media studies and cultural studies. Put bluntly, some scholars in criminology adopt an insular stance that leads, at best, to partial understanding of the issues being studied. In addition to theoretical parochialism, Greer is disparaging about what he describes as the growing distancing between the researcher and the object of enquiry, when 'methods are designed for detached quantification and counting rather than engaged, in-depth understanding, and the main objective is the routinized production of quick, clean datasets' (Greer, 2009: 4). Greer's aversion to *quantitative* methods is shared by Ferrell et al. (2008) who lament that *methodologies* designed explicitly to 'exclude ambiguity, surprise, and "human error" from the process of research result in "lifeless, stale, and inhuman" data' (2008: 165).

Elsewhere I have explored the kinds of research that can be undertaken into the media-crime nexus by breaking the field into four distinct parts (Jewkes, 2010b). In brief, and to take them in reverse order, I discuss the role of *media within the criminal justice system* and the part that research can play in illuminating aspects of a system that is usually not only hidden from public gaze but can also be shrouded in a certain amount of myth and mystique. Unfortunately negotiating access, getting past 'gatekeepers', persuading busy criminal justice professionals and wary 'clients' to grant interviews, and treading fine ethical lines are all potential obstacles to carrying out research in the relatively 'closed' settings of police stations, legal practices, courtrooms and prisons, which is why such projects are arguably the least commonly undertaken (although I discuss exceptions in Jewkes, 2010b). Hardly more straightforward are ethnographic studies into *media organizations*. As we saw in Chapter 2, in the 1970s, 1980s and 1990s several ground-breaking studies were conducted in the newsrooms where crime correspondents worked, but the practicalities of immersing oneself in the field of news production and spending a great deal of time with journalists, both on and off duty, in order to explore the full range of institutional and socio-cultural factors which shape and determine news output, have caused a sharp decline in the number of projects carried out in these environments. That said, no sooner had I posed the rhetorical question; 'where is today's Chibnall?' than Rob Mawby claimed the mantle with a study entitled 'Chibnall revisited: Crime reporters, the police and law and order news' (2010) which drew on data from 18 interviews conducted with journalists who were or had been crime reporters, together with a postal questionnaire survey of the 51 territorial police forces in England, Wales and Scotland.

Rather more easily embarked upon are studies examining *media audiences*. Large-scale postal surveys examining public perceptions of mediated crime are usually beyond the financial means and time constraints of most students, although small-scale questionnaires are popular and can yield valuable responses. Focus groups and semi-structured interviews are also commonly undertaken because they are cheap and relatively easy to organize, and are useful for obtaining rich data in participants' own words and developing deeper insights than would be elicited from a questionnaire. Finally, *media texts* may be the subject of research and content analysis or discourse analysis might be the chosen method. Newspapers, TV news bulletins, films, chat-room exchanges or any other 'readable' text can be studied and this approach is particularly useful for examining the kinds of biases, prejudices and omissions in media reporting that were discussed in the first six chapters of this volume. There now exist several searchable online databases, including *LexisNexis* and newspaper digital archives, for example the *Times* and the *Guardian* and *Observer* which make content and discourse analysis relatively cheap and easy – and therefore attractive to students with limited means and numerous competing pressures on their time and attention.

It is for these reasons that I want to dwell a moment on online news archives and exercise a word of caution. The problem with research tools like *LexisNexis* is that they only provide the researcher with flat text:

> Reduced to words on a computer monitor, printed 'news' becomes decontextualized, shorn of structure and style, disconnected from defining images and surrounding stories – and so, ultimately, left with little similarity to the increasingly spectacular, brilliantly colourful products that media audiences consume on a daily basis. (Greer et al., 2007: 6)

For this reason, newspaper digital archives might be considered superior insofar as a story can be viewed online as a facsimile of the original news page, along with accompanying photographs and other *images*, and the stories composed around it. These aspects of news reporting – images and composition – are important elements to any news story and it is frequently instructive to look beyond a single report and examine other elements that are constructed around it in order to fully grasp the meaning encoded in it. For example, when they were both alive, news reports about the Princess of Wales and Myra Hindley were frequently published alongside each other in the popular press, together with mirroring photographs of the two women (e.g. close-up images of their faces). While the accompanying headline would sometimes make reference to binary oppositions such as 'Angel' and 'Devil', it was not always necessary to spell out so blatantly the intended meaning, given that the juxtaposed images were of the invariably photogenic Diana and the unflattering police mugshot of Myra. Illustrating just how much the popular press held up Hindley as the personification of evil is also illustrated by the ways in which they framed reporting of Maxine Carr by reference to her; sometimes explicitly (with headlines such as 'MYRA MK II'); at other times more subtly, in their use of imagery (Jones and Wardle, 2010). Another common practice, especially in the local and regional press, is to publish lots of small crime stories, often taken from court reports, on a single page to give the impression of a crime wave. The overall effect of this kind of composition is frequently lost if the researcher is using only a keyword search to isolate particular stories.

The importance of the visual

Echoing Greer's concerns about the relative neglect of visual images in media criminology, I have argued (with my colleague, Tammy Ayres) that it is in the realm of the visual – or the 'graphic image', to use the terminology employed in Chapter 2 of this volume on news values – that meaning is most immediately and powerfully conveyed. Any story can be manufactured in such a way that it is deemed newsworthy, but it is the incorporation of images that most directly communicates the intended message. We demonstrated this in a small-scale analysis of UK press coverage of the 'moral panic that never was' – the predicted arrival of a crystal methamphetamine epidemic from the United States. Crystal meth was a drug that British people may have known little about, beyond the fact that self-confessed user Andre Agassi was seemingly able to continue his professional career, appearing on television numerous times, playing and being interviewed, while looking the picture of health and not arousing suspicion. So in their bid to shock readers out of any complacency about the harms caused by crystal meth, several newspapers published lurid 'before and after' pictures of meth addicts; the latter graphically illustrating the facial deformities and chronic ageing effects accompanying use of the drug.

These 'shock pictures of what new danger drug can do to you' (*Mirror*, 2 March 2006; cited in Ayres and Jewkes, 2012: 317) were crucial in conveying the moral message of the story and communicating a sense of awe and fear about the next anticipated crime wave to hit these shores from the United States. As Brown (2009: 23) and Linnemann et al. (2013: 612) have further commented, looking at and judging the lives of others (e.g. meth users) harnesses a 'peculiar energy' bound up in the enduring human fixation on the traumatic and grotesque. In a similar way to passing the scene of an accident and feeling compelled to look, shocking images are a defining feature of spectatorship (Linnemann et al., 2013). More importantly, though, the 'faces of addiction', as they were described, were used as a driver for broader drugs legislation and policy; a highly visible manifestation of the need for an American-style 'war on drugs' to be waged on *all* drugs, including cannabis. Linnemann (2013) calls this 'governance through meth' and argues that it is part of a broader drift toward securitization and crime control. He also notes that analyses of the centrality of visual images to a story like meth use – including an advertising campaign that employed graphic images accompanied by headlines such as '15 Bucks for Sex Isn't Normal. But on Meth It Is' and 'Before meth I had a daughter; now I have a prostitute' – demonstrates what Greer, Ferrell and Jewkes had earlier observed; that 'the visual constitutes perhaps the central medium through which the meanings and emotions of crime are captured and conveyed to audiences ... 'a sort of inflationary spiral of shock and enticement designed to sustain commercial buoyancy' (Greer et al, 2007: 5). In this sense and as Ayres and Jewkes (2012) further note, the mugshots of meth users performed a similar function to the photographs on cigarette packets showing the damaging effects of nicotine. Ostensibly designed to act as a visual deterrent, yet frequently having the opposite effect, especially among young smokers, it might be suggested that the graphic depictions of crystal meth users reproduced in the newspapers had similar intentions and effects.

Taking media-crime research seriously

I would argue that by far the best way to research newspaper content is to get hold of actual newspapers; indeed many believe that the ways in which we engage with the physicality of newspapers are radically different to the ways in which we use online news sources. This is not just because newspapers *have* a physicality (they have a certain smell; they crackle as you turn the pages; they are frequently large and cumbersome, especially if you are trying to read one in a restricted space, such as on a train; some still leave inky marks on your fingers), but it is because when we browse 'real' newspapers, we have a healthy lack of control. By exercising control through our choice of searchable keywords when we conduct research, we limit our opportunities to chance upon stories that are of interest and relevance to our research topic, but which did not contain the words we inputted. On the other hand, 'actual' newspapers can be difficult to get hold of, especially if your desired sample is very large or goes back several years/decades. In any case, it is estimated that more people now get their news online than from old-fashioned newspapers. For example, a US survey found that 37 per cent of Americans go online for news compared to 27 per cent who only read a print newspaper (http://people-press. org/report/444/news-media). People who consume news in this way may interact with the journalist, editor and other readers via comment pages, networking sites and blogs, and they may also access video clips as well as still images; all of which will be absent from a LexisNexis search. I am not saying don't use Nexis, but *do* supplement it with other research tools and approaches.

For example, in the study by Ayres and Jewkes described above, it was impractical to get hold of and analyse actual newspapers. Instead, a two-fold methodological approach was adopted. First, a keyword search was undertaken using both the InfoTrac newspaper database and LexisNexis for the key terms 'crystal meth' and 'crystal methamphetamine'. These searches yielded approximately 1,254 articles in UK national newspapers published between 2004 and 2011, which were then reduced to 537 by removing irrelevant articles and non-news stories (including TV guides, book reviews and quizzes).

Then, the second stage involved a more focused online search in which 52 key articles incorporating visual images were isolated. Of these, 20 (38%) were accompanied by the faces of crystal meth users. At this stage, we emailed the newspapers concerned and requested 'hard copies' of the ones that contained the images we were interested in. This enabled us to conduct a detailed semiotic analysis of the photographs used *and* to consider the relationship between written text and image. We also analysed the pages on which the stories were situated in order to understand intra- and inter-textual relationships, and how news stores are composed and juxtaposed on the page (or across double pages) to subtly suggest a particular ideological worldview (Ayres and Jewkes, 2012). For example, we were able to see how stories about crystal meth were printed alongside stories about other drugs (ranging from cannabis to heroin) and also alongside reports of serious crimes, including gun offences. The overall impression was that experimenting with, say, cannabis, may represent the 'thin end of the wedge', leading unavoidably to addiction to more serious drugs such as meth; and that crime and drug use are inextricably and inevitably linked.

The crystal meth study demonstrates the importance of going beyond a simple textual analysis using word-search software. The message, then, is to take media-crime research seriously; apply the same kind of theoretical and methodological standards as you would to any other area of criminological research while nonetheless exercising your imagination and enthusiasm. Be cognisant of the field's interdisciplinary roots; but be prepared to go beyond a faithful adherence to orthodoxies. In these endeavours we may succeed in (re)conceptualizing the relationship between media and crime in the 21st century.

Stigmatization, sentimentalization and sanctification: the 'othering' of victims and offenders

The notion of (re)conceptualizing the media-crime nexus brings us to some concluding thoughts on what we have learned from this book. Although ostensibly about the relationship between media and crime, this volume has touched on many wider issues which continually circulate in media discourse and partially define contemporary British society – among them, the sexual exploitation of children, the different cultural responses to men and women who kill, racism and bigotry within the police, and the threat of the 'outsider'. This latter concern is perceived as sufficiently troubling to legitimate the demonization of certain individuals and groups – on the basis of age, ethnicity, style and a range of other, usually visible, indicators – and to justify the repressive surveillance of public spaces. The examples discussed throughout the book indicate a clear selectiveness in the mediated constitution of offenders and offences as well as victims who capture the public imagination. If I were able to ask the readers of this book: 'what have been the three most important, significant and newsworthy crime stories reported in the decade since this book was first published?', a relatively small number might immediately respond with the 'War on Iraq'. I imagine that most people's replies would not include the worldwide recall of millions of cars by Toyota in 2009 and 2010 after mechanical defects reportedly caused severe injury and the deaths of 52 people in the United States (*The Times*, 2 March 2010). Nor would I think that most readers would instantly come up with the £1.12 million 'MPs expenses' scandal, even though British politicians' claims for moat cleaning, duck houses and porn movies gained worldwide notoriety, including being lampooned by Jon Stewart on the popular US TV programme *The Daily Show*.

In the second edition of this book, I guessed that readers (in the UK, at least) might respond to my question with the disappearance of Madeleine McCann, the torture and death of 'Baby Peter' and, perhaps, the discovery of a new 'house of horrors' owned by Josef Fritzl in Austria. However, although, shocking and exceptional as this last case seemed when it was revealed, it has arguably been superseded by similarly horrible crimes elsewhere in the world, including the discovery in 2013 of three women and a child held for a decade by Ariel Castro in Cleveland, Ohio. Castro had kidnapped, tortured and raped his victims and was found to be the biological father of the child, born to one of the women in 2006. Facing a life sentence plus 1,000 years in custody, Castro took his own life a month after being convicted. But, actually, as the fourth edition of *Media & Crime* goes into production, it may not be the most recent and 'extreme' examples of human depravity that spring to mind, but the historical and arguably more mundane crimes of newspaper editors who sanctioned phone hacking on a scale so wide and so all-encompassing that some minor celebs knew their five minutes of fame had come to an end when they found that their phones calls were *not* being monitored! Alternatively, in the aftermath of the revelations about Jimmy Savile and the ongoing Operation Yewtree, it may be the sexual offences of 1960s and 70s TV and radio personalities that spring to mind when you think about the most newsworthy crime stories of recent years. Savile's offences, in particular, were extraordinary in their number, their severity and their illustration of the power of celebrity to blind others to very serious crimes taking place right under their gaze – or, even worse, to ensure their silence and complicity.

Such is the nature of news in the 'global village' that all these the cases described above – and indeed, throughout this volume – might also come to the minds of readers in other countries, although there will, of course, be local variations. In the US, there are arguably many more candidates for crimes that have united people in shock and grief in the last decade – the case that introduces this edition, the Boston Marathon bombing, being just one example that had global, as well as national impact. When I have asked American friends to name a landmark criminal case of recent years, many have cited an unusual offence (in the sense that it was a financial crime). Bernard Madoff defrauded thousands of investors and, in June 2009 was given a maximum prison sentence of 150 years. The severity of punishment in itself guaranteed the story's newsworthiness (Madoff's lawyer had pushed for 12 years) but the scale of the invested money lost ($65 billion) in the midst of a global recession and at a time when bankers and financiers were regarded as folk devils, also accounted for the case's widespread coverage.

Readers outside the United States might not be familiar with the details of this crime though and, when it comes to crime news, the US pretty much operates in a void! The people of America are largely oblivious to our tragedies, crises and criminal cases, and we only hear about theirs if journalists assume they will be meaningful to us. As mentioned elsewhere in this volume, the US arguably is a great deal more newsworthy than any other country from a crime news perspective, but it still takes events of a significantly high threshold or magnitude to come to our attention and, conversely, many of our most high-profile criminal cases never get reported in the States. This was brought home to me by the numerous reviews of this book commissioned by the publisher to try and ascertain the merits of contracting me to co-author a dedicated US edition of *Media and Crime* (Jewkes and Linnemann, forthcoming). American reviewers liked the scope, structure and theoretical content of the book, but couldn't relate to the case studies used. They said their students had never heard of James Bulger or Madeleine McCann, so they had to substitute cases such as that of JonBenet Ramsey, a six-year-old girl murdered in her home in Boulder, Colorado in 1996, or Susan Smith, the mother convicted in 1994 of strapping her two young sons into their seats in her car, before pushing it into a lake and then claiming a black man had carjacked the vehicle with the boys inside.

Such crimes may generate pages of sociological analysis and collective soul searching in their countries' news media and frequently they not only shape collective cultural life but also result in new legislation and policy. To take another country and *'mega-case'* (Peelo, 2006) by way of example, Australia has experienced several tragic crimes that poignantly end up carrying their perpetrators' and/or victims' names into books like this. On 22 September 2012, Jill Meagher, a 29-year-old Irish-born woman living in Melbourne was raped and murdered while walking the short distance home from a pub where she had been enjoying a night out with friends. CCTV footage from inside a bridal shop captured Jill walking past and talking to a man wearing a blue hoodie. This man, Adrian Bayley, was convicted and sentenced to 35 years for her murder; five days after she went missing, Bayley led police to her body, buried in a shallow grave. A significant feature of the case was the role of social media in bringing the case to prominent public attention and in helping with the investigation. In the days following her disappearance, Jill's colleagues at broadcast company ABC used Twitter to alert followers to the search and they set up a Facebook group, 'Help us Find Jill Meagher'. Following the charging of a suspect, the police tried, initially unsuccessfully, to have Facebook pages about the case removed and the State Premier suggested that legal reform might be necessary to avoid social media coverage prejudicing the trial. On 30 September 2012, a public march in Jill's memory was organized which attracted a crowd of 30,000 people and there was a great deal of discussion subsequently on online forums, expressing grief for the victim and her family, as well as broader concerns about violence against women. The tragic murder of Jill Meagher may not be familiar to many people outside Australia (and Ireland, the country of her birth, whose news media followed the story closely) but in those countries, and in the state of Victoria in particular, it had a profoundly shocking effect and galvanized many people into publicly stating – and supporting the 'White Ribbon Campaign' initiated by her husband, Tom – that all violence against women is unacceptable.

The point is that in our increasingly individualized culture, where offending is regarded as the inflicting of harms by some individuals onto other individuals, mediated articulations of crime and punishment can still be seen as vehicles for connecting people and making a personal tragedy somehow emblematic of a wider social malaise or cause. As noted in Chapter 4, stories about crime and justice perform a similar role to royal weddings, state funerals and 'must see' television events, in bringing communities together and mobilizing common responses. Yet even the most extreme crime, murder, is subject to differing levels of interest, with only certain murders (of certain victims) containing sufficient human interest to touch everyone with the emotional intensity required to constitute a climate of public vilification and mourning. Appealing to the consensual values of an 'imagined community' (Anderson, 1983), the media stigmatize offenders, sentimentalize victims and sanctify those deemed particularly vulnerable or tragic. And, in relation to the latter, it is not just victims of serious and violent offences that attain such elevated status, but in some cases, their relatives too. Images of Neville and Doreen Lawrence MBE meeting Nelson Mandela, Sara Payne MBE becoming a government advisor on victims' rights, and Kate McCann being granted an audience with the Pope illustrate the point.

The exercise of writing a second edition of a book originally published in 2004 has proved instructive in thinking about how certain crimes come to public attention and stay in the mass consciousness, subtly contributing to our sense of selves, our perceptions of others, our cultural values, our levels of tolerance and our national identity. In the seven years or so since I wrote the first edition of *Media & Crime* new tragedies have come to occupy the collective psyche. Many of the offences inflicted on the victims we all now we feel we 'know' have already passed from being 'current events' to 'historical events', living on in the shared memory and serving to frame future mediated public discourses on crime and punishment. As mediated witnesses to tragic events, we come to occupy a terrain that Peelo terms 'virtual victimhood', which may help to explain the tone of some media coverage (and mediated public opinion) devoted to the new chapter that unfolded in Jon Venables' oddly public-private life in March 2010. When Venables was recalled to prison for allegedly breaching the terms of his life licence, reaction was shocking in its rawness, its visceralness and its vividness. The hatred directed at this 27-year-old man was undiminished by the passage of time: if anything, in the 17 years since his two-year-old victim was left dead on a railway line in Liverpool, strength of feeling had boiled down to a deep and potent poison that spoke of how emotionally involved in some cases we become and how natural it seems to 'take sides' in the social commentary that surrounds brutal offences. Despite the Minister of Justice's decision not to make public the details of the alleged crime for which Venables had been returned to prison (a decision which may have resulted in public imaginings far worse than the truth) the popular press enjoyed a few days of speculation and came up with several versions involving drugs and violent brawls (http://tinyurl.com/yew-6gyn) before alighting on child pornography offences; an allegation they stuck to in the face of the Minister's failure to deny it. What was also interesting about coverage by the red-top newspapers, was that their journalists appeared to have compiled an extensive dossier on both Venables and his co-accused, Robert Thompson, since they were released from custody in 2001. Notwithstanding the new identities given them to try and secure their lifelong anonymity, and the legal injunction preventing the media from releasing any information that might identify them, many newspapers were able to offer considerable detail about their lives, jobs and domestic situations. Of course, the journalists could have made it up. But, whether they fabricated their scoops or really had been keeping these two individuals under surveillance for a decade, it seems unsurprising that other press reports alleged that Venables had been suffering a breakdown in the months prior to his re-arrest and had been behaving recklessly. Descending into a 'persistent state of self-disclosure' his mental state was said to have become 'so fragile that he would regularly reveal his identity to strangers' (*Observer,* 7 March 2010).

Given the populist punitiveness that shaped this case, which included the misidentification of an innocent man on a Facebook page called *John Venables is David Calvert and lives in Fleetwood ... kill the *****, which over 2,500 people reportedly signed up for before the page was removed (http://tinyurl.com/ylr-6zfb), the likelihood of Venables receiving a fair trial seem very slim. As Lynn Chancer argues, when a crime becomes so high-profile that it blurs into a 'social cause', it not only alters the contours of future public discourse about similar events, but it also creates an irresolvable tension when it enters the arenas of the legal system. Put simply, the law cannot be impartial and objective in cases which generate feverish media and public debate; especially those that appear to emphatically lay down markers which highlight broader social problems. Whether intentionally or unwittingly, then, individuals involved in judicial proceedings have a profound influence on understandings of subsequent cases which are tried in the knowledge, and under the influence, of what has occurred previously (Chancer, 2005).

But why does the murder of a two-year-old in 1993 still occupy such a powerful place in the collective psyche when there have been so many similarly brutal crimes since that have failed to register in most minds? Why do only certain criminal events become thrust into the public sphere with sufficient vigour and emotional intensity to shape public fears of victimization? Why do some crimes invoke a public reaction so forceful that they become embedded in the cultural fabric of society, while other, almost identical, incidents fail almost to register on the media radar, still less capture the collective imagination? Why do some very serious crimes cast a much longer shadow than others, and some offenders become iconic representations of pure evil while others fade into quiet obscurity? Why is it, for example, that Harold Shipman, who was almost certainly the most prolific serial killer in British history, was not constantly vilified by the popular media and ascribed the kind of motifs applied to Myra Hindley or Robert Thompson and Jon Venables? And why do paedophiles who target children unknown to them merit such extreme hostility that the deep, enraged seething that bubbles quietly under society's surface occasionally erupts into violent, bloody and frequently indiscriminate action, when the level of abuse occurring within families is largely ignored?

While it does not claim to provide all the answers, this book has attempted to shed light on some of the most troubling questions which continue to vex scholars of media and crime. While I didn't set out to write a book about 'self' and 'other', the finished project has had much to say about the ways in which 'we' – the audience – in an ever expansive mediascape, are influenced in our understandings of those who transgress legal and moral boundaries. I have concentrated on some of those crimes that are most sensationalized by the media and, as a consequence, have a peculiarly strong hold on our national culture and identity. But there are many 'outsiders' – 'the threatening outcast, the fearsome stranger, the excluded and the embittered' (Garland, 1996: 461) – who provide the 'others' against whom we measure ourselves. As Foucault (1988) suggests, we judge the criminal, not the crime, and for all our 'postmodern' sophistication, the beginning of the 21st century finds us still falling back on the positivist discourses of 19th-century criminology. Attributing irrationality, over-sensitization and lesser reasoning to women, children, adolescents, the dangerous classes, those who lead 'unconventional' lifestyles, people from different ethnic backgrounds to our own and people with mental illnesses, it is perhaps not surprising that these 'lesser mortals' are the very groups who are considered to be most susceptible to media 'effects'. It is also they who are most consistently demonized by the media as these ascribed attributes then become the lens through which we view crime and violent behaviour. No-one who lives in today's media-saturated society is immune to the winner–loser/ self–other/insider–outsider culture – little wonder, then, that to many of Britain's citizens the police and criminal justice system are viewed as, at best, ineffective and, at worst, threatening (Reiner et al., 2001).

It has long been established that the media is not a window on the world, but is a prism subtly bending and distorting our picture of reality. In most versions of this argument, the reader, viewer or listener is characterized according to varying degrees of passivity, unarmed and ill-prepared to cogni-tively filter out the prejudices, biases and slants that may be subtly conveyed or overtly apparent. But in this book, I have argued that the relationship between media and audience in defining the parameters of social (in)toler-ance and social control is not only complex, but is one of collusion. To be blunt, crime is constructed and consumed in such a way as to permit the reader, viewer or listener to side-step reality rather than confronting or 'own-ing up' to it. Many of the cases discussed in this volume have been described as the unthinkable and unknowable, but perhaps they simply alert us to our collective unwillingness to think and to know. I have suggested that the crimes which conform to journalistic perceptions of 'newsworthiness' elicit a deep cultural unease that we, as a society, can only confront if we detach ourselves from the perpetrator(s) emotionally, morally and physically. Through a process of alienation and demonization we establish the '*other-ness*' of those who deviate and (re)assert our own innocence and normality (Blackman and Walkerdine, 2001).

Our pre-modern responses to postmodern problems is also evident in the media's overwhelming tendency to denounce acts as 'evil'. Since Cohen popularized the notion of the '*folk devil*' three decades ago, the symbolic potency of that image has been weakened and has, in recent times, been replaced by a more powerful icon – the 'evil monster'. When very serious offences are committed, the evil nature of the act is projected onto the perpe-trators and 'evil' comes to be seen not as the element that sets this crime apart as an abnormal and isolated event, but as the common factor in all crimes that can be reported as components of a single moral panic (Stokes, 2000). Thus, children who kill – in breaching our ideal of childhood innocence – and women who commit very serious crimes – in challenging traditional notions of acceptable femininity – become doubly vilified. Meanwhile, paedophiles are universally condemned as unequivocal folk devils, set apart from 'normal' society, inherently evil and incapable of reform (Critcher, 2003). The com-monly felt emotions of guilt, denial and repression that characteristically follow serious crimes perpetrated by women and children, and by paedo-philes, give their crimes a superordinancy that lifts them above other, equally horrible, crimes and secures for them a powerful symbolic place in the collective psyche. Constructed as evil monsters or sub-human beasts, their complexity can be denied and their evil can be exorcized by their exclusion from society (Kitzinger, 1999; Critcher, 2003).

It is, then, precisely for this reason that the crimes of Dr Harold Shipman, extreme and terrible as they were, failed to spark the interest of the media and public. Although sentenced to 15 consecutive life sentences, and excluded from society in that sense, Shipman did not face the level of fear and loathing that might have been anticipated when his crimes first came to light. The sheer number of victims involved suggests that this should have been one of the most infamous and talked about mediated events in our life-times. Up to 350 victims, most of them elderly, were killed in their own homes or in his small surgery in a suburb of Manchester. In either case, these were environments in which his victims were at their most defenceless and vulnerable, yet felt they were in safe hands. Shipman was so respected and trusted in his community that, even after his conviction, many of his former patients were protesting his innocence and integrity. But Shipman was unmitigatingly ordinary, bland even. He went to work, took holidays abroad, enjoyed a pint at his local, spent time with his family, just like all of us. As Heidkamp puts it, in relation to a different case which involved medical professionals 'putting to sleep' their elderly patients: 'how could murder have become banal, normal?' (1993: 220). The point, then, is this. Crimes like those of Dr Shipman do not become the stuff of media sensation precisely because the constitutive features of the case (a middle-class, profes-sional male perpetrator; elderly, mostly female victims; non-violent means of death) cannot be consigned to the unknown and unknowable margins. They invite society to recognize that it is not simply 'evil' or 'mad' people who are capable of killing, and this is an unpalatable truth that society is simply not ready to contemplate.

It would also seem that media-orchestrated infamy is shaped by the repre-sentational resources available to report a case. Since the infamous 'Watergate' tapes that brought down an American president, mediated sounds and images have themselves frequently become part of a crime story, and help not only to elevate public awareness at the time, but also to ensure that a crime remains in the collective imagination long after the trial is over. There are many exam-ples of chilling-with-hindsight snippets and snapshots from audio tape, film, mobile phone cameras and CCTV which help to explain the potent symbolic resonance of certain crimes. The audio tape played in court of one of the child victims of Ian Brady and Myra Hindley crying and begging to go home; the hoax tapes broadcast on national television that taunted police investigating the 'Yorkshire Ripper', and led them to focus their inquiries almost exclusively on suspects with a 'Geordie' accent; the Bootle shopping centre CCTV footage of a toddler holding hands with the little boys who would kill him; the ama-teur video film of Rodney King being brutally beaten by the LA police; the photographs of Holly Wells and Jessica Chapman in their matching Manchester United shirts standing in front of a kitchen clock, literally frozen in time; the television footage shot from a police helicopter of O. J. Simpson driving slowly down the highway trying to evade the LA police which was seen on television by approximately 100 million viewers; the 14-minute tape played in court of Nicole Brown Simpson pleading for help from a 911 emergency operator as O. J. could be heard in the background threatening and abusing her. All these haunting moments are seared on the memories of those who have witnessed them.

Of course, many of the criminal cases discussed in this volume have no such audio-visual 'extras' and it is not being suggested that crime stories must have these media adjuncts in order to be deemed newsworthy. Nonetheless it has become virtually impossible in contemporary society to separate the real from the mediated, and every 'true crime' that comes to public attention becomes inseparable from the media discourses and images that communicate it which, once again, underlines the importance of a holistic approach to media-crime research. There is no CCTV footage of the murder of Stephen Lawrence, but that case is virtually impossible to imagine without recourse to the memories of the *Daily Mail*'s (14 February 1997) front page carrying the photographs of the five men who were acquitted, under the one-word headline 'Murderers', or of the same five men snarling and jeering at the crowd and television cameras as they left the Macpherson inquiry (cf. Hayward and Presdee, 2010).

As a final thought, it must be remembered that in order to construct offenders as 'others', their 'outsider' status must be unequivocal and incontestable. All mediated discourses are narrative devices, but there are always counternarratives, even if they are not represented by the media. Revenge is a common theme in the defences of many notorious killers and many claim that they acted out of a sense of grievance which they perceive as legitimating their crimes. Tracey Wigginton claimed that her murder of a man she had never previously met was not the act of a blood-seeking vampire, but a consequence of her violent and abusive childhood. Aileen Wuornos' explanation for her murder of seven men was that she had acted in self-defence; Thomas Hamilton who, in March 1996, massacred 16 children and their teacher in a primary school in Dunblane, Scotland, was said to have acted out of revenge against a community from which he felt persecuted and ostracized. Timothy McVeigh who killed 168 people when he planted a bomb in a government building in Oklahoma, described it as a 'retaliatory strike, a counter attack' against the US Government for their botched raid on a cult headquarters in Waco, Texas, and their treatment of Iraqis and their own troops through the use of chemicals (*Observer*, 6 May 2001). Numerous perpetrators of crimes which are, at one and the same time, so horrific that they result in life prison sentences, yet so mundane (because committed by men against women and children) that they barely register a flicker of interest from the media, were either neglected in childhood or grew up in care and, in either case, were frequently the victims of sexual and physical abuse by adults in whom they should have been able to trust. Even Jon Venables and Robert Thompson, while not mature enough at the time of their trial to offer a motive for killing James Bulger, might be said to have had extenuating circumstances which included dysfunctional and, in the latter's case, violent home lives. They formed an alliance which gave them a feeling of power in lives in which cruelty was the norm, and their two-year-old victim may have been a surrogate for their loathing of their siblings or the vessel on to which they projected all their feelings of disappointment and rage (Morrison, 1997).

Of course, all these defences can be read as cynical ploys by the actors involved, or their supporters, to shift their status from that of offender to that of victim. But the crucial point is that, in downplaying their defences, the media demonstrate the profound discomfort and denial with which our culture views these counter narratives. Whether this denial arises from a fear of the potential for 'evil' that is within all of us, or more generally of the unwillingness to accept that, sometimes, horror lies beneath the most ordinary facades is debatable. But the fact remains that the truly 'unthinkable' and 'unknowable' are those crimes that take place behind closed doors and never reach public attention.

Summary

This chapter has sought to do two things in conclusion to *Media & Crime*:

- First, it has offered some thoughts on how an interest in media criminology might extend to conducting research (perhaps for a dissertation or thesis) into some or other aspect of the media-crime nexus. It has also highlighted some of the criticisms of existing scholarship in the field and warned against taking certain shortcuts when carrying out your own study.
  Second, the chapter has attempted to draw together some of the main themes that have emerged from the discussions throughout this volume. It has noted that not all offenders, victims and crimes are treated equally by the media and that, there is a tendency to concentrate on the most unusual, serious and atypical offences and report them in such a way as to characterize the offenders as 'absolute others' with no hope of rehabilitation or redemption. At the same time the victims of these horrible but thankfully rare offences are sentimentalized sometimes to the point of sanctification. All these processes ensure that 'mega-cases' take on a significance far greater than might be the case for other criminal events. They become socially, culturally, politically and historically important, bringing audiences together as 'mediated witnesses' or 'virtual victims' and uniting them in an imagined community.

STUDY QUESTIONS

1. Given the criticisms raised here about media criminology sometimes lacking methodological rigour and theoretical interdisciplinarity, what do you think might provide fruitful areas for future research?

2. What do you imagine might be some of the barriers to conducting the kind of research that cultural criminologists like Jeff Ferrell and his colleagues have undertaken?

3. Compile a list of 'mega-cases' or 'signal crimes'. How would you characterize their place in the collective psyche and what kinds of wider social, cultural and legal implications have they had?

4. Are mega-cases always brutal homicides or do other types of offences have the capacity to move from being 'current events' to 'historical events', living on in the collective memory and serving to frame future mediated public and legal discourses on crime and punishment? Can you think of any state crimes, corporate crimes, eco-crimes or cybercrimes that could be described as mega-cases?

FURTHER READING

There are not many books devoted specifically to the relationship between media and crime, but the one I would most strongly recommend is: Greer, C. (2009) *Crime and Media: A Reader* (Routledge) which is a collection of 'classic' and more unusual readings accompanied by insightful original commentaries written by the editor. In a similar vein is Jewkes, Y. (2009) *Crime and Media: Three Volume Set* (Sage). A good edited collection of essays on many of the topics covered in this volume is P. Mason (ed.) (2003) *Criminal Visions: Media Representations of Crime and Justice* (Willan/Routledge). As its title suggests, Carrabine, E. (2008) *Crime, Culture and the Media* (Polity) goes beyond the media to analyse the role of crime in other cultural forms, including art and literature. An engaging and thought-provoking collection that demonstrates the importance of the visual in crime reporting is Hayward, K. and Presdee, M. (2010) *Framing Crime: Cultural Criminology and the Image* (Glasshouse-Routledge). Finally, *Crime, Media, Culture: An International Journal* (http://cmc.sagepub. com) should be required reading for all students studying media and crime and is still one of the few 'criminology' journals to incorporate photographs, cartoons and other graphic illustrations.

Glossary

adultification – a term that hints at the ill-defined and variable nature of childhood, referring to the tendency to see children and young people as possessing similar capacities of reasoning and knowledge as adults. While this may be to their advantage in human rights terms, it also leads to an inclination – in the UK, at least – to criminalize children at a very young age.

agency – the notion that individuals act independently out of a sense of moral choice and free will, as opposed to being 'acted upon' by social forces and structures.

agenda-setting – the ways in which those who work within the media decide what is important enough to be reported and what is ignored, thus setting public agendas of debate. Crime is a particularly striking example of the agenda setting process because it is considered to be inherently **newsworthy** – although certain types of crimes, offenders and victims are more prominent on the news agenda than others.

anomie – a concept deriving from the work of Durkheim and developed by Merton, who suggest that anomie characterizes certain groups who experience a conflict between culturally desired goals (for example, material wealth) and legitimate means of attaining such goals. It is sometimes held that the media and culture industries are among the primary culprits in creating a desire for success, wealth and so on, which is unobtainable by means other than criminal or deviant.

audience – the assumed group at whom media **texts** are aimed. Recent media theory has reconceptualized the notion of audience from an agglomeration of individual receivers who are fragmented and passive, to one of sophisticated and active meaning-makers. In the light of developments in 'reality television', it might be argued that the lines between producers and audiences are becoming increasingly blurred.

behaviourism – an empiricist approach to psychology developed by J.B. Watson in the early years of the 20th century. Becoming the dominant perspective in psychology in the 1960s, this school is concerned with the objective study of observable behaviour and represents an antithetical challenge to psychoanalysis.

binary oppositions – the notion that the media (picking up on a human inclination to do the same) presents the world through polarized constructions of **difference** which are fixed and immutable – man/woman, black/white, good/evil, **tragic victim/evil monster** and so on. The media's tendency to deal largely in binary oppositions is said to further entrench biased or prejudiced public attitudes towards marginalized groups.

carceral society – the idea (derived from Foucault, 1977) that systems of surveillance are extending throughout society so that many more areas of social life are becoming subject to observation, categorization and control, resulting in an increasingly compliant population.

catharsis – sometimes held to be a media 'effect' and used to counter the argument that there is too much violence in the media, catharsis literally means 'cleansing' or 'purging' and implies that consuming violent media content allows viewers to release their feelings of anger, frustration or aggression in a vicarious but safe manner. The designers of violent computer games are among proponents of catharsis theory, arguing that their products constitute a harmless outlet for players' negative emotions.

celebrity – one of the 12 cardinal **news values** of the late 20th/early 21st century referring to a person who is globally famous. Celebrity is said to carry cultural weight as a key signifier of how media culture operates (Osborne 2002), and it intersects with crime in so far as celebrities who commit offences, or who are victims of crime, are eminently **newsworthy**, while some 'ordinary' offenders and victims become celebrities by virtue of the crimes associated with them.

children – a relatively neutral term (compared to the more negative ascriptions 'adolescents', 'youths' and 'juveniles'), which nonetheless is inclined to take on somewhat sinister undertones in the aftermath of serious crimes committed by the very young.

citizen journalism – a form of democratic participation brought about by mass ownership of mobile phones with built-in cameras, image-sharing networking sites including YouTube and Twitter, and the popularity of blogs **User-generated content** from citizen journalists has transformed news particularly of events where either professional journalists and cameramen have been unable to get to the scene quickly enough or where reporters are banned for political or military reasons.

consensus – the achievement of social unity through shared agreement. **Critical criminologists** suggest that, far from being conceived in terms of consensus, societies are actually characterized by *conflicts* between social groups and classes whose interests are opposed and incompatible. Some of these groups exercise power and hold positions of advantage over others. In this interpretation, consensus is seen as constructed and imposed in order to maintain the privileged position of dominant groups. Consensus might thus be achieved subtly and **hegemonically**.

control of the body – an aspect of surveillance achieved via an interface of technology and corporeality that can range from direct physical contact between flesh and technological device, to more oblique or covert methods of monitoring and codifying the body.

crime – conventionally crime is a violation of the law, but this is not a unitary concept and it has been extended to incorporate social harms. Its meaning is historically and culturally relative, and depends to a large extent on the theoretical position adopted by those defining it.

crime film – here used simply to denote a film made for cinema release or television which has a narrative/visual reference to criminal activity and/or criminal justice.

crime news – news stories about **crime** are ubiquitous in modern society and are invariably 'novel' and 'negative' in essence. In addition, crime news conforms to 12 **news values** which not only help us to understand the relationship between journalists, editors and the **audience**, but also tell us much about prevailing cultural and ideological assumptions.

criminalization – the application of the label 'criminal' to particular behaviours or groups, this term reflects the state's power – transmitted via the media, among other institutions – to regulate, control and punish selectively.

critical criminology – a Marxist-inspired, 'radical' school of criminology that emphasizes the relationship between routine, everyday life, and the surrounding social structures. Critical criminology has parallels with the political economy approach within media studies in their common emphasis on the connections between class, state and crime control.

cultural criminology – an approach that embraces postmodernism's concerns with the collapse of meaning, immediacy of gratification, consumption, pleasure and so on, and emphasizes the cultural construction of crime and crime control, and the role of image, style, representation and performance among deviant subcultures.

cyberbullying – a 'catch-all' term describing any form of abusive behaviour online which threatens, harasses or harms others, particularly over a sustained period of time.

cybercrime – any criminal activity that takes place within or by utilizing networks of electronic communication such as the Internet.

cyberspace – the interactional space or environment created by linking computers together into a communication network.

cyber-terrorism – activity that seeks to realize political ends by unlawful (and usually violent) means, and that (1) utilizes electronic communication networks to further those ends (such as the dissemination of propaganda, fund-raising or recruitment) and/or (2) targets computer networks and information systems for attack.

dangerousness – a term that sums up widespread fear of individuals and groups who appear to pose a significant threat to order or to individuals' personal safety (references to the 'dangerous classes' were common in 19th century Britain), but is increasingly supplanted by the actuarial and politically-charged concept of **risk**.

demonization – the act of labelling individuals or groups whose norms, attitudes or behaviour are seen to constitute 'evilness'. Those who are demonized are traditionally characterized as **folk devils** and are the subjects of **moral panic** (Cohen, 1972/2002), although it is arguable that ascriptions of 'pure evil' are becoming more salient than the rather less potent image of folk devilry.

deviance – a social, and usually moral (as opposed to legal), concept to describe rule-breaking behaviour.

deviancy amplification spiral – the moral discourse established by journalists and various other authorities, opinion leaders and moral entrepreneurs, who collectively demonize a perceived wrong-doer (or group of wrong-doers) as a source of moral decline and social disintegration, thus setting off a chain of public, political and police reaction.

difference – a concept often used in a negative sense to encapsulate cultural diversity, whereby the patterns of behaviour of certain groups are identified as 'differing' from some presumed norm. Cultural difference – most unequivocally expressed in **binary oppositions** – is frequently seen as the key factor in designating some groups as 'others', 'outsiders' or 'strangers', all of which can lead to **criminalization** and **demonization**.

documentary – usually a visual genre that has a claim to realism; i.e. is based on the attempt, in some form or other, to document 'reality' (although the line between 'fact' and 'fiction' can be somewhat blurred).

doli incapax – the principle that children under a certain age are incapable of understanding the difference between right and wrong, and therefore cannot be held criminally responsible for their actions.

'effects' research – a tradition of research that focuses on the impact or effects of media texts on audience attitudes or behaviour. Although a popular explanation for serious and juvenile crime (particularly and, somewhat ironically, within the media), much effects research has been discredited for isolating media influence from all other variables.

essentialism – the belief that behaviour is determined or propelled by some underlying force or inherent 'essence'. Essentialism informs many 'common sense' views on crime and criminality and provides the basis of a great deal of stereotyping about offenders.

ethnocentrism – when a country's news organizations value their own nation over others. In a famous study originally published in 1979 by Herbert J. Gans, ethnocentrism was found to be the enduring value in American news. He describes it as coming through most explicitly in foreign news 'which judges other countries by the extent to which they live up to or imitate American practices and values' (2004: 42). The clearest expression of ethnocentrism in all countries appears in war news which relies on unsubtle and unmitigated notions of 'the enemy'.

evil monsters – a (post)modern version of **folk devils** whereby media, political and legal discourses intersect to construct serious offenders in **essentialist** terms as absolute **others** and beyond the normal values that bind the **moral majority** together.

familicide or **family annihilation** – reported to be an increasingly common phenomenon whereby a man is driven by fear of failure to kill himself and his family. It is often characterized as 'misguided altruism', or a matter of masculine honour and pride in the face of overwhelming social expectations concerning men's responsibilities for their families' wellbeing. The relatively sympathetic coverage afforded by the media to men who commit familicide is in contrast to media reporting of women who kill, and demonstrates public tolerance to men's violence.

fear of crime – a state of anxiety or alarm brought about by the feeling that one is at risk of criminal victimization. Much discussion of individuals' fear of crime centres on whether such fear is rational (that is, that there is some tangible basis to the fear, such as previous experience of victimization) or irrational (that is, that fear is engendered by overblown and sensational media reporting of serious but untypical crimes).

feminism – in criminology, feminism emerged in the 1970s to challenge traditional approaches and their inhability, or unwillingness, to explore the relationship of sex/gender to crime or criminal justice systems. Feminist criminologies are diverse and evolving, and have been instrumental in introducing theories from psychoanalysis and cultural studies into criminology. One recent concern has been the portrayal of offending women as active agents exercising choice and free will, rather than simply as passive victims of male oppression.

fifth estate – traditionally used to describe the poor, it now usually refers to social media users and bloggers, who are not part of the mainstream media, but has also been used, in a film of the same name, about WikiLeaks.

filicide – the killing of a child by its parent or step-parent, filicide is the only type of homicide that women and men commit in approximately equal numbers.

film noir – a highly stylized cinematic crime genre usually characterized by a hard-boiled cynicism (on the part of the police officer, detective or private eye) and sexual motivations (on the part of a ubiquitous femme fatale).

folk devils – the term popularized by Cohen (1972/2002) to describe an individual or group defined as a threat to society, its values and interests, who become the subjects of a media-orchestrated **moral panic**. Folk devils are frequently young people who are stereotyped and scapegoated in such a fashion as to epitomize them as *the* problem in society.

fourth estate – although it's meaning has changed over time, it is generally regarded as being the press, in the form of powerful press barons like Lord Beaverbrook, William Randolph Hearst and latterly Rupert Murdoch.

framing – the shared cultural narratives and myths that a news story conveys via recourse to visual imagery, stereotyping and other journalistic 'short-cuts'.

genre – a category of usually musical, literary or media composition characterized by a particular style, form or content.

governmentality – Foucault coined this term to describe the growing inclination of the state to intervene in the lives of its citizens, not only via overt forms of regulation such as surveillance systems, but also through the dynamic relations of power and knowledge circulated intellectually and liguistically across institutions.

hegemony – a concept derived from Gramsci that refers to the ability of the dominant classes to exercise cultural and social leadership and thus to maintain their power by a process of consent, rather than coercion. The notion of hegemony is typically found in studies which seek to show how everyday meanings and representations (for example, to be 'tough on crime') are organized and made sense of in such a way as to render the class interests of the dominant authorities into a natural, inevitable and unarguable general interest, with a claim on everybody.

heteropatriarchy – a society in which the heterosexual, male/masculine is assumed to be the norm, and anyone or anything that differs from this is defined as '**other**' and is subject to censure or discrimination.

hypodermic syringe model – an unsophisticated model of media **effects** whereby the media are seen as injecting ideas, values and information directly into the passive receiver, thus producing a direct and unmediated effect.

ideology – a complex and highly-contested term referring to the ideas that circulate in society, and how they represent and misrepresent the social world. Ideology is often reduced to the practice of reproducing social relations of inequality in the interests of the ruling class.

imagined community – a term suggesting collective identity based on, and encompassing attitudes to, class, gender, lifestyle and nation. An imagined community is sustained via its representation, expression and symbolization by various social and cultural institutions, including the media.

infanticide – the homicide of an infant under 12 months by its mother while she is affected by pregnancy or lactation.

infantilization – while recent times have seen a certain **'adultification'** of children, particularly in legal and criminal discourses, they have simultaneously been subjected to a much greater degree of protective control and regulation than in former times. In addition, social, political and economic forces have resulted in many young people having to delay the 'rites of passage' (marriage, home ownership and so on) that have traditionally marked the transition from adolescence to adulthood, thus condemning them to a prolonged period of infantilization.

labelling – a sociological approach to crime and deviancy made famous by Becker (1963) that refers to the social processes by which certain groups (politicians, police, the media and so on) classify and categorize **others**. Deviance is thus not inherent in any given act, but is behaviour that is so labelled.

late modernity – a term used to describe the condition or state of highly-developed, present day societies which denotes their state as a continuation or development of what went before ('modernity'), rather than as a distinct new state ('post-modernity').

left realism – a 'radical' criminological perspective that emerged in Britain in the 1980s which views crime as a natural and inevitable outcome of class inequalities and patriarchy, and which proposes to take both **crime** and **fear of crime** seriously.

legitimacy – the process by which a group or institution achieves and maintains public support for its actions. For example, **critical criminologists** have argued that while the media frequently construct violence by protesters as unacceptable and deviant, violence on the part of the police is legitimated on the grounds that it is seen as necessary and retaliatory.

marxism – a theoretical approach that proposes that the media – like all other capitalist institutions – are owned by the ruling bourgeois élite and operate in the interests of that class, denying access to oppositional or alternative views. Crime is regarded as one of the ways in which class conflicts are played out within a stratified society.

mass media – the term used to describe the means of mass communication via electronic and print media made popular following the rise of the mass circulation newspaper in the 19th century and fully realized with the growth of radio in the 20th century. 'Mass media' encapsulates the notion of large numbers of individuals being part of a simultaneous audience, hence – in this book – it has been used sparingly. In the postmodern media environment, the plurality of media **texts** available and the increasing move towards narrowcasting' rather than 'broadcasting', makes the notion of a 'mass' media increasingly untenable.

mass society – a term from sociology suggesting that in industrial/capitalist societies individuals are directly controlled by those in power, and are atomized and isolated from traditional bonds of locality or kinship, making them particularly susceptible to the harmful **effects** of the **mass media**.

media criminology – the academic study of the relationship between the media and crime in all their forms.

mediated – in general usage, to mediate is to connect, not directly, but through some other person or thing. In this book the term 'mediated' is used throughout to mean 'mediated via the media'. While semantically incorrect, this avoids using the clumsier, but perhaps less ambiguous, 'mediatized'.

mega-cases – are those that take on a significance far greater than might the case for other criminal events. They become socially, culturally, politically and historically important, bringing audiences together as 'mediated witnesses' or 'virtual victims' and uniting them in an **imagined community**.

moral majority – a term that encapsulates the **imagined community** to which the popular press address themselves. Encompassing notions of conservativeness, respect for the law and its enforcers, and a certain version of 'Britishness', it assumes **consensus** on the part of the readership and can be summed up as the *Daily Mail* view of the world.

moral panic – hostile and disproportional social reaction to a condition, episode, person or group defined as a threat. According to some, crime has moved so emphatically to the centre of the media agenda, and has become so commercialized, that a virtual permanent state of moral panic exists.

narrative arc – the pattern of progression in a storyline; put simply, a beginning, middle and end.

newsworthiness – a term that encapsulates the perceived 'public appeal' or 'public interest' of any potential news story. Newsworthiness is determined by **news values**; the more news values a potential story conforms to, the more newsworthy it is perceived to be.

news values – the professional, yet informal, codes used in the selection, construction and presentation of news stories.

otherness – the term 'other' denotes a symbolic entity (for example, one or more individuals) located outside of the self. Otherness involves the perception of the self as distinct from the not-self, the latter being a vast category subdivided according to learned **differences**. Otherness is frequently used as an explanation for the **demonization** and **criminalization** of those who differ in background, appearance and so on from oneself or 'us' and relies on notions such as **moral majority, imagined community** and so forth to provide the norm against which others are perceived and judged.

paedophiles – in clinical psychology 'paedophilia' denotes an erotic preference for prepubescent children – that is, those under 11 years of age. In common currency 'paedophile' refers to adults who are sexually attracted to children of any age, including pubescents of 12 years or older, although these individuals are more accurately described as 'hebephiles'. Applied indiscriminately to both 'lookers' (for example, those who download abusive images of children from the Internet) and 'doers' (those who actually abuse children themselves) the media also frequently refer to offenders as 'convicted paedophiles', although no such offence exists in law.

panopticon and **panopticism** – the Panopticon was a prison design, created by Jeremy Bentham, that has been used as a blueprint for analysis of surveillance, social control and the exercise of power within society as a whole. Panopticism can be summed up as 'the few observing the many'.

paradigm – a shared set of ideas; the dominant pattern of thinking at any given time. Movements in theoretical understanding (for example, from modernity to postmodernity or from Marxism to pluralism) are often referred to as 'paradigm shifts'.

penal populism – the notion that, with declining faith in the formal structures and procedures of the criminal justice establishment and growing alarm that crime is out of control, the public support more punitive and retributive crime control and sentencing policies.

persistent offending – the notion that a small group of (usually young) offenders is responsible for a disproportionately large amount of crime in a given locale.

pluralism – an idea, deriving from sociology, suggesting that all opinions and interests should be equally represented and equally available. The promotion of a plurality of ideas has led some to criticize pluralism as a factor in the 'dumbing down' of culture.

police and **policing** – the term 'policing' refers to a diverse array of tasks, skills and procedures involving monitoring, regulation, protection and enforcement. Even 'the police' themselves are becoming part of a more diverse assortment of bodies with such functions, and the array of activities we term 'policing' is increasingly diffuse. Policing has come to be understood as a set of semiotic practices enmeshed with mediated culture; an activity that is as much about symbolism as it is about substance.

political economy – a sociological tradition that analyses society and social phenomena, including the media, in terms of the interplay between politics, economics and ideology.

populism/populist punitiveness – 'populism' means an appeal to the masses; 'populist punitiveness' is a term often used interchangeably with **penal populism**, referring to the perception that the public demands more punitive justice and punishment strategies to deter would-be offenders from committing crime.

positivism – the 19th century theoretical approach that argues that social relations can be studied scientifically and measured using methods derived from the natural sciences. In criminology it draws on biological, psychological and sociological perspectives in an attempt to identify the causes of crime which are generally held to be beyond the individual's control. In media studies, positivism has also been influential in the development of experimental, especially **behaviourist**, research, and has been particularly central to studies of media **effects**.

postmodernism – postmodernism embraces a rejection of claims to truth proposed by the 'grand theories' of the past and challenges us to accept that we live in a world of contradictions and inconsistencies which are not amenable to objective modes of thought. Postmodernism is arguably most prominent in cultural studies where it is used to emancipate meanings from their traditional usage, and emphasize pleasure, feelings, carnival, excess and dislocation. Within criminology, postmodernism implies an abandonment of the concept of crime and the construction of a new language and mode of thought to define processes of criminalization and censure.

profit – in the context of this book, 'profit' has been highlighted as a key term in relation to surveillance and social control. Surveillance and **security** represent big business and are driven largely by profit-motivated corporations who want to make their products attractive to the 'right kind' of consumer.

psychoanalysis – a theoretical approach developed by Freud and more recently popularized through the work of Lacan, psychoanalysis studies people's unconscious motivations for their actions and has been especially influential as a theory of constructions of sexuality and of masculinity/femininity.

psychosocial explanations – perspectives that draw on both **psychoanalysis** and social/sociological understandings, particularly in the pursuit of knowledge about gendered identities. It is often useful to employ psychoanalytic concepts in conjunction with sociologically-informed ideas from, for example, feminism, media studies and cultural studies, in order to explore why some individuals generate a level of media-orchestrated and publicly-articulated hysteria and vilification disproportionate to their actual crimes.

public appeal/public interest – two related but different concepts that are frequently confused. 'Public appeal' can be measured quantitatively in sales figures and ratings and is frequently used to justify the growing dependence on stories with a dramatic, sensationalist or celebrity component. 'Public interest' may involve qualitative assessments of what the public should and should not be made aware of. It therefore connotes interference from corporations or, more commonly, politicians.

rationality/irrationality – in debates about public fear of crime, it has frequently been proposed that such fears are irrational because the crimes that people fear most are those they are least likely to fall victim to. However, in recent years **left realists** and **cultural criminologists** have argued that there is a rational core to most people's anxieties. For example, the former suggest that people will fear crime if they have previously been victimized, while the latter argue that the modern media are so saturated with images of, and discourses about, crime, that it is increasingly difficult to separate the 'real' from the 'mediated'.

realism – an approach to painting, literature, film-making etc. that attempts to describe something 'as it is' without idealization or romantic subjectivity.

reception analysis – an alternative term for 'audience research' that has taken an increasingly sophisticated view of the 'receivers' of media **texts**. No longer are **audiences** conceived in terms of what the media *do* to them but, rather, the concern of reception analysts is 'what do audiences *do with* the media?'.

remakes – generally refers to a movie which uses an earlier film as the main source material, as opposed to a second, later movie based on the same source e.g. a novel or comic book), although remakes do not necessarily share the same title as the original.

representation/misrepresentation – the ways in which meanings are depicted, communicated and circulated. Although the media are sometimes conceptualized as a mirror held up to 'reality', in fact they are arguably more accurately thought of as a means of representing the world within coherent, if frequently limited and inaccurate, terms.

revenge porn – linked to **cyberbullying** and **sexting**, a typical scenario is that a boy shares sexually explicit images of a former girlfriend, who has ended their relationship, with his friends and threatens to circulate it more widely. In some cases, such images have gone viral and have resulted in the victim committing suicide.

risk – a concept that emerged to dominate discussions of late modernity in the 1990s, the term 'risk society' was coined by Beck to denote the social shift from the pre-industrial tendency to view negative events as random acts of God or nature, to the post-industrial preoccupation with man-made dangers and harms. The media are frequently conceptualized as the most prominent articulators of risk (and thus the primary source of people's **fear of crime**) because of their seeming obsession with health scares, panics over food and diet and, of course, **crime**.

scopophilia – the pleasure of looking; the desire to see.

security – one of the five aspects of surveillance that has significant social and cultural implications. Paradoxically, surveillance technologies may make people feel both more secure and more paranoid about their personal safety.

sexting – one of the fastest-growing harms involving young people; a form of peer-to-peer grooming or exploitative behaviour in which sexually explicit messages and images are shared on mobile phones, via texting, instant messaging or social networking sites. The phenomenon is linked to **cyberbullying** because victims are often threatened or blackmailed, and **revenge porn** when used as retaliation.

signal crime – bearing some similarity to **moral panics** and the theory of 'broken windows', signal crimes are incidents or offences that, when seen or experienced, may trigger a change in public beliefs or behaviour. It has become a familiar concept in policing because signal crimes can have a negative disproportionate impact on public perceptions of security.

social constructionism – a perspective that emphasizes the importance of social expectations in the analysis of taken-for-granted and apparently natural social processes. Constructionism avoids the conventional **binary opposition** of **representation**/reality by suggesting that there is no intrinsic meaning in things, but that meaning is conferred according to shared cultural references and experiences.

social networking – The practice of encountering, interacting and forming social relations with others using Internet-based sites or services designed for this purpose.

social reaction – the social process characterizing responses to crime and deviance. Encompassing public, political, criminal justice and media reactions, the term is often used to signify the processes of **labelling**, **stereotyping** and **stigmatizing** of certain individuals and groups.

spousal homicide – the unlawful killing of an individual by their spouse or partner, this offence has led to a great deal of research, especially within **feminist** criminology, regarding the mediating factors that have to be taken account of in studies of offending and **victimization**.

stereotyping – the process of reducing individuals or groups to over-simplified or generalized characterizations resulting in crude, and usually negative categorizations.

stigmatizing – the process by which an individual or group is discredited because of some aspect of their appearance or behaviour. Stigmatization helps to explain why some perceived **deviants** are subjected to marginalization and social exclusion and are the recipients of hostile reporting and censure by the media.

subculture – generally used to describe groups of young people whose apearance, norms and behaviour differ from those of the mainstream or 'parent' culture.

surveillant assemblage – the depth, or intensity, of surveillance that is achieved via the connection of different and once discrete technologies (for example, digitized CCTV systems and computer databases) and institutions (for example, the police and private security companies) (Haggerty and Ericson, 2000).

synopticism – an emerging theme in the sociological and criminological literature on surveillance, synopticism describes a situation where the many observe the few (as opposed to **panopticism** where the reverse is true). The ate modern trend towards synopticism is evident in the development of the **mass media** and is exemplified by the 'reality television' boom that has taken place in recent years.

errorism – a notoriously slippery and contested term. In its most conventional sense, it denotes the use of violence or the threat of violence in pursuit of political ends. See also **cyber-terrorism**.

ext – a media text is any media product (for example, film, advertisement, television programme, Internet home page, radio jingle, newspaper article) in which meaning is inscribed, and from which meaning can be inferred.

ragic victims – the term frequently used in **binary opposition** to that of **evil monsters**, whereby the innocence and vulnerability of a victim of crime becomes the primary aspect of their representation in the media to the point of sentimentalization and sanctification.

rolling – formerly known as 'flaming', the posting of defamatory and/or threatening messages on online forums, including personal Twitter accounts. Internet trolls divide opinion. Some maintain that freedom of speech, however tasteless or offensive, must be preserved. Others argue that the prison sentences handed out to trolls who have targeted **newsworthy** victims are justified.

unconscious – the term used in **psychoanalysis**, and central to the work of Freud, to refer to that which is repressed from consciousness.

user-generated content or UGC refers to various kinds of media content that is publicly available and is produced by end-users. In news contexts these end-users are known as **citizen journalists**.

victimization – the experience of being a victim of crime. The study of the relationship between the victim and the offender – or 'victimology' – has become a key concern and might be said to constitute a sub-discipline within criminology.

voyeurism – orignally used to describe the act of watching the sexual activities of others, voyeurism is now used more widely to describe spectatorship of what is usually held to be a private world.

youth – the imprecise period between infancy and adulthood. In media reporting of crime, youth tends to be more frequently linked to offending than victimization.

References

Aas, K. F. (2005) *Sentencing in the Age of Information: From Faust to Macintosh*, Glasshouse-Cavendish.

Aas, K. F. (2013) *Globalization and Crime* 2nd edn, London: Sage.

Agnew, R. (2012) 'The ordinary acts that contribute to ecocide: a criminological analysis', in N. South and A. Brisman (eds) *Routledge International Handbook of Green Criminology*, London: Routledge

Alder, C. M. and Polk, K. (1996) 'Masculinity and child homicide', *British Journal of Criminology*, 36 (3): 396–411.

Aldridge, M. (2003) 'The ties that divide: regional press campaigns, community and populism', *Media, Culture & Society*, 25: 491–509.

Anderson, B. (1983) *Imagined Communities: Reflections on the Origins and Spread of Nationalism*, London: Verso.

Apted, M. (2009) 'Michael Apted responds', *Ethnography*, 10 (3): 359–67.

Ashenden, S. (2002) 'Policing perversion: the contemporary governance of paedophilia', *Cultural Values*, 6 (1 and 2): 197–222.

Ball, K. (2003) 'Editorial. The labours of surveillance', *Surveillance and Society*, 1 (2): 125–37.

Bannister, J., Fyfe, N. and Kearns, A. (1998) 'Closed circuit television and the city', in C. Norris, J. Moran and G. Armstrong (eds) *Surveillance, Closed Circuit Television and Social Control*, Aldershot: Ashgate.

Barak, G. (1994) 'Media, society, and criminology', in G. Barak (ed.) *Media, Process, and the Social Construction of Crime*, New York: Garland.

Barker, V. (2009) *Politics of Imprisonment: How the Democratic Process Shapes the Way America Punishes Offenders*, Oxford: Oxford University Press.

Barthes, R. (1973) *Mythologies*, London: Paladin.

Bartky, S. L. (1988) 'Foucault, femininity, and the modernization of patriarchal Power', in I. Diamond and L. Quinby (eds) *Feminism and Foucault: Reflections of Resistance*, Boston: Northeastern University Press.

Baudrillard, J. (1981) *For A Critique of the Political Economy of the Sign*, St Louis: Telos.

Baudrillard, J. (1983) *Simulations*, New York: Semiotext(e).

Bauman, Z. (1992) *Intimations of Postmodernity*, London: Routledge.

Bauman, Z. (1997) *Postmodernity and its Discontents*, Cambridge: Polity Press.

Beck, U. (1992) *Risk Society*, London: Sage.

Becker, H. (1963) *Outsiders: Studies in the Sociology of Deviance*, New York: Free Press.

Benedict, H. (1992) *Virgin or Vamp*, Oxford: Oxford University Press.

Benn, M. (1993) 'Body talk: the sexual politics of PMT', in H. Birch (ed.) *Moving Targets: Women, Murder and Representation*, London: Virago.

Bennett, J. (2004) 'Life lessons: Rex Bloomstein's Lifer films', *Journal for Crime, Conflict and the Media*, 1 (3): 43–54. Available at http://www.jc2m.co.uk/Issue%203/Bennett.pdf

Bennett, J. (2006a) 'Undermining the simplicities: the films of Rex Bloomstein', in P. Mason (ed.) *Captured by the Media: Prison Discourse in Popular Culture*, Cullompton: Willan.

Bennett, J. (2006b) '"We might be locked up, but we're not thick": Rex Bloomstein's Kids Behind Bars', *Crime, Media, Culture: An International Journal*, 2 (3): 268–85.

Bennett, J. (2009) 'The interview: Paul Hamann', *Prison Service Journal*, 184: 45–50.

Berman, M. (1983) *All that is Solid Melts into Air: The Experience of Modernity*, London: Verso.

Berntzen, L. E. and Sandberg, S. (2014) 'The Collective Nature of Lone Wolf Terrorism: Anders Behring Breivik and the Anti-Islamic Social Movement', *Terrorism and Political Violence*, published online: 5 February 2014

Birch, H. (1993) 'If looks could kill: Myra Hindley and the iconography of evil', in H. Birch (ed.) *Moving Targets: Women, Murder and Representation*, London: Virago.

Blackman, L. and Walkerdine, V. (2001) *Mass Hysteria: Critical Psychology and Media Studies*, Basingstoke: Palgrave.

Bloomstein, R. (2008) 'Crime and the camera: making prison documentaries: the work of Rex Bloomstein', presentation as part of the Scarman Lecture Series, Department of Criminology, University of Leicester, 5 November.

Blumler, J. (1991) 'The new television marketplace', in J. Curran and M. Gurevitch (eds) *Mass Media and Society*, London: Arnold, pp. 194–215.

Bocock, R. (1993) Consumption, London: Routledge.

Bok, S. (1998) *Mayhem: Violence as Public Entertainment*, Reading, MA: Addison-Wesley.

Bowling, B. and Phillips, C. (2002) *Racism, Crime and Justice*, Harlow: Longman.

Box, S. (1983) *Power, Crime and Mystification*, London: Tavistock.

Boyne, R. (2000) 'Post-panopticism', *Economy and Society*, 29 (2): 285–307.

Brake, M. (1980) 'The sociology of youth culture and youth subcultures: sex and drugs and rock 'n' roll', London: Routledge & Kegan Paul.

Bright, M. (2002) 'The vanishing', *Observer Magazine*, 15 December.

Browne, A. (1987) *When Battered Women Kill*, New York: Macmillan/Free Press.

Burawoy, M. (2009) 'Public ethnography as film: Michael Apted and the *Up!* Series', *Ethnography*, 10 (3): 317–19.

Burney, E. (1990) *Putting Street Crime in its Place: A Report to the Community/Police Consultative Group for Lambeth*, London: Goldsmiths College.

Cameron, D. and Frazer, E. (1987) T*he Lust to Kill: A Feminist Investigation of Sexual Murder*, Cambridge: Polity Press.

Campbell, D. (2000) 'Echelon: world under watch, an introduction', 29 June www.zdnet.co.uk/news/specials/2000/06/echelon/

Campbell, M. (1995) 'Partnerships of perversion under study', *The Globe and Mail* [Toronto], 9 February.

Cantril, H. (1997) 'The invasion from Mars', in T. O'Sullivan, T. and Y. Jewkes (eds) *The Media Studies Reader*, London: Arnold. Originally published in 1940 as *The Invasion from Mars: A Study in the Psychology of Panic*, with H. Gaudet and H. Herzog (Princeton University Press).

Carrabine, E. (2008) *Crime, Culture and the Media*, Cambridge: Polity.

Carrington, K. and Hogg, R. (eds) (2002) *Critical Criminology: Issues, Debates, Challenges*, Cullompton: Willan.

Carter, C. (1998) 'When the "extraordinary" becomes "ordinary": everyday news of sexual violence', in C. Carter, G. Branston and S. Allen (eds) *News, Gender and Power*, London: Routledge.

Cavender, G. and Mulcahy, A. (1998) 'Trial by fire: media constructions of corporate deviance', *Justice Quarterly*, 15 (4): 697–719.

Cere, R. Jewkes, Y. and Ugelvik, T. (2013) 'Media and crime: a comparative analysis of crime news in the UK, Norway and Italy', in M. Hough et al. (eds.) *The Routledge Handbook of European Criminology*, London: Routledge

Chadwick, K. and Little, C. (1987) 'The criminalisation of women', in P. Scraton (ed.) *Law, Order and the Authoritarian State*, Buckingham: Open University Press.

Chakraborti, N. and Garland, J. (2009) *Hate Crime: Impact, Causes, and Consequences*, London: Sage.

Chancer, L. S. (2005) 'In re the legal system', in *High-Profile Crimes: When Legal Cases Become Social Causes*, Chicago: University of Chicago Press.

Cheatwood, D. (1998) 'Prison movies: films about adult, male, civilian prisons: 1929–1995', in F. Bailey and D. Hale (eds) *Popular Culture, Crime and Justice*, Belmont: Wadsworth.

Chermak, S. (1994) 'Crime in the news media: a refined understanding of how crimes become news', in G. Barak (ed.) *Media, Process, and the Social Construction of Crime*, New York: Garland.

Chesney-Lind, M. and Eliason, M. (2006) 'From invisible to incorrigible: the demonization of marginalized women and girls', *Crime Media Culture: An International Journal*, 2 (1): 29–47.

Chibnall, S. (1977) *Law and Order News: Crime Reporting in the British Press*. Originally published by Tavistock 1977, republished in 2001 in Tavistock Classics series by Taylor and Francis.

Chibnall, S. (2006) 'The anti-heroines of Holloway: the prison films of Joan Henry and J. Lee Thompson', in P. Mason (ed.) *Captured by the Media: Prison Discourse in Popular Culture*, Cullompton: Willan.

Cohen, N. (1999) *Cruel Britannia: Reports on the Sinister and the Preposterous*, London: Verso.

Cohen, S. (1972/2002) *Folk Devils and Moral Panics: The Creation of Mods and Rockers*, London: MacGibbon and Kee; 3rd edn with revised Introduction, London: Routledge.

Cohen, S. (1980) *Folk Devils and Moral Panics: The Creation of Mods and Rockers*, Oxford: Martin Robertson; 2nd edn with revised Introduction.

Cohen, S. (1985) *Visions of Social Control: Crime, Punishment and Classification*, Cambridge: Polity Press.

Cohen, S. and Young, J. (1973) *The Manufacture of News: Deviance Social Problems and the Mass Media*, London: Constable.

Coleman, C. and Norris, C. (2000) *Introducing Criminology*, Cullompton: Willan.

Coleman, R. and McCahill, M. (2010) *Surveillance and Crime*, London: Sage.

Coleman, R. and Sim, J. (2000) '"You'll never walk alone": CCTV surveillance, order and neo-liberal rule in Liverpool city centre', *British Journal of Criminology*, 41 (4): 623–39.

Connell, I. (1985) 'Fabulous powers: blaming the media', in L. Masterman (ed.) *Television Mythologies*, London: Comedia.

Connell, R. W. (1987) *Gender and Power: Society, the Person and Sexual Politics*, Cambridge: Polity.

Coward, R. (1990) 'Innocent pleasure', *New Statesman & Society*, 13 April: 12–14.

Cowburn, M. and Dominelli, L. (2001) 'Masking hegemonic masculinity: reconstructing the paedophile as the dangerous stranger', *British Journal of Social Work*, 31: 399–415.

Crawford, A., Jones, T., Woodhouse, T. and Young, J. (1990) *Second Islington Crime Survey*, London: Middlesex Polytechnic.

Creed, B. (1996) 'Bitch queen or backlash? Media portrayals of female murderers', in K. Greenwood (ed.) *The Things She Loves: Why Women Kill*, Sydney: Allen & Unwin.

Critcher, C. (2003) *Moral Panics and the Media*, Buckingham: Open University Press.

Cross, S. (2014) 'Mad and bad media: populism and pathology in the British tabloids', *European Journal of Communication*, 29(2): 204-217

Cullen, D. (2003) 'Child porn list leaked to *Sunday Times*', www.theregister.co.uk

Curran, J. (2010) 'Reinterpreting Internet history', in Y. Jewkes and M. Yar (eds) *Handbook of Internet Crime*, Cullompton: Willan.

Curzon-Brown, D. (2000) 'The teacher review debate part II: the dark side of the Internet', in D. Gauntlett (ed.) *Web.studies: Rewiring Media Studies for the Digital Age*, London: Arnold.

Davies, J. and Smith, C. R. (1997) *Gender, Ethnicity and Sexuality in Contemporary American Film*, Edinburgh: Keele University Press.

Davies, P. (2003) 'Women, crime and work: gender and the labour market', *Criminal Justice Matters*, 53, Autumn: 46–7.

Davies (2009) http://www.guardian.co.uk/media/2009/apr/27/ipcc-police-g20-death-media

Davis, M. (1994) *Beyond Blade Runner: Urban Control – the Ecology of Fear*, Open Magazine Pamphlet series, New York: The New Press.

Debord, G. (1967/1997) *The Society of the Spectacle*, London: Verso.

De Certeau, M. (1984) *The Practice of Everyday Life*, California: University of California Press.

Denning, D. E. (2010) 'Terror's web: how the Internet is transforming terrorism', in Y. Jewkes and M. Yar (eds) *Handbook of Internet Crime*, Cullompton: Willan.

Ditton, J., Bannister, J., Gilchrist, E. and Farrall, S. (1999) 'Afraid or angry? Recalibrating the "fear" of crime', *International Review of Victimology*, 6 (2): 83–99.

Ditton, J. and Duffy, J. (1983) 'Bias in the newspaper reporting of crime news', *British Journal of Criminology*, 23 (2).

Dobash, R. and Dobash, R. (1992) *Women, Violence and Social Change*, London: Routledge.

Dobash, R., Dobash, R. and Gutteridge, S. (1986) *The Imprisonment of Women*, Oxford: Blackwell.

Dobash, R., Dobash, R. and Noaks, L. (eds) (1995) *Gender and Crime*, Cardiff: University of Wales Press.

Douglas, M. (1966) *Purity and Danger: An Analysis of Concepts of Pollution and Taboo*, London: Routledge and Kegan Paul.

Dovey, J. (1996) 'The revelation of unguessed worlds', in J. Dovey (ed.) *Fractal Dreams: New Media in Social Context*, London: Lawrence & Wishart.

Downes, D. (1988) 'The sociology of crime and social control in Britain, 1960–87', in P. Rock (ed.) *A History of British Criminology*, Oxford: Oxford University Press.

Downes, D. and Rock, P. (1988) *Understanding Deviance: A Guide to the Sociology of Crime and Rule Breaking*, Oxford: Oxford University Press.

Duneier, M. (2009) 'Michael Apted's *Up!* series: Public sociology or folk psychology through film?', *Ethnography*, 10 (3): 341–5.

Durkheim, E. (1893/1933) *The Division of Labour in Society*, Glencoe, IL: Free Press.

Durkheim, E. (1895/1964) *The Rules of Sociological Method*, New York: Free Press.

Edwards, L., Rauhofer, J. and Yar, M. (2010) 'Recent developments in UK cybercrime law', in Y. Jewkes and M. Yar (eds) *Handbook of Internet Crime*, Cullompton: Willan.

Ericson, R., Baranek, P. and Chan, J. (1987) *Visualising Deviance: A Study of News Organisations*, Buckingham: Open University Press.

Ericson, R., Baranek, P. and Chan, J. (1989) *Negotiating Control: A Study of News Sources*, Buckingham: Open University Press.

Ericson, R., Baranek, P. and Chan, J. (1991) *Representing Order: Crime, Law and Justice in the News Media*, Buckingham: Open University Press.

Ericson, R. V. and Haggerty, K. D. (1997) *Policing the Risk Society*, Oxford: Oxford University Press.

Espiner, T. (2007) 'EU To Launch Scam Crackdown', 26 February, http://news.zdnet. co.uk/security/0,1000000189,39286068,00.htm

Farrall, S. and Gadd, D. (2004) 'The frequency of the fear of crime', *British Journal of Criminology*, 44 (1): 127–32.

Farrell, G. and Pease, K. (2007) 'Crime in England and Wales: more violence and more chronic victims', *Civitas Review*, June, 4 (2).

Ferrell, J. (1996) *Crimes of Style: Urban Graffiti and the Politics of Criminality*, Boston: Northeastern University Press.

Ferrell, J. (2001) 'Cultural criminology', in E. McLaughlin and J. Muncie (eds) *The Sage Dictionary of Criminology*, London: Sage.

Ferrell, J. (2002) *Tearing Down the Streets: Adventures in Urban Anarchy*, New York: Palgrave/St Martins.

Ferrell, J., Hayward, K. and Young, J. (2008) *Cultural Criminology: An Invitation*, London: Sage.

Fiddler, M. (2007) 'Projecting the Prison: The Depiction of the Uncanny in *The Shawshank Redemption*', *Crime, Media, Culture: An International Journal*, 3 (2): 192–206.

Finch, E. (2003) 'What a tangled web we weave: identity theft and the Internet', in Y. Jewkes (ed.) *Dot.cons: Crime, Deviance and Identity on the Internet*, Cullompton: Willan.

Finch, E. (2003) 'The problem of stolen identity and the Internet', in Y. Jewkes (ed.) *Crime Online*, Cullompton: Willan.

Finch, E. (2007) 'The problem of stolen identity and the Internet', in Y. Jewkes (ed.) *Crime Online*, Cullompton: Willan.

Fishman, M. (1981) *Manufacturing the News*, Austin, TX: University of Texas Press.

Fiske, J. (1982) *Introduction to Communication Studies*, London: Routledge.

Fiske, J. (1987) *Television Culture*, London: Routledge.

Fiske, J. (1989) *Reading the Popular*, London: Routledge.

Foucault, M. (1977) *Discipline and Punish*, London: Allen Lane.

Foucault, M. (1988) *Politics, Philosophy, Culture: Interviews and Other Writings, 1977–1984*, London: Routledge.

Fowler, R. (1991) *Language in the News*, London: Routledge.

Frayn, M. (1965) *The Tin Men*, London: Collins.

Freeman, M. (1997) 'The James Bulger tragedy: childish innocence and the construction of guilt', in A. McGillivray (ed.) *Governing Childhood*, Aldershot: Dartmouth.

Furedi, F. (1997) *Culture of Fear: Risk-Taking and the Morality of Low Expectation*, London: Cassell.

Furedi, F. (2013) *Moral Crusades in an Age of Mistrust: The Jimmy Savile Scandal*, London: Palgrave Pivot.

Furnell, S. (2010) 'Hackers, viruses and malicious software', in Y. Jewkes and M. Yar (2010) *Handbook of Internet Crime*, Cullompton: Willan.

Gadd, D., Farrell, S., Dallimore, D. and Lombard, N. (2003) 'Male victims of domestic violence', *Criminal Justice Matters*, 53, Autumn.

Galtung, J. and Ruge, M. (1973) 'Structuring and selecting the news', in S. Cohen and J. Young (eds) *The Manufacture of News: Deviance, Social Problems and the Mass Media*, London: Constable.

Gandy, O. (1993) *The Panoptic Sort*, Boulder, CO: Westview Press.

Gans, H. J. (1979/2004) *Deciding What's News*, 2nd edn, Chicago, IL: Northwestern University Press.

Garland, D. (1996) 'The limits of the sovereign state: strategies of crime control in contemporary society', *British Journal of Criminology*, 36 (4): 445–71.

Garland, D. (2008) 'On the concept of moral panic', *Crime, Media, Culture: an International Journal*, Vol. 4 (1): 9–30.

Garside, R. (2001) 'Putting the emotion back into crime: or how we can start to win the war of the headlines', *Criminal Justice Matters*, 43, Spring: 32–3.

Geertz, C. (1983) *Local Knowledge: Further Essays in Interpretive Anthropology*, New York: Basic Books.

Gelsthorpe, L. and Morris, A. (eds) (1990) *Feminist Perspectives in Criminology*, Buckingham: Open University Press.

Geraghty, C. (n.d.) www.frameworkonline.com/42cg.htm

Gergen, K. J. (1991) *The Saturated Self*, New York: Basic Books.

Gibson, G. (2006) 'Warning to chatroom users after libel award for man labelled a Nazi', 23 March, at http://www.guardian.co.uk/media/2006/mar/23/digitalmedia.law

Gillespie, M. and McLaughlin, E. (2002) 'Media and the making of public attitudes', *Criminal Justice Matters*, 49, Autumn: 8–9.

Girling, E., Loader, I. and Sparks, R. (2000) *Crime and Social Change in Middle England: Questions of Order in an English Town*, London: Routledge.

Girling, E., Loader, I. and Sparks, R. (2002) 'Public sensibilities towards crime: anxieties of affluence', in A. Boran (ed.) *Crime: Fear or Fascination*, Chester: Chester Academic Press.

Glancey, J. (2002) 'Image that for 36 years fixed a killer in the public mind', Guardian, 16 November.

Golding, P. and Murdock, G. (2000) 'Culture, communications and political economy', in J. Curran and M. Gurevitch (eds) *Mass Media and Society*, revised 3rd edn, London: Arnold.

Goldson, B. (2003) 'Tough on children ... tough on justice'. Paper presented to Tough On Crime Tough on Freedoms, The European Group for the Study of Deviance and Social Control Conference, Centre for Studies in Crime and Social Justice, Edge Hill College, Liverpool, 22–24 April.

Goode, E. and Ben-Yehuda, N. (1994) *Moral Panics: The Social Construction of Deviance*, Oxford: Blackwell.

Goodman, M. (1997) 'Why the police don't care about cybercrime', Harvard Journal of Law and Technology, 10: 465–94.

Graber, D. (1980) *Crime, News and the Public*, New York: Praeger.

Graef, R. (1989) *Talking Blues*, London: Collins.

Grabosky, P. (2001) 'Virtual criminality: old wine in new bottles?', *Social & Legal Studies* 10: 243–9.

Gramsci, A. (1971) *Selections from Prison Notebooks*, London: Lawrence & Wishart.

Green, D. A. (2008a) 'Suitable vehicles: Framing blame and justice when children kill a child', *Crime, Media, Culture: An International Journal*, Vol. 4 (2): 197–220.

Green, D. A. (2008b) *When Children Kill Children: Penal Populism and Political Culture*, Oxford: Oxford University Press.

Green, N. (2009) Are readers being robbed of the facts? *MediaGuardian*, 7 December, p. 6.

Greer, C. (2003) *Sex Crime and the Media: Sex Offending and the Press in a Divided Society*, Cullompton: Willan.

Greer, C. (2004) 'Review of F. Leishman and P. Mason (2003) Policing and the Media: Facts, Fictions and Factions, Cullompton: Willan', *British Journal of Criminology*, 44 (2).

Greer, C. (2009) *Crime and Media: A Reader*, London: Routledge.

Greer, C. and Jewkes, Y. (2005) 'Images and processes of social exclusion', *Social Justice*, 32 (1): 20–31.

Greer, C., Ferrell, J. and Jewkes, Y. (2007) 'It's the image that matters: style, substance and critical scholarship', *Crime, Media, Culture: An International Journal*, 3 (1): 5–10.

Haggerty, K.D. and Ericson, R.V. (2000) 'The surveillant assemblage', *British Journal of Sociology*, 51(4): 605–22.

Hall, S. (1978) 'The treatment of football hooliganism in the press', in R. Ingham (ed.) *Football Hooliganism*, London: Inter-Action.

Hall, S., Critcher, C., Jefferson, T., Clarke, J. and Roberts, B. (eds) (1978/2013) *Policing the Crisis: Mugging, the State and Law and Order*, London: Macmillan.

Hall, S. and Jefferson, T. (eds) (1975) *Resistance Through Rituals: Youth Subcultures in PostWar Britain*, London: Hutchinson.

Halloran, J. (1970) *The Effects of Television*, London: Panther.

Halloran, J., Elliott, P. and Murdock, G. (1970) *Demonstrations and Communication: A Case Study*, Harmondsworth: Penguin.

Hamelink, C. J. (2000) *The Ethics of Cyberspace*, London: Sage.

Hayward, K. and Presdee, M. (eds) (2010) *Framing Crime: Cultural Criminology and the Image*, Abingdon: Glasshouse-Routledge.

Hebdige, D. (1979) *Subculture: The Meaning of Style*, London: Routledge.

Hebdige, D. (1989) 'After the masses', *Marxism Today*, January.

Heidensohn, F. (1985) *Women and Crime*, New York: New York University Press.

Heidensohn, F. (2000) *Sexual Politics and Social Control*, Buckingham: Open University Press.

Heidkamp, B. (1993) '"Angels of death": the Lainz Hospital murders', in H. Birch (ed.) *Moving Targets: Women, Murder and Representation*, London: Virago.

Hellawell, K. (2002) *The Outsider*, London: HarperCollins.

Henry, S. and Milovanovic, D. (1996) *Constitutive Criminology*, London: Sage.

Herman, E. and Chomsky, N. (1992) *Manufacturing Consent: The Political Economy of Mass Media*, New York: Vintage.

Hornby, S. (1997) Challenging Masculinity in the Supervision of Male Offenders, Social Work Monograph 157, University of East Anglia, Norwich.

Horton, D. and Wohl, R. (1956) 'Mass communication and para-social interaction', *Psychiatry*, 19: 215–19.

Hough, M. and Roberts, J. (1998) Attitudes to Punishment, Home Office Research Study no. 179, London: HMSO.

Innes, M. (2003) 'Signal crimes: media, murder investigations and constructing collective memories', in Mason, P. (ed.) *Criminal Visions: Media Representations of Crime and Justice*, Cullompton: Willan.

Innes, M. (2004) 'Crime as signal, crime as memory', *Journal for Crime, Conflict and the Media*, 1 (2): 15–22.

Jarvis, B. (2004) *Cruel and Unusual: A Cultural History of Punishment in America*, London: Pluto.

Jarvis, B. (2007) 'Monsters Inc.: Serial killers and consumer culture', *Crime, Media, Culture: An International Journal*, 3 (3): 326–44.

Jefferson, T. (2002) 'For a psychosocial criminology', in K. Carrington and R. Hogg (eds) *Critical Criminology: Issues, Debates, Challenges*, Cullompton: Willan.

Jenkins, P. (1992) *Intimate Enemies: Moral Panics in Contemporary Great Britain*, New York: Aldine de Gruyter.

Jenkins, P. (2001) Beyond Tolerance: Child Pornography on the Internet, New York: New York University Press.

Jenkins, P. (2008) 'Failure to launch: why do some social issues fail to detonate moral panics?' *British Journal of Criminology*, 49 (1): 35–47.

Jenkins, P. (2009) 'Failure to launch: why do some social issues fail to detonate moral panics?' *British Journal of Criminology*, 49 (1): 35–47.

Jermyn, D. (2003) 'Photo stories and family albums: imaging criminals and victims on Crimewatch UK', in P. Mason (ed.) *Criminal Visions: Media Representations of Crime and Justice*, Cullompton: Willan.

Jewkes, Y. (2002) *Captive Audience: Media, Masculinity and Power in Prisons*, Cullompton: Willan.

Jewkes, Y. (ed.) (2003a) *Dotcons: Crime, Deviance and Identity on the Internet*, Cullompton: Willan.

Jewkes, Y. (2003b) 'Policing the net: crime, regulation and surveillance in cyberspace', in Y. Jewkes (ed.) *Dot.cons: Crime, Deviance and Identity on the Internet*, Cullompton: Willan.

Jewkes, Y. (2007) *Crime Online*, Cullompton: Willan.

Jewkes, Y. (2008) 'Offending media: the social construction of offenders, victims and the probation service', in S. Green, E. Lancaster and S. Feasey (eds) *Addressing Offending Behaviour*, Cullompton: Willan.

Jewkes, Y. (2010a) 'Much ado about nothing? Representations and realities of online soliciting of children', *Journal of Sexual Aggression*, 16 (1): 5–18.

Jewkes, Y. (2010b) 'The media and criminological research', in P. Davies, P. Francis and V. Jupp (eds) *Doing Criminological Research* 2nd edn, London: Sage.

Jewkes, Y (2014) 'Punishment in black and white: Penal "hell-holes", popular media and mass incarceration', *Atlantic Journal of Communication* special issue on 'Reframing Race and Justice in the Age of Mass Incarceration' 22(1): 42-60

Jewkes, Y. and Andrews, C. (2005) 'Policing the filth: the problems of investigating online child pornography in England and Wales', *Policing & Society*, 15 (1): 42–62.

Jewkes, Y. and Sharp, K. (2003) 'Crime, deviance and the disembodied self: transcending the dangers of corporeality', in Y. Jewkes (ed.) *Dot.cons: Crime Deviance and Identity on the Internet*, Cullompton: Willan.

Jewkes, Y. and Wykes, M. (2013) 'Reconstructing the sexual abuse of children: "Cyber-paeds", panic and power', *Sexualities* 15(8): 934–52

Jewkes, Y. and Yar, M. (eds) (2010) *Handbook of Internet Crime*, Cullompton: Willan.

Jones, C. and Wardle, P. J. (2008) 'No emotion, no sympathy: the visual construction of Maxine Carr', in *Crime, Media, Culture*, Vol. 4 (1): 53–71.

Katz, J. (1990) *Seductions of Crime: Moral and Sensual Attractions in Doing Evil*, New York: Basic Books.

Keating, M. (2002) 'Media most foul: fear of crime and media', in A. Boran (ed.) *Crime: Fear or Fascination*, Chester: Chester Academic Press.

Kennedy, H. (1992) *Eve Was Framed*, London: Chatto & Windus.

Kidd-Hewitt, D. (1995) 'Crime and the media: a criminological perspective', in D. Kidd-Hewitt and R. Osborne (eds) *Crime and the Media: The Post-Modern Spectacle*, London: Pluto.

Kidd-Hewitt, D. and Osborne, R. (eds) (1995) *Crime and the Media: The Post-Modern Spectacle*, London: Pluto.

Kitzinger, J. (1999) 'The ultimate neighbour from hell? Stranger danger and the media framing of paedophiles', in B. Franklin (ed.) *Social Policy, the Media and Misrepresentation*, London: Routledge.

Knopf, T. (1970) 'Media myths on violence', *Columbia Journalism Review*, Spring: 17–18.

Koskela, H. (2006) '"The other side of surveillance": webcams, power and agency', in Lyon, D. (ed.) *Theorizing Surveillance: The Panopticon and Beyond*, Cullompton: Willan.

Krutnik, F. (1991) *In A Lonely Street: Genre, Film Noir, Masculinity*, London: Routledge.

Lacey, N. (1995) 'Contingency and criminalisation', in I. Loveland (ed.) *Frontiers of Criminality*, London: Sweet & Maxwell.

Langford, B. (2005) *Film Genre: Hollywood and Beyond*, Edinburgh: Edinburgh University Press.

Langman, L. (1992) 'Neon cages: shopping for subjectivity', in R. Shields (ed.) *Lifestyle Shopping: The Subject of Consumption*, London: Routledge.

Larke, G. S. (2003) 'Organized crime: mafia myths in film and television', in P. Mason (ed.) *Criminal Visions: Media Representations of Crime and Justice*, Cullompton: Willan.

Lea, J. and Young, J. (1984) *What is to be Done about Law and Order?* Harmondsworth: Penguin.

Lea, J. and Young, J. (1993) *What is to be Done about Law and Order? Crisis in the Nineties*, London: Pluto Press.

Leacock, V. and Sparks, R. (2002) 'Riskiness and at-risk-ness: some ambiguous features of the current penal landscape', in N. Gray, J. Laing and L. Noaks (eds) *Criminal Justice, Mental Health and the Politics of Risk*, London: Cavendish.

Le Bon, G. (1895/1960) *The Crowd: A Study of the Popular Mind*, New York: Viking.

Lee M. (2007) *Inventing Fear of Crime: Criminology and the Politics of Anxiety*, London: Routledge

Lee M. and McGovern, A. (2014) *Policing and Media: Public Relations, Simulations and Communications*, London: Routledge.

Leishman, F. (2008) From Dock Green to Life on Mars: Continuity and Change in TV Copland, Inaugural lecture, University of Gloucestershire, 7 May.

Leishman, F. and Mason, P. (2003) Policing and the Media: Facts, Fictions and Factions, Cullompton: Willan.

Leitch, T. (2002) *Crime Films*, Cambridge: Cambridge University Press.

Lemert, E. (1951) *Social Pathology: A Systematic Approach to the Theory of Sociopathic Behaviour*, New York: McGraw-Hill.

Leveson Inquiry (2012) Report into the culture, practices and ethics of the press. Available at http://www.official-documents.gov.uk/document/hc1213/hc07/0780/0780.asp

Linnemann (2013) 'Governing through meth: local politics, drug control and the drift toward securitization ', *Crime, Media, Culture: An International Journal* 9(1): 38–60.

Linnemann, T., Hanson, L. and Williams, L. S. (2013) '"With Scenes of Blood and Pain": crime control and the punitive imagination of The Meth Project', *British Journal of Criminology* 53 (4): 605–23.

Lloyd, A. (1995) *Doubly Deviant, Doubly Damned: Society's Treatment of Violent Women*, Harmondsworth: Penguin.

Lombroso, C. (1876) *L'uomo delinquente* (The Criminal Man), Milan: Hoepli.

Lombroso, C. and Ferrero, W. (1895) *The Female Offender*, London: Unwin.

Lowenstein, A. (2005) *Shocking Representation: Historical Trauma, National Cinema, and the Modern Horror Film*, New York: Columbia University Press.

LSE (n.d.) *Reading the Riots: Investigating England's Summer of Disorder* http://eprints. lse.ac.uk/46297/1/Reading%20the%20riots(published).pdf

Lyon, D. (2001) *Surveillance Society: Monitoring Everyday Life*, Buckingham: Open University Press.

Lyon, D. (2003) 'Surveillance as social sorting: computer codes and mobile bodies', in D. Lyon (ed.) *Surveillance As Social Sorting: Privacy, Risk and Digital Discrimination*, London: Routledge.

Lyon, D. (2006) 'The search for surveillance theories', in D. Lyon (ed.) *Theorizing Surveillance: The Panopticon and Beyond*, Cullompton: Willan.

Lyon, D. (2007) *Surveillance Studies: An Overview*, Cambridge: Polity Press.

McCahill, M. (2002) *The Surveillance Web: The Rise of Visual Surveillance in an English City*, Cullompton: Willan.

McCahill, M. (2003) 'Media representations of surveillance', in P. Mason (ed.) *Criminal Visions: Media Representations of Crime and Justice*, Cullompton: Willan.

McCahill, M. and Norris, C. (2002) Literature Review: Working Paper No. 2, at www. urbaneye.net/results/ue_wp2.pdf

McCahill, M. and Norris, C. (2003) 'Estimating the extent, sophistication and legality of CCTV in London', in M. Gill (ed.) *CCTV*, Leicester: Perpetuity Press.

MacKay, C. (1841/1956) *Extraordinary Popular Delusions and the Madness of Crowds*, New York: Harmony Books.

McLaughlin, E. and Muncie, J. (eds) (2001) *The Sage Dictionary of Criminology*, London: Sage.

McLean, G. (2003) 'Family fortunes', *Guardian*, 30 July.

McNair, B. (1998) *The Sociology of Journalism*, London: Arnold.

McQuail, D. (2010) *McQuail's Mass Communication Theory: An Introduction*, 4th edn, London: Sage.

McRobbie, A. and Thornton, S. (1995) 'Rethinking "moral panic" for multi-mediated social worlds', *British Journal of Sociology*, 46 (4): 559–74.

Mander, J. (1980) *Four Arguments for the Elimination of Television*, New York: Harvester.

Macnab, G. (2009) 'The Taking of Pelham 123 – Why remake a Seventies classic?', *Independent* 12 June. Available at http://tinyurl.com/m3tl9e

Manning, P. (1997) *Police Work*, 2nd edn, Prospect Heights, IL: Waveland Press.

Manning, P. (2001) *News and News Sources: A Critical Introduction*, London: Sage.

Marx, G. T. (1995) 'Electric eye in the sky: some reflections on the new surveillance and popular culture', in J. Ferrell and C. R. Sanders (eds) *Cultural Criminology*, Boston: Northeastern University Press.

Marx, G. T. (2002) 'What's new about the "new surveillance"? Classifying for change and continuity', *Surveillance & Society*, 1 (1): 9–29.

Mason, D., Button, G., Lankshear, G. and Coats, S. (2000) On the Poverty of a Priorism: Technology, Surveillance in the Workplace and Employee Responses, pre-publication draft, Plymouth: University of Plymouth.

Mason, P. (1992) *Reading The Bill: An Analysis of the Thames Television Police Drama*, Bristol: Bristol Centre for Criminal Justice.

Mason, P. (ed.) (2003a) *Criminal Visions: Media Representations of Crime and Justice*, Cullompton: Willan.

Mason, P. (2003b) 'The screen machine: cinematic representations of prison', in P. Mason (ed.) *Criminal Visions: Media Representations of Crime and Justice*, Cullompton: Willan.

Mason, P. (ed.) (2006) *Captured By the Media: Prison Discourse in Popular Culture*, Cullompton: Willan.

Mason, P. (2008) Entries in Y. Jewkes and J. Bennett (eds) *Dictionary of Prisons and Punishment*, Cullompton: Willan.

Mathiesen, T. (1997) 'The viewer society: Michel Foucault's "Panopticon" revisited', *Theoretical Criminology*, 1 (2): 215–34.

Mathiesen, T. (2001) 'Television, public space and prison population: a commentary on Mauer and Simon', *Punishment & Society*, 3 (1): 35–42.

Mathiesen, T. (2013) *Towards a Surveillant Society: The Rise of Surveillance Systems in Europe*, Hook, Hampshire: Waterside Press

Matza, D. (1964) *Delinquency and Drift*, New York: Wiley.

Mawby, R. C. (2002) Policing Images: Policing, Communication and Legitimacy, Cullompton: Willan.

Mawby, R. C. (2010) 'Police corporate communications, crime reporting and the shaping of policing news', *Policing & Society*, 20 (1): 124–39.

Mawby, R. C. (2010) 'Chibnall revisited: crime reporters, the police and "law and order news"', *British Journal of Criminology*, 50 (6): 1060–76.

Merton, R. K. (1938) 'Social structure and anomie', *American Sociological Review*, 3: 672–82.

Millbank, J. (1996) 'From butch to butcher's knife: film, crime and lesbian sexuality', *Sydney Law Review*, 18 (4): 451–73.

Miller, V. (2010) 'The Internet and everyday life', in Y. Jewkes and M. Yar (eds) *Handbook of Internet Crime*, Cullompton: Willan.

Minsky, R. (1998) *Psychoanalysis and Culture: Contemporary States of Mind*, Cambridge: Polity Press.

Monahan, T. (2006) 'Counter-surveillance as Political Intervention?' *Social Semiotics*, 16 (4): 515–34.

Morley, D. (1992) *Television Audiences and Cultural Studies*, London: Routledge.

Morris, A. (1987) *Women, Crime and Criminal Justice*, Oxford: Blackwell.

Morris, A. and Wilczynski, A. (1993) 'Rocking the cradle: mothers who kill their children', in H. Birch (ed.) *Moving Targets: Women, Murder and Representation*, London: Virago.

Morrison, B. (1997) *As If*, London: Granta.

Morrissey, B. (2003) *When Women Kill: Questions of Agency and Subjectivity*, London: Routledge.

Mulgan, G. (1989) 'A tale of two cities', *Marxism Today*, March: 18–25.

Muncie, J. (1999) *Youth and Crime: A Critical Introduction*, 1st edn, London: Sage.

Muncie, J. (2001) 'The construction and deconstruction of crime', in J. Muncie and E. McLaughlin (eds) *The Problem of Crime*, 2nd edn, London: Sage.

Muncie, J. (2009) *Youth and Crime: A Critical Introduction*, 3rd edn, London: Sage.

Muncie, J. and McLaughlin, E. (eds) (2001) *The Problem of Crime*, 2nd edn, London: Sage.

Mythen, G. and Walklate, S. (2006) 'Communicating the terrorist risk: harnessing a culture of fear?' *Crime, Media, Culture: An International Journal*, 2 (2): 123–42.

Narey, M. (2002) 'Human rights, decency and social exclusion', Prison Service Journal, 142: 25–8.

Naylor, B. (2001) 'Reporting violence in the British print media: gendered stories', Howard Journal, 40 (2): 180–94.

Nelkin, D. and Andrews, L. (2003) 'Surveillance creep in the genetic age', in D. Lyon (ed.) Surveillance As Social Sorting: Privacy, Risk and Digital Discrimination, London: Routledge.

Nellis, M. (1982) 'Notes on The American prison film', in M. Nellis and C. Hale (eds) The Prison Film, London: RAP.

Nellis, M. (2006) 'Future punishment in American science fiction films', in P. Mason (ed.) Criminal Visions: Media Representations of Crime and Justice, Cullompton: Willan.

Nellis, M. and Hale, C. (eds) (1982) The Prison Film, London: RAP.

Newburn, T. (1996) 'Back to the future? Youth crime, youth justice and the rediscovery of "authoritarian populism", in J. Pilcher and S. Wagg (eds) Thatcher's Children, London: Falmer.

Newburn, T. and Hayman, S. (2001) Policing, Surveillance and Social Control: CCTV and Police Monitoring of Suspects, Cullompton: Willan.

Newson, E. (1994) 'Video violence and the protection of children', University of Nottingham, reprinted as Memorandum 13 in House of Commons Home Affairs Committee, Video Violence and Young Offenders, Session 1993–4, 4th Report, London: HMSO, pp. 45–59.

Norris, C. (2003) 'From personal to digital: CCTV, the panopticon, and the technological mediation of suspicion and social control', in D. Lyon (ed.) Surveillance As Social Sorting: Privacy, Risk and Digital Discrimination, London: Routledge.

Norris, C. and Armstrong, G. (1999) The Maximum Surveillance Society: The Rise of CCTV, Oxford: Berg.

Oakley, A. (1986) From Here to Maternity: Becoming a Mother, Harmondsworth: Penguin.

Office of the Data Protection Commissioner (2000) The Use of Personal Data in Employer/Employee Relationships, draft report, Winslow: ODPC.

O'Leary, N. (2003) 'An examination of the nature and influence of media representations of policing on the police themselves'. Unpublished MA thesis, University of Hull.

O'Malley, P. (2001) 'Governmentality', in E. McLaughlin and J. Muncie (eds) The Sage Dictionary of Criminology, London: Sage.

Osborne, R. (1995) 'Crime and the media: from media studies to post-modernism', in D. Kidd-Hewitt and R. Osborne (eds) Crime and the Media: The Post-modern Spectacle, London: Pluto.

Osborne, R. (2002) Megawords, London: Sage.

O'Sullivan, T. and Jewkes, Y. (eds) (1997) The Media Studies Reader, London: Arnold.

Parker, M. (2009a) 'Tony Soprano on management: the Mafia and organizational excellence', Journal of Cultural Economy, 2 (3): 379–92.

Parker, M. (2009b) 'Pirates, merchants and anarchists: representations of international business', Management and Organizational History, 4 (2): 167–85.

Parker, M. (2011) Alternative Business: Outlaws, Crime and Culture, London: Routledge.

Pearson, G. (1983) Hooligan: A History of Respectable Fears, Basingstoke: Macmillan.

Pearson, P. (1998) When She Was Bad: How and Why Women Get Away With Murder, Toronto: Random.

Peelo, M. (2006) 'Framing homicide narratives in newspapers: mediated witness and the construction of virtual victimhood', Crime, Media, Culture: An International Journal, 2 (2): 159–75.

Perry, B. (2001) *In the Name of Hate: Understanding Hate Crimes*, New York: Routledge.

Petley, J. (1997) 'In defence of video nasties', in T. O'Sullivan and Y. Jewkes (eds) *The Media Studies Reader*, London: Arnold. Originally published in 1994 in *British Journalism Review*, 5 (3): 52–7.

Philo, G. (ed.) (1995) *The Glasgow University Media Group Reader, Vols. I and II*, London: Routledge.

Polk, K. (1993) 'Homicide: women as offenders', in P. Easteal and S. McKillop (eds) *Women and the Law*, Canberra: Australian Institute of Criminology.

Pollak, O. (1950/61) *The Criminality of Women*, New York: Perpetua.

Poster, M. (1990) *The Mode of Information*, Chicago: University of Chicago Press.

Pratt, J. (2007) *Penal Populism*, London: Routledge.

Presdee, M. (1986) Agony or Ecstasy: Broken Transitions and the New Social State of Working-class Youth in Australia, South Australian Centre for Youth Studies Occasional Paper.

Presdee, M. (2000) *Cultural Criminology and the Carnival of Crime*, London: Routledge.

Punch, M. (1996) *Dirty Business: Exploring Corporate Misconduct*, London: Sage.

Qi, M. Wang, Y. and Xu, R. (2009) 'Fighting cybercrime: legislation in China', *International Journal of Electronic Security and Digital Forensics*, 2 (2): 219–27.

Radford, L. (1993) 'Pleading for time: justice for battered women who kill', in H. Birch (ed.) *Moving Targets: Women, Murder and Representation*, London: Virago.

Rafter, N. (2000) *Shots in the Mirror: Crime Films and Society*, Oxford: Oxford University Press.

Rafter, N. (2007) 'Crime film and criminology: recent sex-crime movies', *Theoretical Criminology*, 11 (3): 403–20.

Rayner, J. (2003) 'Masculinity, morality and action: Michael Mann and the heist movie', in P. Mason (ed.) *Criminal Visions: Media Representations of Crime and Justice*, Cullompton: Willan.

Regan, P. M. (1996) 'Genetic testing and workplace surveillance: implications for privacy', in D. Lyon and E. Zureik (eds) *Computers, Surveillance and Privacy*, Minneapolis: University of Minnesota Press.

Reiner, R. (2000) *The Politics of the Police*, 3rd edn, Oxford: Oxford University Press.

Reiner, R. (2001) 'The rise of virtual vigilantism: crime reporting since World War II', *Criminal Justice Matters*, 43, Spring.

Reiner, R., Livingstone, S. and Allen, J. (2001) 'Casino culture: media and crime in a winner–loser society', in K. Stenson and R. R. Sullivan (eds) *Crime, Risk and Justice: the Politics of Crime Control in Liberal Democracies*, Cullompton: Willan.

Ronson, J. (2009) 'Gary McKinnon: Pentagon hacker's worst nightmare comes true', *Guardian*, 1 August 2009: available at http://www.guardian.co.uk/world/2009/aug/01/gary-mckinnon-extradition-nightmare

Roshier, B. (1973) 'The selection of crime news by the press', in S. Cohen and J. Young (eds) *The Manufacture of News*, London: Constable.

Sandberg, S., Oksanen, A., Berntzen, L. E. and Kiilakoski, T. (2014) 'Stories in action: the cultural influences of school shootings on the terrorist attacks in Norway', *Critical Studies on Terrorism*

Schechter, D. (2003) 'How media has changed since "the day that changed everything"', ColdType.net, pp. 2–8.

Schlesinger, P. and Tumber, H. (1994) *Reporting Crime: the Media Politics of Criminal Justice*, Oxford: Clarendon.

Schlesinger, P., Tumber, H. and Murdock, G. (1991) 'The media politics of crime and criminal justice', *British Journal of Sociology*, 423: 397–420.

Scraton, P. (2003) 'The demonisation, exclusion and regulation of children: from moral panic to moral renewal', in A. Boran (ed.) *Crime: Fear or Fascination*, Chester: Chester Academic Press.

Signorielli, N. (1990) 'Television's mean and dangerous world: a continuation of the cultural indicators project', in N. Signorielli and M. Morgan (eds) *Cultivation Analysis: New Directions in Media Effects Research*, Newbury Park, CA: Sage.

Silverman, J. and Wilson, D. (2002) *Innocence Betrayed: Paedophilia, the Media and Society*, Cambridge: Polity.

Simon, J. (1997) 'Governing through crime', in G. Fisher and L. Friedman (eds) *The Crime Conundrum: Essays on Criminal Justice*, Boulder, CO: Westview Press.

Simon, J. (2009) 'Governing through crime', paper presented to Architecture and Justice conference, University of Lincoln, 27 November.

Slapper, G. and Tombs, S. (1999) *Corporate Crime*, London: Longman.

Smith, J. (1997) *Different for Girls: How Culture Creates Women*, London: Chatto & Windus.

Smith, R. (2010) 'Identity theft and fraud', in Y. Jewkes and M. Yar (eds) *Handbook of Internet Crime*, Cullompton: Willan.

Smith, S. J. (1984) 'Crime in the news', *British Journal of Criminology*, 24 (3).

Soothill, K. and Walby, S. (1991) *Sex Crime in the News*, London: Routledge.

Sounes, H. (1995) *Fred and Rose*, London: Warner Books.

South, N. and Brisman, A. (eds) (2012) *Routledge International Handbook of Green Criminology*, London: Routledge.

Sparks, R. (1992) *Television and the Drama of Crime: Moral Tales and the Place of Crime in Public Life*, Buckingham: Open University Press.

Sparks, R. (1996) 'Masculinity and heroism in the Hollywood "Blockbuster": the culture industry and contemporary images of crime and law enforcement', *British Journal of Criminology*, 36 (3): 348–60.

Sparks, R. (2001) '"Bringin' it all back home": populism, media coverage and the dynamics of locality and globality in the politics of crime control', in K. Stenson and R. R. Sullivan (eds) *Crime, Risk and Justice: the Politics of Crime Control in Liberal Democracies*, Cullompton: Willan.

Sparks, R., Girling, E. and Loader, I. (1999) *Crime and Social Change in Middle England: Questions of Order in an English Town*, London: Routledge.

Stalder, F. and Lyon, D. (2003) 'Electronic identity cards and social classification', in D. Lyon (ed.) *Surveillance As Social Sorting: Privacy, Risk and Digital Discrimination*, London: Routledge.

Stanko, E. A. (1985) *Intimate Intrusions: Women's Experience of Male Violence*, London: Routledge.

Stenson, K. (2001) 'The new politics of crime control', in K. Stenson and R. R. Sullivan (eds) *Crime, Risk and Justice: the Politics of Crime Control in Liberal Democracies*, Cullompton: Willan.

Stokes, E. (2000) 'Abolishing the presumption of doli incapax: reflections on the death of a doctrine', in J. Pickford (ed.) *Youth Justice: Theory and Practice*, London: Cavendish.

Surette, R. (1994) 'Predator criminals as media icons', in G. Barak (ed.) *Media, Process, and the Social Construction of Crime*, New York: Garland.

Surette, R. (1998) *Media, Crime and Criminal Justice*, Belmont, CA: West/Wadsworth.

Taylor, P. A. (2003) 'Maestros or misogynists? Gender and the social construction of hacking', in Y. Jewkes (ed.) *Dot.cons: Crime, Deviance and Identity on the Internet*, Cullompton: Willan, pp.126–46.

Taylor, I., Walton, P. and Young, J. (1973) *The New Criminology: For a Social Theory of Deviance*, London: Routledge & Kegan Paul.

Thompson, K. (1998) *Moral Panics*, London: Routledge.

Thorne, B. (2009) 'The Seven Up! films: connecting the personal and the sociological', *Ethnography*, 10 (3): 327–40.

Tierney, J. (1996) *Criminology: Theory and Context*, Harlow: Pearson.

Tombs, S. and Whyte, D. (2007) *Safety Crimes*, Cullompton: Willan.

Townsend, M. (2003) 'Panic-room is a must-have for rich and famous', *Observer*, 23 June.

Upton, J. (2000) 'The evil that women do', *Guardian*, 17 October: 6.

Valier, C. (2004) *Crime and Punishment in Contemporary Culture*, London: Routledge.

van der Ploeg, I. (2003) 'Biometrics and the body as information: normative issues of the socio-technical coding of the body', in D. Lyon (ed.) *Surveillance As Social Sorting: Privacy, Risk and Digital Discrimination*, London: Routledge.

Verhoeven, D. (1993) 'Biting the hand that breeds: the trials of Tracey Wigginton', in H. Birch (ed.) *Moving Targets: Women, Murder and Representation*, London: Virago.

Waddington, P. A. J. (1986) 'Mugging as a moral panic: a question of proportion', *British Journal of Sociology*, 37 (2).

Walden, I. (2010) 'Computer forensics and the presentation of evidence in criminal cases', in Y. Jewkes and M. Yar (eds) *Handbook of Internet Crime*, Cullompton: Willan.

Wall, D. S. and Yar, M. (2010) 'Intellectual property crime and the Internet: Cyber-piracy and "stealing" informational intangibles', in Y. Jewkes and M. Yar (eds) *Handbook of Internet Crime*, Cullompton: Willan.

Walklate, S. (2001) *Gender, Crime and Criminal Justice*, Cullompton: Willan.

Walters, R. (2010) *Eco-Crime and Genetically Modified Food*, London: Routledge-Cavendish.

Ward Jouve, N. (1988) *The Street-Cleaner: the Yorkshire Ripper Case on Trial*, London: Marion Boyars.

Ward Jouve, N. (1993) 'An eye for an eye: the case of the Papin sisters', in H. Birch (ed.) *Moving Targets: Women, Murder and Representation*, London: Virago.

Watney, S. (1987) *Policing Desire: Pornography, Aids and the Media*, London: Methuen.

Weaver, C. K. (1998) 'Crimewatch UK: keeping women off the streets', in C. Carter, G. Branston and S. Allen (eds) *News, Gender and Power*, London: Routledge.

Welsh, B. C. and Farrington, D. P. (2008) Effects of Closed Circuit Television Surveillance on Crime. Campbell Systematic Reviews: 17. Available from www.campbellcollaboration.org

Whiteacre, K. (undated) The Cultural Milieu of Criminology and Drug Research, www.lindesmith.org/docUploads/milieu.pdf (accessed 1 November 2003).

White, R. (2013) *Environmental Harm: An Eco-Justice Perspective*, Bristol: Policy Press.

Wilczynski, A. (1997) 'Mad or bad? Child killers, gender and the courts', *British Journal of Criminology*, 37 (3): 419–36.

Willis, P. (1982) 'Male school counterculture', in *U203 Popular Culture*, Milton Keynes: Open University Press.

Wilkins, L. (1964) *Social Deviance: Social Policy, Action and Research*, London: Tavistock.

Williams, P. and Dickinson, J. (1993) 'Fear of crime: read all about it?', *British Journal of Criminology*, 33 (1).

Willis, P. (2009) 'The accidental ethnographer and the accidental commodity', *Ethnography*, 10 (3): 347–58.

Wilson, D. and O'Sullivan, S. (2004) *Images of Incarceration: Representations of Prison in Film and Television*, Winchester: Waterside Press.

Wilson, P. (1988) 'Crime, violence and the media in the future', *Media Information Australia*, 49: 53–7.

Winfield, B. H. and Peng, Z. (2005) 'Market or party controls?: Chinese media in transition', *International Communication Gazette*, 67 (3): 255–70.

Wood, B. (1993) 'The trials of motherhood: the case of Azaria and Lindy Chamberlain', in H. Birch (ed.) *Moving Targets: Women, Murder and Representation*, London: Virago.

Worrall, A. (1990) *Offending Women*, London: Routledge.

Wykes, M. (1995) 'Passion, marriage and murder', in R. Dobash, R. Dobash and L. Noaks (eds) *Gender and Crime*, Cardiff: University of Wales Press.

Wykes, M. (1998) 'A family affair: the British press, sex and the Wests', in C. Carter, G. Branston and S. Allen (eds) *News, Gender and Power*, London: Routledge.

Wykes, M. (2001) News, Crime and Culture, London: Pluto.

Wykes, M. and Gunter, B. (2004) *Looks Could Kill: Media Representation and Body Image*, London: Sage.

Wykes, M. with Harcus, D. (2010) 'Cyber-terror: construction, criminalization and control', in Y. Jewkes and M. Yar (eds) *Handbook of Internet Crime*, Cullompton: Willan.

Yar, M. (2006) *Cybercrime and Society*, London: Sage.

Yar, M. (2010) 'Public perceptions and public opinion about internet crime', in Y. Jewkes and M. Yar (eds) *Handbook of Internet Crime*, Cullompton: Willan.

Young, J. (1971) *The Drug Takers: The Social Meaning of Drug Use*, London: MacGibbon and Kee/Paladin.

Young, J. (1974) 'Mass media, drugs and deviance', in P. Rock and M. McKintosh (eds) *Deviance and Social Control*, London: Tavistock.

Young, J. (1987) 'The tasks facing a realist criminology', *Contemporary Crises*, 11: 337–56.

Young, J. (1992) 'Ten points of realism', in J. Young and R. Matthews (eds) *Rethinking Criminology: the Realist Debate*, London: Sage.

Young, J. (1999) *The Exclusive Society*, London: Sage.

Younge, G. (2002) 'The politics of partying', *Guardian*, 17 August, www.guardian.co.uk

Zittrain, J. and Edelman, B. (2003) 'Empirical analysis of Internet filtering in China', IEEE Internet Computing, March/April; also available at http://cyber.law.harvard.edu/filtering/china/

Zureik, E. (2003) 'Theorizing surveillance: the case of the workplace', in D. Lyon (ed.) *Surveillance As Social Sorting: Privacy, Risk and Digital Discrimination*, London: Routledge.

INDEX

ACOP (Association of Chief Officers of Probation), 118
ACPO (Association of Chief Police Officers), 178, 232
Adebolajo, M., 5
Adorno, T., 19
adultification, 112-113, 293
Agassi, A., 280
agency, 152, 293
agenda-setting, 45, 46, 293
Agha-Soltan, N., 74
Aktenzeichen XY ... Ungelost (German television programme), 180
al Qaeda, 52-53
Allitt, B., 145, 147-148, 149, 153
America's Most Deadly Prison Gangs (documentary), 207
America's Most Wanted (television show), 180
Amnesty International, 255
Andress, U., 199
Andrews, T., 141, 143-144, 147-148
anomie, 19-21, 38-39, 293
anti-social behaviour orders, 89
anti-Vietnam demonstrations, 51
The Apprentice (NBC show), 37
Apted, M., 205, 206, 207
Armstrong, G., 226
Armstrong, L., 57-58
Ashenden, S., 119
Ashes to Ashes (BBC series), 170, 172
assassin movies, 199
Association of Chief Officers of Probation (ACOP), 118
Association of Chief Police Officers (ACPO), 178, 232
Atkinson, M., 114
audience, 45, 100-102, 293
Ayres, T., 280-281

Baby Peter, 261
Baidu, 255
Baldock, E., 147
Balls, E., 114
Bandura, A., 15-16
Banksy, 37

Barings, 54
Battle Royale (film), 217
Bauman, Z., 237, 239
Bayley, A., 284-285
BBC, 46, 57-59, 75-76. *See also specific programmes*
Bebo, 270
Beck, V., 139-140, 141, 144, 147-148, 154
Becker, H., 22, 83, 300
behaviourism, 12, 14-17, 294
Belgium, 117
Ben-Yehuda, N., 90
Benedict, H., 135
Bennett, J., 208, 209
Bentham, J., 225
Bentley, D., 205
Berman, M., 91
Bernardo, P., 139-140
Between the Lines (BBC show), 172-173
Bhutto, B., 75
Bierne, P., 26
Big Brother (TV show), 65
The Big House (film), 202
The Bill (ITV series), 172, 174
binary oppositions, 53, 279, 294
biological determinism, 150
biometrics, 229
Birch, H., 146
Birmingham Evening Mail (newspaper), 143
Birmingham Six, 173-174
Blackman, L., 53
Blair, T., 69-70, 89
The Blair Witch Project (film), 216
Blanchard, C., 145
Bloomstein, R., 208-210
Blow (film), 197
The Blue Lamp (film), 171-172
Blue Velvet (film), 201
Blumler, J., 29
Bogarde, D., 171-172
Bok, S., 167
Borden, L., 134
Boston (US magazine), 2
Boston marathon bombings (2013), 1-4, 283-284

The Bourne Identity (film), 199
Bournemouth Echo (newspaper), 100
Box, S., 25, 165–166
Boyle, D., 201
Brady, I., 59, 151–152
Breivik, A., 53–54, 71–73, 234
British Crime Surveys, 143, 168, 189
Brosnan, P., 196
Brown (2009), 280
Bulger case
  Blair and, 89
  Calvert and, 261
  Child's Play 3 and, 18
  construction of childhood and, 113–116
  current resonance of, 286–287
  government and, 120
  graphic imagery and, 66
  Internet and, 261–262
  James' mother and, 144
  Major on, 52
  Morrison on, 270
  news values and, 67–68
  reactions to, 121
Burawoy, M., 206
Bush, G.W., 23

Cage, N., 203–204
Calvert, D., 261
Campbell, S., 56
Captive Audience (Jewkes), 31
carceral society, 228, 294
carnival, 35–36
Carr, M., 151, 262, 279
Carrabine, E., 98
Casino Royal (film), 199
Castro, A., 283
catharsis, 294
Ceausescu, N., 236
celebrity or high-status persons, 57–60, 70,
    71–72, 157, 294
Cellan-Jones, R., 73–74
censorship, 18
Central Intelligence Agency (CIA), 223
Cere, R., 72–73
Certeau, M. de, 238
Chafer, P., 181
Chamberlain, L., 144, 147–148
Chancer, L. S., 286–287
Chaplin, C., 240–241
Chapman, J., 62, 121
Chesney-Lind, M., 136
Chibnall, S., 47, 48, 78
Chicago School, 20
Chicago Tribune (newspaper), 3
Child Exploitation and Online Protection
    (CEOP) Centre, 268

child pornography, 267–268
child safety orders, 89
Childline (charity), 118
children and young people
  collective sense of guilt and, 120–123
  community and, 124–126
  definition of, 294
  as 'evil monsters', 110–116, 126–127
  fear of crime and, 167
  Internet and, 267–271
  as news value, 66–68, 71
  as social construction, 67
  as 'tragic victims', 110–111, 116–120, 127
  women as bad mothers and, 143–146
  See also paedophilia
Child's Play 3 (film), 18
China, 23, 74, 254–259
Chomsky, N., 23
Christian Dior Couture, 265
citizen journalism, 73–76, 256, 294–295
classicism, 111
Clifford, M., 59
Climbié, V., 116
closed circuit television (CCTV)
  Boston marathon bombings and, 1–2, 3
  Crimewatch UK and, 180, 240
  entertainment and, 240
  Meagher case and, 284
  news values and, 65–66, 67
  policing and, 177
  profit and, 236–239
  surveillance and, 224, 226
  See also surveillant assemblage
Cohen, N., 89
Cohen, P., 35
Cohen, S.
  cultural criminology and, 35
  on folk devils, 288
  on moral panics, 82, 84, 85, 93, 96, 98, 103,
      105, 124, 276–277
  on newsworthiness, 104
  on surveillance, 225–226
  on youth, 92, 111
Coleman, C., 20
Coleman, R., 244, 260
common sense, 18
community, 124–126
community policing, 169
computer-generated imagery (CGI), 216
Con Air (film), 203–204
Connell, R. W., 200
Connery, S., 196
consensus, 88–89, 100–102, 295
conservative ideology, 68–70, 71, 72, 88
Consumer Protection Cooperation Network, 263
control of the body, 228–229, 295

cop films, 197, 199, 215, 217
COPS (Community Oriented Policing
    Services), 175–176, 179
corporate crime, 25–27
Cox, T., 122
Craig, D., 196, 199
Crawford, A., 166
Creed, B., 148
crime, 295
Crime and Disorder Act (1998), 89, 117,
    126–127
crime films
  appeal of, 195–197
  cities in, 201, 214
  definition of, 295
  documentary films, 29–30, 205–210
  evolution of, 214–217
  masculinity in, 197–200
  prison films, 201–205
  remakes, 210–214
  types of, 194–195
  women in, 199–200
crime news, 44–47, 295. See also news values
Crime Survey for England & Wales, 12–13,
    164, 189
Crimes of Style (Ferrell), 37
Crimewatch UK (BBC series), 165, 179–187,
    226, 227, 240
criminal justice system, 278
criminal responsibility, age of, 112, 112,
    113–114, 115
The Criminality of Women (Pollak), 150
criminalization, 22, 295
critical criminology, 22–27, 35, 165–166, 295
crystal methamphetamine, 280, 282
cultural criminology, 35–38, 39–40, 64, 296
cultural proximity, 60–63
cyber-bullying, 262, 270
cyber-terrorism, 257–259, 266, 296
cyber-warfare, 257, 266
cyberbullying, 296
cybercrimes
  child pornography and online grooming,
      267–268
  in China, 256–257
  definition of, 296
  eBay fraud, 264–265
  electronic theft and abuse of intellectual
      property rights, 259–260
  hacking and loss of sensitive data,
      265–267
  hate crime, 260–262
  invasion of privacy, defamation and identity
      theft, 262–264
cyberspace, 296
cybersurveillance, 232–236

Dacre, P., 29
Daily Express (newspaper), 145
Daily Mail (newspaper), 29, 51, 113, 290
Daily Mirror (newspaper), 137, 141
The Daily Show (US TV programme), 283
Daily Star (newspaper), 50, 114
Daily Telegraph (newspaper), 140
Daley, T., 262
Damon, M., 199
Dando, J., 180, 227
dangerousness, 113, 296
Darwin, A., 147–148
Davies, J., 198–199
Davis, M., 231
Dead Man Walking (film), 205
death penalty, 2
defamation, 263
Defense Intelligence Agency (DIA), 223
demonization, 101, 282–291, 296
denial of service attacks, 257
Dennehy, J., 147–148
Denning, D. E., 257
Depp, J., 197–198, 199
deviance, 93–95, 99, 131, 296
deviancy amplification spiral, 86–89, 87,
    93–95, 101, 296
Diana, Princess of Wales, 66, 279
difference, 131–132, 297
Ditton, J., 56
Dixon of Dock Green (BBC series), 170–171,
    172, 174
DNA testing, 180, 229, 231–232
documentary films, 29–30, 205–210, 297
doli incapax, 114, 297
domestic violence, 142–143
dominant ideology, 22–27, 39
Douglas, M., 239
Dovey, J., 239, 244–245
Dowler, M., 62, 63, 77
Downes, D., 169–170
Dr No (film), 199
Duffy, J., 56
Duggan, M., 177–178
Duneier, M., 206
Durkheim, E., 293
Dylan, B., 241

E-mails You Wish You'd Never Sent
    (BBC series), 243
eBay, 253, 264–265
Echelon, 235–236
Edwards, M., 139
effects research, 12–19, 38, 167–168, 188, 297
electronic theft, 259–260
Eliason, M., 136
Enoch, D., 153

environmental harm and justice, 26–27
Ericson, R.V., 66, 226, 227, 244, 247
Escape From New York (film), 214
essentialism, 297
ethnocentrism, 61, 297
ethnography, 206–210
European Court of Human Rights, 231
Europol, 234
evil monsters, 297
Experian, 264

Facebook, 101–102, 175, 252, 253, 261, 263
familicide (family annihilation), 155,
    297–298
Farrall, S., 98
Farrell, G., 143
fathers and fatherhood, 145, 155
FBI, 235
fear of crime, 103–104, 165–170, 298
Federal Trade Commission (US), 263–264
Feltham Sings (documentary), 207–208
feminism and feminist research, 25, 131,
    133–135, 157–158, 298
Fergus, D., 114, 144
Ferrell, J., 35, 37, 278
Fifth Estate, 298
filicide, 149, 153, 298
film noir, 198, 217, 298
Finch, E., 233
flaming, 262
Fletcher, Y., 173–174
Flynn, E., 197–198
folk devils
    children and young people as, 110–116
    definition of, 298
    deviancy amplification spiral and, 88
    'evil monsters' and, 288–289
    global recession and, 284
    media effects and, 19
    news values and, 59
    paedophiles as, 119
    women as, 136
    See also moral panics
Folk Devils and Moral Panics (S. Cohen), 82,
    93, 96, 98, 103
The Football Factory (film), 200
Foster, H., 185
Foucault, M., 204, 225, 237, 287, 294, 299
Fourniret, M., 144
Fourteen Days in May (documentary), 208
fourth estate, 298
Fowler, R., 46
framing, 45, 46–47, 299
Frankfurt School, 16, 19
Frayn, M., 61

Freedom of Information Act (FOI), 263
freedom of speech, 75
Freud, S., 131–132
Fritzl, J., 123
Fry, S., 253
Fukasaku, K. [Kenta], 217
Fukasaku, K. [Kinji], 217
Furedi, F., 98, 112–113
Furnell, S., 266

G20 protests (London, 2009), 177
Gadd, D., 98
Galtung, J., 47, 48, 64–65, 78
Gandolfini, J., 214
Gandy, O., 237
gang cultures, 97
gangster movies (mob movies), 196–197, 217
Garland, D., 105
Garside, R., 169
Gaza strip, 52
GCHQ (Government Communications
    Headquarters), 223–224
genre, 299
George, B., 227
George, V., 145
Gergen, K. J., 97
Gillespie, M., 186, 245
Gillick, V., 95
Girling, E., 104
Glasgow University Media Group (GUMG),
    22–23
Glenister, P., 173
The Godfather Trilogy (film), 196–197
Gone Baby Gone (film), 216
Goode, E., 90
Goodfellas (film), 196–197
Google, 253, 255, 257
Gorky Park (film), 205
governance, 230–232
governmentality, 230–232, 299
Graef, R., 207, 215
graffiti, 37
Gramsci, A., 18, 21–22, 299
graphic imagery, 64–66, 71–72, 157, 280–281,
    289–290
green criminology, 26–27
Green, N., 177
Greer, C., 56, 64–65, 277–278, 279
Guardian (newspaper)
    citizen journalism and, 76
    on Duggan case, 177–178
    on Hindley, 146
    on Internet in China, 255–256
    news values and, 51
    on surveillance activities, 222–223

hacking, 265–267
Haggerty, K.D., 66, 226, 227, 244, 247
Hall, S., 22, 24, 30, 33, 35, 66, 103
Hamann, P., 208
Hamilton, T., 290
Harvey, L., 141
Harvey, M., 157
Hasan, M., 29
Hassrick, P., 198
hate crime, 260–262
Hayward, K., 37
Heartbeat (ITV series), 172–173
Hebdige, D., 32–33
hegemonic masculinity, 200
hegemony, 21–22, 299
Heidkamp, B., 289
heist movies, 198, 217
Henry, S., 39
heteropatriarchal culture, 137–138, 155, 299
Hindley, M.
   as bad mother, 145–146
   Bulger case and, 114
   as evil manipulator, 151–152
   as folk devil, 158–159
   graphic imagery and, 157
   juxtaposed to Diana, Princess of Wales, 279
   as mythical monster, 146
   news values and, 59–60
   as non-agent, 154
   sexuality and, 138–139
Hitchcock, A., 241
Holdsworth, A., 181
Holloway (documentary), 208
Homolka, K., 139–140, 141, 147–148,
   151, 154
Homolka, T., 151
Hopkins, A., 195
Horkheimer, M., 19
Hornby, S., 142
Horrocks, P., 75
Hough, M., 168–169
Huffington Post (newspaper), 29
The Hunger (film), 147
Huntley, I., 151
Hussein, S., 114, 236
hypodermic syringe model, 16, 299
hysteria, 149

I am a Fugitive from a Chain Gang (film), 202
Identity Fraud Steering Committee, 264
identity theft, 233–234
ideological values, 46
ideology, 22, 299
imagined community, 125, 299
incest, 122–123

Independent Broadcasting Authority, 185
Independent Police Complaints Commission
   (IPCC), 177
individualism, 53–55, 70, 71, 157
infanticide, 148–149, 153, 299
infantilization, 113, 300
inner city riots, 173–174
intellectual property rights, 259–260
International Institute for Strategic Studies
   (IISS), 257–258
Internet
   in China, 254–259
   evolution of, 271–272
   fear of crime and, 168
   paedophilia and, 101–102, 119
   penetration of, 254
   rise of, 252
   See also cybercrimes; social media; social
      networking
Iraq, 61
Irving, B., 182

James Bond film series, 196, 199, 205
Japan, 115
Jarvis, B., 216
Jeffreys, A., 231
Jenkins, P., 66–67, 102, 120
Jermyn, D., 183
Jewkes, Y., 31, 102, 119, 203, 281
Jim'll Fix It (BBC show), 58
Johnson, E. E., 208
Jones, C., 151
Jones, D., 56
Journal of International Peace Studies, 47
Juliet Bravo (BBC series), 172–173

Kanka, M., 117
Katz, J., 35
Kennedy, H., 134, 158
Kennedy, J. F., 61
Kercher, M., 62, 247
Kerviel, J., 54
Kidd-Hewitt, D., 93, 184
kidnap films, 217
King, R., 66, 178
Kitzinger, J., 118, 120
Knox, A., 62, 65, 247
Koskela, H., 270
Kouao, M. T., 116
The Krays (film), 197

labelling theory, 22, 32, 82, 89, 300
LaBianca, L., 215
LaBianca, R., 215
Laming, Lord, 116

late modernity, 31–35, 90–91, 300
Law and Order News (Chibnall), 47
Lawrence, C., 183
Lawrence, S., 173–174, 178, 290
Le Bon, G., 124–125
Lea, J., 30
Lee M., 168, 176
Lee-Potter, L., 51
Leeson, N., 54
left realism, 30, 120–121, 166, 300
legitimacy, 171, 300
Leishman, F., 174
Leitch, T., 198, 212
Lemert, E., 83
lesbianism, 137–139, 147, 151
Let Him Have It (film), 205
Leveson Inquiry, 77–78
Lexis Nexis, 175
Life on Mars (BBC series), 170, 172, 173
Lifer (documentary), 209
Lifer – Living With Murder (documentary), 209
The Lights of New York (film), 201
Linnemann, T., 65, 280
Lloyd, A., 133, 155
Loader, I., 104
Lock Stock and Two Smoking Barrels (film),
    196–197
Lombroso, C., 14–15
London, S., 46
Longhurst, J., 267–268
Louis Theroux: Behind Bars (documentary), 207
Louis Vuitton Malletier, 265
Lynch, D., 201
Lyon, D., 233–234, 239, 246, 247

Ma, J., 255
MacKay, C., 124–125
Maclean, R., 140
Macnab, G., 211, 213, 214
Madoff, B., 54, 284
Major, J., 52, 69–70, 101
Malicious Communications Act (1998/2003), 262
malicious software, 257
Malkovich, J., 204
The Maltese Falcon (film), 198
Man On Wire (film), 201
Manning, C. [Carl], 116
Manning, C. [Chelsea, formerly Bradley], 244
Manson, C., 215
Marsh, C., 139
Marx, G. T., 240–242, 244, 246
Marx, K., 21–22
Marxism, 21–22, 300
masculinity, 197–200
Mason, D., 245

Mason, P., 37, 174, 202–203, 204–205
mass media, 300–301
mass society theory, 12, 13–14, 88, 301
Mathiesen, T., 204, 234, 247
Matthau, W., 211
Matza, D., 83
Mawby, R. C., 176–177, 278
McCahill, M., 239, 240, 243, 245, 260
McCann, M., 62, 66, 70–71, 183, 216
McGovern, A., 176
McGrail, J., 142
McIntosh, M., 20
McKinnon, G., 266–267
McLaren, M., 96
McLaughlin, E., 186, 245
McLean, G., 156
McNair, B., 33
McRobbie, A., 94, 103
McVeigh, T., 290
Meadows, S., 200–201
Meagher, J., 284–285
Medea, 146
media audiences, 278
media criminology, 10–12, 276–279,
    281–282, 301
media effects, 12–19, 38, 167–168, 188,
    287–288
media organizations, 278
media texts, 278–279
mediated discourse, 28, 301
Medusa, 146
mega-cases, 83, 99, 301
Megan's Law (US, 1996), 117
Merkel, A., 224
Merton, R. K., 20, 293
microblogging sites, 254–255. *See also* Twitter
The Military Balance 2010 (IISS), 257–258
Millbank, J., 138
Miller, V., 254
Milovanovic, D., 39
Miners' Strike (1984), 173–174
Minority Report (film), 241
Minsky, R., 132
Miranda Rights, 3
Mirror (newspaper), 140
misrepresentation, 305
mobile media, 1–2, 4–5, 175–179
Mochrie, R., 155–156
Modern Times (film), 240–241
Monahan, T., 178
Moore, R., 196
moral majority, 68, 124, 301
moral panics
    background to, 84–93, *87*
    The Blue Lamp and, 172

moral panics *cont.*
  community and, 124–126
  criticism of, 93–102
  current perspectives on, 103–105, 276–277
  definition of, 301
  mugging and, 24, 103
  origins and use of term, 82–83
  paedophilia as, 116–120, 124, 268, 288–289
  youth and, 91–93, 96–98, 172
morality, 95–96
morality campaigns, 66–67
MORI, 168, 169
Morley, D., 30–31, 33
Morrison, B., 114, 121, 270
Morrissey, B.
  on legal and media institutions, 132–133
  on women, 139, 141, 143, 153, 154, 156
mugging, 24, 103
Mulgan, G., 238–239
Mulvey, L., 199
Munchausen's syndrome by proxy (MSBP), 149, 153
Muncie, J., 94
Murdoch, R., 77
Mythen, G., 52, 53

Narey, M., 209
narrative arc, 301
National Campaign to Prevent Teen and Unplanned Pregnancy, 269
National Security Agency (NSA), 223–224
Naylor, B., 56–57
Nellis, M., 202, 203
The New Criminology (Taylor et al.), 22
New Statesman (newspaper), 29
New York Times (newspaper), 29
News of the World (newspaper), 77–78, 100, 118, 169
news values
  crime news production and, 76–78
  Crimewatch UK and, 179
  definition of, 301
  examples of newsworthy stories, 70–73
  moral panics and, 86
  overview, 46–49, 78–79
  women and, 157
news values, list of
  celebrity or high-status persons, 57–60, 70, 71–72, 157
  children, 66–68, 71
  conservative ideology, 68–70, 71, 72
  individualism, 53–55, 70, 71, 157
  predictability, 50–51, 70, 71, 86, 157
  proximity, 60–63, 70, 72
  risk, 54, 55, 70, 71, 116, 157

news values, list of *cont.*
  sex, 56–57, 70, 71, 117, 157
  simplification, 51–53, 70, 71, 86, 157
  threshold, 49–50, 70, 71, 86, 157
  violence, 63–64, 70, 72, 86
  visual spectacle and graphic imagery, 64–66, 71–72, 157, 280–281
Newson, E., 18–19
newspapers, 279, 281–282. *See also specific newspapers*
newsworthiness, 45–46, 70–73, 104, 284, 301. *See also* news values
Norris, C., 20, 226
Northern Ireland, 117
Norway, 115
Notting Hill Carnival, 51

Obama, B., 23
Observer (newspaper), 124, 233
Office for National Statistics, 12–13, 164
Office of the Data Protection Commissioner, 245–246
O'Leary, N., 174
Olivier, M., 144, 147–148
online databases, 279, 281–282
online dating scams, 263
online grooming, 101–102, 267–268
Operation Yewtree, 58–59, 283. *See also* Savile, J.
Operational Policing Review, 170
Orwell, G., 224–225
Osborne, R., 34, 93, 179
otherness, 130–133, 154–159, 302
outlaw movies, 199, 217
Oxfam, 60–61

paedophilia
  definition of, 302
  in films, 216
  incest and, 122–123
  as moral panic, 101–102, 116–120, 124, 268, 288–289
Pakistan, 75
Panic Room (film), 233
panopticon and panopticism, 224–226, 242–243, 302
para-social interaction, 125
paradigm, 302
paradigm shift, 21
Parker, M., 199–200
Pavlov, I., 14
Paxman, J., 58–59
Payne, S., 62, 118, 121, 169
Pearson, G., 13
Pease, K., 143

Peelo, M., 286
peer-to-peer (P2P) file-sharing, 259–260
penal populism, 302
Pennington, S., 227–228
persistent offending, 302
Petit, P., 201
phishing, 263
physical attractiveness, 140–141
Pirate Bay, 260
pirate films, 197–198, 199, 217
Pirates of the Caribbean film series, 197–198, 199
pluralism, 27–30, 32, 39, 302
Polanski, R., 215
police, 169–170, 170–175, 186–187, 303
Police Executive Research Forum (PERF), 175–176
Police Five (ITV show), 180
policing, 171, 175–179, 303
Policing the Crisis (Hall et al.), 22, 24, 30
political economy, 22, 303
Pollak, O., 150
Popplewell, Justice, 142
populism, 75, 303
populist punitiveness, 303
pornography, 267–268
positivism, 14, 303
positivist criminology, 14–15
post-panopticism, 246
Poster, M., 227
postmodernity, 31–35, 39, 90–91, 97, 303
Power, T., 197–198
Pratt, J., 76, 125
pre-menstrual syndrome (PMS), 150
predictability, 50–51, 70, 71, 86, 157
Presdee, M., 36, 37, 64, 238
pressure groups, 33
Prime Suspect (television show), 172–173
Prism, 223–224
prison documentaries, 207
prison films, 201–205
The Prisoner (television series), 241
privacy, 262–264
private eye films, 215, 217
profit, 303
prostitution, 137–138
proximity, 60–63, 70, 72
psychoanalysis
    behaviourism and, 14
    definition of, 304
    women and, 131–133, 138, 143, 148–150
psychosocial explanations, 131, 304
public appeal, 46, 304
The Public Enemy (film), 197
public interest, 46, 304
Pulp Fiction (film), 197, 212

quantitative methods, 277–278

radical criminology, 22
Rafter, N., 195, 217
Ramsbotham, D., 144
Ramsey, J., 284
rape, 139–140
rationality and irrationality, 166, 304
realism, 304
reality TV, 239–240
Rear Window (film), 241
reception analysis, 30–31, 32, 304
Record Industry Association of America (RIAA), 260
Regulation of Investigatory Powers Act (RIPA) (2000), 235
Reiner, R., 54
Reith, Lord, 77
remakes, 210–214, 304–305
representation, 305
Reservoir Dogs (film), 197, 212
revenge porn, 305
Rigby, L., 5, 65, 66
risk
    definition of, 305
    individualism and, 54
    moral panics and, 90–91, 98
    as news value, 54, 55, 70, 71, 116, 157
Ritchie, G., 196–197
Ritchie, J., 139
Robbins, T., 202
Roberts, J., 168–169
Robocop (film), 215
Robson, M., 253
Rock, P., 20
Rolling Stone (magazine), 2
Ronson, J., 266–267
Ross, N., 185
Ruge, M., 47, 48, 64–65, 78
runaways, 95, 121–122
Rushdie, S., 69

Sandberg, S., 73
Sargent, J., 211
Savile, J., 57–59, 101, 283
Scarface (film), 197
Schechter, D., 52
Schlesinger, P., 181, 182, 185
Schwarzenegger, A., 215
scopophilia, 305
Scott, T., 211
Scraton, P., 89, 116, 126
The Secret Policeman (documentary), 178–179
security, 305
Seductions of Crime (Katz), 35
Self, W., 77

September 11 terrorist attacks (2011), 34, 61
serial killer movies, 199, 216
Seven Up! (documentary), 205
sex, as news value, 56–57, 70, 71, 117, 157
Sex Offenders Act (1997), 117
sexting, 269, 305
sexual abuse, 67, 145. See also paedophilia
sexuality and sexual deviance, 95, 135–140
Shallow Grave (film), 201
The Shawshank Redemption (film), 202
Shipman, H., 131, 289
Sichuan earthquake (2008), 256
signal crimes, 83, 305
Signorielli, N., 166
The Silence of the Lambs (film), 195
Sim, J., 244
Simm, J., 173
simplification, 51–53, 70, 71, 86, 157
Simpson, O.J., 66
Slumdog Millionaire (film), 201
Smart, C., 133
Smith, C. R., 198–199
Smith, C. S., 208
Smith, J., 158
Smith, R., 264
Smith, S. J., 56
Smith, S., 134, 139, 284
Snowden, E., 223–224, 234, 244
social constructionism, 306
social media and social networking
    Boston marathon bombings and, 1–4
    definition of, 306
    fear of crime and, 168
    Meagher case and, 284–285
    paedophilia and, 101–102
    policing and, 175–179
    rise of, 4–5, 28, 252–253
    surveillance and, 246–247
    See also Facebook
social reaction, 88, 306
social retreat, 269
Société Générale, 54
Sollecito, R., 247
Sophos, 257
South, N., 26
spamming, 262
Sparks, R., 103–103, 181–182, 188, 189, 199
spatial proximity, 60–63
Spielberg, S., 196, 241
spousal homicide, 142, 153, 306
Stalder, F., 233–234
Stein, Lord, 158
Stenson, K., 230–231
stereotyping, 29, 306
Stewart, J., 283
stigmatizing, 95, 306

Sting, 240
strain theory, 19–21, 38–39
Strangeways (documentary), 208–209
style, 96–98
Style Wars (documentary), 37
subcultures, 84, 306
Sun (newspaper), 76, 77, 147
Sunday Mail (Australian newspaper), 141
Sunday Mercury (newspaper), 270–271
Sunday Times (newspaper), 115
super-panopticism, 246
supermale syndrome, 150
surveillance
    panopticism and, 224–226, 242–243
    power and, 243–247
    recent revelations on, 222–224
surveillant assemblage
    control of the body and, 228–229
    cybersurveillance and, 232–236
    definition of, 306
    entertainment and, 239–242
    governance and, 230–232
    overview, 226–228
    profit and, 236–239
Sutcliffe, P., 59, 137. See also Yorkshire
    Ripper case
Sutcliffe, S., 137
The Sweeney (ITV series), 172
Swire, C., 243
Symantec, 257
synopticism, 213, 239–242, 246, 306–307

tagging, 37
The Taking of Pelham One Two Three (1974
    film), 211–214
The Taking of Pelham 123 (2009 film), 199,
    201, 211–214
Tanner, J., 140
Taobao, 255
Tarantino, Q., 196–197, 198–199, 212, 217
Tate, S., 215
Taylor, D., 62–63, 66, 116, 169
Taylor, I., 22
Telegraph (newspaper), 76, 153, 244
television, 29, 31
The Terminator (film), 215
terrorism, 33–34, 52–53, 69, 233–235, 307
text, 307
Thatcher, M., 5, 173–174
theft of personal identity, 263–264
This is England (film), 200–201
Thompson, R., 113–116, 127, 261–262, 286,
    291. See also Bulger case
Thornton, S., 94, 103, 142
threshold, 49–50, 70, 71, 86, 157
Tierney, J., 12

The Times (newspaper), 47, 76
Todd, M., 179
Tombs, S., 25–26
Tomlinson, I., 177
Top of the Pops (BBC show), 58
tragic victims, 307
Trainspotting (film), 201
Travolta, J., 199, 211
trolling, 262, 307
Trump, D., 37
Tsarnaev, D., 2, 3–4
Tsarnaev, T., 2
Tumber, H., 181, 182, 185
Twitter, 73–74, 252–253, 253

unconscious, 132, 307
Uniting and Strengthening of America to
    Provide Appropriate Tools Required to
    Intercept and Obstruct Terrorism Act
    (USA PATRIOT Act) (2001), 235
Up! documentary series, 205–207
Upton, J., 137, 158
user-generated content (UGC), 73–76,
    256, 307

Valier, C., 236
vampires, 147
Venables, J., 113–116, 127, 236, 261–262, 286,
    291. *See also* Bulger case
Verhoeven, D., 138, 147
victimization, 153, 164, 166, 307
violence, 63–64, 70, 72, 86
Virgin or Vamp (Benedict), 135
visual spectacle, 64–66, 71–72, 157, 280–281,
    289–290
Vodafone, 222
voyeurism, 239–242, 307

Waddington, P. A. J., 85
Walkerdine, V., 53
Walklate, S., 52, 53
War of the Worlds (Wells), 16–17, 91
Wardle, P. J., 151
Washington, D., 211
Watney, S., 103
Watson, J.B., 14, 294
Watts, B., 139–140, 144
Weaver, C. K., 184
Weibo, 254–255
Welles, O., 16–17
Wells, H., 62, 121
Wells, H.G., 16–17
Wells, O., 91
West, F., 117, 136–137, 140

West, R.
    as bad mother, 144
    Hindley and, 139
    as mythical monster, 147–148
    as non-agent, 154
    paedophilia as moral panic and, 117
    physical attractiveness and, 141
    sexuality and, 136–137
Westerns, 198, 199
Westwood, V., 96
Whyte, D., 25–26
Wigginton, T., 137–138, 140–141, 147–148, 290
Wikipedia, 253
Wilczynski, A., 149
Wilding, R., 187
Williams, H., 63
Williams, T., 263
Willis, P., 183, 207
Wiseman, F., 208
women
    as bad mothers, 143–146, 150
    as bad wives, 141–143
    in crime films, 199–200
    in *Crimewatch UK*, 186
    as evil manipulators, 150–152
    feminist perspectives on, 133–135, 157–158
    Internet and, 271
    as mad cows, 148–150
    as mythical monsters, 146–148
    news values and, 56–57
    as non-agents, 152–154
    as 'other', 130–133, 154–159
    physical attractiveness and, 140–141
    psychoanalytic perspectives on, 131–133,
        138, 143, 148–150
    sexuality and, 135–140
Women, Crime and Criminology (Smart), 133
The World Is Not Enough (film), 205
Wuornos, A., 138, 147–148, 290
Wykes, M., 102, 119, 136–137, 140, 143,
    258–259

Yar, M., 258, 268
Yorkshire Ripper case, 59, 137, 173–174, 289
Young, J., 30, 35, 95–96, 166
youth, 91–93, 96–98, 307. *See also* children
    and young people
youth culture, 19
YouTube, 74, 175, 253
Yukou Tudou, 255

Z Cars (BBC series), 172
Zuckerberg, M., 252
Zureik, E., 245